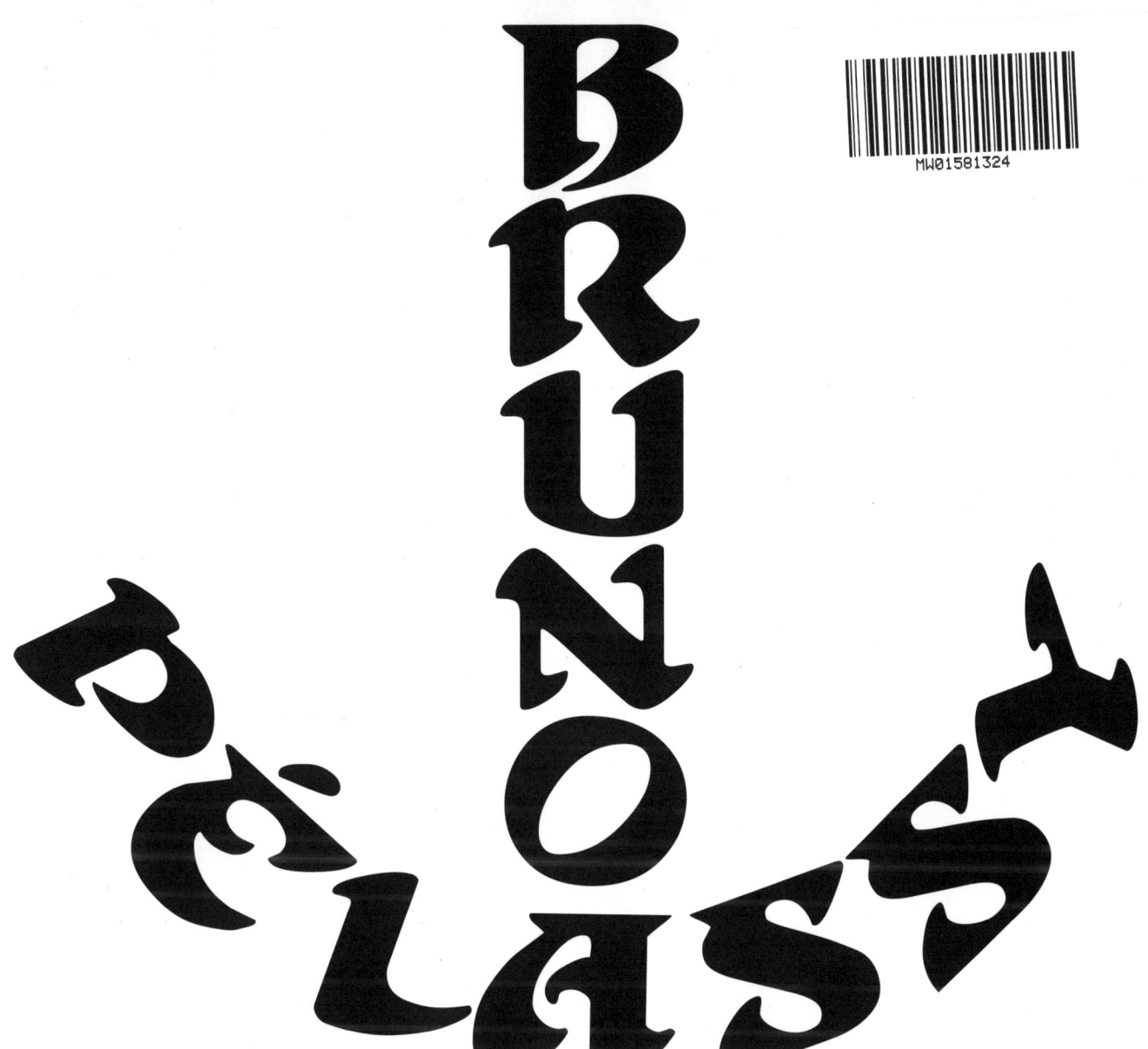

MOUSSE PUBLISHING

TABLE OF CONTENTS

5   *Remembering Bruno Pélassy (Encore)*
Laura Cottingham

11   *Glitches and Modesty*
Marie Canet

17   *The Pilgrim of Angkor*
Baptiste Pinteaux

195   *Ligne du Temps*
Florence Bonnefous

199   Bookshelf
Bruno Pélassy

Remembering Bruno Pélassy (Encore)

Laura Cottingham

They say the past never changes. But in fact, the past is always changing.
Our present-day perspective alters how we think and feel about the past. Of course, gaps and distortions will appear and disappear in our memories. Our understanding of the past also changes when we acquire new information, experiences, and beliefs. The images and feelings I recall of my friend Bruno Pélassy—while often consistent with what I wrote or spoke or photographed more than twenty years ago—are nonetheless different today. I'm feeling less Jean Genet, more Marcel Proust. Less humor, camp, and curiosity, more pathos, pain, and confusion. I feel the heaviness and see the long, dark shadow of those who, like Bruno, die young. I understand more about what he was reaching for in his art and how his *Lust for Life* intensified as he looked death in the eye. In the summer of 1997 in Nice, when the majority of my recollections were formed, Bruno was living with AIDS and five years away from the end of his life. I wasn't involved in his daily life or professional activities. For a few weeks in 1997, when I was a guest at the Villa Arson, I was a guest in his life, *An American Friend.* Some life experiences, including friendships, are high-impact, supercharged, and destined to leave lasting impressions, like the memory of an incredible musical performance, or if you've ever seen a shooting star. One feels buoyed up, carried away, extraordinary, during and after these encounters. Bruno and I had a lot of things in common, and we shared certain affinities in our tastes in art, music, and politics.

It seemed then that the closer Bruno got to death, the closer he got to life. He had so much energy. He introduced himself to me as a "Garbage Man," but when he said it, he spoke like a King. His junkyard of jewels wasn't just the collection of stuff he hoarded and transformed into art; it was also the diamonds and rust in his mind. He was an alchemist of the soul. He was his own Balzacian character. One night in Nice, after a particularly boisterous dinner party (this may or may not have been the same night that the neighbors upstairs unsuccessfully tried to quiet us by pouring a bucket of water out over the balcony), Bruno convinced me to stay late to watch his film *Sans titre, Sang titre, Cent titres* (1995). I was exhausted and wanted to leave. He insisted. His fatal illness was guiding him in the philosophy of the now, of living in the moment, of taking nobody and nothing for granted. He wasn't so much wistful as he was invigorated—determined, even. He was focused on the quality of his steps, and not, as so many of us are, on where we are going (more aptly, where we think we are going).

Reluctantly, I agreed to stay. And I was astounded by this cinematic *objet trouvé* on VHS tape. I still am. When I came back to New York, I told all my friends about it (I was making videos then, and we were looking for new approaches). When *Sans titre, Sang titre, Cent titres* screened in New York in 2018 in the *Song Cycle* exhibition curated by Nick Irvin, I told all my friends about it and watched it again. I had the same amazed response. I think of it as an autobiographical work about Bruno's life found in the mirror of the movies and television shows he saw. Memory is the origin of photography and cinema. Aren't we all projecting ourselves and our lives onto everything we see, including the movies we watch?

The clip from John Waters's *Female Trouble* (1974) with French subtitles is the ultimate camp.

On another evening in Nice, Bruno showed me a film by Claude Nuridsany and Marie Pérennou, *Microcosmos: Le peuple de l'herbe* (1996), which uses microscopic cinematography to reveal insect dramas that are mostly invisible to the human eye. Aware that the inevitable result of his chronic illness would be death, Bruno was interested in the reality of our senses: what it means to see, touch, feel. He was also interested in making the invisible visible. We talked about how trees can communicate through their root systems, and how fascinatingly mysterious mushrooms are.

We shared a rapport with nature. We were among the last generation of children given an opportunity to connect directly and frequently with the intricacies and mysteries of the countryside, before human experience became increasingly dominated by computerized images and information. Our connection to the natural world as children was enhanced by the fact that we had both enjoyed the luxury of freely roaming about sparsely cultivated areas. We shared memories of running through open fields, searching for birds' nests, picking wild flowers, collecting rocks, playing with insects. Bruno told me that in his childhood, a boy in the village (Mons, France) was bitten by a snake, and some of the elders said it was the child's fault, that he should have known how to walk through a field of tall grass in a way to warn the snake such that the snake would never have bitten him. I remember at the time thinking that this was an intelligent way for humans to live alongside other life forms, including and perhaps especially those with the potential to harm us.

One afternoon in Mons, Bruno took me to one of his favorite places in the forest. It was a natural spring sealed off and surrounded by large boulders that were themselves surrounded by tall, skinny, coniferous trees. The current in this small body of water was so strong that it was challenging to swim just a few meters. But you could swim to the center, against the current, then allow the natural movement to push you back up against the rocks, sometimes gently, sometimes forcefully, usually unpredictably. Then we could relax with our backs to the rocks as the centrifugal force of the vortex swirled about and a faint glow of sunlight pierced through the pines.

He had a friend who owned the pizza parlor in the center of the village. Bruno described her to me as a "lavender heiress," and, sure enough, when we met, she was wearing a small silver flask around her neck that contained lavender oil her ancestors harvested centuries ago. It was like a moment from a fairy tale. He also took me to the Church of Saint Agnes in Mons and showed me his family name carved into the wall there. He told me about Saint Agnes, her martyrdom and hagiography. We shared secrets about how Catholic priests in our respective childhoods, in France and United States, abused their power, and in particular sought to subjugate and repress the historical contributions and contemporary realities of women. We both felt we had excellent reasons to reject the values and beliefs of the religion of our ancestors.

Kitsch and Catholicism are two variations of the sacred and the profane in Bruno's artworks. The cacophony of often-contradictory tones and tensions, highs and lows, comedy and eros, are like a visual re-orchestration of a Karlheinz Stockhausen score: intoxicating and inexplicable simultaneously. Illness, death, laughter, phallic symbols, regal gestures, morbid, decadent, anthropomorphic, luxurious, abject, decorative, Americana, trashy, ironic, cinematic, threatening, sexual, macabre, gaudy, fashionable — how are we to understand and make sense of so many juxtapositions and disjunctions? And so many wigs? How many keys do we need to unlock the meaning of all of this? Or what if we were to allow these indecipherables to remain mysteries, to just accept this artist's unique and peculiar range?

This is a body of work born in a candy store on the coast of a morbid serendipity near the French border. The seemingly discordant pieces in a wide range of media and materials arrange themselves exclusively within the unique and individual personality of the artist. What you see is what you get. This is not "official art," this is not "art-school art," this is not "gallery art." This is individualism. Enveloped in a surrealistic atmosphere, the playful deployment of sexualized and gender-ized images and things has an infinity with the Jungian ideal of androgynous creativity, where concepts of men/women, or masculine/feminine, are synthesized and equivalated. Bruno's photographs of himself as a "fashion model" made in collaboration with Natacha Lesueur display the artist as an awkward androgyne whose toes are made cloven like the Devil's as he attempts to force, like Cinderella's evil stepsisters, his big feet into tight high heels.

Bruno and I shared an enthusiasm for popular music of the late 1970s and early 1980s, in particular the punk and New Wave bands that developed and cross-pollinated between New York and London at that time. I think he was the only other person I ever met who had a copy of *The Flying Lizards* (1979). We also talked about Sid Vicious, the bassist for the Sex Pistols who died a drug-related death in New York at age twenty-one (and to this day is still thought to haunt the Chelsea Hotel with his girlfriend, Nancy Spungen). Punk was dark, antiauthoritarian, decadent, and nihilistic, and the English variant had a strong twist of neo-Victorianism. Many of Punk's leading practitioners and fans, like Sid and Nancy, were, like the Victorians, obsessed with death (a fascination frequently accentuated and even realized by regular heroin usage and the consequent fatal overdoses).

Under Queen Victoria's reign (1837–1901), the mortality rate in England was extremely high. Death was a regular occurrence, and managing it a frequent topic of conversation. It was a commonly held belief that the dying one's fate in the afterlife (Heaven or Hell) was decided during the last moments of life and the "beginning" of death. For those like Bruno who contracted AIDS before the medical advances of the twenty-first-century, it could be said that the "beginning" of death usually lasted a long time. Punk Victoriana seems to inspire his sculptures that look like reliquaries and coffins. The velvet, the gloves, the gold gilt, and the fur create a sense of macabre luxury or divine death. The gemstones (many colored ruby red, like blood, and others milky white, like semen, or clear, like tears and sweat) glisten like bodily fluids. Fluids and movement are not just metaphors for human life.

So many of us who are living are not really living at all. We don't seem to know the value of life and get lost in the struggle to survive and the snake in the grass. One of the fundamental contradictions of our human experience on Earth—that there is so much beauty alongside so much suffering here—animates Bruno's work.

Glitches and Modesty

Marie Canet

In 1979, something went wrong in the operating theater of the Saint George clinic in Nice. The doctor made a mistake—a bit like going in for a pacemaker and ending up with a knee replacement. Everyone was talking about it. Bruno Pélassy was then thirteen years old, and when he was taken to this same hospital to urgently have his appendix removed, reality glitched like a neon light badly wired. He didn't trust them; he feared human error. He did not want to surrender to fate, so he decided to write on his forehead, in permanent marker, in capital letters:

APPENDICITIS

. . . to avoid any confusion.

During the "Art and Virality" seminar at the École supérieure d'art d'Aix-en-Provence in May 2022, we had a hard time showing the video *Sans titre, Sang titre, Cent titres*, created by Pélassy in 1995. This cut-up work, produced and distributed on VHS, is composed of pirated fragments of cult films such as Gus Van Sant's *My Own Private Idaho* (1991), René Clair's *Sous les toits de Paris* (1930), and Stanley Kubrick's *The Shining* (1980). The artist drew from more than thirty works to create this allegorical and performative piece, one of whose themes is the notion of fate. Today, the damage caused by time and the chemical erosion of the magnetic tape have transformed its structure, visibility, and accessibility.

Although I was familiar with the work, I was almost dazzled, and a little distressed, by the new effects I was discovering: only a third of the images remained. The glitches produced by the artist during the editing process (through the juxtaposition of images, harsh cuts, the presence of signal-free parts on the tape, and luminous variations between PAL and SECAM video formats) seemed to shatter. The VCR playback, necessary to the exhibition process, was further damaging the work. It had lost more of its shine and texture. Grays and blacks often invaded the screen. The video flickered uncontrollably, like a faulty neon sign. The glitches led to a loss of signal. This lack of information was traced back to the cable that connected the VCR to the projector. The latter jammed. The encoding of the images was too disturbed and the technological basis of the signal was transformed. The VCR would look for the source, splutter, and then restart. I must say that the audience received these mechanical stumbles with varying degrees of enthusiasm. In fact, the projector stopped working on several occasions. Without any clear data to display, it would simply resign, following which one would read, on the auditorium screen that had turned electric blue, an impassive

SAMSUNG

. . . and then it would resume, until the next disruption.

A glitch is a technological error, a mechanical malfunction. It appears, as the author and curator Legacy Russell explains, to warn that "something has gone wrong."[1] It disrupts the way we read and look. Its recurrence accentuates its disruptive power. It makes you blink and sometimes gnash your teeth. The illusion of fluidity is broken because something has occurred. For Russell, the glitch is disruptive, encrypting reality in a new way, for it is both an error within a technological system

1
Legacy Russell, *Glitch Feminism: A Manifesto* (London, New York: Verso Books, 2020).

(on screens) and a break within the social realm. In this respect, it is even capable of exposing racist and sexist aspects of patriarchy. Thus, whether in virtual or real spaces, glitching exposes the tangible failings of the ideal fluidity of the world and meaning. That's why the glitch can also be considered a form of assertive dissidence. According to Russell, the phenomenon has a viral potential, for it corrupts computer data, diminishes the performance of machines, and threatens profit, efficiency, work, and the apparent stability of data. In Bruno Pélassy's pre-internet work, this viral dimension of glitches destroys meaning while simultaneously wrecking the work's already dysfunctional communication network. When glitches occur, they create turmoil in an already precarious system of information dissemination.

The queer performative machine *Sans titre, Sang titre, Cent titres* (tape + VCR + projector) is a malfunctioning physical and symbolic chain. Glitches damage the material and the figures featured. In fact, the latter are also narratively marked by precariousness. I'm thinking of Edmund, the suicidal child in Roberto Rossellini's *Germany, Year Zero* (1948), of the rebellious teenager with his fist raised in Pier Paolo Pasolini's *Salò, or the 120 Days of Sodom* (1975), of the young woman hanging like a piece of meat from a butcher's hook in Tobe Hooper's *The Texas Chainsaw Massacre* (1974). Pélassy compulsively repeated the same sequences, which are often very violent. These figures send out signals from the fictional narratives they inhabit. In the artwork, they indirectly inform the social and intimate history provoked by the emergence and spread of AIDS in the 1980s and 1990s. To me, they evoke youth that will never age. They tell of the shock, the contamination, as well as the semantic and often ordinary social violence surrounding the discovery of the disease. Today, these memories remain intact for many people. For a generation like mine, who did not directly experience the catastrophe of the AIDS epidemic during those years, Pélassy's disappearing images hold considerable memorial weight, and although eaten away by magnetic injuries, they prove surprisingly resistant.

Pélassy was born in 1966 in Vientiane, Laos, where his father was a military officer. He died in Nice in 2002. He studied textile and jewelry design in Paris. He found out that he was HIV positive in 1987. His work spans more than a decade. It seems to me that it can be divided into two periods, the first being rather materialistic and esoteric, followed by a second period dominated by animal iconography. In both, the artist addressed issues of adornment and technology—their visual, performative, and narrative dimensions.

During the first period, Pélassy developed a dark, mortuary, at times grandiose aesthetic, for example the *Reliquaires* series, which consists of imposing cases protecting large jewelry-objects. He began working on this series in the early 1990s. The heavy necklaces (made of glass, crystal, or stone beads with pendants or rhinestones) are placed like relics in large boxes made of carved chipboard, covered in gold. The jewelry pieces usually rest on velvet cushions. The series is inspired by religious goldsmithed items dating from the Middle Ages, which were frequently adorned with precious and semiprecious gemstones and protected in majestic shrines, such as those held at the Abbey Church of Sainte-Foy in Conques, France, which the artist greatly admired.

Pélassy presented this series for the first time in 1995 at Art Concept gallery in Nice. The works were suspended in the space, and the walls were covered with black hangings. The gallery was bathed in blue thanks to the smoke of the incense burned every day, coating it with fragrant and religious density. In a corner, the artist had placed an audio player that was emitting a sound work made from cut-up film recordings. Over time, the jewelry-objects began to free themselves from the boxes in order to be worn directly on the body, as with the *Untitled* (1992–1993) tiara made of colored glass beads and enameled bronze.[2] Important works from this period also include the video *Sans titre, Sang titre, Cent titres*, of which there is only one copy (apart from the one used for screenings), and the *Bestioles* (Beasties). The first works of the latter series were made with synthetic wigs mounted on cheap toy robots. These crawling objects are rather sinister. They resemble animated scalps. The series began after a long hospital stay, and the works became increasingly sophisticated while retaining the body-horror aesthetics of his early experiments.

The later beasties, adorable pet works, are dressed in red mink, ermine, or leather and wear gold chains, jewelry, or gemstones. Pélassy couldn't resist beautiful materials. Some of them wiggle; others rub, rush, and bang against the walls, dancing with their erect pearl penises. They squeak, laugh, and whine. The mechanical and synthetic noises they produce as well as their repetitive, jerky movements reinforce their technically and psychically messed-up object status. In 1994, the artist filmed them in motion as part of the *Freaky Pets Shop* exhibition presented at Galerie Chez Valentin. The event took place in a vacant, derelict flat in Clichy, on the outskirts of Paris.[3] In the video, we can see the works in motion amid rubbish and filth. Pélassy filmed them discreetly, as if he didn't want to disturb them. In the shower pan or in the bedroom, the sculptures wriggle, mewl, and splutter. Like bacteria or gremlins, they appear to be the landlords of this marginal environment, which fosters, or shelters, their proliferation.

All these works are fragile and require ongoing care and attention in both their display and their preservation. They often have to be parked in order to avoid losing them in the exhibition space. During the artist's last exhibition during his life, in Nice in 2002 at Galerie Vigna (titled *Shim*, a queer contraction of "she" and "him"), they were displayed on plinths with raised edges, as if each had its own stage or small clearing, alongside three aquariums of varying sizes containing works from the *Créatures* series (all produced between 2000 and 2001). Here again, Pélassy reappropriated the art of clothing and the formal challenges of haute couture but worked at the scale of a pocket handkerchief, as he did with the *Bestioles*, which are all more or less the size of a Chihuahua.

These pieces bear a certain resemblance to pet artwork. They are aquatic objects, evolving voluptuously and silently in domestic ponds. For the exhibition, the artist lit them strongly from beneath using halogen construction-site lamps placed directly on the floor. As a result, the shadows

---

2 The artist worked in particular with gemstones and jewelry. His major gem works include the emblematic *Untitled* (1997) gorgon helmet made with "aurora borealis" Swarovski crystals. Pélassy worked for the brand as a freelancer for a short period. Uncomfortable with the stakes of the industry and that of trade (particularly regarding artists' rights), he was later able to take advantage of the materials and crystals made available to him by the brand in order to experiment and produce his own works, for instance his *Ouroboros* sculptural snake necklaces, which were hung on the wall, suspended on vine shoots like hunting trophies. All these objects made with glass beads, pendants, and crystals were produced in 1997.

3 In the last part of the video *Bruno Pélassy, family & friends* (available at https://vimeo.com/116850313), edited by Brice Dellsperger on the occasion of the artist's retrospective exhibition at Le Crédac, Ivry-sur-Seine, France, in 2015, we can see footage Pélassy shot at *Freaky Pets Shop*.

of their translucent dresses' floating movements, driven by the slow water circulation, traveled all the way up to the gallery ceiling. The visual effect was most spectacular at night. With these works, Pélassy managed to free himself from the weight of the body, from carrying the garment/work, by reducing the scale. The use of rather basic mechanical devices compensated for the static nature of the sculpture. They shook up surfaces and textures. The *Bestioles* move like Robert Breer's rugs. They are a little less suspicious, however, for they are faster and more ferocious, evoking visual parasites. Indeed, as they scan the space, they also animate it with contradictory dynamics. Personally, I prefer them being free in the gallery. I remember being startled at Le Crédac in Ivry-sur-Seine on the evening of the 2015 opening there: one of them (a wig) had been unleashed. Deceitful, it was waiting for me, hiding in the dark behind a pole. Surprised by its squeaking and rather creepy appearance, I was unable to hold back an

AH!

... while being dramatic, there was also something comical about it.

On the artist's page, which is still available on the Document d'artistes PACA website, the *Créatures* series appears alongside the *Bestioles*.[4] The darker works from the first period, prior to 1996, have disappeared. Christine Finizio, the website director at the time, explains that Pélassy made the selection himself—preferring, I suppose, the provocation, seduction, and creepy camp humor of his later work to his overly baroque, silent, grandiloquent early-1990s work.

Yet what we are missing today are the artist's words to shed light upon these assumptions. Of course there are the images, the works, the materials, but there are few if any texts, no direct accounts. Nothing. The artist's voice is missing. And it's too late. How can we explain this absence? Likewise, he rarely spoke of his health problems. Here again, something is missing. Things were said, but Pélassy didn't want to make a big deal of it. He probably sought to preserve the magic of the show. I feel that his relationship to language and intimacy can be perceived in a small composition from 2000: Pélassy covered a female figure sculpted in synthetic stone with a cream-colored goatskin glove. He tied the glove around the figure, and so her expression can only be guessed. She is folding her arms over her face as if hiding.

UNTITLED

Did Pélassy ever shift away from the arts of jewelry and dressmaking? He officially left the world of fashion (as well as Paris) after designing a children's clothing collection. Although he was in contact with Christian Lacroix for the launch of a jewelry collection and with the brand Swarovski, for whom he designed the spring/summer 1998 collection, he quite quickly abandoned the constraints of the industry, preferring to create unique, smaller, more personal pieces. This enabled him to use expensive, very beautiful materials given the very limited amounts required, for example white mink, red fox, beige leather, snakeskin, ermine, and silk, but also much more common materials such as raffia, sequins,

[4] http://www.documentsdartistes.org/artistes/pelassy/repro.html.

and artificial flowers—it's like a Joris-Karl Huysmans list.[5] Often these materials were scavenged from the bins of haute couture houses in Paris, or from the *Secours populaire* in Nice. They were bought, exchanged, and infinitely desired.

Pélassy loved theatricality. Leaving the fashion industry enabled him to escape the relations of power and money without giving up rarity or his signature. He didn't want to abandon his copyright or be consumed by capitalism as a creator. In his work, he often combined and juxtaposed materials to create tactile and (preferably) moving or surprising surfaces. One archival photograph shows him at home, sitting at his kitchen table. A *Bestiole* is on a tray. When he claps his hands, the garment comes to life, dancing to electronic music. It's also a show for children. Sometimes in Nice, the artist organized fashion shows during which he presented his creations for his own enjoyment and that of friends who would wear his clothing. In one of these fashion shows, he is seen dressed in his famous white bullfighter costume adorned with black and green embroidery.

A wedding dress he made—cream-colored, made from canvas, cotton, latex, and rhinestones—is now held at the Palais Galliera in Paris. It is adorned, in its center, with an open vulva within the folds of the fabric, in the heart of which appears a large molded penis that runs up the stomach. In archival pictures of this dress being worn on the runway, Pélassy is seen holding the bride's arm. He is bare-chested under his breastplate, wearing a boxing champion's belt and a large rhinestone necklace. Two long metal rods, held in place thanks to magnets fixed under his brow ridge, keep his eyes wide open in an excessive manner. In another photograph, he is unblinkingly staring at the camera. His implants keep him in a state of compulsory visual tension. He is an ultra-queer creature. He glitches, but above all he resists. He looks worn out. His features are marked by a day's work, the heat, the performance. In fact, he doesn't just transmit effects; he *is* the effect, the experienced malfunction. He produces a highly unique form of resistance and shimmering—one that is physical, aesthetic, informational, and political.

That evening, he was also wearing a pair of boots with rigged heels that made him tiptoe, like a satyr, as if he had hooves. Bearing such garish and erotic power, he thus maintained his deviant status. As a cripple himself, he joined the other cripples he loved and paid tribute to in *Sans titre, Sang titre, Cent titres*: the uncontrollable delinquent Dawn Davenport in John Waters's *Female Trouble* (1974), the delusional young Tommy in Ken Russell's 1975 eponymous film, the community of weirdos in Tod Browning's *Freaks* (1932). He glitches and resists with them, it's pretty obvious. Together they are glitching and resisting the times, for the sake of reality and their children's future.

VIVA LA MUERTE

[5] I am thinking here of Joris-Karl Huysmans's *À rebours* (1884). This novel, a manifesto of the French Decadent movement, tells the story of a person who definitively turns his back on life and transforms his existence into a work of art. Huysmans uses accumulation to produce sensual descriptions of the many objects in the life of Jean des Esseintes, the sickly and eccentric protagonist.

The Pilgrim of Angkor

Baptiste Pinteaux

In 1987, while he was finishing his training as a tailor, Bruno Pélassy was living in a studio apartment on the rue du Croissant in the 2nd arrondissement in Paris, amid a cluttered cascade of needles, lace, and fur that his mother routinely brought him from Nice. On his television set, various VHS tapes played on endless repeat: *The Exorcist* (1973), *Female Trouble* (1974), *Fox and His Friends* (1975). Sometimes he would turn the TV volume down and play his vinyl records: "Madame Butterfly" by Malcolm McLaren (1984), a recording of Ingrid Caven at Le Pigall's (1978), anything by Madonna. On a pine shelf, a Chanel perfume bag and the beginnings of a library: *La Nuit juste avant les forêts* (1977), *Dans la solitude des champs de coton* (1985), *Le Retour au désert* (1988). Like Bernard-Marie Koltès, the author of these books, Pélassy was gay and had been born into a Catholic family with a military father and a housewife mother. The two shared a weakness for exotic dreams (Pierre Loti in particular) and distant countries that served as spaces for the discovery of desire and the marvelous, as well as of the depths of human and political evil.

Pélassy was born in 1966 in Vientiane, Laos, where his father worked as a mechanic in the air force. The family returned to France a year later, and he grew up amid the souvenirs his parents brought back with them: lengths of fabrics bought at markets, photographs of Khmer temples, stories of Buddhist funeral rites. "Néo Laos": years later, Pélassy inscribed this pun (phonetically *né au Laos*, or "born in Laos") in a notebook.[1] This witticism evokes his works' visual syncretism and appears at the same time as an attempt by Pélassy to set himself apart from his contemporaries by articulating his place outside or beyond his immediate world.

Koltès was a passionate reader of Arthur Rimbaud, and perhaps had in mind the poet's desire to "swim, trample grass, hunt, smoke... drink liquor hard as boiling metal"[2] when he wrote to his mother in Togo from his Jesuit boarding school in France: "I went paddling in a canoe with you, all afternoon. Isn't the water beautiful, and the reeds, too! The sky is emerald and the water a sparkling diamond. I saw children laugh, little black pebbles on the riverbed... I saw it all, through your eyes—at least, as long as my imagination would let me escape from the black snow of the city."[3] Pélassy never returned to Laos. Perhaps he feared suffering the same disappointment that Koltès felt when he traveled to Africa for the first time in the late 1970s: in a letter to his friend Henri Gignoux from Ahoada, Nigeria, on February 11, 1978, Koltès described how, as he left Lagos airport, he saw a cowering taxi driver being beaten by three policemen, cheered on by a jeering crowd. His wonder at the beauty of the men and the bougainvillea quickly darkened as he discovered the injustice and cruelty all around him: the idleness of the colonists and their craving for domination, and the reflection of this corruption in a government made up of "shameless puppets of American imperialism."[4]

Pélassy also shared with Koltès the experience of illness. Both were HIV-positive and both would die of AIDS-related illnesses within thirteen years of one another. On the night of Wednesday, November 25, 1987, Pélassy, then aged twenty-one, wrote the following lines:

---

1 From an undated text in a notebook belonging to Bruno Pélassy, collection of Brigitte Pélassy.

2 Arthur Rimbaud, "Bad Blood," trans. Bertrand Mathieu, in *Illuminations* (New York: BOA Editions, 1991), 9.

3 From a letter from Koltès to his mother, March 5, 1965, reprinted in Bernard-Marie Koltès, *Lettres* (Paris: Minuit, 2009), 32. Original translations for this article unless otherwise stated.

4 Koltès, *Lettres*, 316.

I am so tired again, so tired.
My nights are endless now, I stay awake until six in the morning.
I want peace, heat, real contact, without false hypotheses.
Afraid of seeing myself nude, I overdress, and now, I don't even know how these rags are meant to be organized!
I can no longer stop myself from diving into lives that are not my own.
Goodnight.[5]

Copi died on December 14, 1987, Guy Hocquenghem on August 28, 1988, Koltès on April 15, 1989. A whole generation and a way of being a faggot died along with them. Their deaths also pointed to a lethal horizon for those who had more recently seroconverted. The three men had long lived on rue Cauchois, a few streets away from the studio on rue des Trois Frères where Pélassy lived at the end of the 1980s. Aged twenty-three, he had just presented his degree show, featuring a suit in Prince of Wales check designed as an homage to the first collections of Vivienne Westwood and Jean Paul Gaultier, worn by a model on a catwalk beneath the arcades of the Palais-Royal.

On the night of January 7, 1989, while staying in Nice, Pélassy wrote a poem, a litany that he threw away as soon as he was finished but which his mother saved from the wastepaper basket. "No, I won't leave! / To go where? To see who, what?" he wrote:

I will leave, tomorrow, in a month, never,
When I want, nothing is written, everything is still to be done
My destiny will be what I make of it.[6]

Amid the silence that followed Pélassy's death—during his lifetime he gave no interviews and left only a few sparse notes and handwritten texts—these nocturnal expressions (the above note begins "alone—three in the morning") can perhaps allow us to understand something of the shock he felt at being confronted with the idea of death at so young an age. This was the start of what Laura Cottingham calls Pélassy's "Lazarus" stage, which also coincided with the beginning of his oeuvre.[7] Rather than living in suspense, Pélassy instead chose play, a certain mental plasticity, the pleasure of cloaking himself in lives other than his own and traversing other eras and other geographies: the mountains of Laos, the Paris of the nineteenth century, the Baltimore of John Waters. It is unlikely that Pélassy could have read the following letter, which Koltès sent to his mother in 1968, since it was published after the author's death. Yet in this letter, I recognize the same energy, the same promise that the two men made to themselves at the same age, something which might fit between the slogans that Pélassy wove into two beaded curtains created a year apart: *Viva la Muerte* (1995) and *Gracias a la Vida* (1996):

Dear Mum, I got your article on "turning twenty." You seem to have an even more pessimistic view of life than I do... Why are

5 Untitled note by Bruno Pélassy, November 25, 1987, collection of Brigitte Pélassy.

6 Untitled note by Bruno Pélassy, January 7, 1989, collection of Brigitte Pélassy.

7 Laura Cottingham, "Remembering Bruno Pélassy," in *Bruno Pélassy* (Nice: Musée d'art moderne et d'art contemporain, 2004), 30.

you so insistent that this age is the ugliest period of a person's life? It's an age that comes with its share of difficulties, of course, an age of indecision. But personally, I remain convinced that life is what you make of it, and that there is no age that is particularly unhappy, except maybe the age at which you give up—and you can give up at any age. I'll find life ugly the day I "sit down" and never want to get up again. For the moment—as far as I'm concerned—twenty is the age of great decisions; it's the age at which I'm risking my life, my future, my soul, everything, in the hope of achieving more; it's the age at which I'm working "without a safety net.". . . I only want one thing: to be able to take risks all my life, without ever wanting to stop along the way.[8]

8 Letter from Koltès to his mother, Strasbourg, March 26, 1968, in *Lettres*, 56.

From 1990 to 1994, Pélassy lived between Nice and Paris; in the latter city, he received treatment at the Hôpital Saint Louis. He surrounded himself with a group of friends who gravitated around the Villa Arson: Florence Bonnefous, who had graduated in 1989 from the École du Magasin and had just opened the first exhibition at the gallery she founded with Edouard Merino, Air de Paris (*Les Ateliers du Paradise*, 1990), as well as the two Jean-Lucs (Blanc and Verna), Brice Dellsperger, Ingrid Luche, little Natacha (Altman) and big Natacha (Lesueur). When he wasn't crashing with them, he would go back to his parents' house, a ground-floor apartment to the north of Nice, a world away from his Parisian hovel. There, immaculate lace covered the headrests of the armchairs parked in front of the television, and a crested canary sang on the terrace. He would sometimes borrow the keys to their house in Mons, a village further inland, near Fayence, and go hiking alone in the mountains. When he got back to town, Florence would be waiting for him in her flat, just two minutes away from Coco Beach, Nice's best queer beach. When he felt what Koltès, an avid reader of Jack London, referred to as "the call of the wild," he would go out and wander along Avenue Jean Lorrain to find a lover before coming home and climbing into bed with Florence.

The local aesthete who gave his name to this cruisy promenade was no stranger to Pélassy: flamboyant and sleazy in equal measure, Jean Lorrain was one of his tutelary figures and an influence that shone across his entire oeuvre. Born in 1855, Lorrain embodied better than anyone the decadent spirit of the late nineteenth century which Pélassy held so dear. In the Parisian salons he would regale others with tales of his sordid adventures with butchers' boys from Les Halles. He was known for his candor and his vulgarity, for the scent of patchouli that hung around him and the wax that slicked his hair flat, for his close-fitting suits, his fistfuls of extravagant rings, his outrageous makeup. Feared by his contemporaries, who dreaded becoming the target of his vicious chronicles of high society and worldly letters, Lorrain also wrote novels with evocative titles—*Le Vice errant* (1902), *Princesses d'ivoire et d'ivresse* (1902), *Fards et poisons* (1905), *Le Crime des riches* (1906)—full of figures drawn from biblical folklore and the dark underbelly of Romanticism. These were stories of vengeance and murder, of curses and spells. An ardent admirer of Gustave Flaubert and Jules Barbey d'Aurevilly, Lorrain depicted the many vices of the aristocracy with comic fervor and fearsome incisiveness.

Pélassy shared much with Lorrain. Charming and extravagant, he distinguished himself with his humor and his wit (like his close friend Didier Bisson, he adored puns, and kept a well-read copy of the Larousse dictionary of French and popular slang in his library) and an elegance that turned on a sharp sense of contrast. His ever-present jewelry—plastic and rhinestones, but who's checking?—was offset by his punk rags (Derek Jarman's muses, and the first Westwood T-shirts embroidered with chicken bones). The glittering mess amid which he lived was always providing opportunities for creating some new accessory, image, or décor. Lorrain was a great drinker of ether, a habit that earned him no fewer than nine ulcers and finally a plot in a graveyard in Fécamp.[9] Pélassy, for his part, spent his days smoking charas, which unleashed his sense of humor and taste for phantasmagoria.

Just as Pélassy was definitively settling in Nice in 1994, Florence and Edouard decided to move their gallery to Paris. Having given up the lease to her apartment, while waiting to move Florence lived at the Hôtel Windsor, near the Promenade des Anglais, and invited Pélassy to join her there. You can picture them in fits of laughter, coming out of their smoke-filled room in their best outfits to join their friends at Le Blue Boy. At the hotel reception, they would pass by the owner of the premises in the arms of his adoptive son, a young Nepalese cook who he had made head of kitchen, and who would soon be the hotel's director. It could be the beginning of a film by Rainer Werner Fassbinder or one of Lorrain's tales set on the Riviera, where "all the world's mad, all the world's unbalanced and all the world's hysterics arrange to meet."[10] Nice is where penniless aristocrats and smallpox-ravaged countesses came to die. As the sun set, the town would fill with an androgynous bestiary—strixes, toads, jellyfish—and the sea with thousands of creatures that seemed to have slipped out of a painting by Gustave Moreau. A scene not unlike Lorrain's "Galatée": her "head crowned with wrack and bitter coral," "clumsy madrepores," and "mother of pearl shells and thick seaweed."[11]

For his first exhibition at Art Concept in 1993, Pélassy covered the gallery's walls with long black drapes and suspended reliquaries of gold-painted wood from the ceiling. Small architectures of glass beads—a tiara, a collar, a scepter—sparkled in the darkness. Never mind the clay tiles, the wires hanging from the ceiling, or the papier-mâché appearance of the gilded cases: visitors stepped into the gallery as if they were entering a mausoleum, the crypt of a Gothic cathedral, or the grotto of a sickly prince. One of Pélassy's acid-wash denim jackets was presented alongside the reliquaries, carefully folded, with a vermilion flaming heart embroidered on its chest. Like most of the sculptures he was making at the time—gloves in leather and chain mail, a mother-of-pearl vase adorned with bird heads—these glass relics could have been those of a dying aesthete, and the list of their materials would be enough for even the most mediocre of poets to write a passable sonnet: mother-of-pearl, coral, velvet, rock crystal, tassels, vine tendrils, ermine, mink, rhinestones, and *Posidonia oceanica*, a seaweed long used

9 Jean Lorrain, *Contes d'un buveur d'éther* (1895, repr., Paris: Mercure de France, 2015).

10 Jean Lorrain, *Le Crime des riches* (1905; repr., Paris, L'Harmattan, 1996), 32–33.

11 Jean Lorrain, "Galathée" (1893), a poem inspired by Gustave Moreau's painting *Galatée* (ca. 1880), published in *L'Ombre Ardente* (1897) and republished in Jean Lorrain, *Poésie complète*, ed. Philippe Martin Horie (Paris: Éditions du Sandre, 2015), 663.

for packing crates containing fragile glass that came to be known as "Venetian straw."

Though they are a brilliant example of the decadent spirit, Pélassy's works are also a searing, camp (self-)parody of it. For evidence of this, we only need look to the enormous beaded penis, *Bye Bye Jeff* (1998), created in homage to Jeff Stryker using a dildo cast from the porn star himself, which Paul McCarthy had gifted Pélassy four years earlier. Or to the schoolboy humor of a pair of testicles, which, speared by a silver fork, became a Surrealist object (*Sans titre* [2000]). We could just as well read the cruel portraits of frail dandies that Lorrain sacrificed to his penchant for caricature: the Count Noronsoff, for example, who is "ravaged and riddled by tuberculosis, worn down by neurosis," and finds "a fearsome joy in recounting his ailments," "sarcasm and pride in the nomenclature of his afflictions."[12] Or the Princess Ilsée, "a small, futile creature, ferociously selfish and madly in love with herself," whose life consists of little more than "bathing, perfuming, primping, dressing, and endlessly trying on jewels, tunics, and veils, smiling at herself and dreaming of the next new dress, the sudden pose or the as-yet-unknown fabric that would allow her to stand out from the crowd and distinguish her from other women."[13]

Pélassy took from dandyism not only its folklore but also the idea of the individual's capacity to change themselves, something akin to what Michel Foucault had named ten years earlier *le souci de soi*, the care of the self:[14] "intentional and voluntary practices through which individuals fix rules of conduct for themselves and seek to transform themselves, changing their singular being."[15] Not an aestheticized retreat, but a way of being oneself and one's own object throughout one's existence.[16] "Liberation in every way, everything we want, experimenting with voluntary overdose, bohemia, mc me me," to use the very different terms chosen by Guillaume Dustan some years later.[17] The fin-de-siècle spirit was only one guise among others: saint, pimp, faggot, colonel, or *fils de pute*, son of a bitch; Pélassy proudly embroidered this last persona onto a perfumed velvet curtain (*Sans titre, Figlio di puttana* [1993–1994]).

Pélassy's library constitutes a condensed treatise of faggot stylistics through which he wandered freely, borrowing here an idea, there a way of being, or a temperament that he would stitch together with others. We find Hervé Guibert and Roland Barthes; Pier Paolo Pasolini's little hoodlums (*Ragazzi di vita* [1955]) and Wilhelm von Gloeden's Sicilian ephebes; the hyper-virility of Bret Easton Ellis (*American Psycho* [1991]) and the first novel by porn star Aiden Shaw (*Brutal* [1996]), which Dustan dreamed of publishing in translation in his Rayon collection.[18] The other members of his pantheon lie dormant in his vinyl collection and in the boxes of VHS tapes that once littered the floor of his apartments: Jacques Demy (*Lola* [1961]), Kenneth Anger (*Eaux d'artifice* [1953]), Andrzej Zulawski (*L'important c'est d'aimer* [1975]). These tapes and many others formed the material for the film he made in 1995, *Sans titre, Sang titre, Cent titres*. This fragile montage on a videocassette is destined to be erased a little more each time it is played. The methods deployed to make this film—collage, mirroring, collision—are exactly those

---

[12] Jean Lorrain, *Les Noronsoff* (Paris: Éditions des Autres, 1979), 53.

[13] Jean Lorrain, "La princesse au sabbat," in *Princesse d'ivoire et d'ivresse* (1902; repr., Paris: Union générale d'éditions, 1980), 23.

[14] Michel Foucault, "L'éthique du souci de soi comme pratique de la liberté," *Concordia. Revista internacional de filosofia*, no. 6 (July–December 1983), republished in Michel Foucault, *Dits et Ecrits II* (Paris: Gallimard, 1998), 99–116.

[15] Michel Foucault, *L'Usage des plaisir* (Paris: Gallimard, 1984), 90.

[16] See Marielle Macé's reading of Foucault and redefinition of dandyism in *Styles, critique de nos formes de vie* (Paris: Gallimard, 2016).

[17] *Nietzsche*, directed by Guillaume Dustan (2002), DVD.

[18] In his novel *Nicolas Pages*, trans. James Horton and Peter Valente (1999; repr., Los Angeles: Semiotext(e), 2023), Guillaume Dustan mentions his intention to publish a French translation of "the first novel by Aiden Shaw, also a gay porn star, with a violent theme centered around AIDS, sex, and drugs, [which] is worth reading for its frankness and the emotion that emerges from it" (186).

through which Pélassy thought of himself as an individual: as an accumulation of discordant signs, whose slapdash finish and visible seams mattered little.

Of all the authors with whose books he surrounded himself, it was Jean Genet with whom Pélassy had perhaps the most obvious affinity. The similarities between the author's texts and the artist's works are sometimes so striking that the latter appear as commentary on the former. First and foremost, we find in Pélassy's constructions the outrageous eroticism of Genet's characters: the way they extend the realm of sensuality to every aspect of their lives, transforming it into the prism through which the world is read and experienced. There is also the taste for oxymoron, the luxury of "apartments of garnet-red velvet [and] large beveled mirrors, ornamented with candelabra and their crystal pendants," which serve as a backdrop for stupidity, filth, and a vulgar, scatological poetry reminiscent of François Villon (Genet's Mignon announces that he has "dropped a pearl" when he breaks wind).[19] But above all, in Genet's work, there is the construction of a faggy grammar that, through close observation and a sharply honed sense of caricature, offers a repertoire of archetypes perfect for copying, reproducing, and parodying. From the convicts in *Miracle de la Rose* (1946) to the captain in *Querelle* (1947), whose voice emerges like "a marble column . . . that [supports] him and on which he [leans],"[20] to Divine, the mad and joyous "Toute-Froufrouteuse" in *Notre-Dame-des-Fleurs* (1943).

Like Divine, who "ran from boy to girl, and the transitions from one to the other—because the attitude was a new one—were made stumblingly,"[21] Pélassy was alternately a toreador, a biker, a pimp, a gangster, and sometimes (though more rarely) an androgynous creature—a 1960s *yé-yé* girl or a Californian stoner. He more readily took on muscular expressions of virility—bad boys, criminals, soldiers—and all their emblems: cocks, balls, boots, leather. While there is unquestionably something of the pleasure of play and of comedy, of cross-dressing, of subverting the cliché by caricaturing it, for Pélassy this transvestitism spoke to another need. It was a means of accompanying (or of accentuating, or of masking) the changes his body was undergoing as he became more and more ill. In contrast to Jean Des Esseintes's narrow and hieratic dandyism, Pélassy's entire body of work emphasizes rupture, change, and alteration. In 1994, barely out of chemotherapy, he began a series of portraits based on models found in a hairdressing magazine. Their faces were missing eyes, covered in pustules, perforated, and seemingly on the verge of putrefaction. He titled them with typical verve: *We're gonna have a good time* (1994).

With Pélassy's work, one has to pay close attention, because what seems dead might just be asleep, or mesmerized,[22] be it his gloves that seem on the verge of coming to life or the beads on his necklaces soaked in water and blood. His series of relics—a wooden box in which a passport photo is endlessly reflected between two mirrors (*By the Sea* [1997]), or his *Relaxing Balls* (1995), two obese wax testicles covered in pubic hair nestled in a box of *qigong* balls—are less macabre than they first appear. They are not so much relics, a celebration of a vanished life,

Dustan's collection at Balland, "Le Rayon," was conceived as "a must-read selection of gay culture in all its forms, always at its best" (185).

19
Jean Genet, *Notre-Dame-des-Fleurs* (1942; repr., Paris: Gallimard, 1976), 28, 51.

20
Jean Genet, *Querelle de Brest* (1947; repr., Paris: Gallimard, 2013), 74.

21
Genet, *Notre-Dame-des-Fleurs*, 125.

22
In 1997, Pélassy created a sumptuous *casque de méduse* using Swarovski "aurora borealis" beads. On the figure of Medusa and the role of snakes in Pélassy's oeuvre, see Marie Canet, "Bruno Pélassy, Realife," in *NOIT-3* (London: Camberwell Press, 2016), 23–39, published on the occasion of Pélassy's and Marc Camille Chaimowicz's exhibition *Tears Shared*, Flat Time House, London, 2016.

as cuttings from which other forms of existence might sprout or take root. Five years later, the two wax balls metamorphosed into an organic creature covered in lace and tulle, drifting majestically around an aquarium of silicone and distilled water (*Relaxing Ball* [2000–2001]). Just as Genet's language immediately alters any object it describes through the images that it conveys, Pélassy's sculptures celebrate the power of fantasies that spill over into the real—nothing lasts, everything changes (an antique becomes a toy, a natural material becomes synthetic, a scepter becomes a dildo)—and turn it inside out like a glove. Not even the most fervent heterosexual can escape this movement, as Pélassy would prove to his friends every time they went out together.

Pélassy moved into his last apartment in 1996: a small studio on rue Clément Roassal in Nice, where he lived until his death. There, he worked hard and worked a lot, in a marvelous pigsty and a fog of images, with his music on full blast and clouds of smoke from the joints he chain-smoked. It could just as easily have been a clandestine sweatshop as the study of a ruined aesthete or the safehouse of a thug about to make love on top of his loot. As he became weaker, he surrounded himself with a crowd of small creatures, a "freaky pet shop"[23] installed in the comfort of his own home. After the graceful, silent aquatic phantoms who paraded their silvery rags around silicone aquariums like Genet's angels ("neither mind nor matter, white, filmy and frightening, like the translucent bodies of ghosts")[24] came a crowd of extraordinarily endearing critters whose fur covered the wind-up mechanisms of children's toys. Once set in a motion, they wriggled and cried out hysterically. What better company could one ask for? After the mysterious creature that we dream of fishing out of the sea and bringing home without depriving it of oxygen, here was the mouse that keeps the condemned man company in the darkness of his cell. Sometimes Pélassy would find his wind-up creatures missing a leg, broken apart under the weight of their heavier siblings, or crushed underfoot after he trod on them while half asleep. He paid little mind to their demise, though. They weren't meant to outlive him.

Pélassy lived fast, supplying himself thanks to Nice's secondhand stores, where he made off with the best clothes and the best books, as well as with the help of friends, family, and a disability pension from the state. When his health allowed, he would put in appearances at fabulous parties, like the one at the villa in Antibes where he spent all evening in the pool reading tarot cards for the other guests, or the costume ball organized by Brice Dellsperger in 1998. There, the theme was "1983," a celebration of the golden age of Italo-disco at Les Bains Douche ("Dolce vita" by Ryan Paris, the soundtrack of *Scarface* by Giorgio Moroder) and the vampire apotheosis of Bowie (in *Furyo* by Nagisa Oshima and Tony Scott's *Predators*). That year was also the twilight of a period, its last hurrah. Derek Jarman wrote a few years later in his 1990 film *The Garden*:

> I have no words
> My shaking hand
> Cannot express my fury
> Sadness is all I have
> Cold, cold, cold you died so silently

23
In 1993, Pélassy showed his work in an exhibition entitled *Freaky Pets Shop* at Chez Valentin in the Parisian suburb of Clichy.

24
Genet, *Notre-Dame-des-Fleurs*, 10.

Klaus Nomi died on August 6, 1983, in New York, while in France, the Institut Pasteur isolated the virus that causes AIDS for the first time, a year after the Center for Disease Control in the United States did so.

When Dellsperger's party was in full swing, Pélassy was still busy preparing his friends' looks. Dresses, fake eyelashes, hairspray—everything had to be perfect. When he finally arrived, he was wearing a loose silver tunic, a necklace of white pearls, and a crown that was a replica of those worn by the Aspara nymphs in the Laos of his earliest childhood. Just as he was getting ready to walk down the steps, welcomed and cheered on by a small crowd, a hand darted out of the darkness and snatched his headpiece. His friends stared in horror: he had just completed chemotherapy, and his eyebrows and hair fell to the floor. He met their gaze, laughing. Too bad! If you can't be a goddess, be a monk!

That evening, having left first, long before the others, as was now his habit, Pélassy might have stopped on Lorrain's promenade to find a lover in front of the seahorses and starfish—one way among many others of honoring both the epitaph that he carved into a marble headstone a year before his death and the promise that he had made himself aged twenty: [I'm gonna have] *FUN* (2001).

Many thanks to Florence Bonnefous, Ingrid Luche, and Brigitte Pélassy for generously sharing their memories with me.

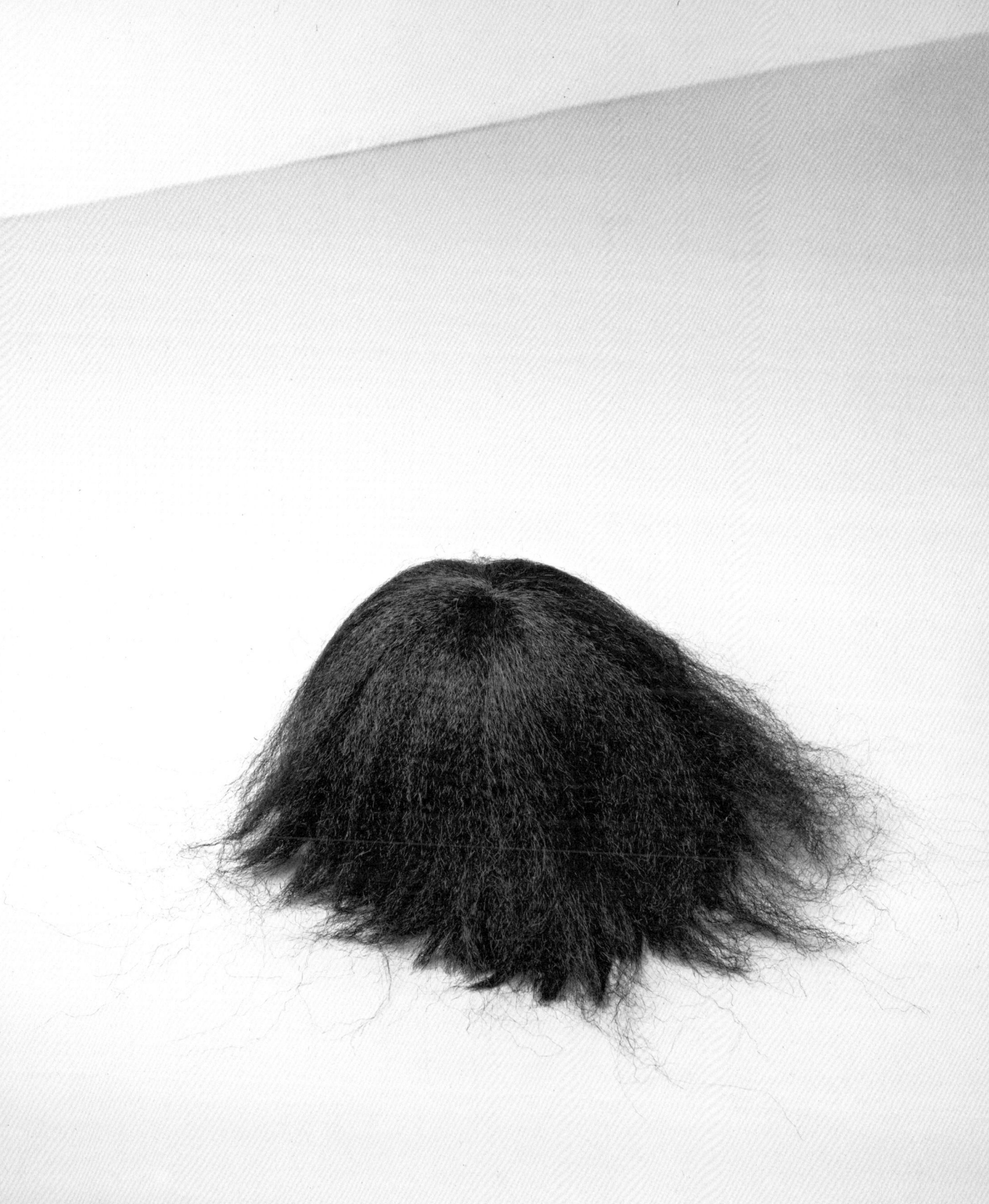

27   *Untitled*, 1994, from the *Bestioles* series. Black wig, plastic, toy mechanism, batteries, 30 × 20 × 18 cm

Untitled, 1994, from the *Bestioles* series. Ash blonde wig, plastic, toy mechanism, batteries, 40 × 30 × 22 cm

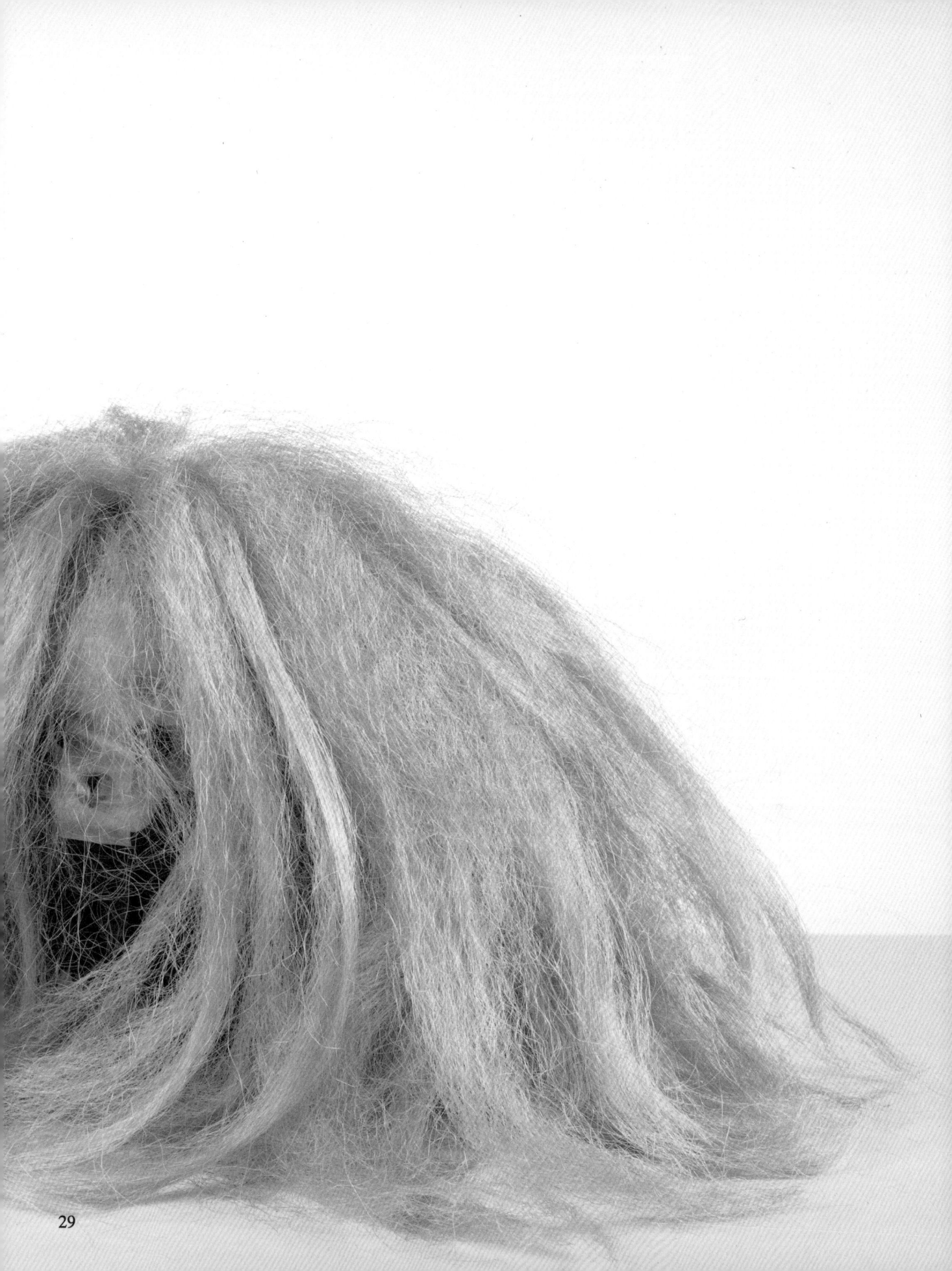

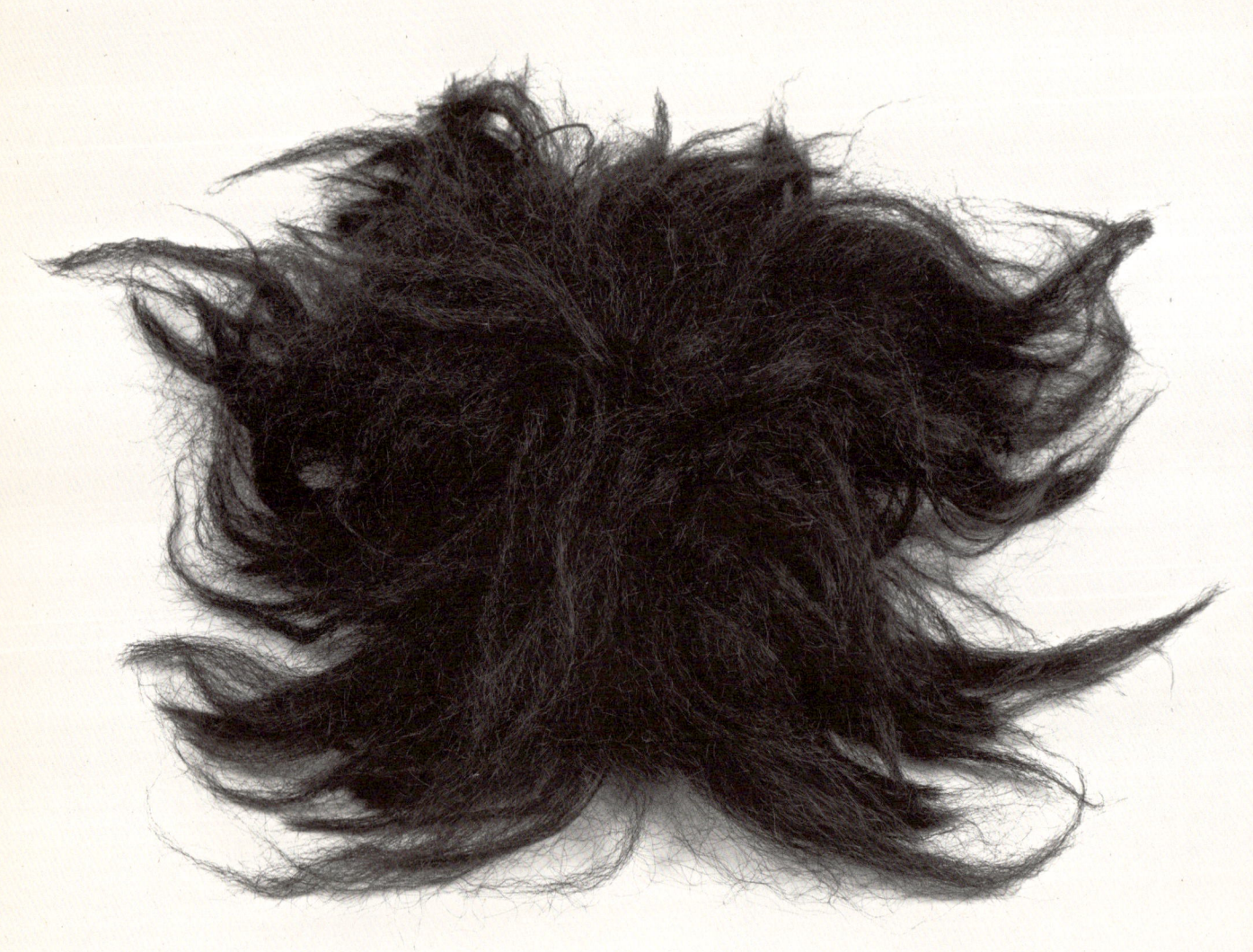

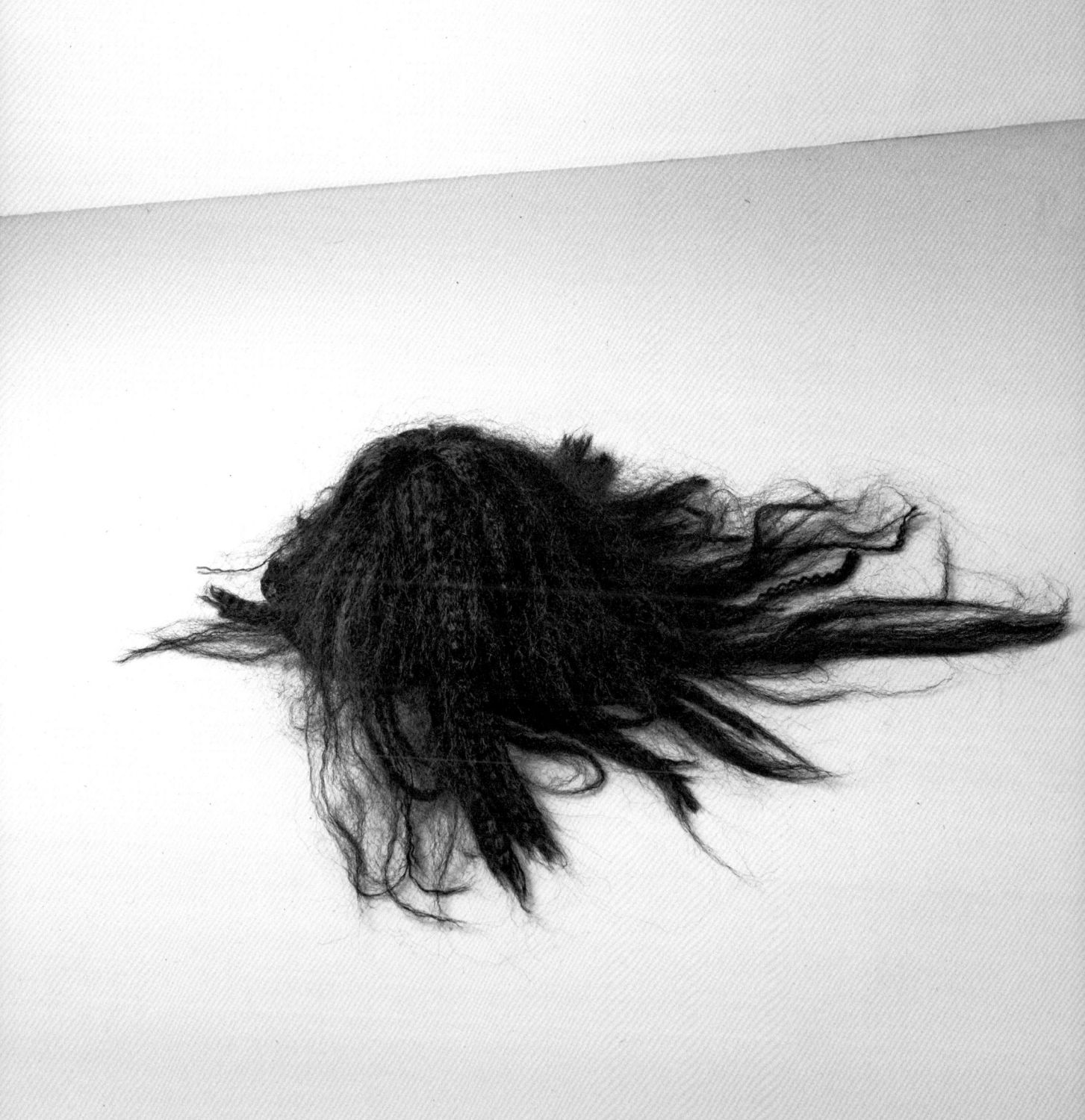

Untitled, 1994, from the *Bestioles* series. Black wig, plastic, toy mechanism, batteries, 55 × 30 × 22 cm

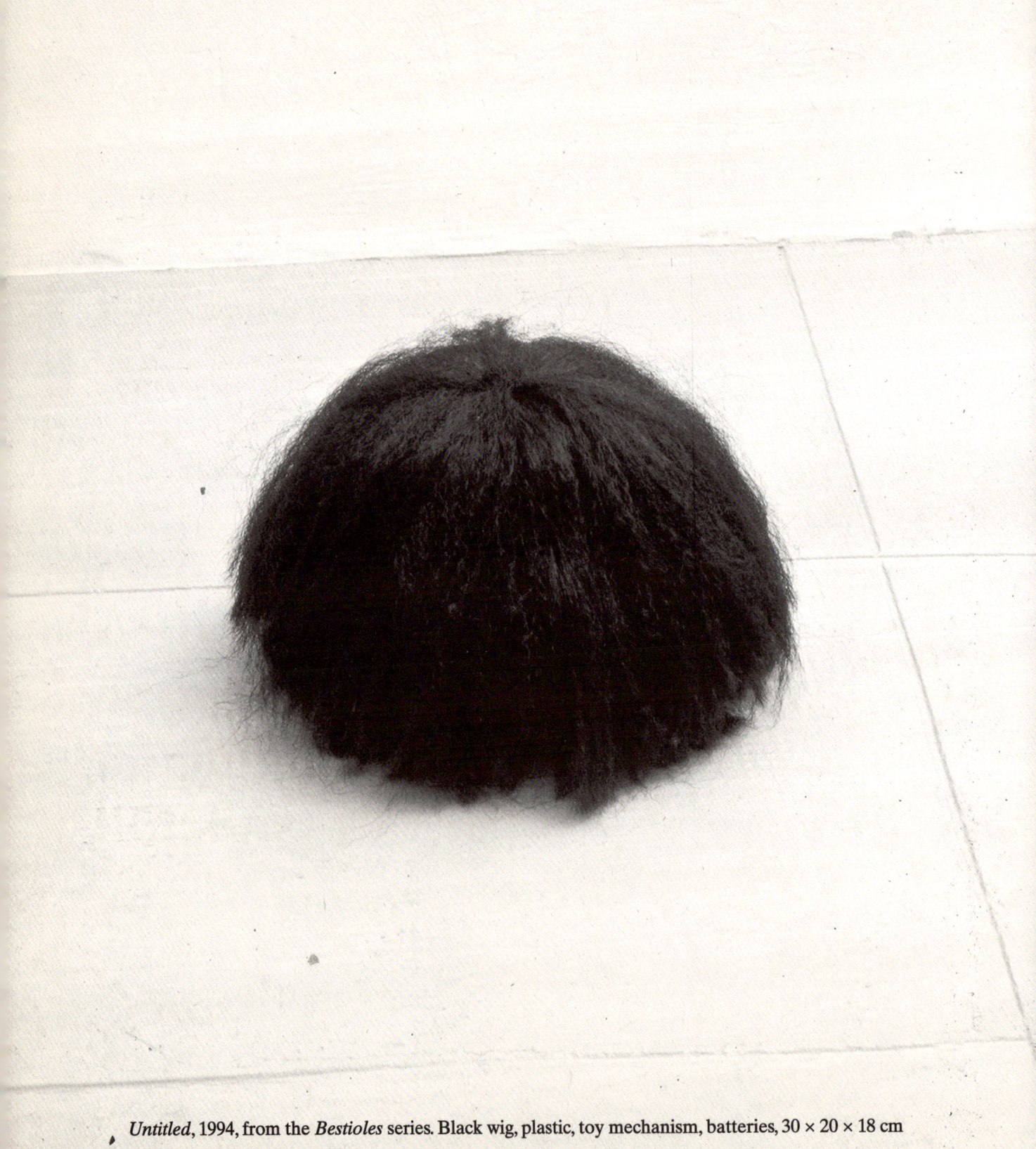

Untitled, 1994, from the *Bestioles* series. Black wig, plastic, toy mechanism, batteries, 30 × 20 × 18 cm

Untitled, 2000–2001, from the *Créatures* series. Silk, lace, silicone, beads, mirror, aquarium and plinth, spotlight, 175.5 × 90 × 40 cm

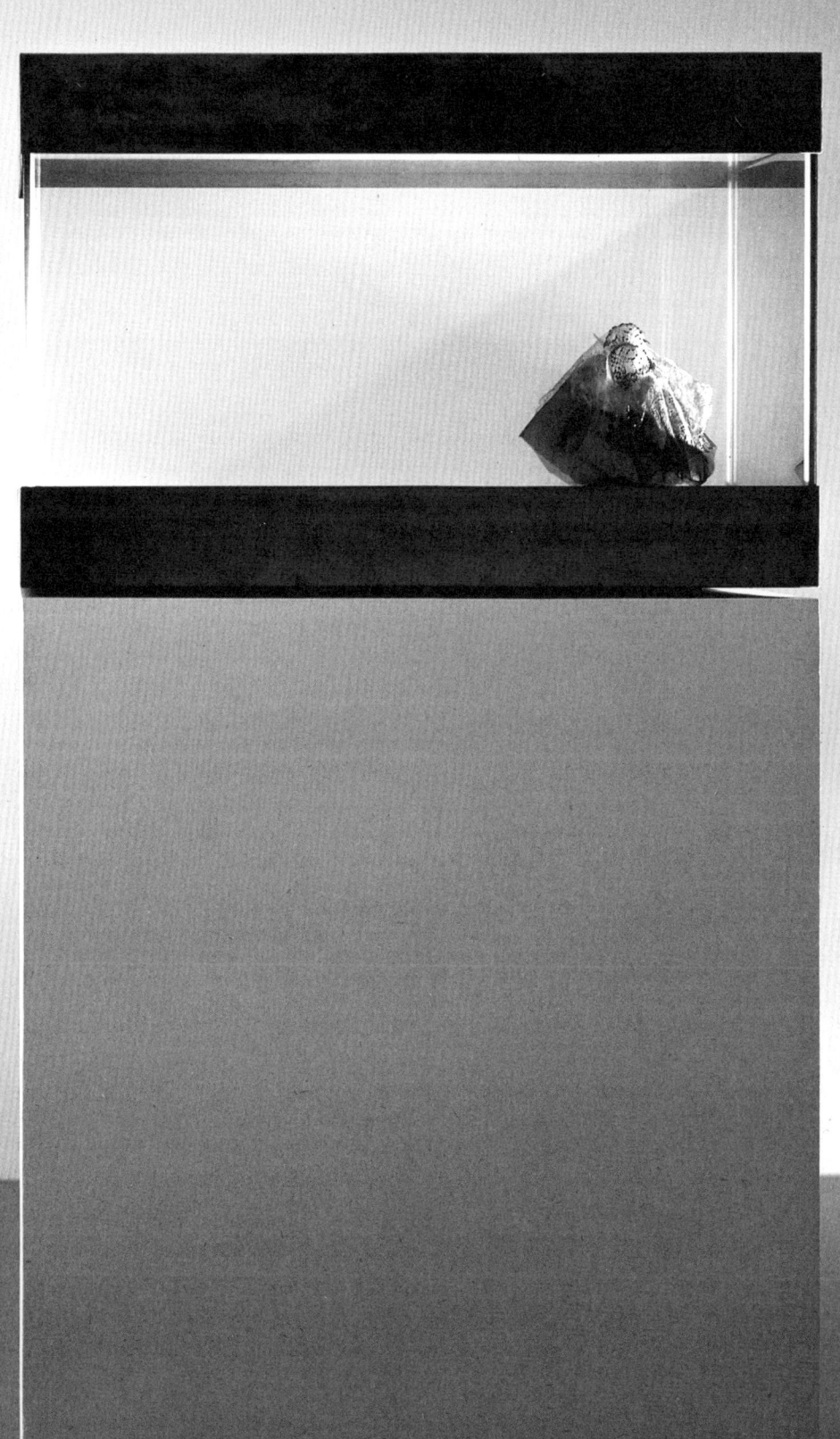

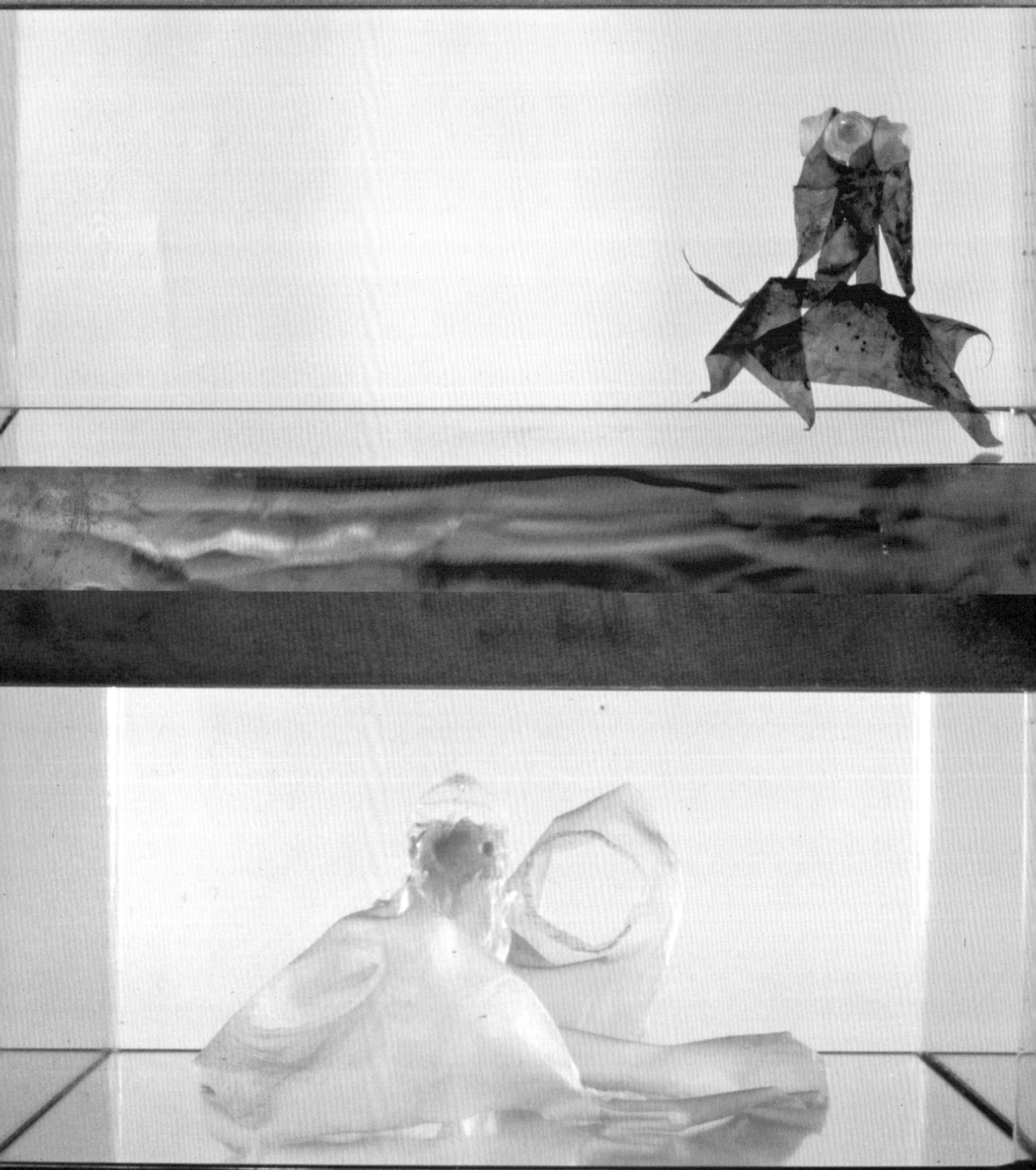

Untitled, 2000–2001, from the *Créatures* series. Silk, silicone, plastic, mirror, aquarium and plinth, spotlight, 175.5 × 90 × 40 cm

Untitled, 2001, from the *Créatures* series. Silk, silicone, crystal, mirror, aquarium and plinth, spotlight, 175.5 × 90 × 40 cm. Collection MAMCO Genève

Untitled, 2000–2001, from the *Créatures* series. Silk, silicone, lace, pearls, mirror, aquarium and plinth, spotlight, 175.5 × 90 × 40 cm. Collection MAMCO Genève

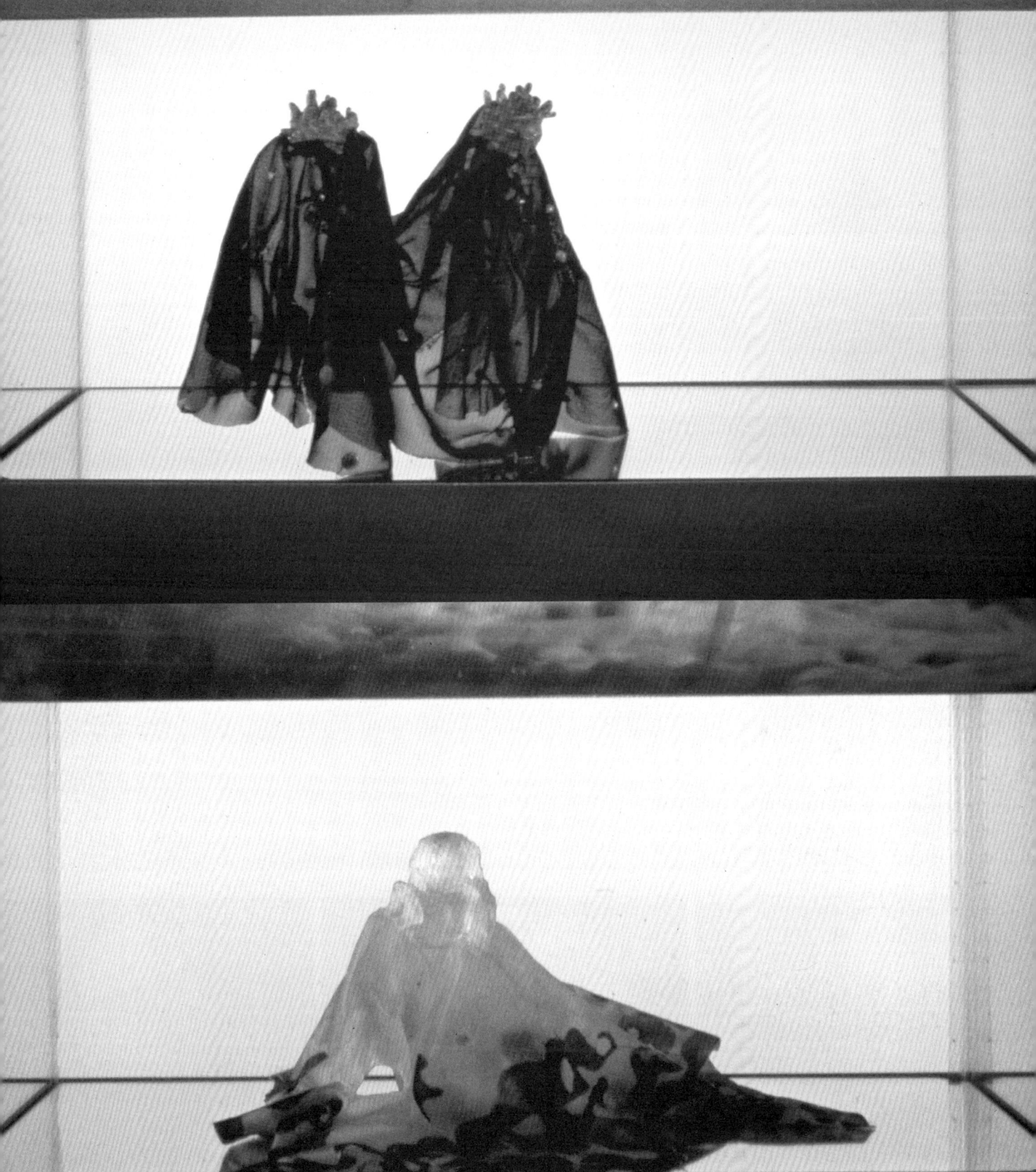

Untitled, 2000–2001, from the *Créatures* series. Silk, silicone, mirror, aquarium and plinth, spot light, 175.5 × 90 × 40 cm

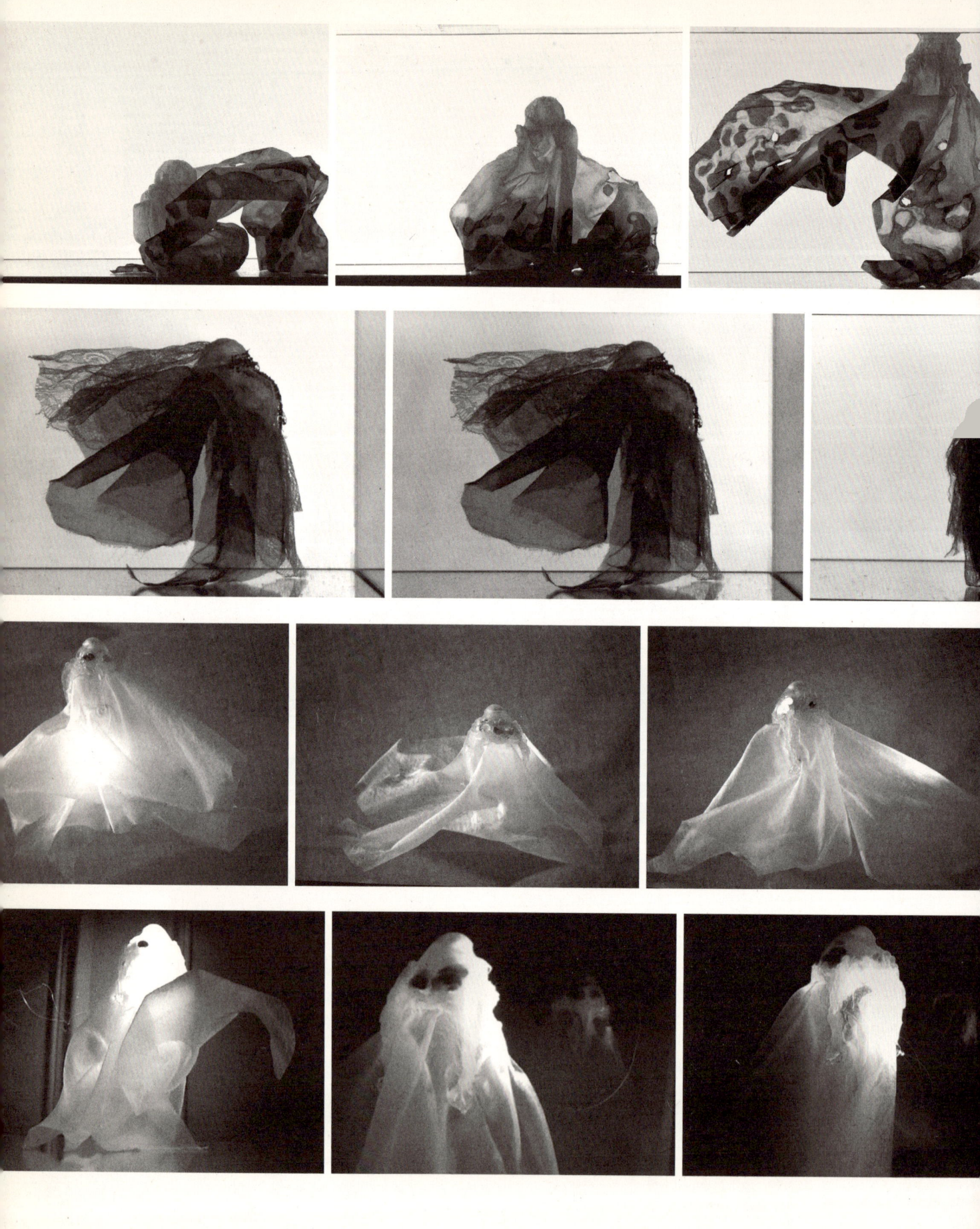

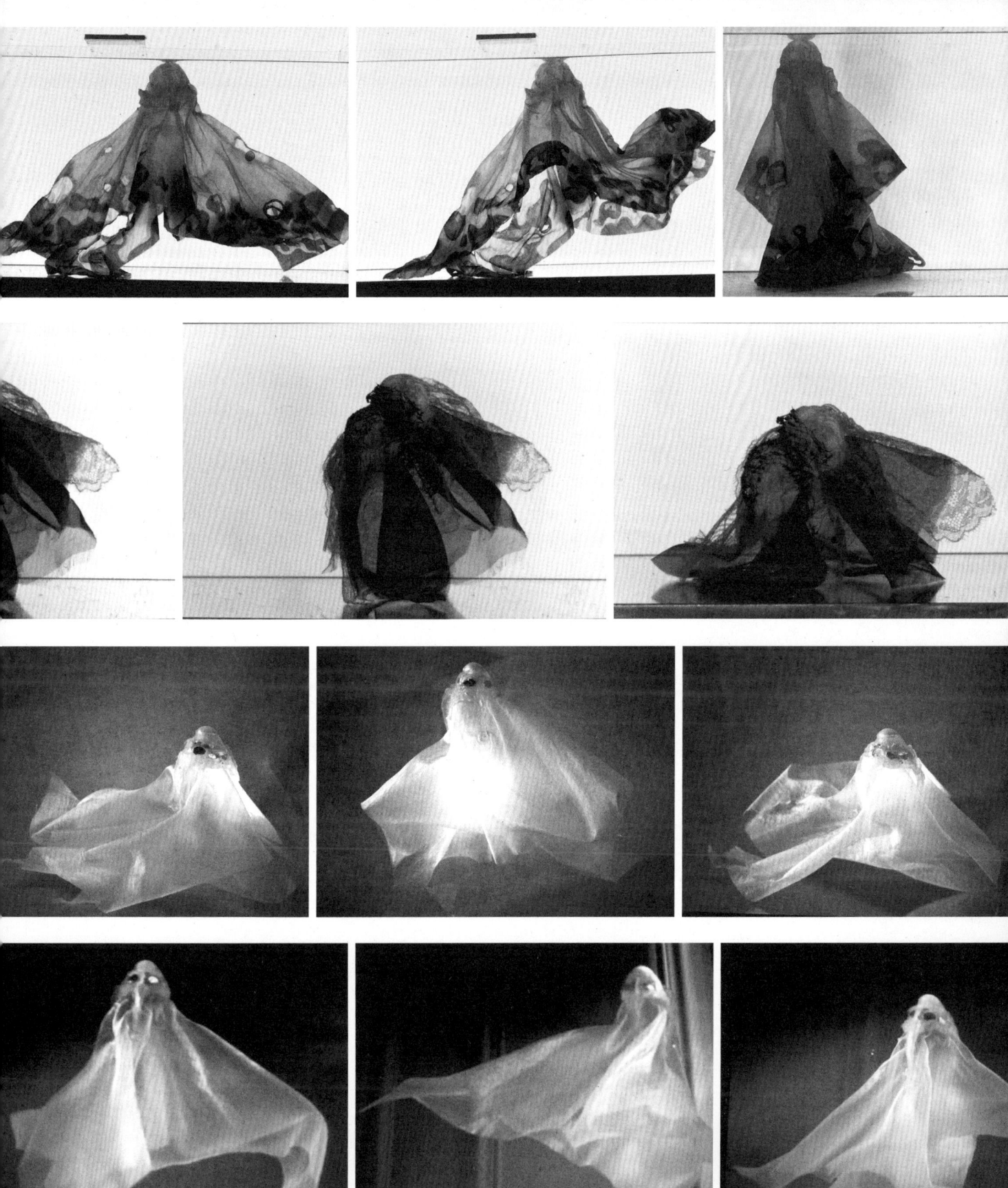

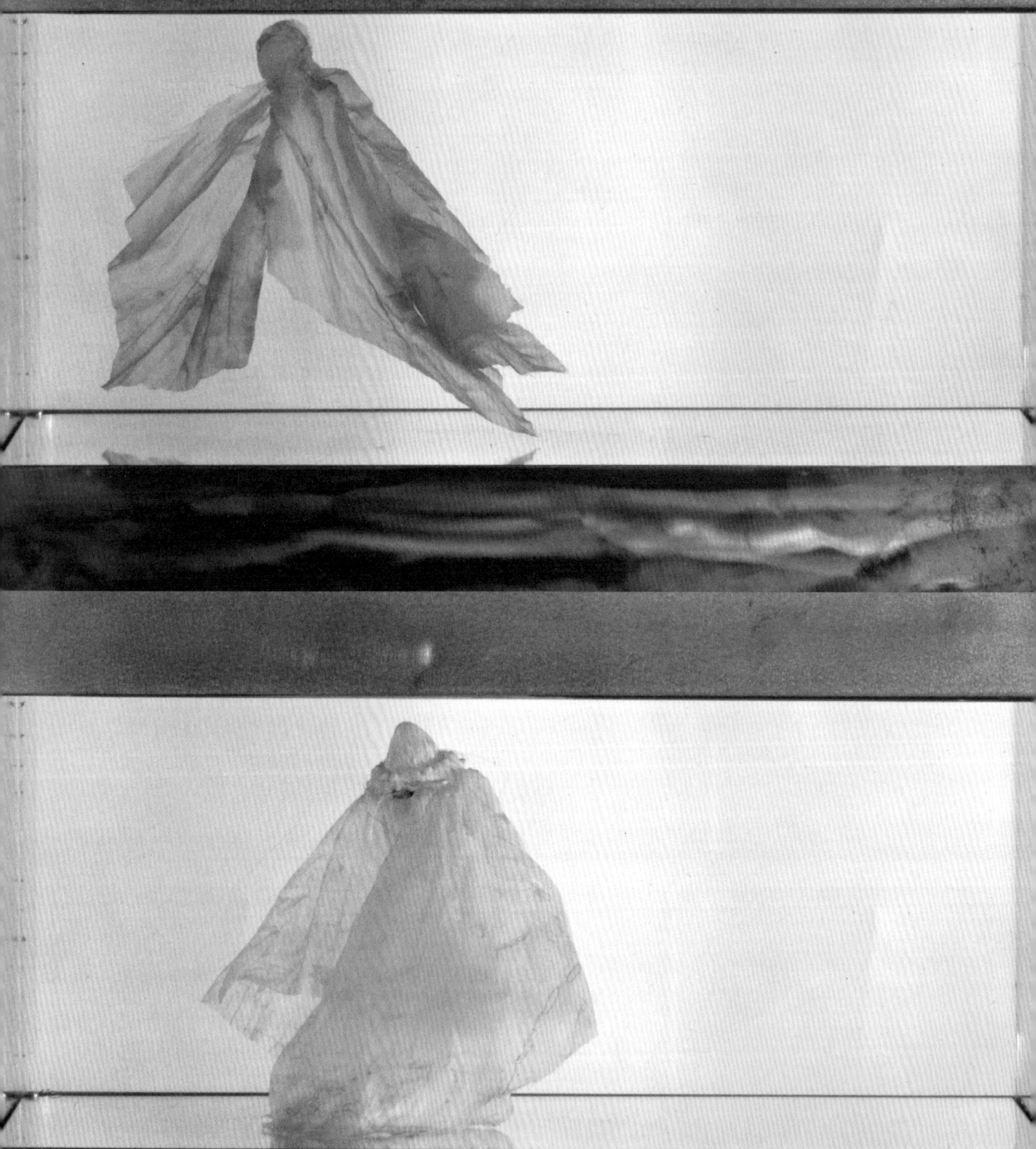

Untitled, 2000–2001, from the *Créatures* series. Silicone, iridescent silk, silver paint, mirror, aquarium and plinth, spotlight, 175.5 × 90 × 40 cm

Untitled, 2000–2001, from the *Créatures* series. Silk, silicone, lace, pearls, mirror, aquarium and plinth, spotlight, 175.5 × 90 × 40 cm

Untitled, 2000, from the *Créatures* series. Silicone, black lace fishnet, beads, mirror, aquarium and plinth, spotlight, 175.5 × 90 × 40 cm

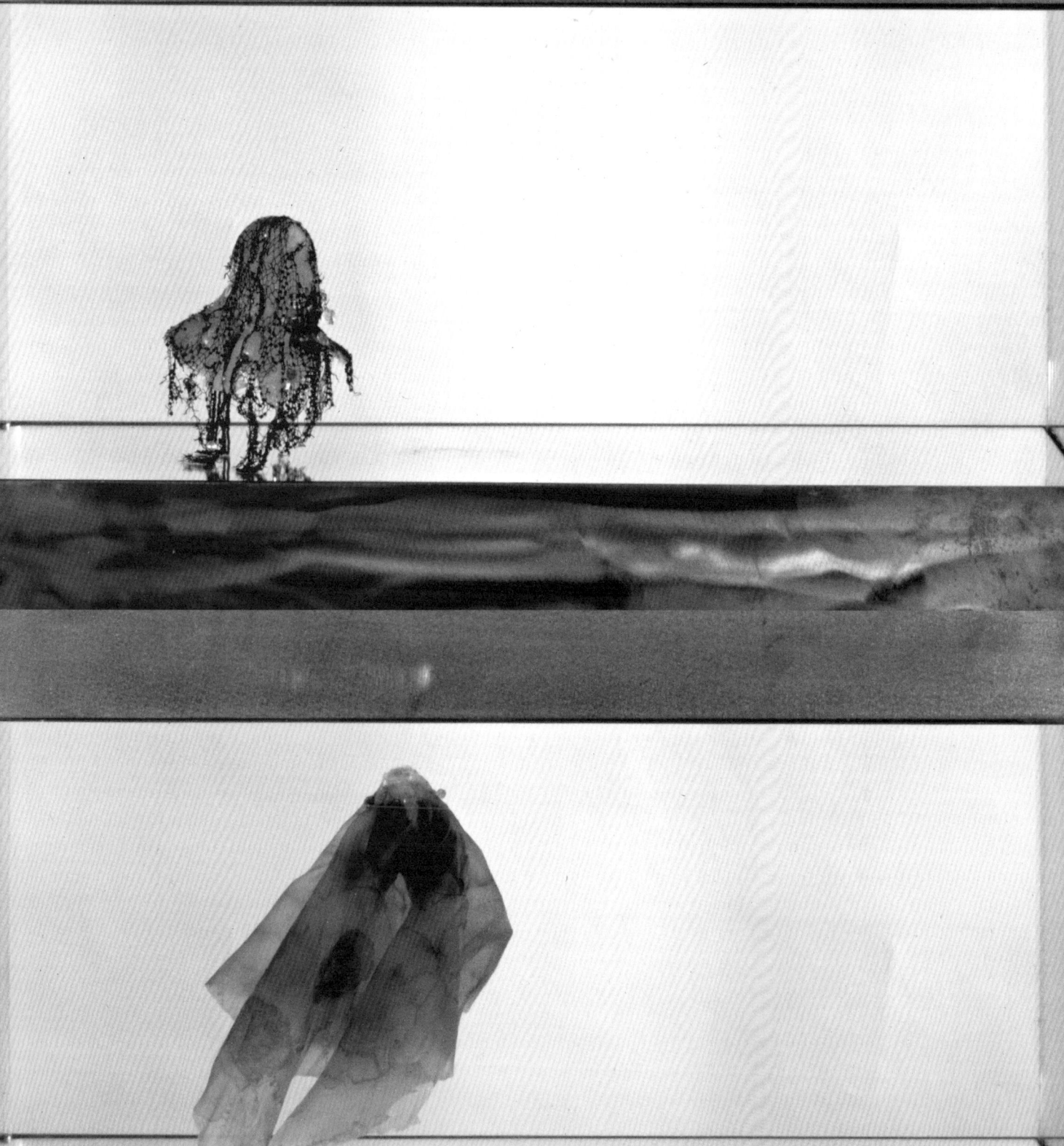

Untitled, 2000–2001, from the *Créatures* series. Silicone, silk, gold paint, tulle, pearls, mirror, aquarium and plinth, 53 × 90 × 40 cm (aquarium), 122.5 × 90 × 40 cm (plinth)

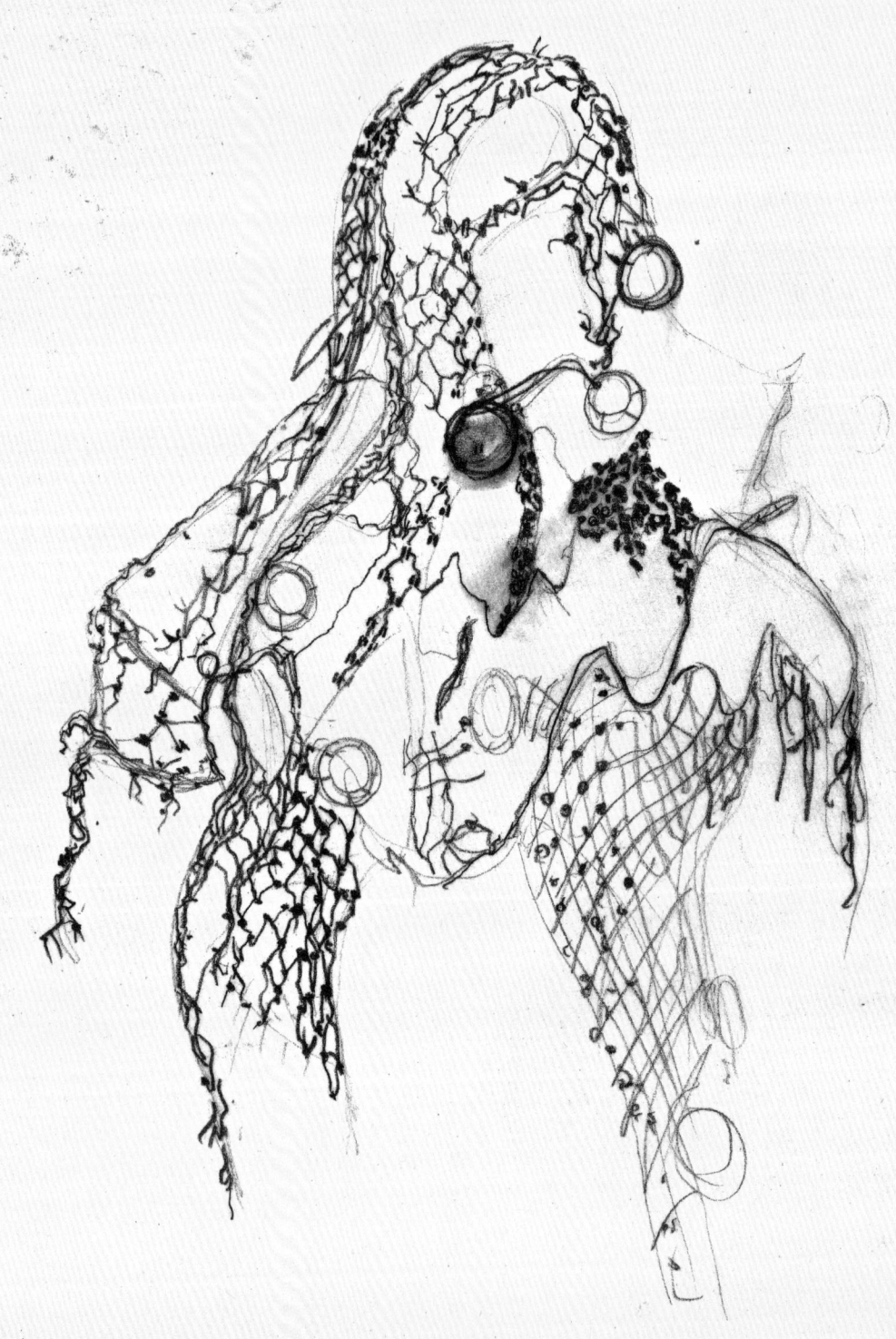

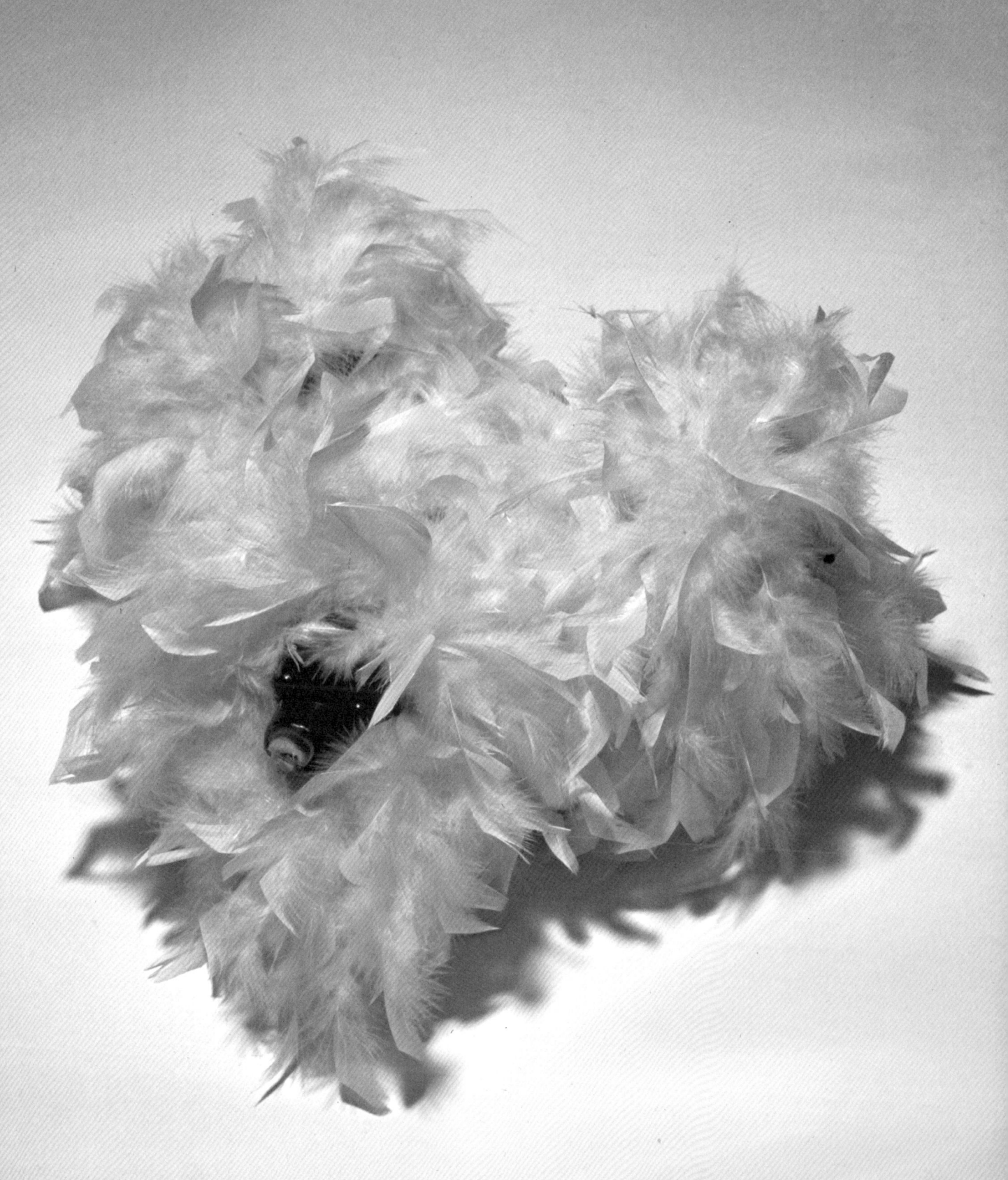

Untitled, 2001, from the *Bestioles* series. Light pink boa feathers, plastic, sound toy mechanism, 20 × 45 × 34 cm. Collection FRAC Lorraine, Metz

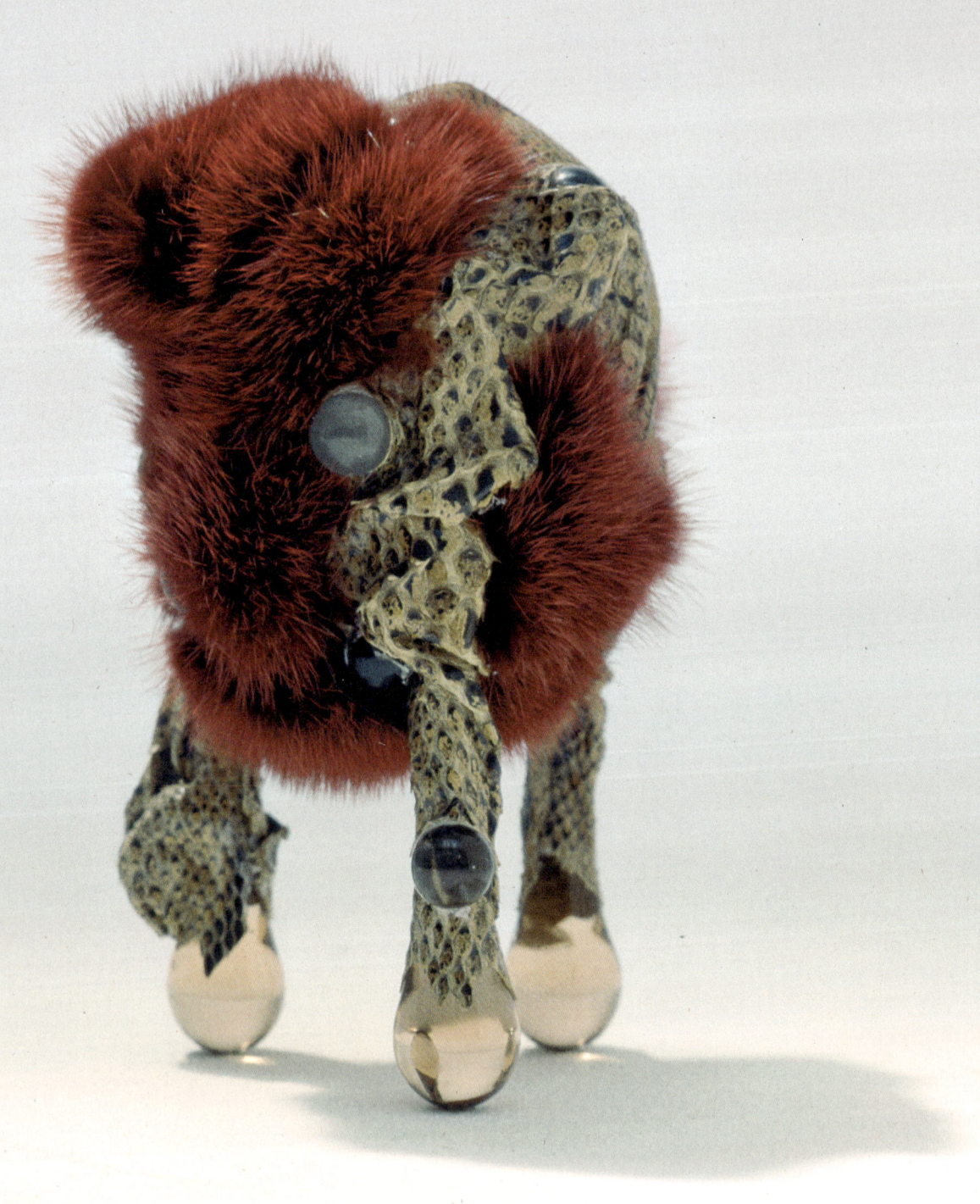

Untitled, 2001, from the *Bestioles* series. Crystal, mink, python, glass, sound toy mechanism, batteries, 19 × 10 × 10 cm. Collection Olivier Petrilli, Paris

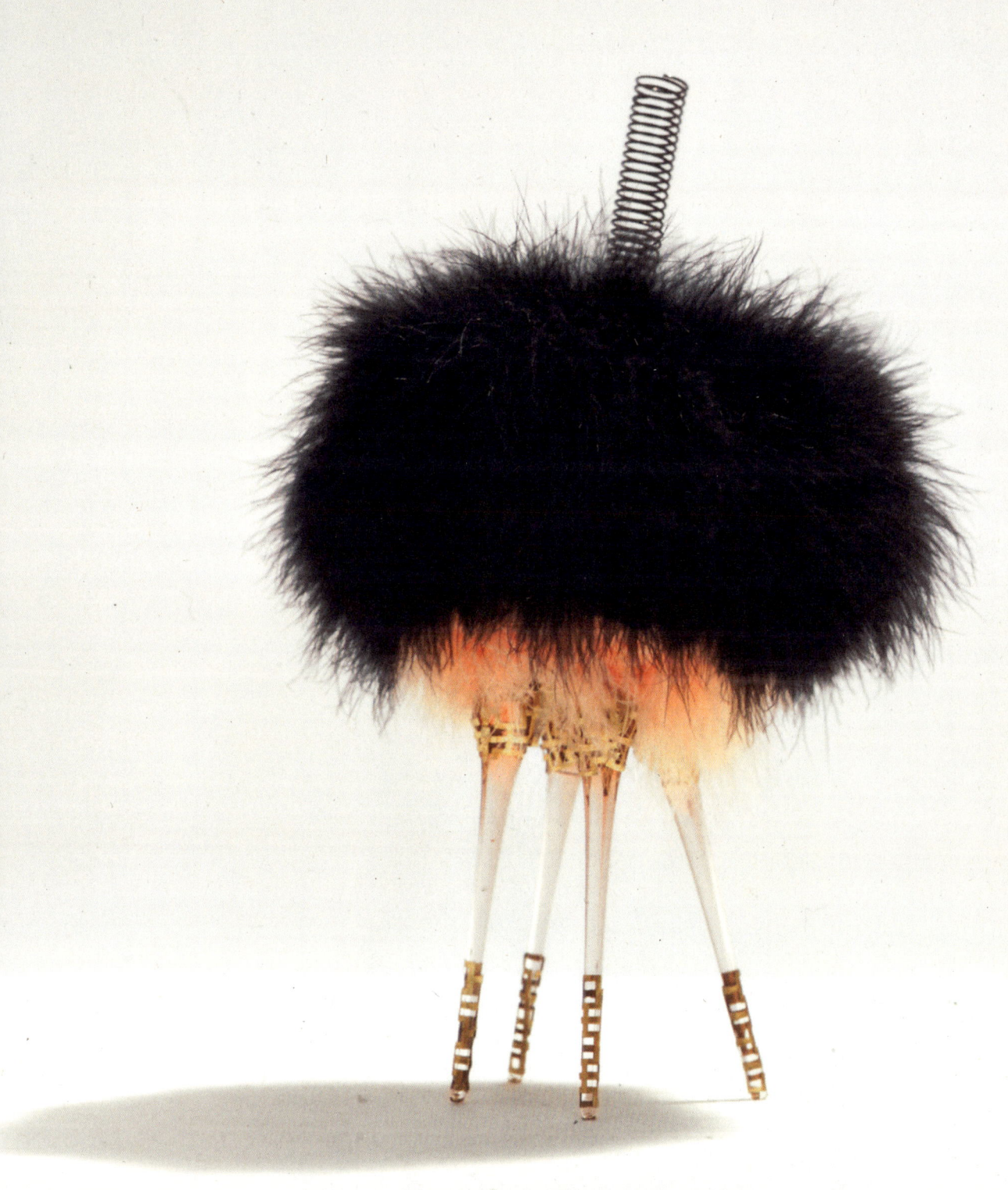

Untitled, 2001, from the *Bestioles* series. Crystal, fur, metal, sound toy mechanism, batteries, 40 × 15 × 15 cm. Collection Ben & Annie Vautier, Nice

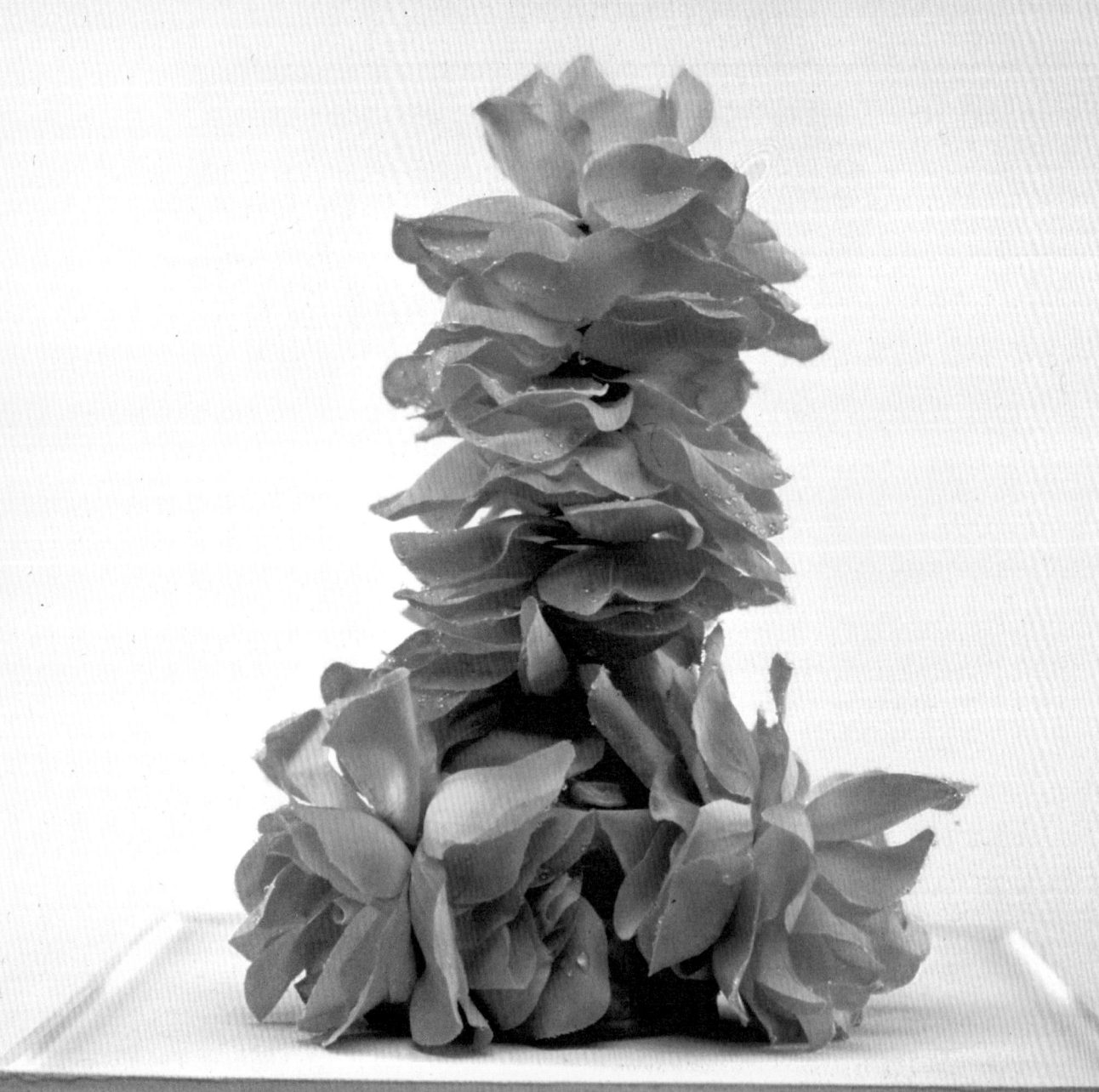

Untitled, 2001, from the *Bestioles* series. Artificial flowers, plastic, sound toy mechanism batteries, 28 × 21 × 15 cm. Collection Andrea Busto, Turin

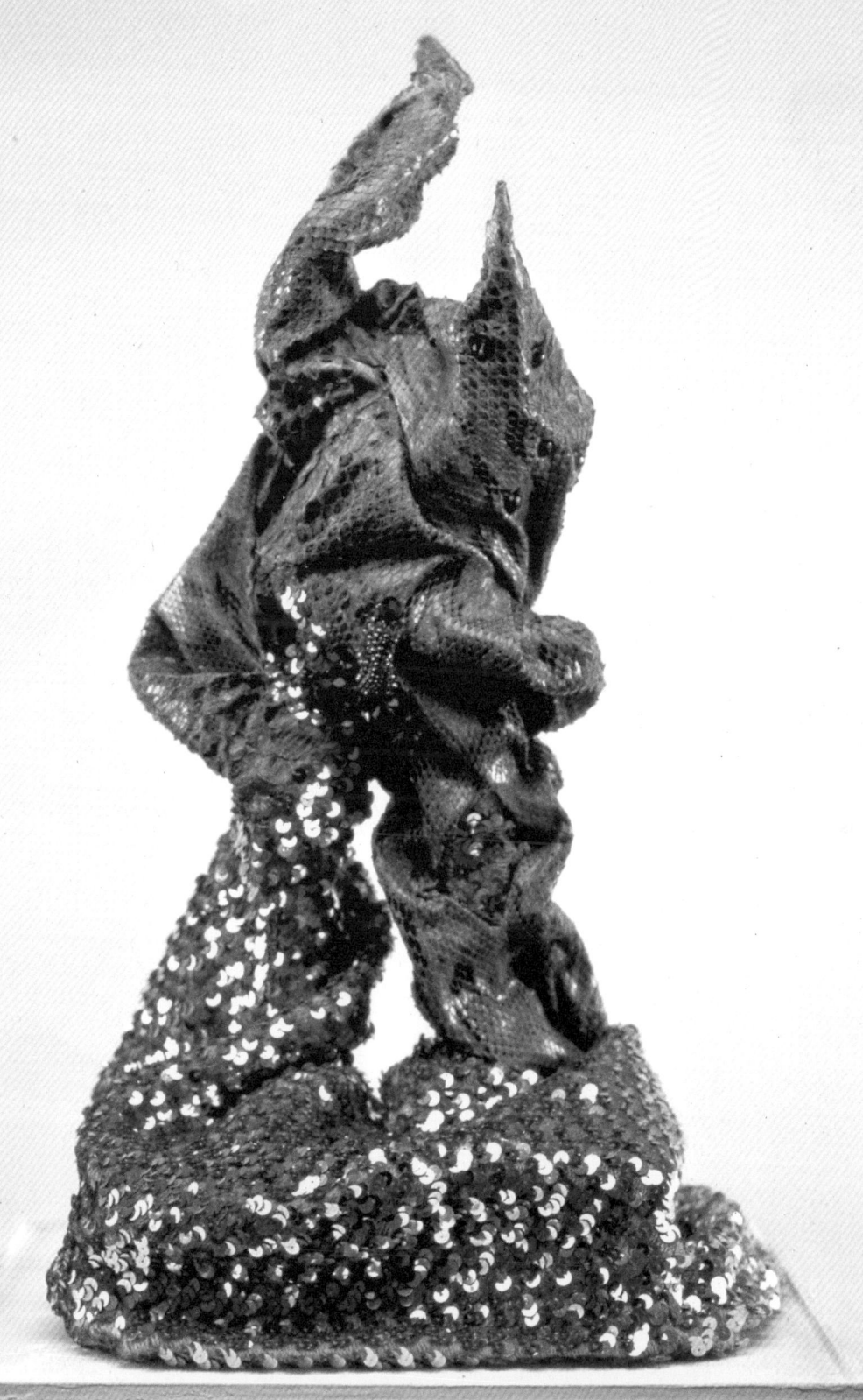

Untitled, 2001, from the *Bestioles* series. Python, sequins, crystal, glass, sound toy mechanism, batteries, 50 × 23 × 20 cm. Collection Ben & Annie Vautier, Nice

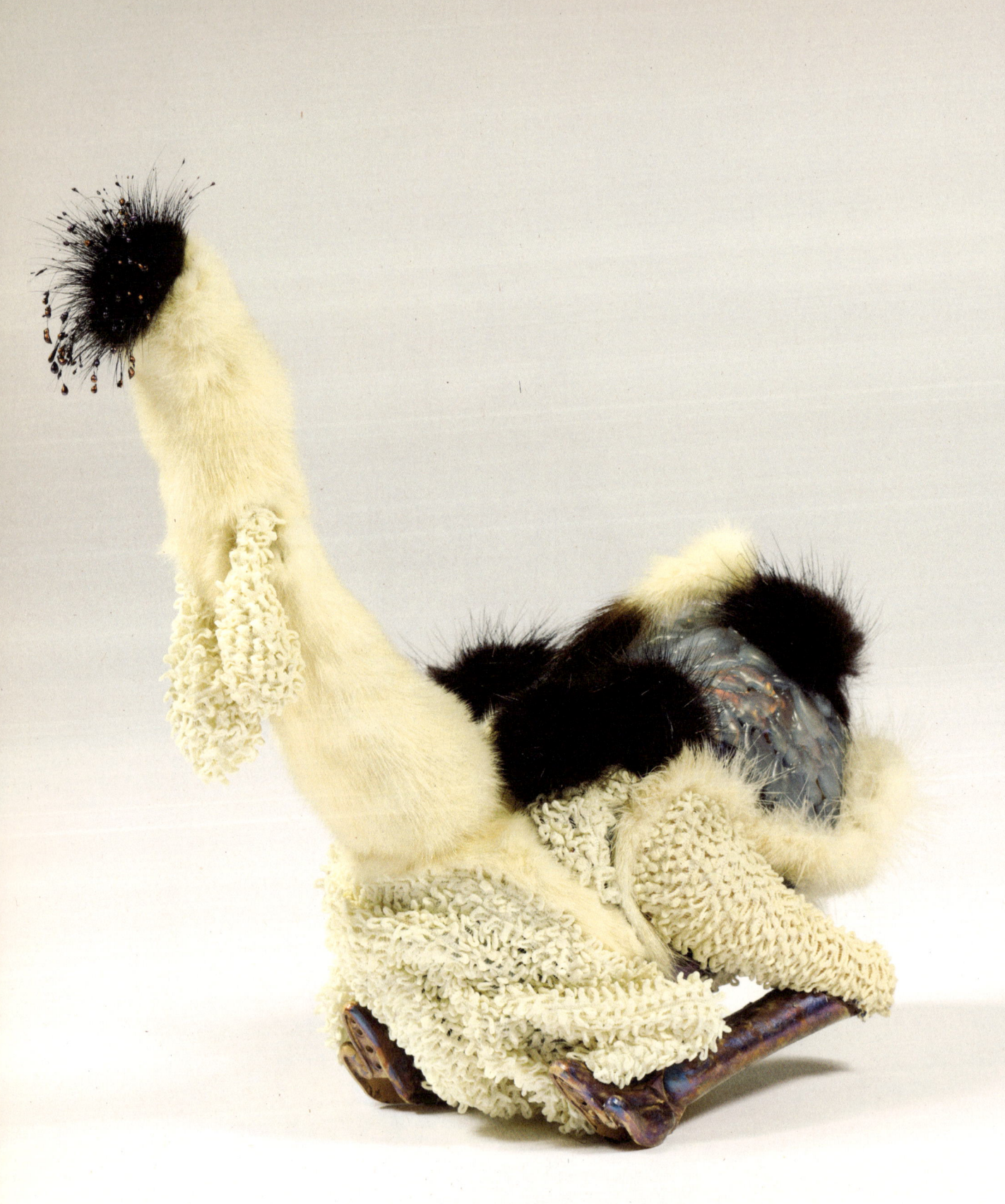

Untitled, 2001, from the *Bestioles* series. Ermine, mink, lace, silicone, plastic, sound toy mechanism, batteries, 33 × 23 × 11 cm. Collection Roselyne & Patrick Michaud, Nice

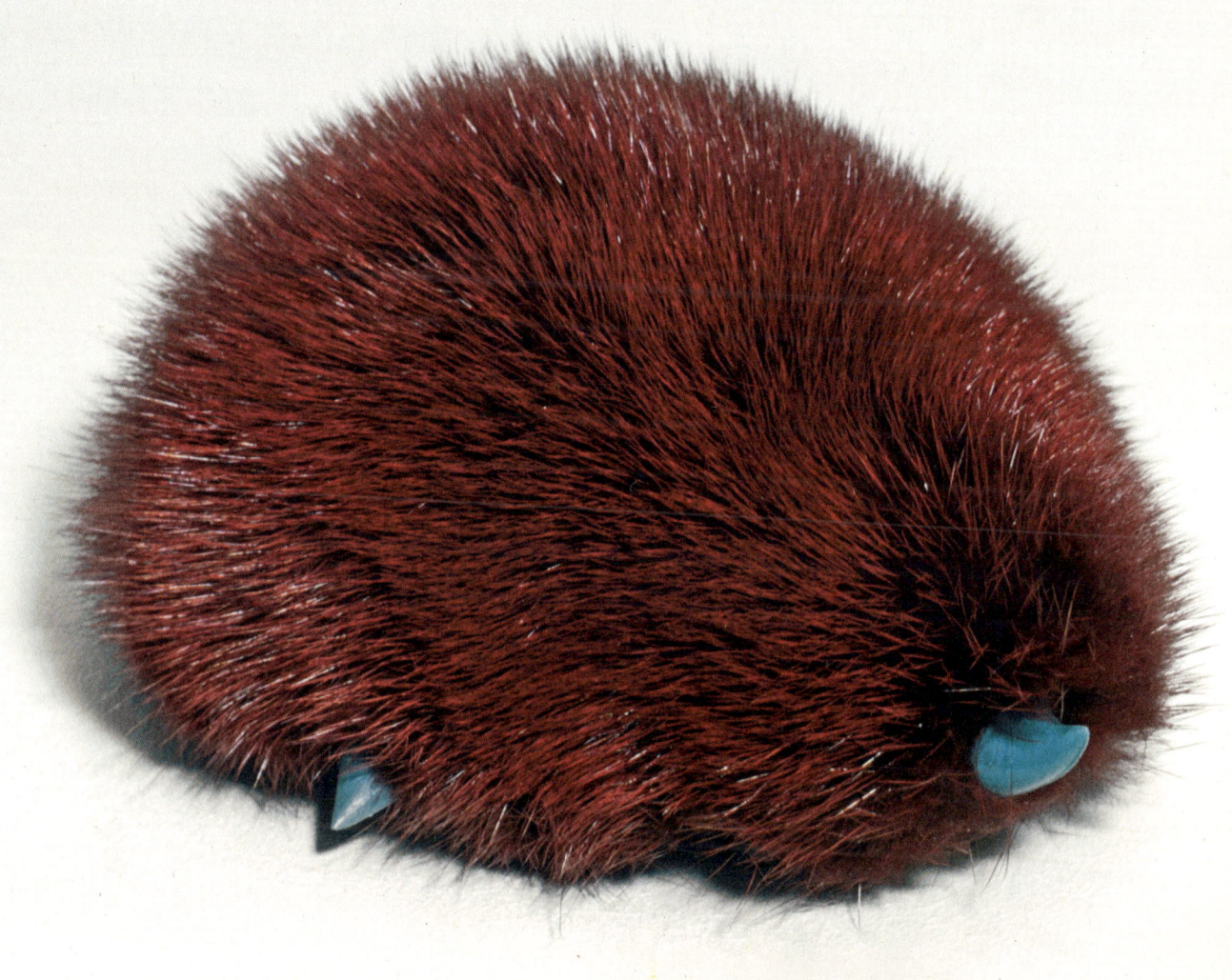

Untitled, 2001, from the *Bestioles* series. Red mink, plastic, sound toy mechanism, batteries, 7.5 × 12 × 16 cm. Collection Brigitte Pélassy, Nice

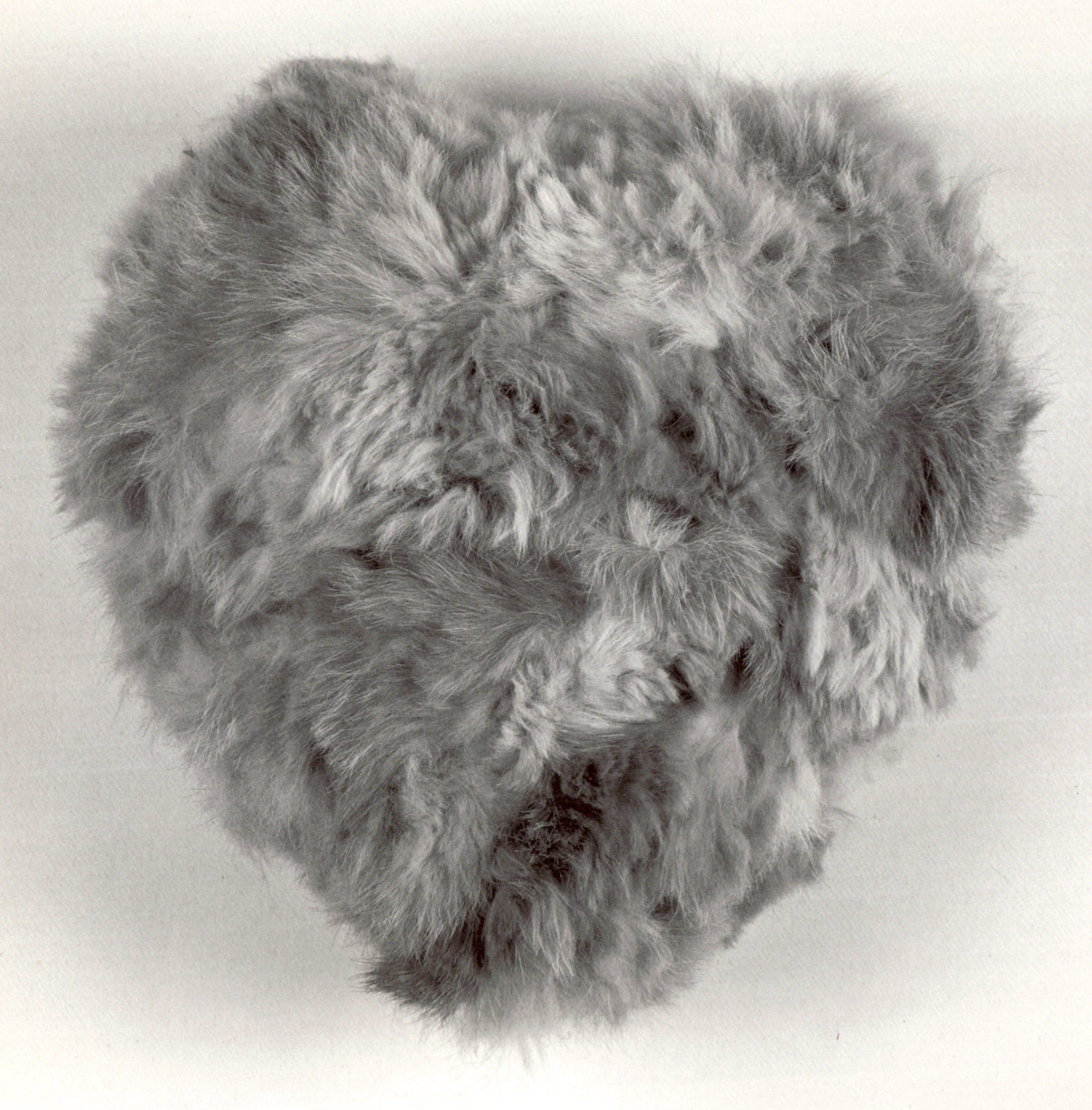

Untitled, 1997, from the *Bestioles* series. Rabbit fur, metal, plastic, sound toy mechanism, 11 × 20 × 20 cm. Collection Michel Coen, Nice

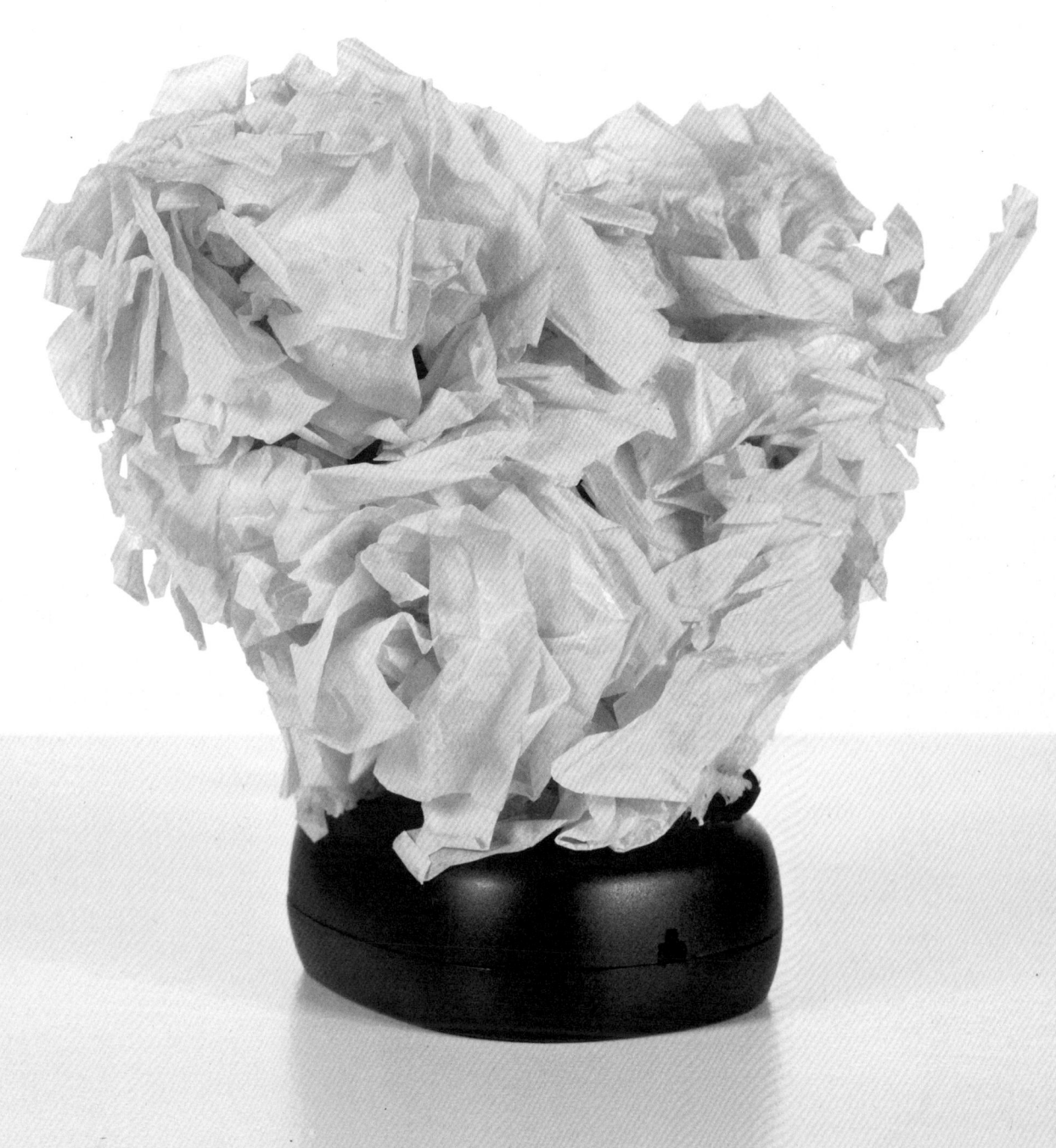

Untitled, 1998, from the *Bestioles* series. Cigarette paper, plastic, glue, sound toy mechanism, batteries, 16 × 18 × 10.5 cm. Collection Fanny Hilaire, Saint-Paul-de-Vence

Untitled, 2001, from the *Bestioles* series. Marabou feather, Venice straw, mirror, plastic, sound toy mechanism, batteries, 10 × 25 × 12 cm. Collection Ben & Annie Vautier, Nice

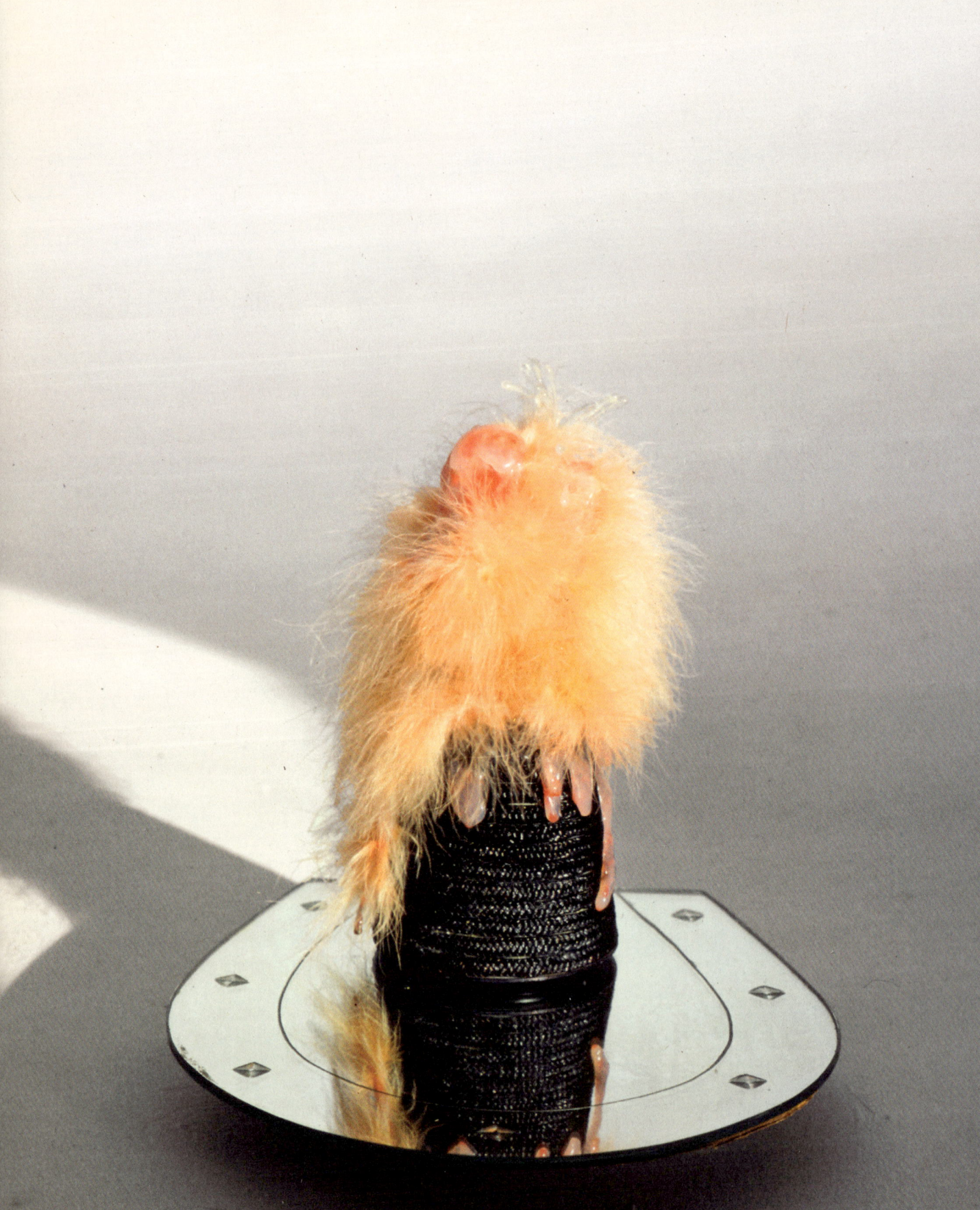

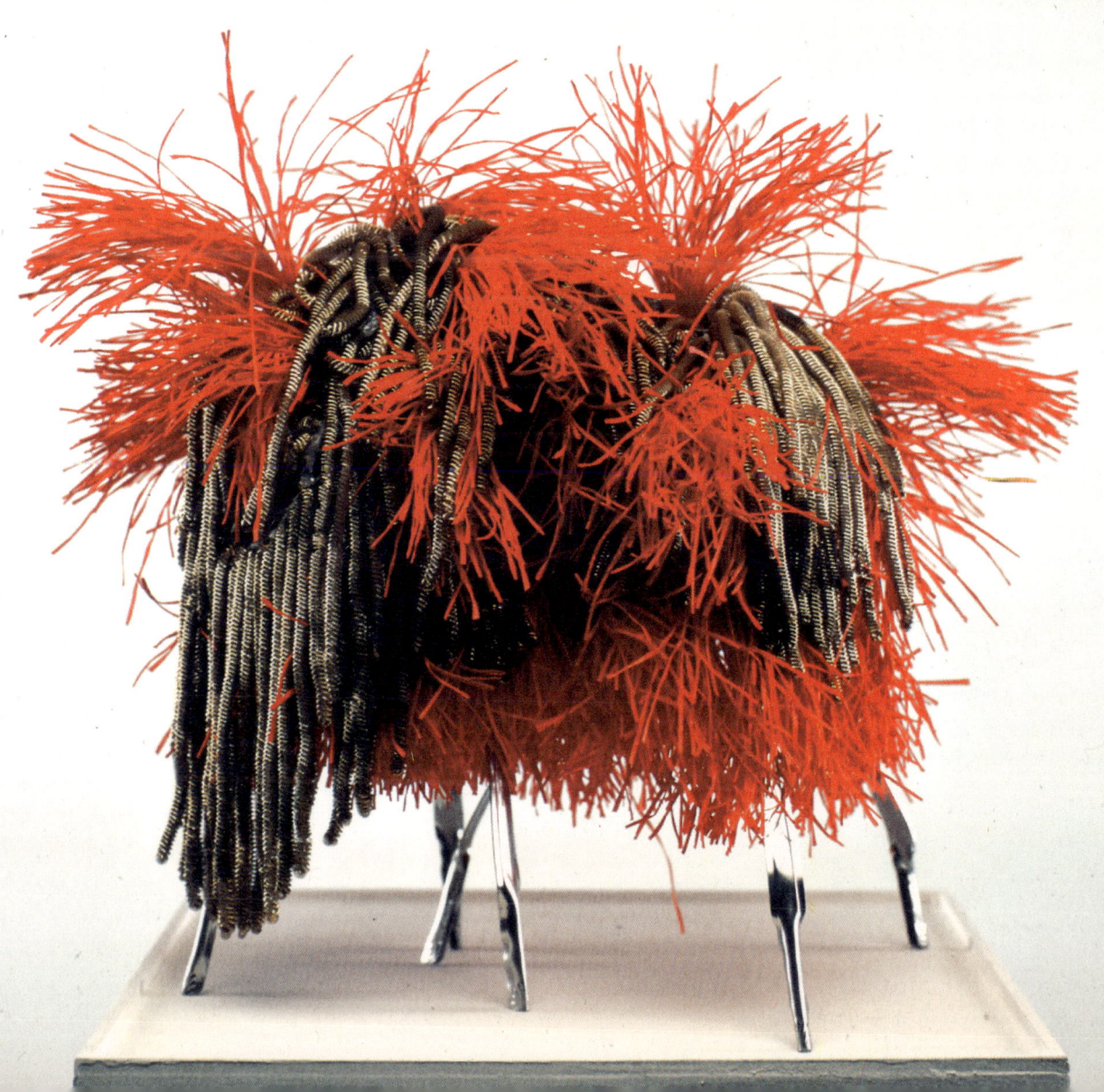

Untitled, 2001, from the *Bestioles* series. Raphia, metal, plastic, sound toy mechanism, batteries, 30 × 27 × 25 cm. Collection Olivier Sidet & Natacha Lesueur, Paris

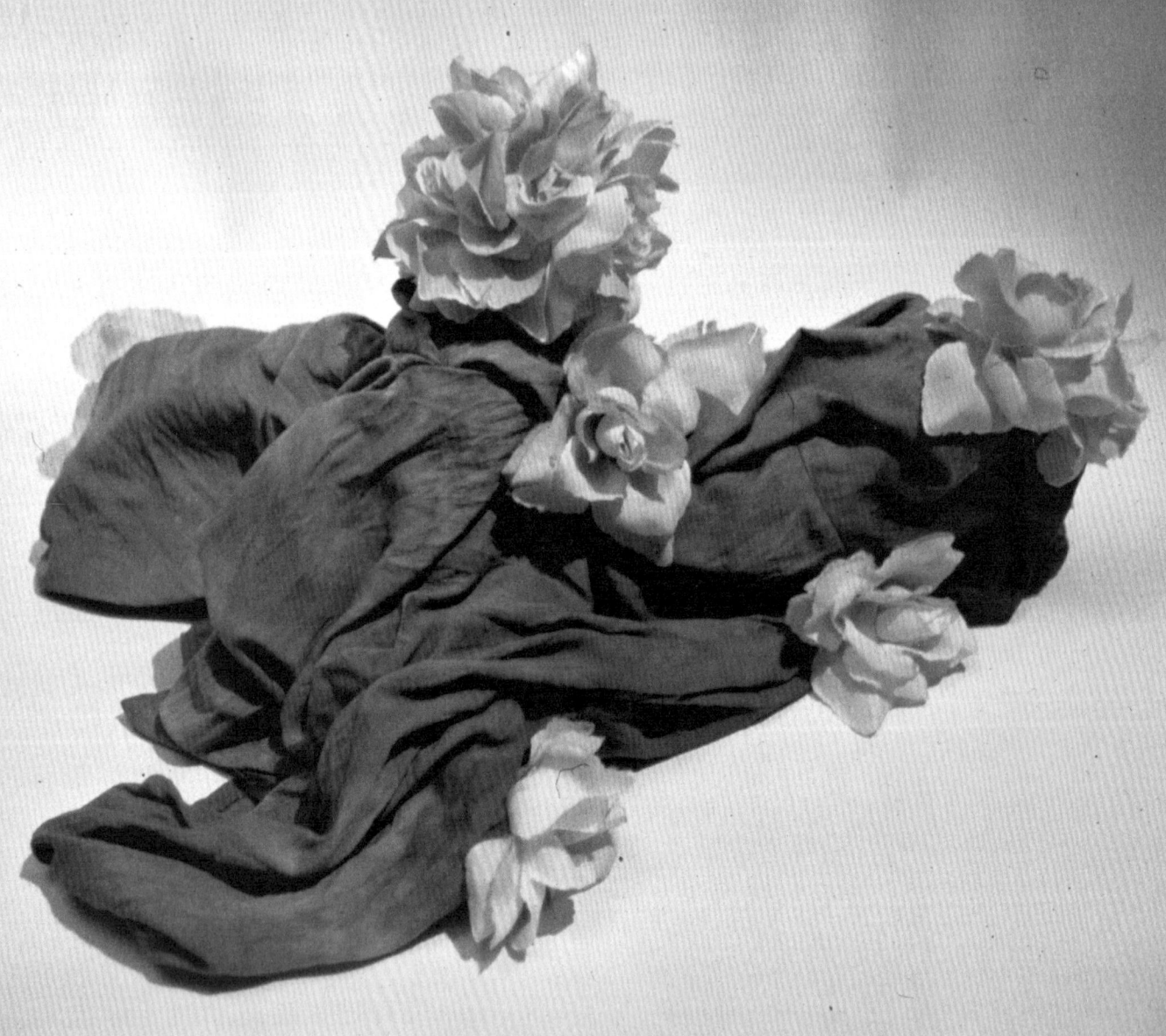

Untitled, 2001, from the *Bestioles* series. Artificial flowers, fabric, sound toy mechanism, batteries, 25 × 40 × 20 cm. Collection Sylvain Peyran & Yoko Nakamura, Paris

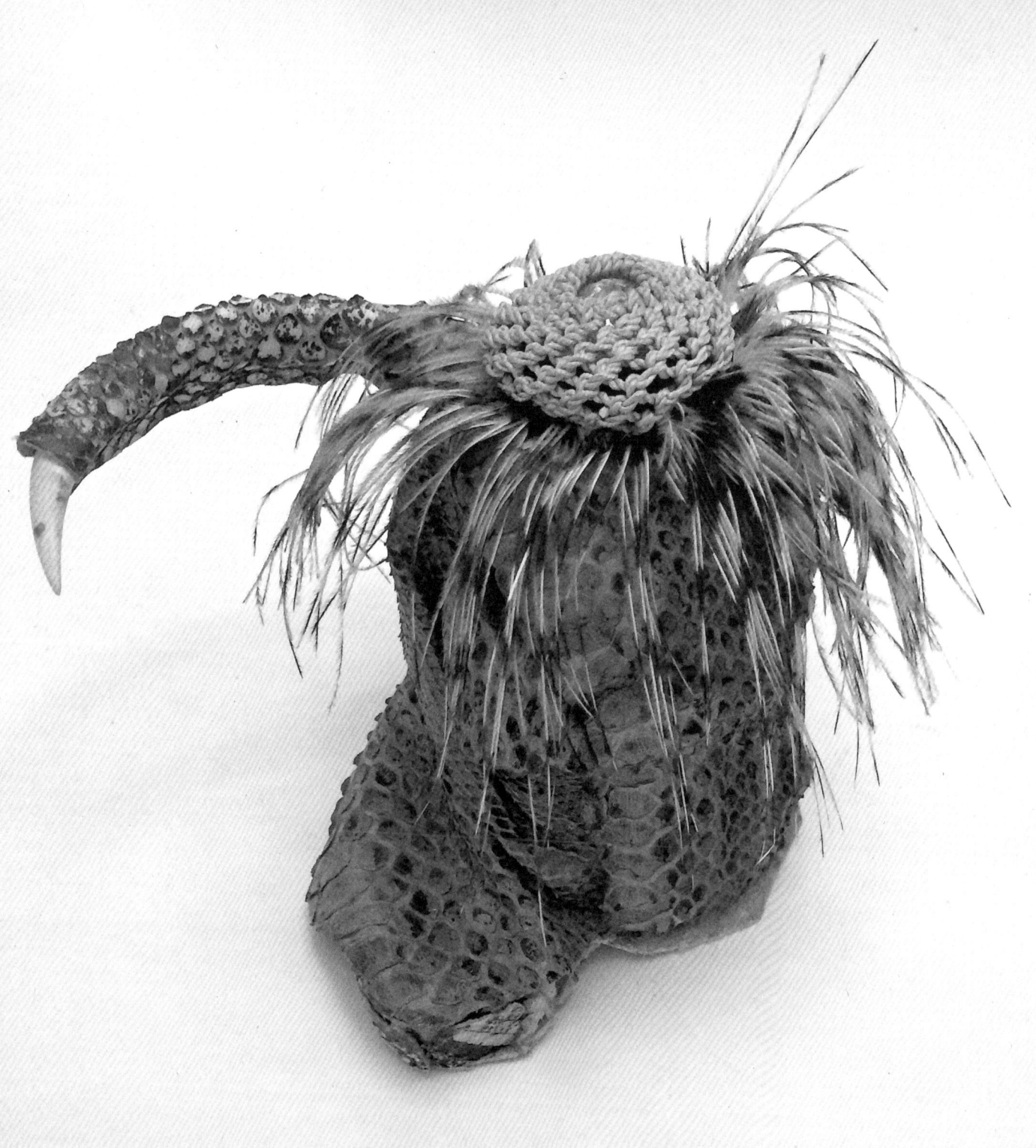

Untitled, n.d., from the *Bestioles* series. Rabbit fur, metal, plastic, sound toy mechanism, height 13 cm. Collection Olivia Boudet, New York

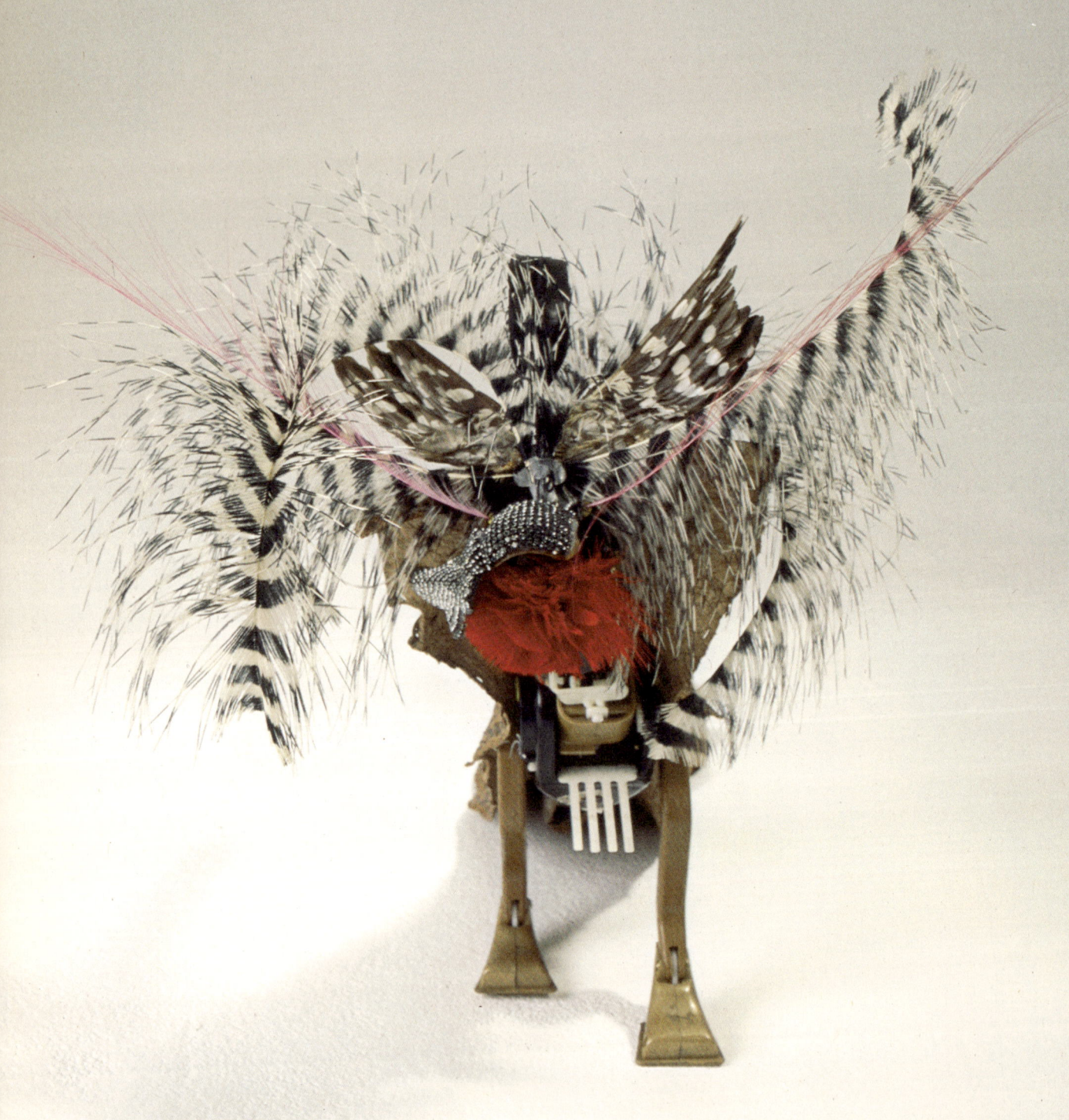

Untitled, 2001, from the *Bestioles* series. Snake skin, feathers, toy mechanism (unfinished work), 50 × 38 × 112 cm. Collection FRAC Lorraine, Metz

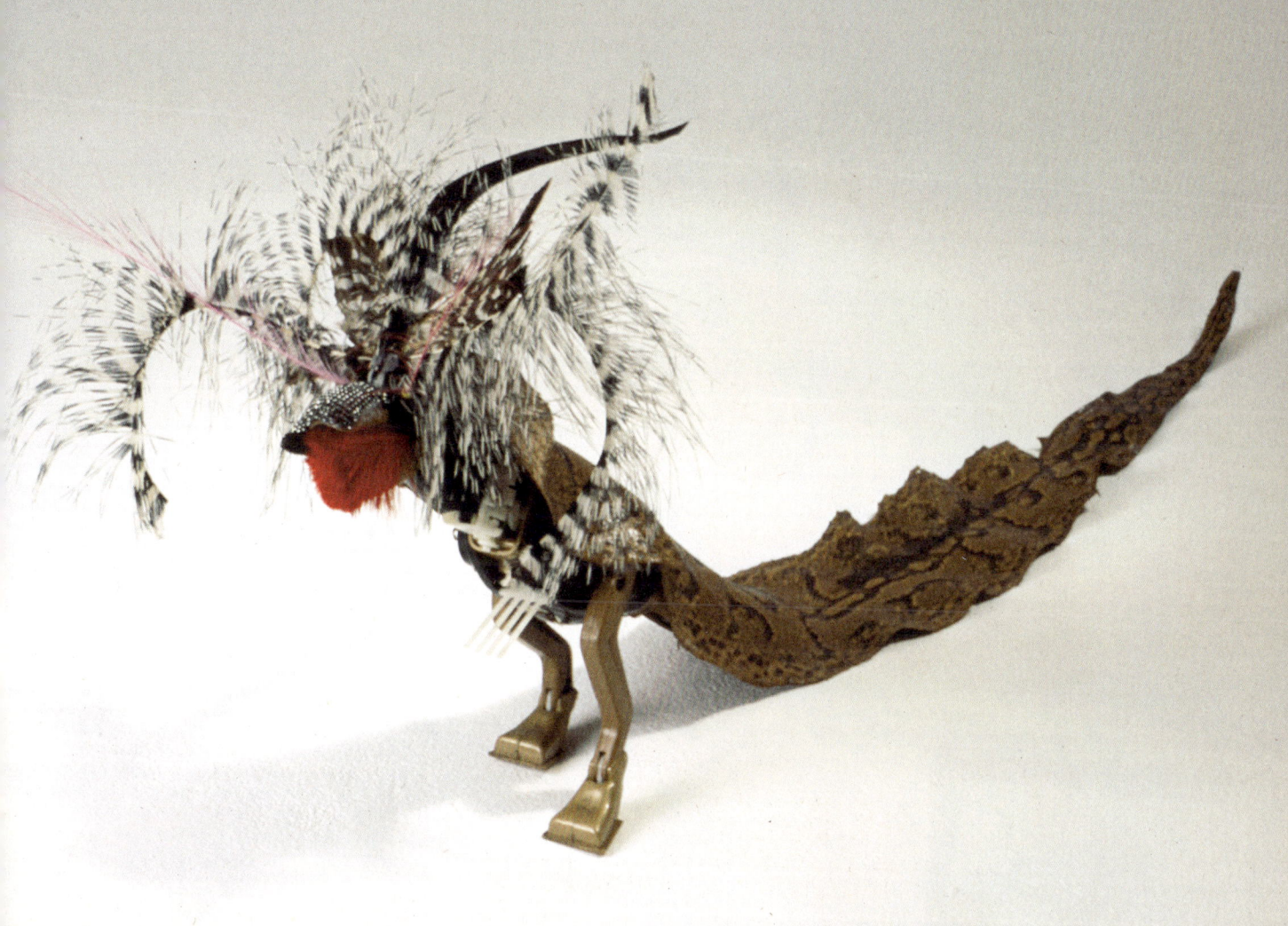

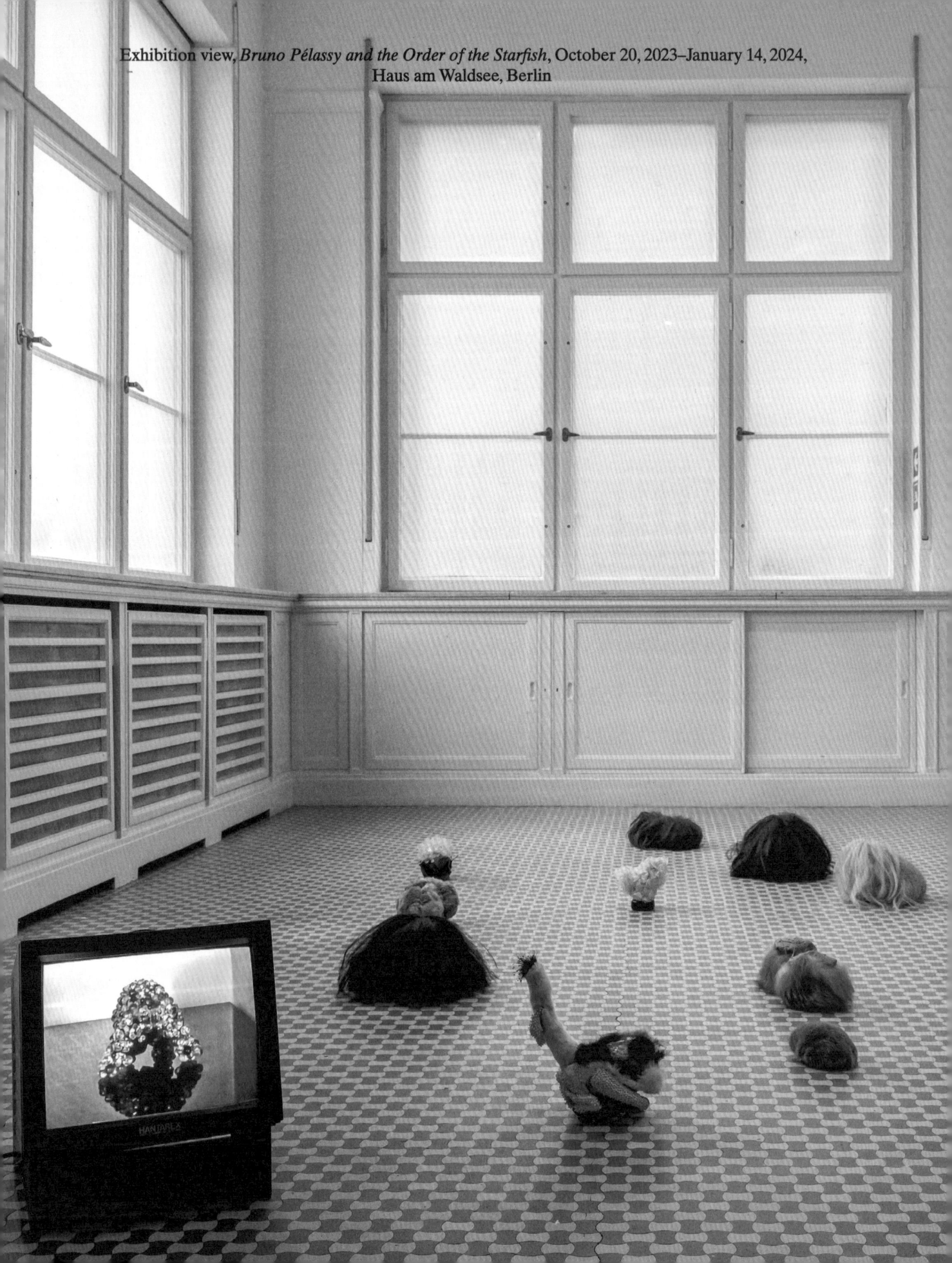

Exhibition view, *Bruno Pélassy and the Order of the Starfish*, October 20, 2023–January 14, 2024, Haus am Waldsee, Berlin

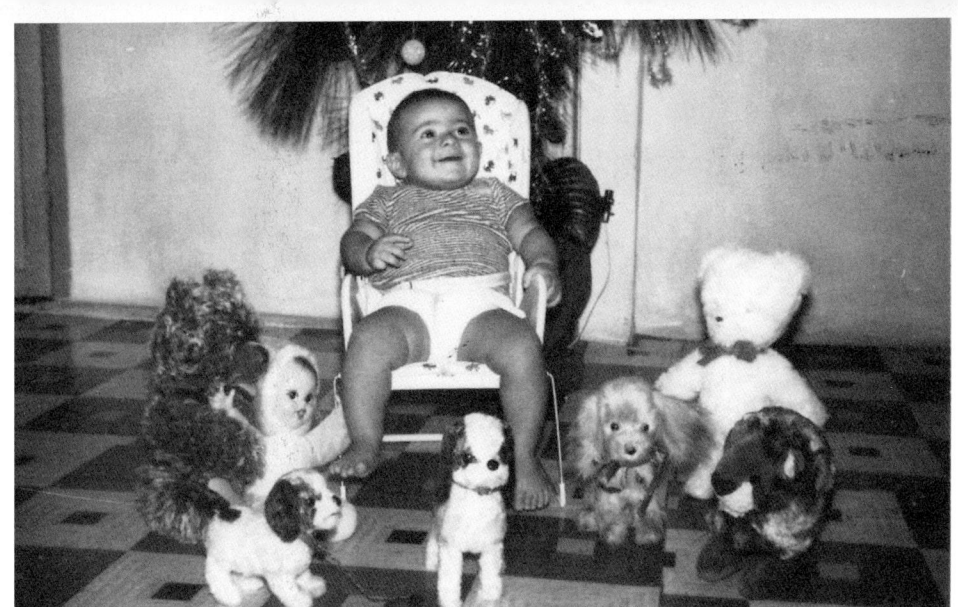

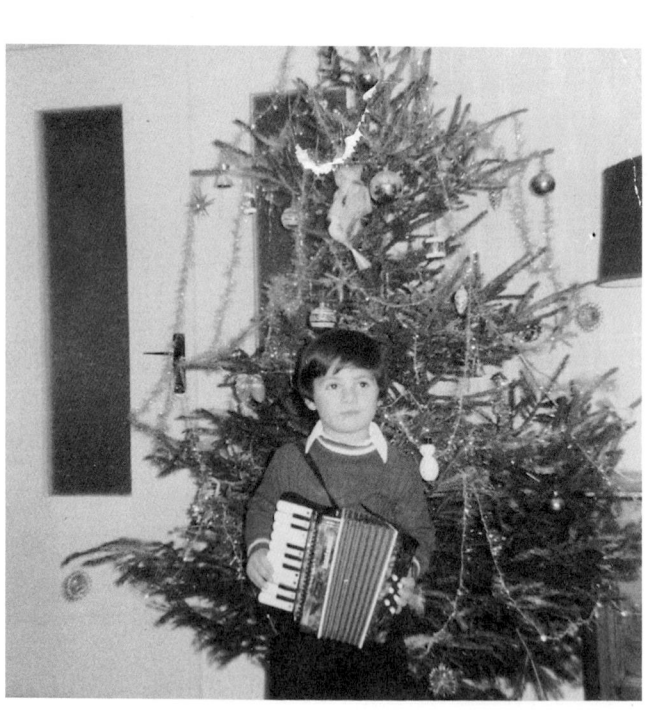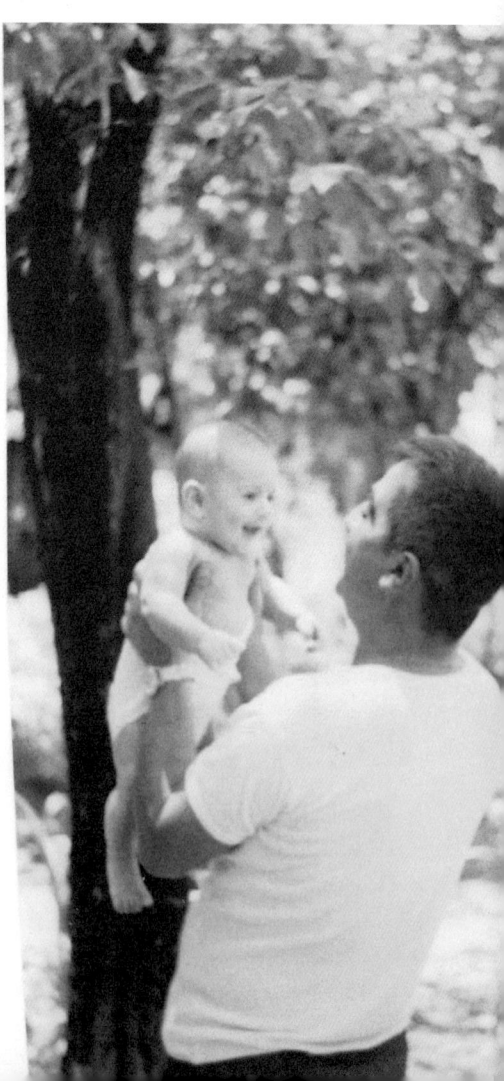

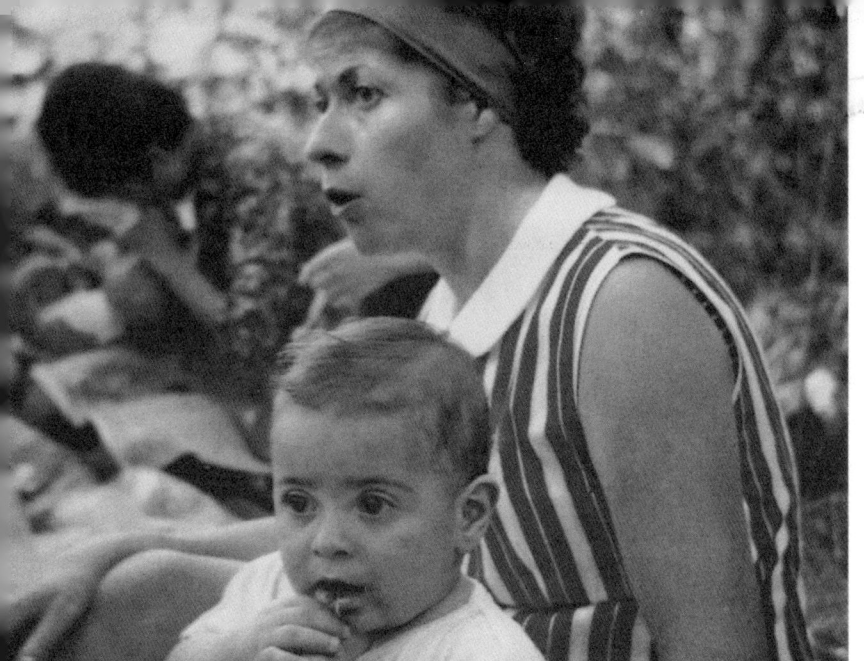
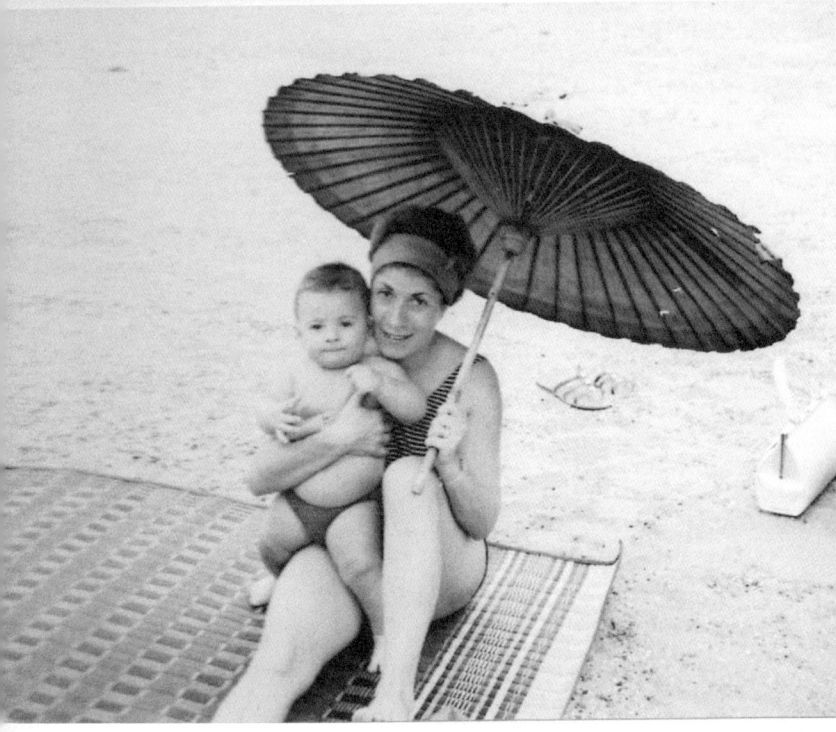

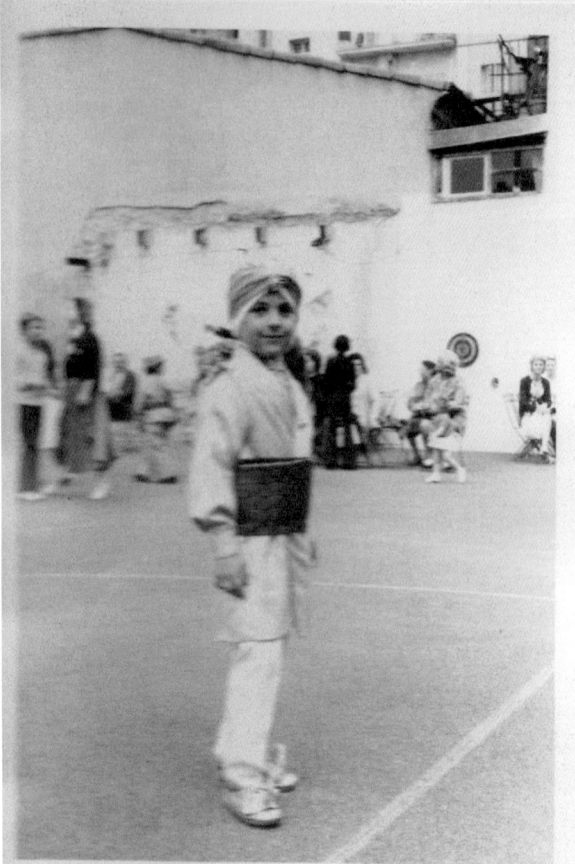 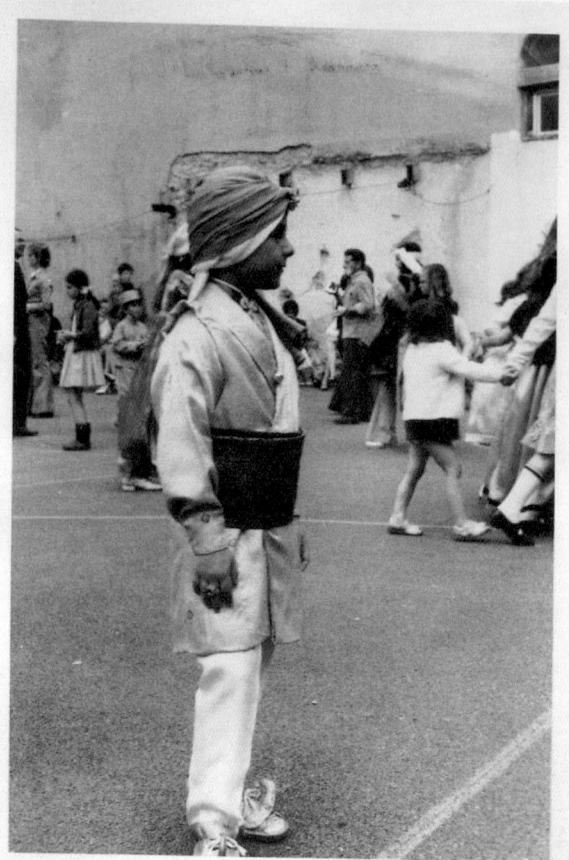

Mardi Gras NICE. 1971

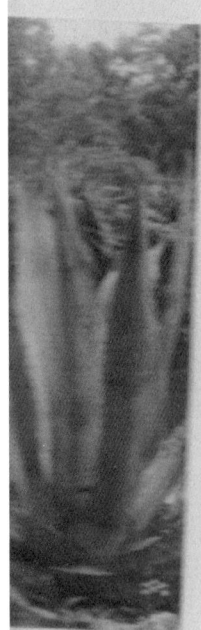 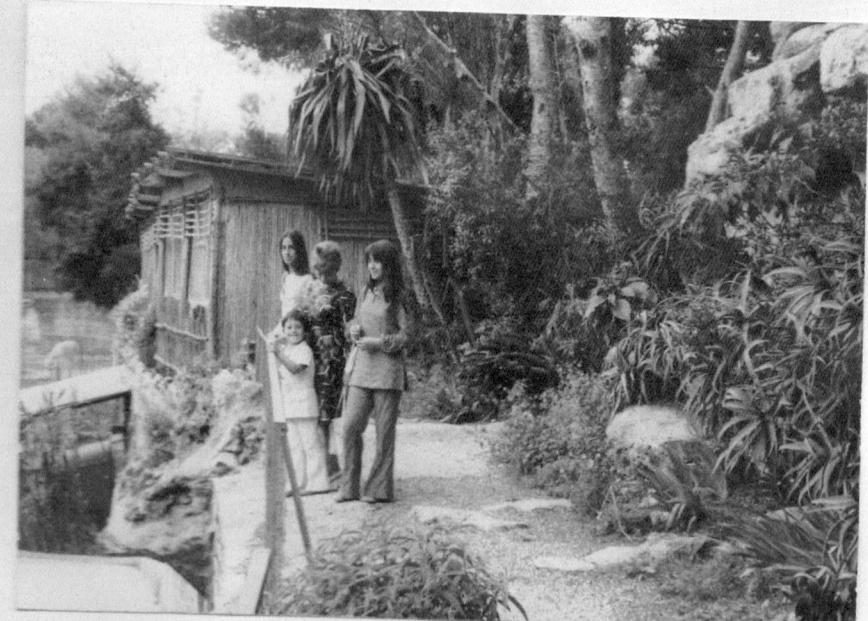

Zoo " S Jean cap Ferrat "
1971

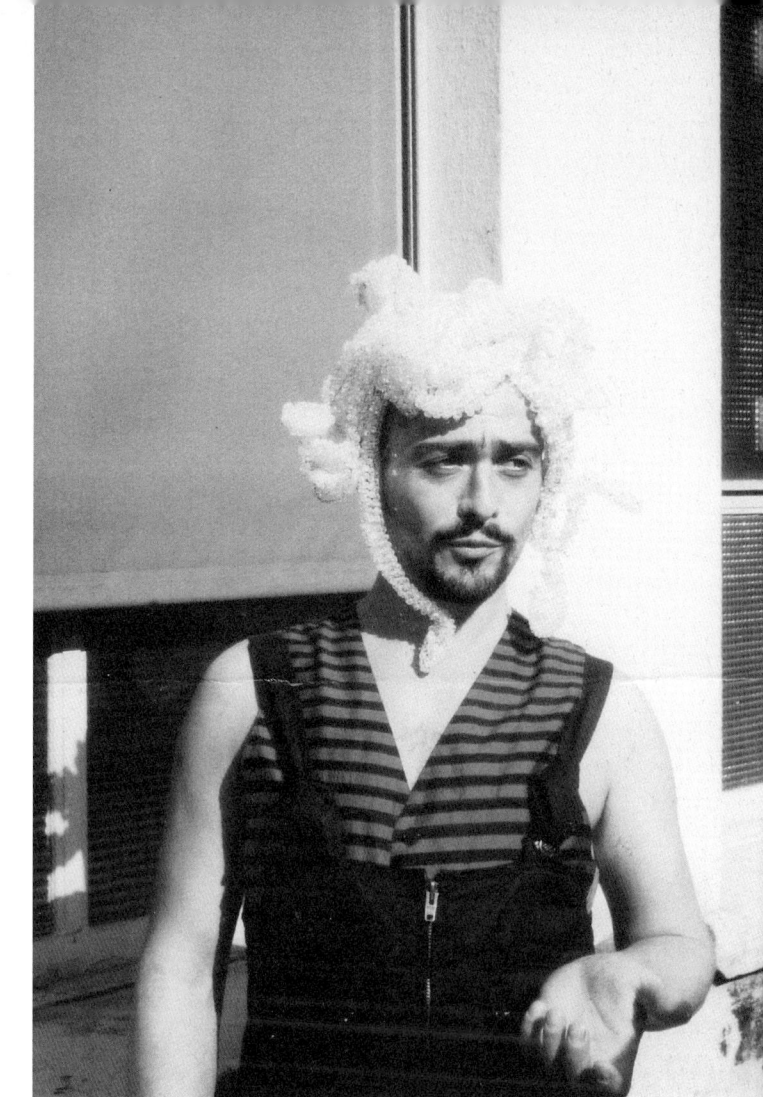
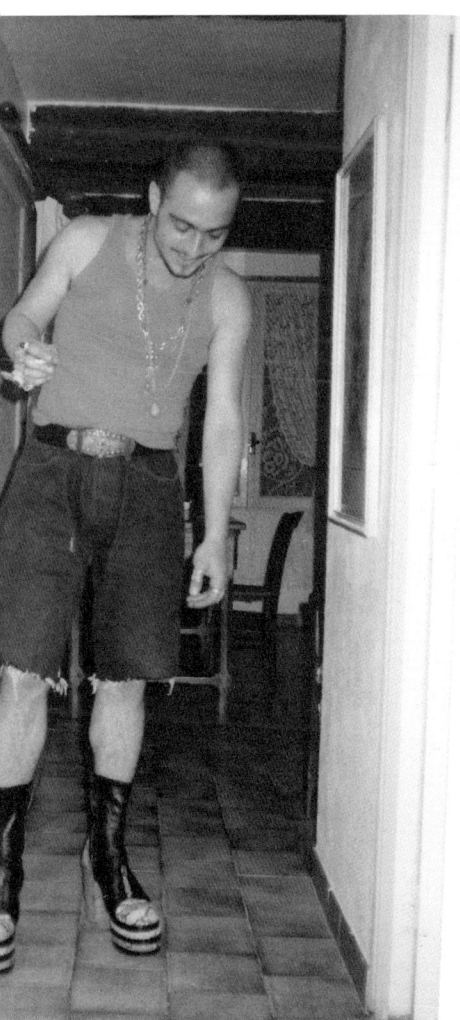

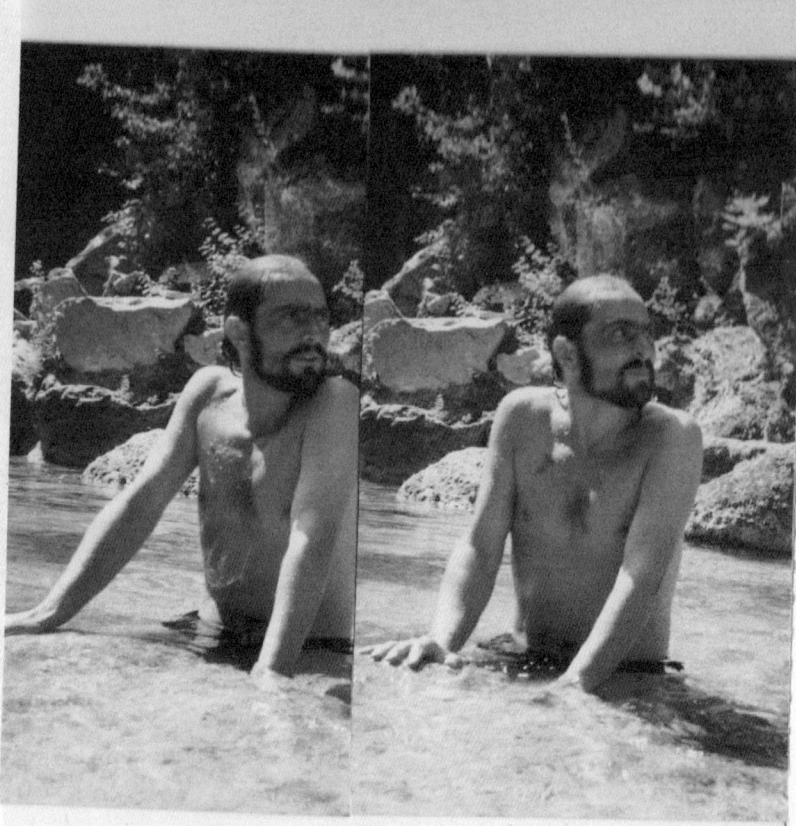

Juillet 2001

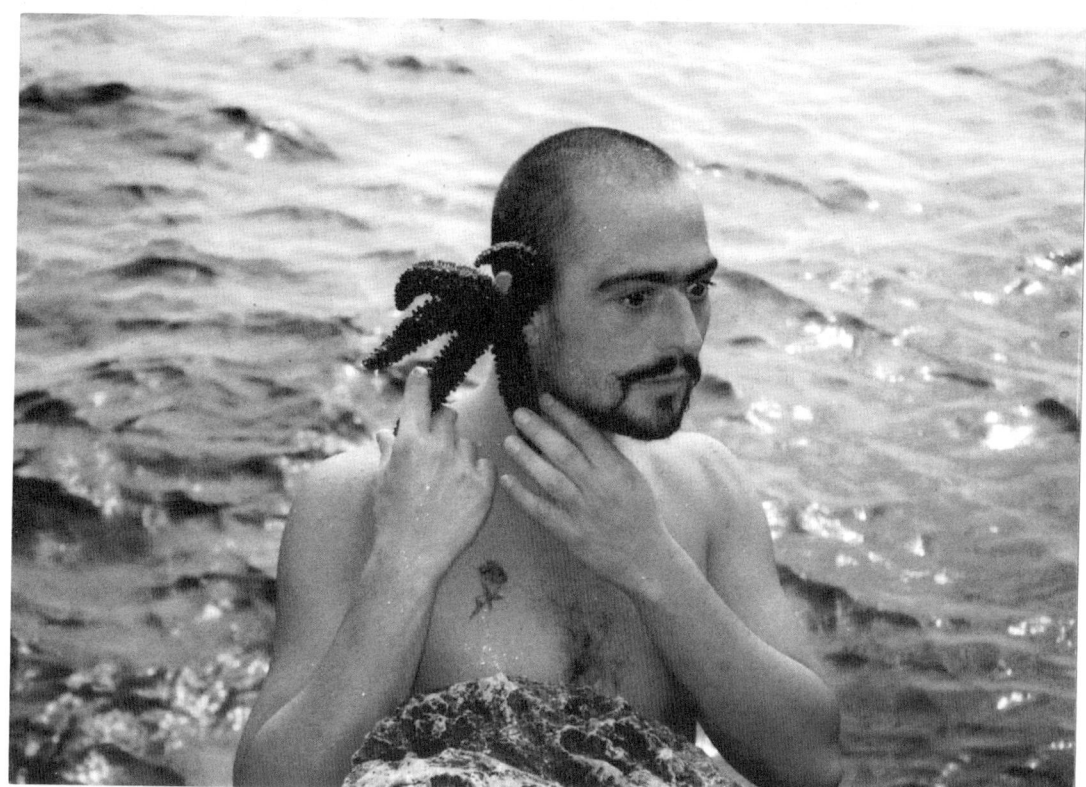
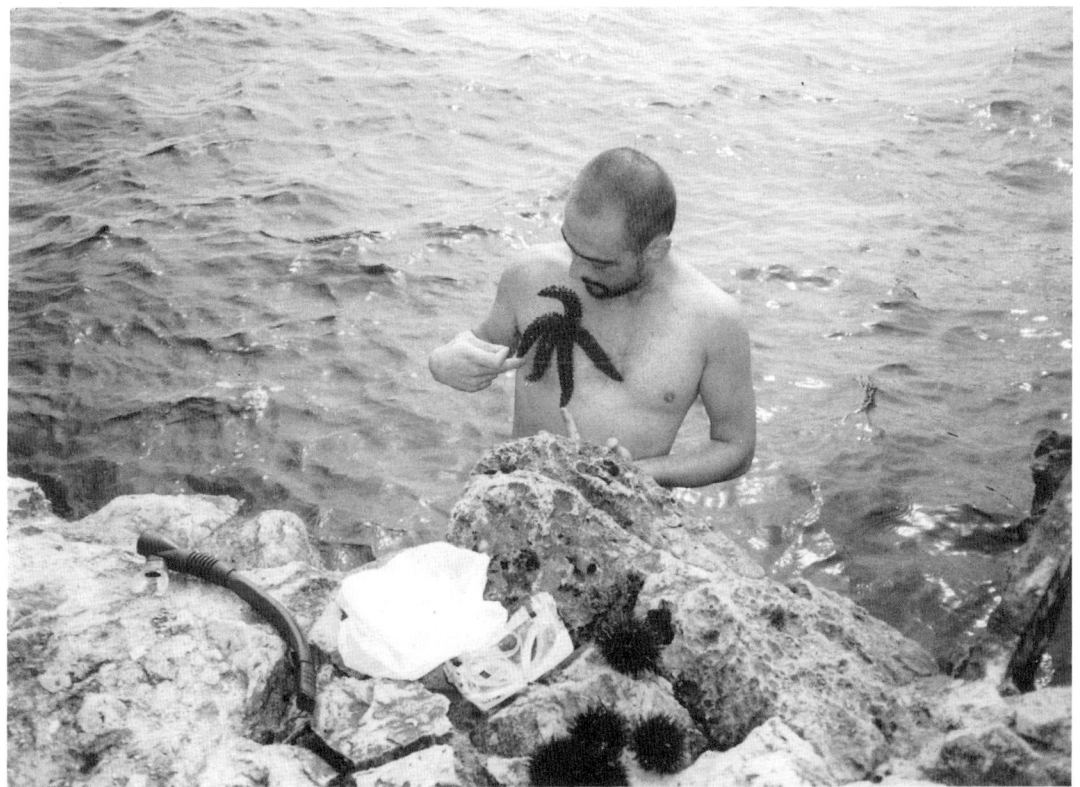

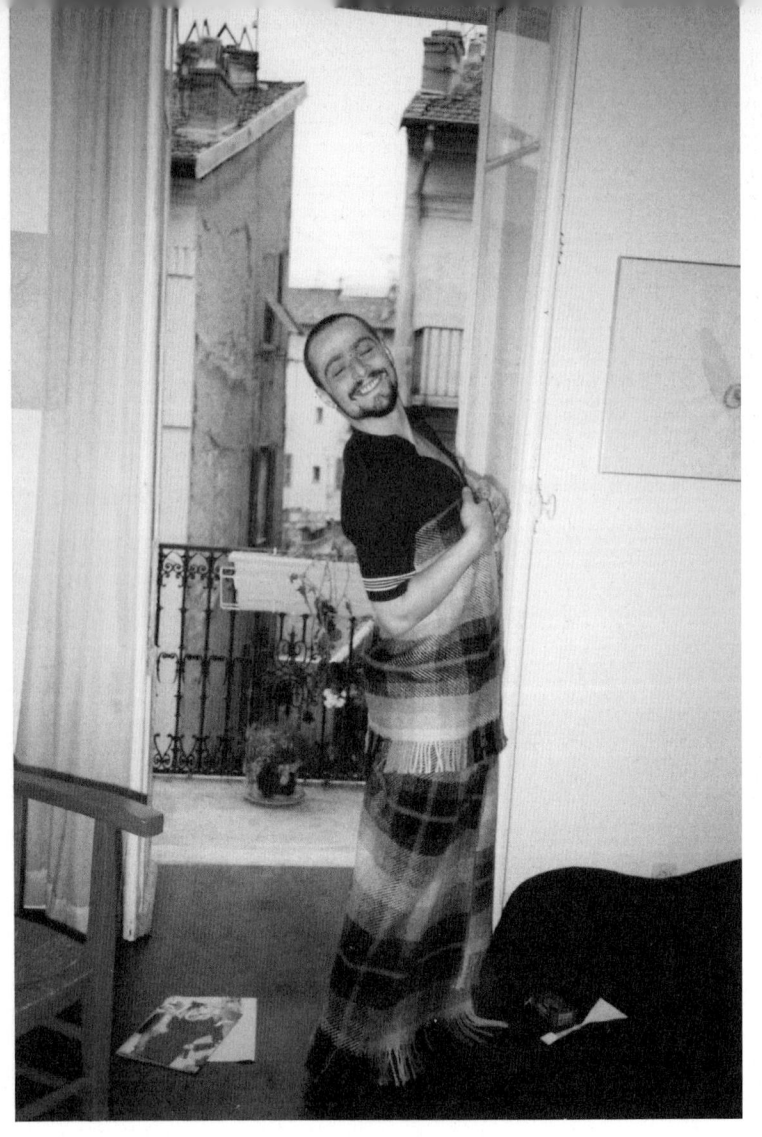
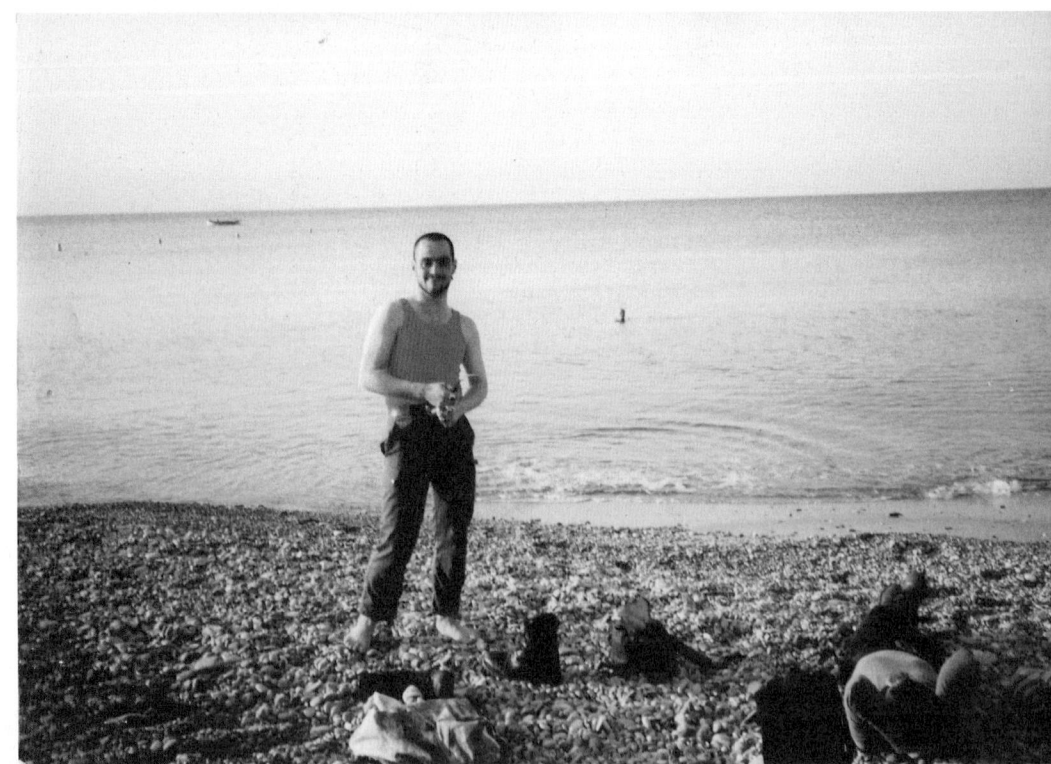

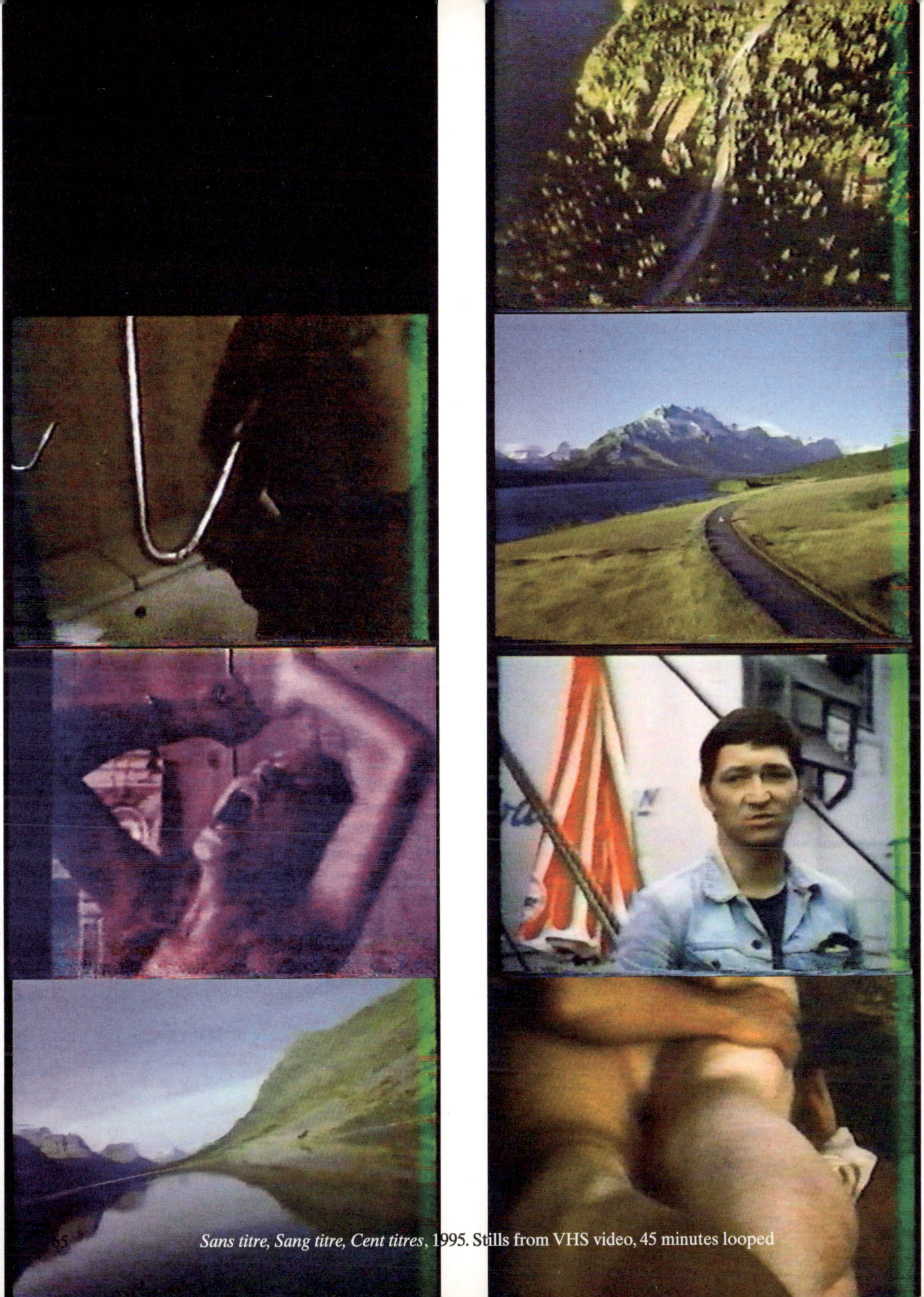

Sans titre, Sang titre, Cent titres, 1995. Stills from VHS video, 45 minutes looped

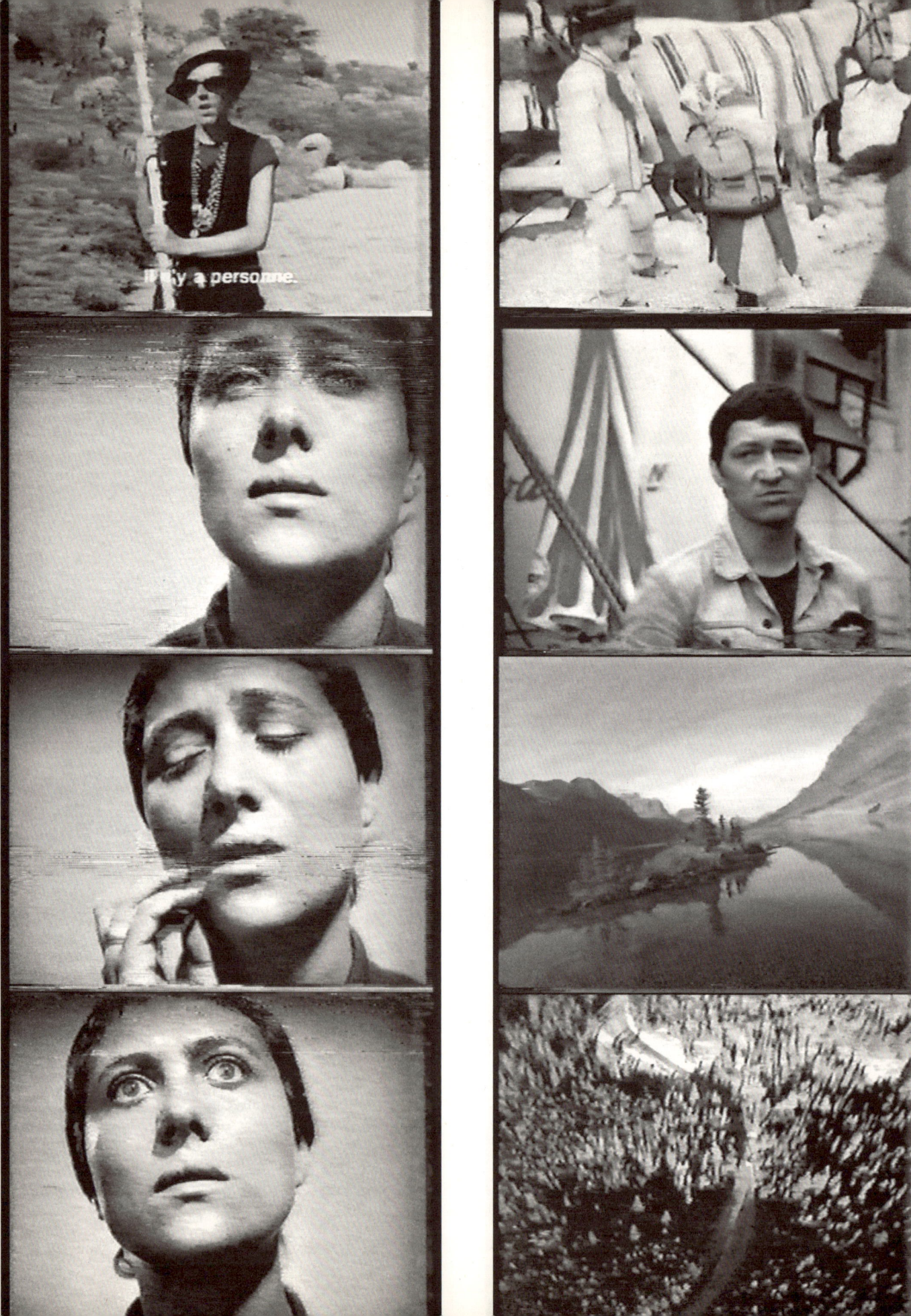

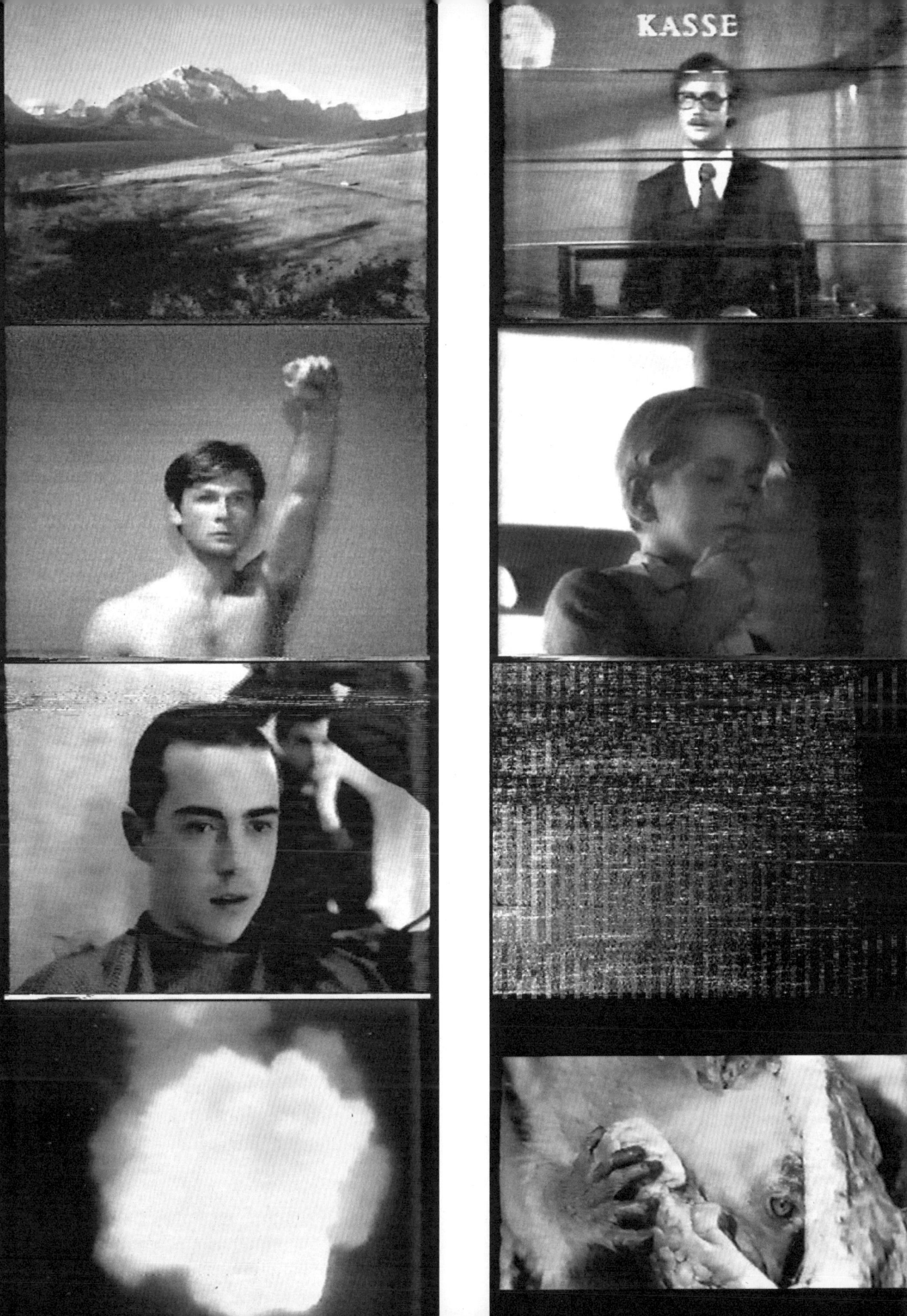

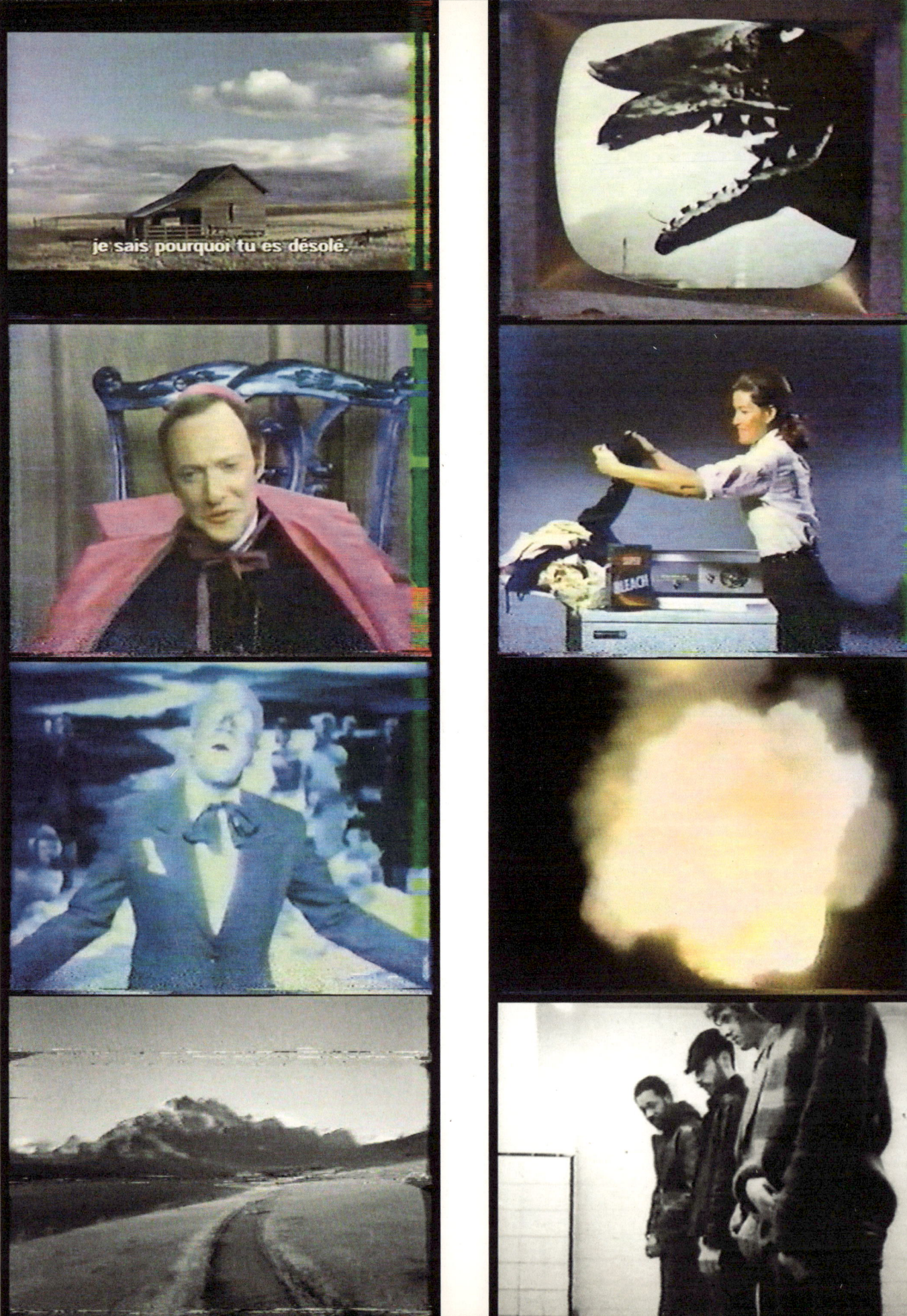

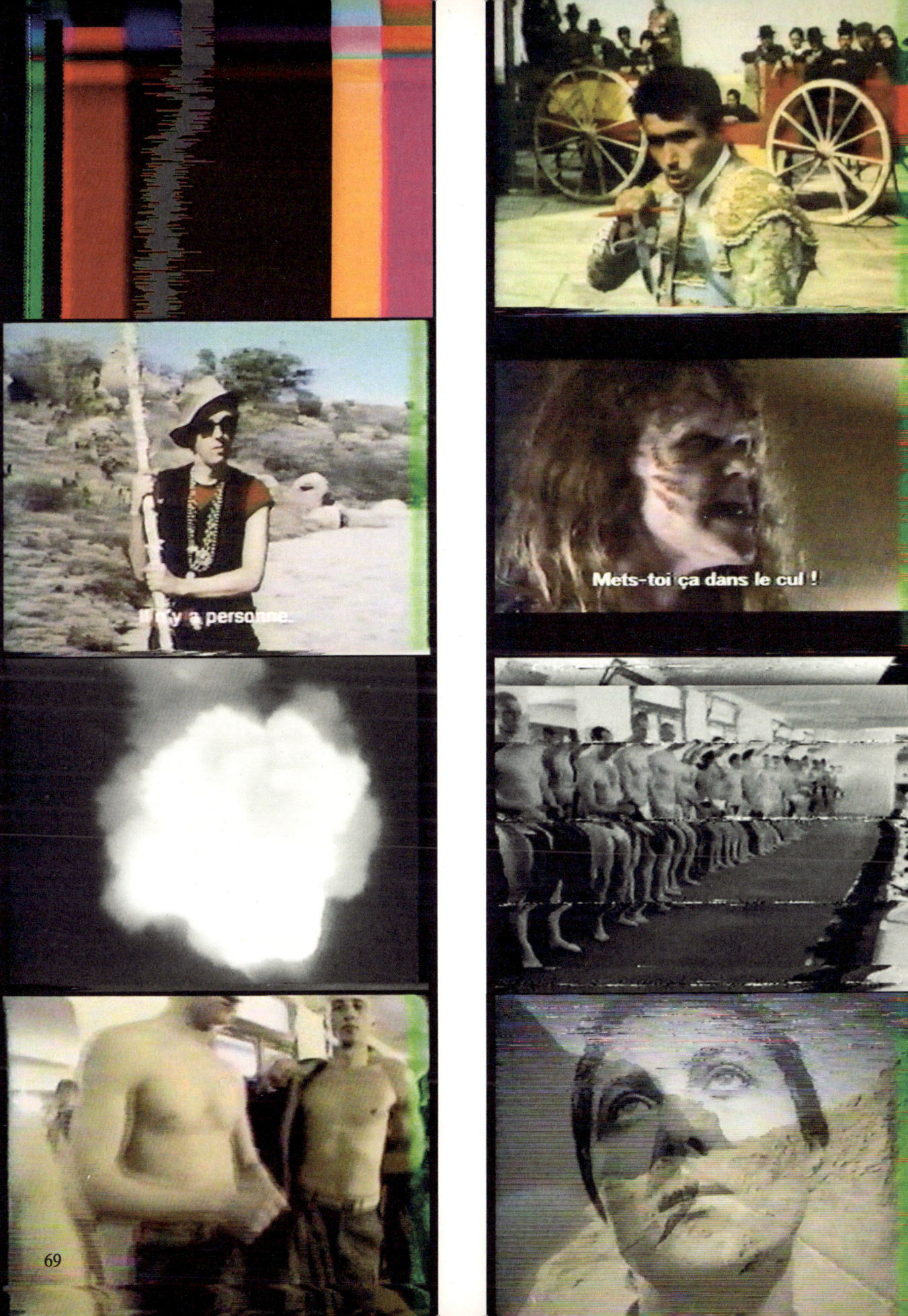

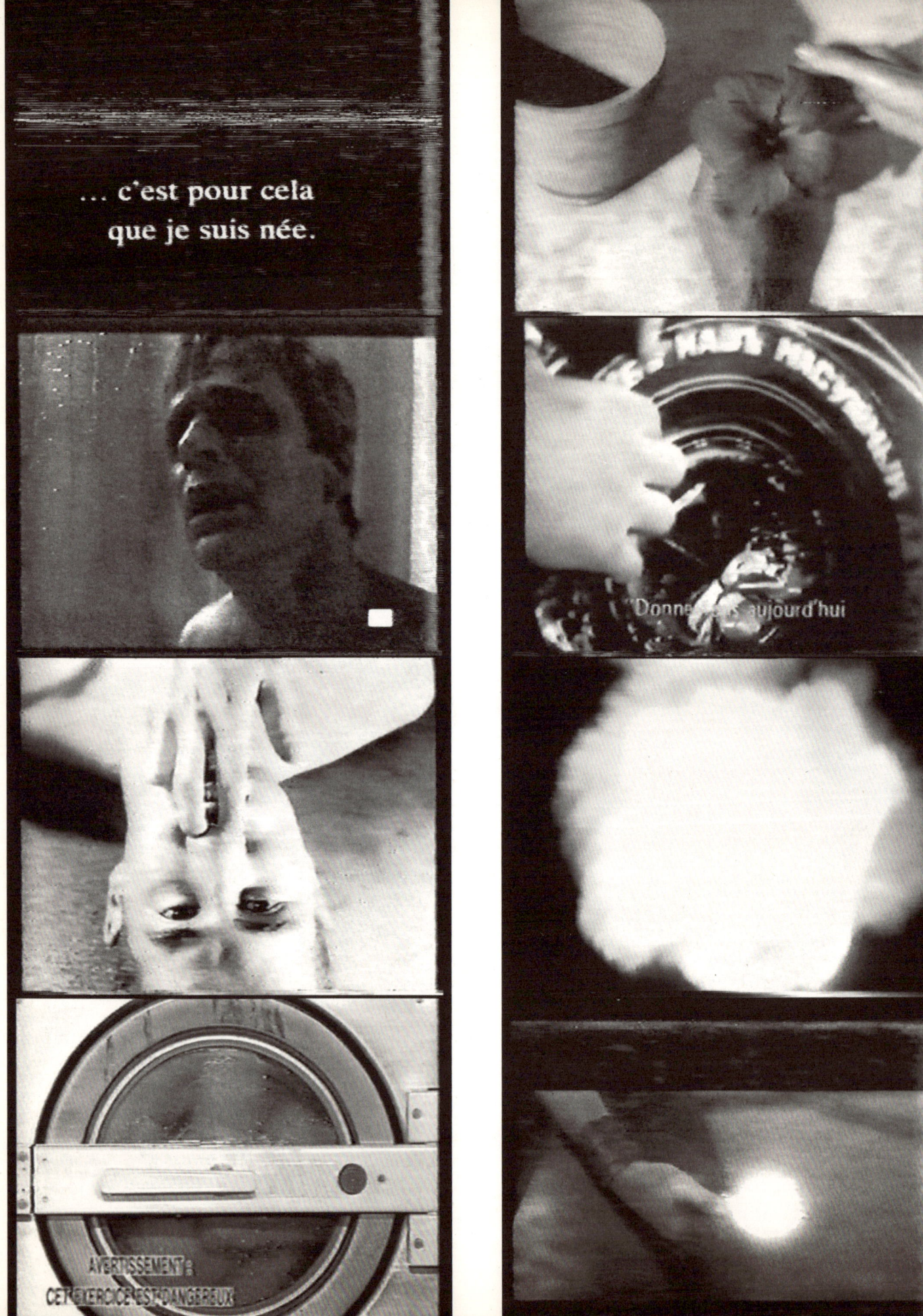

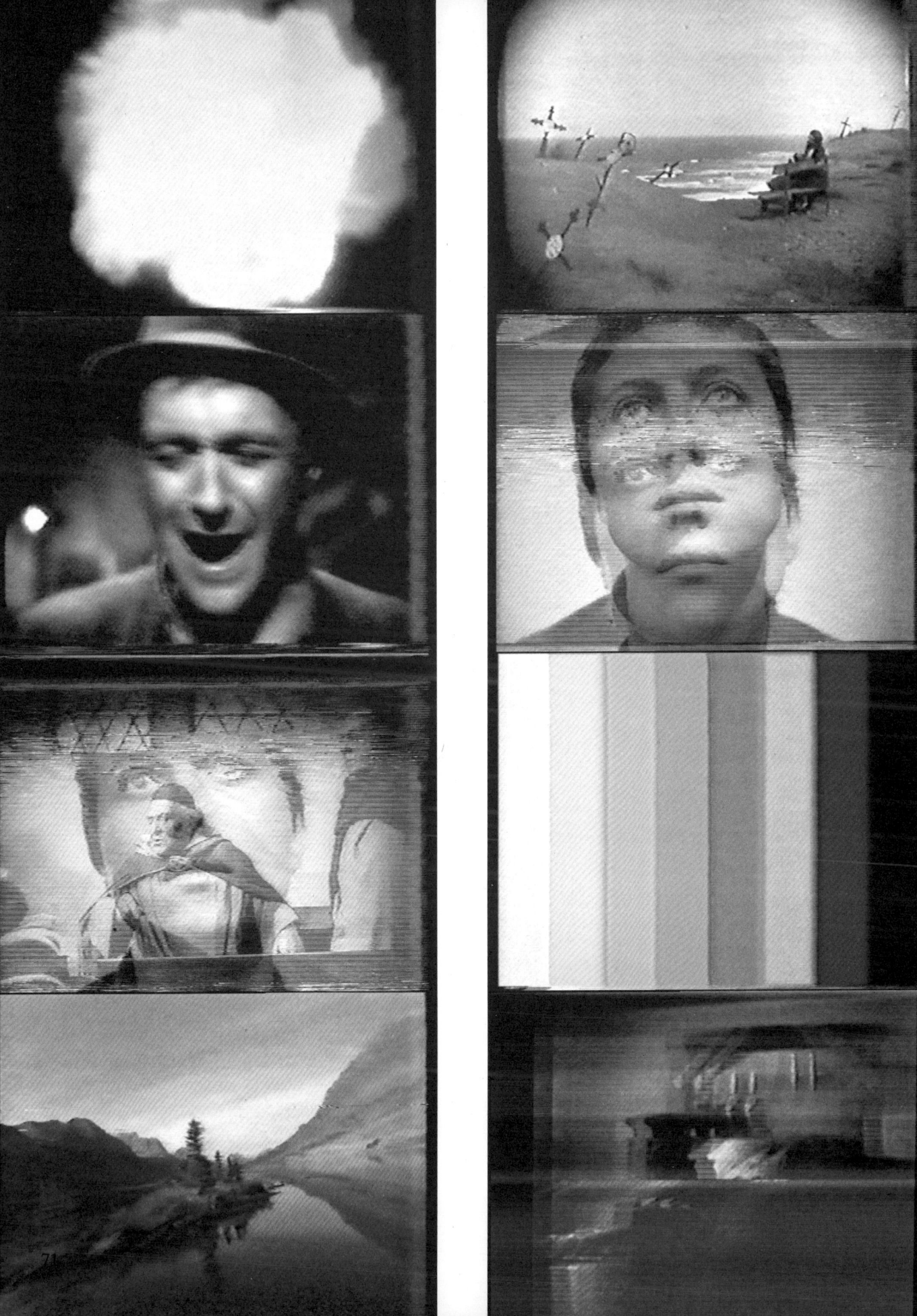

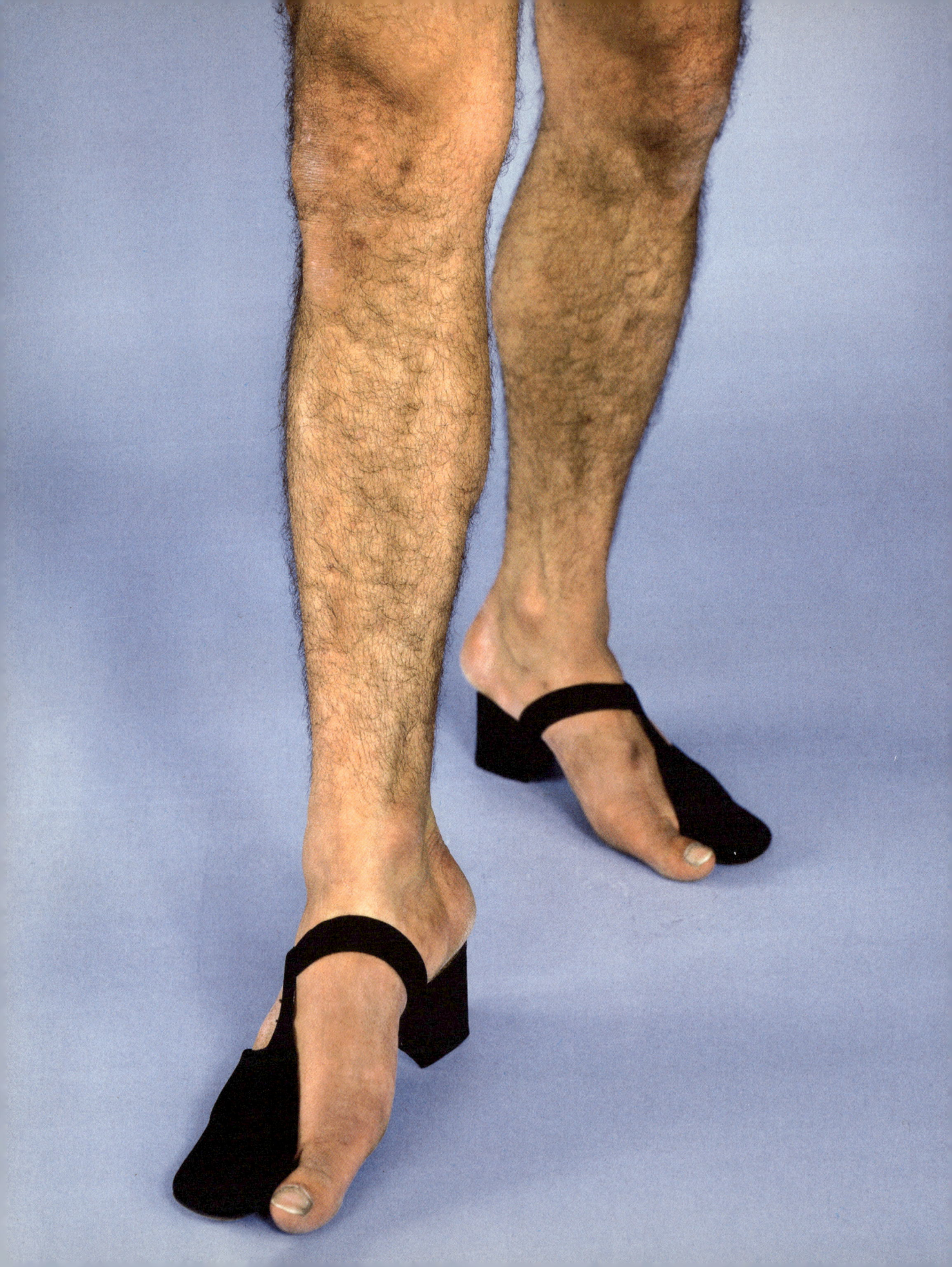

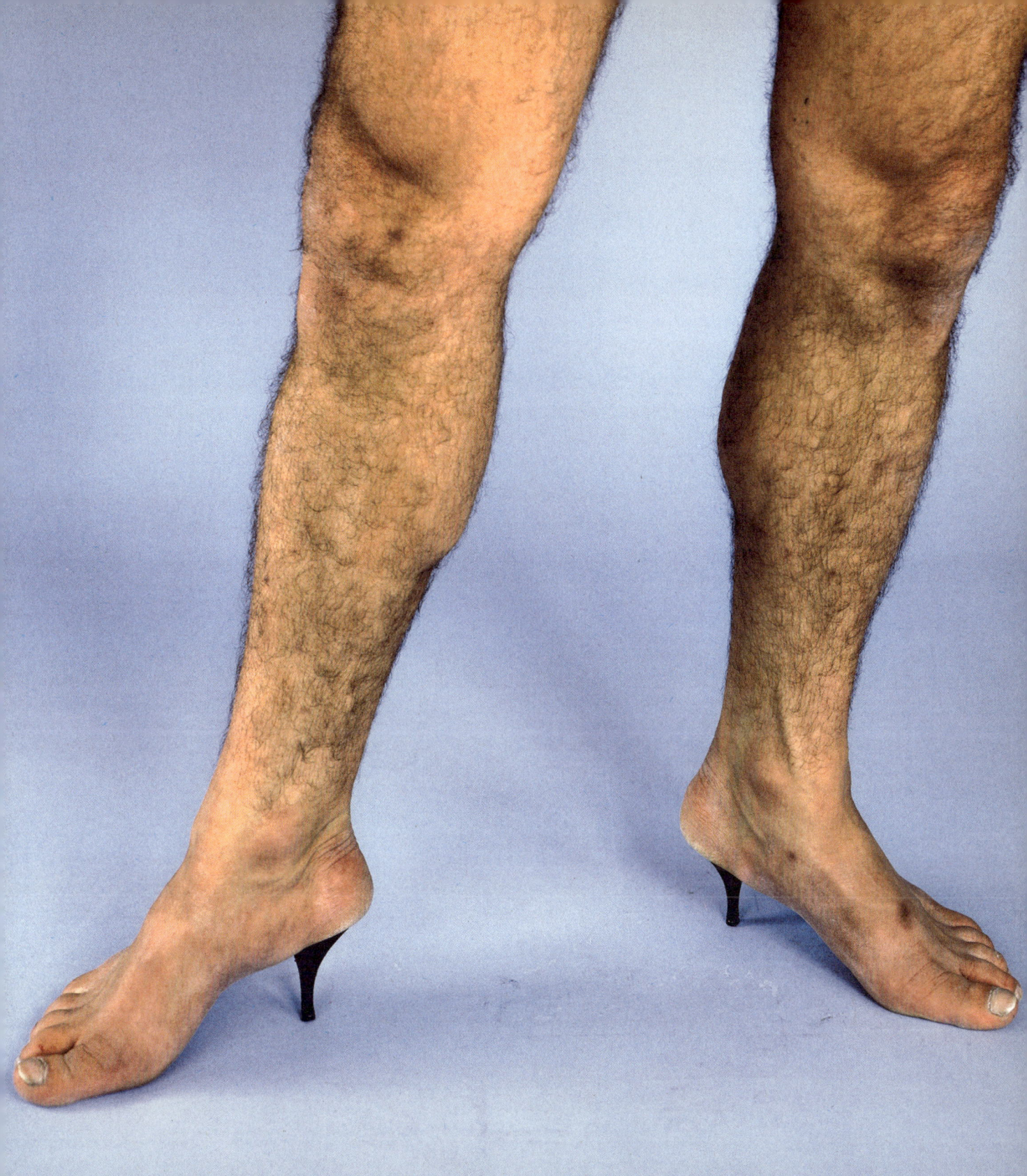

73 *Untitled*, 2000, with Natacha Lesueur. Chromogenic print on aluminium, 122 × 122 cm

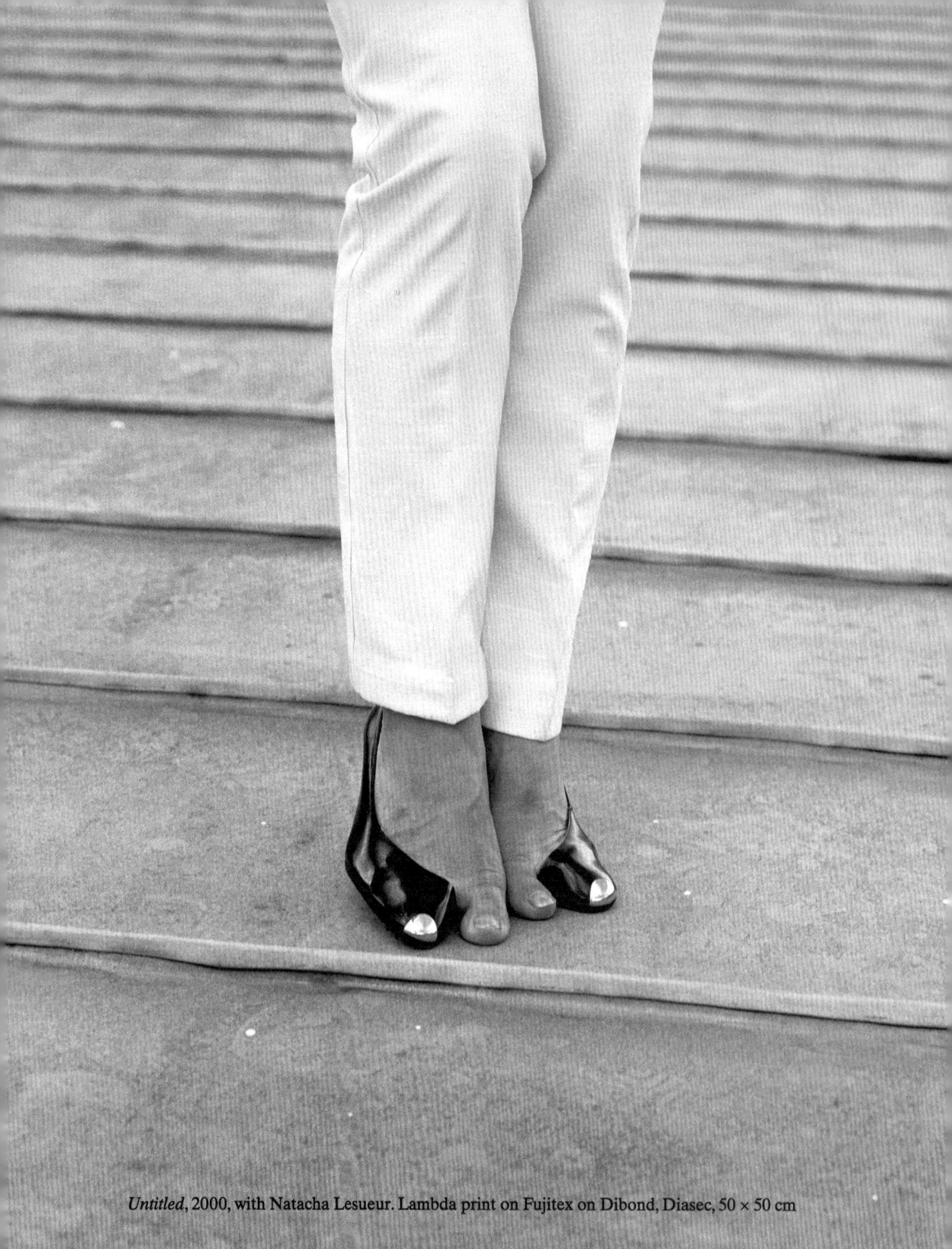

Untitled, 2000, with Natacha Lesueur. Lambda print on Fujitex on Dibond, Diasec, 50 × 50 cm

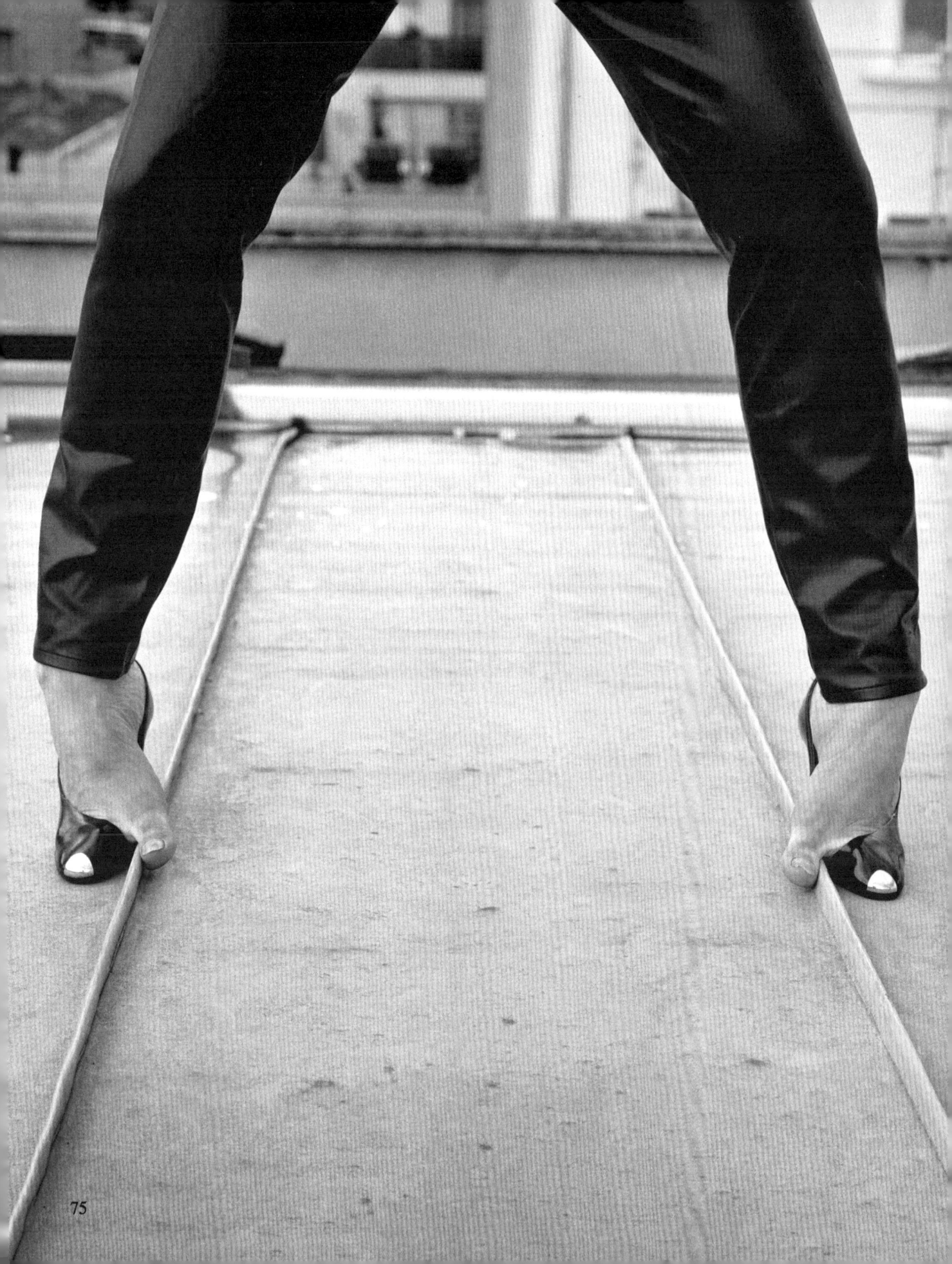

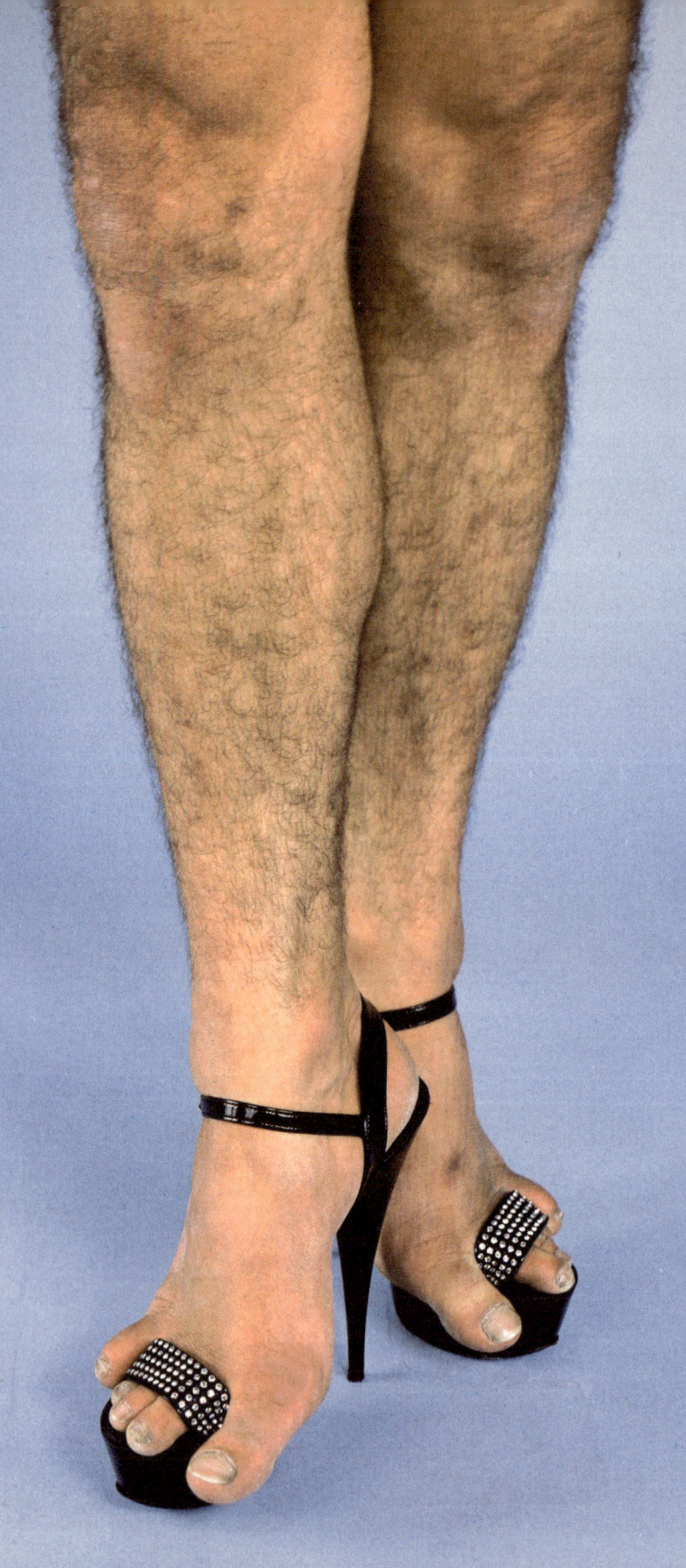

Untitled, 2000, with Natacha Lesueur. Chromogenic print on aluminium, 122 × 122 cm

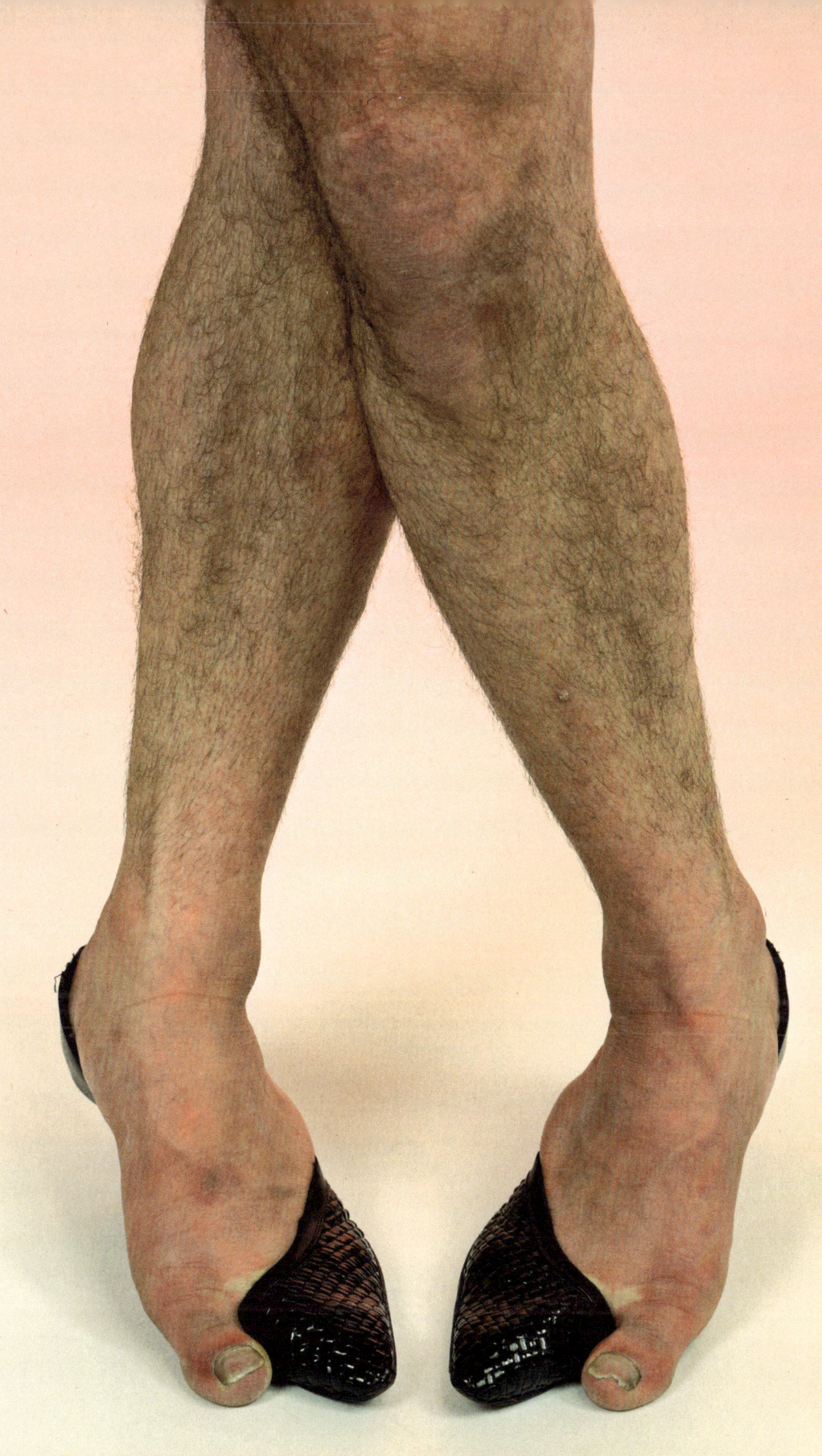

Untitled, 2000, with Natacha Lesueur. Chromogenic print on aluminium, 125 × 100 cm

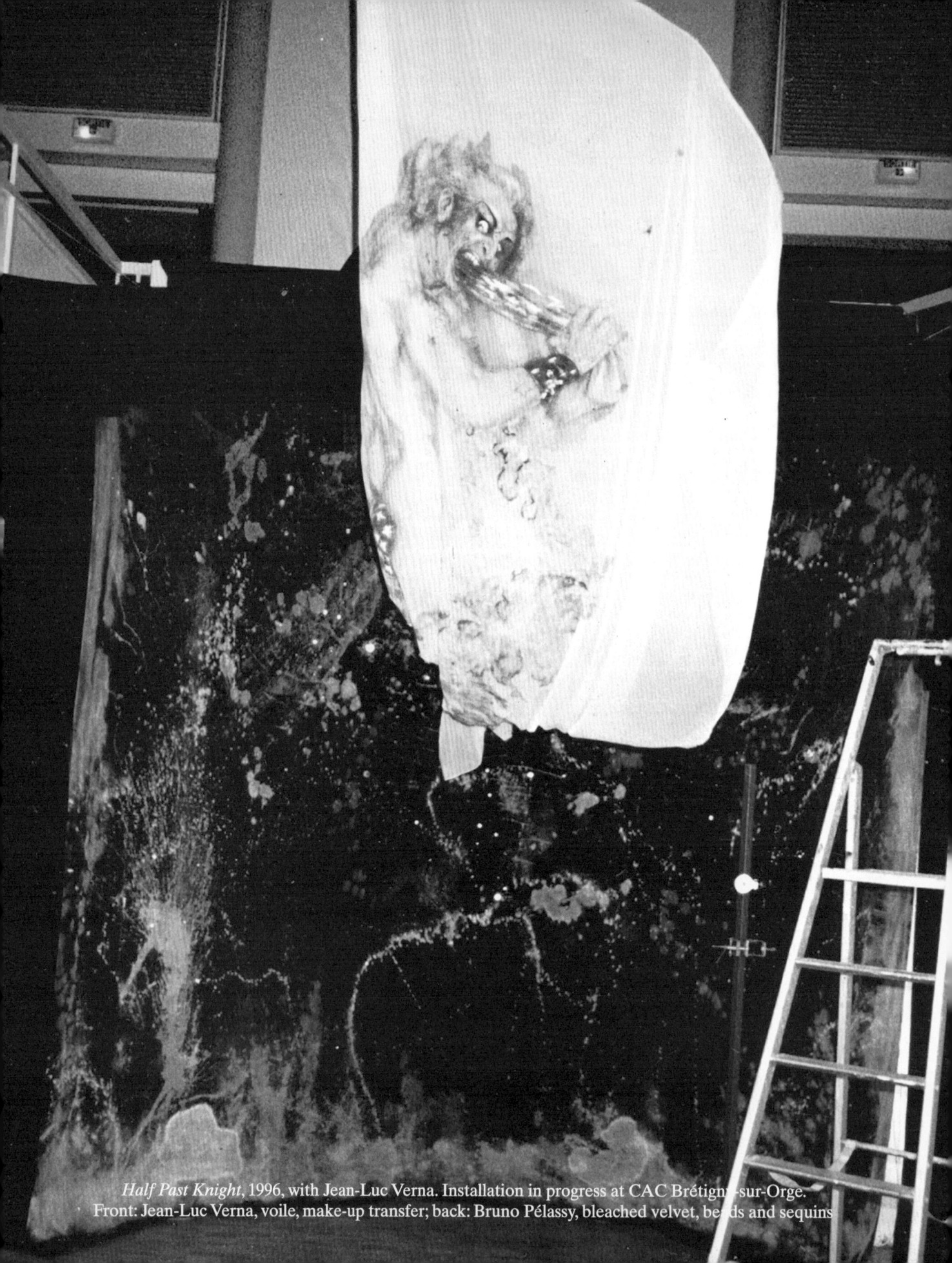

Half Past Knight, 1996, with Jean-Luc Verna. Installation in progress at CAC Brétigny-sur-Orge.
Front: Jean-Luc Verna, voile, make-up transfer; back: Bruno Pélassy, bleached velvet, beads and sequins

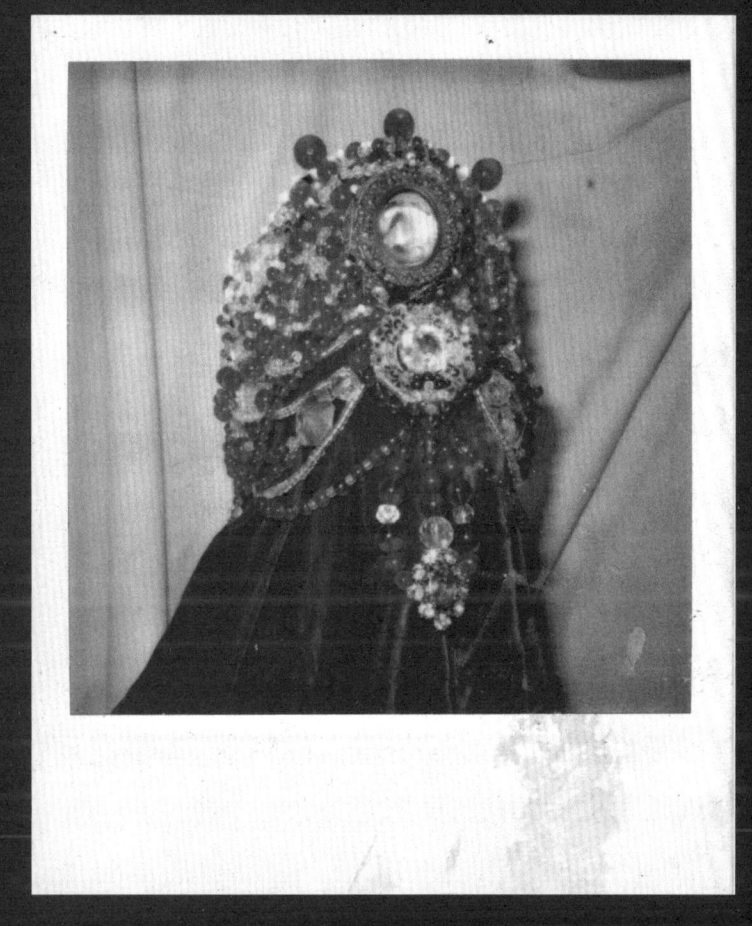

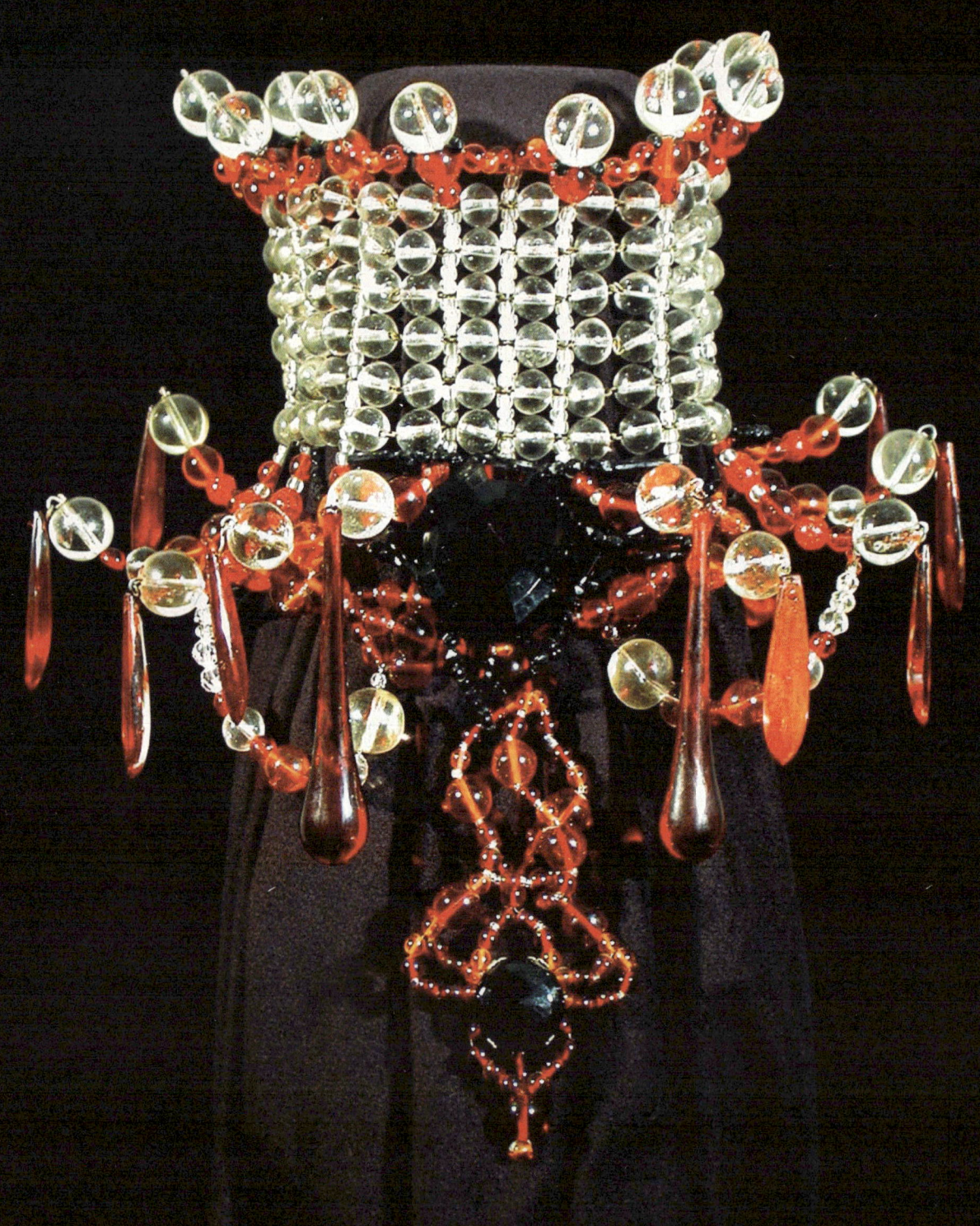

Minerve, 1992–1993. Glass beads, black cabochons, metal wire, approx. 28 × 23 × 35 cm

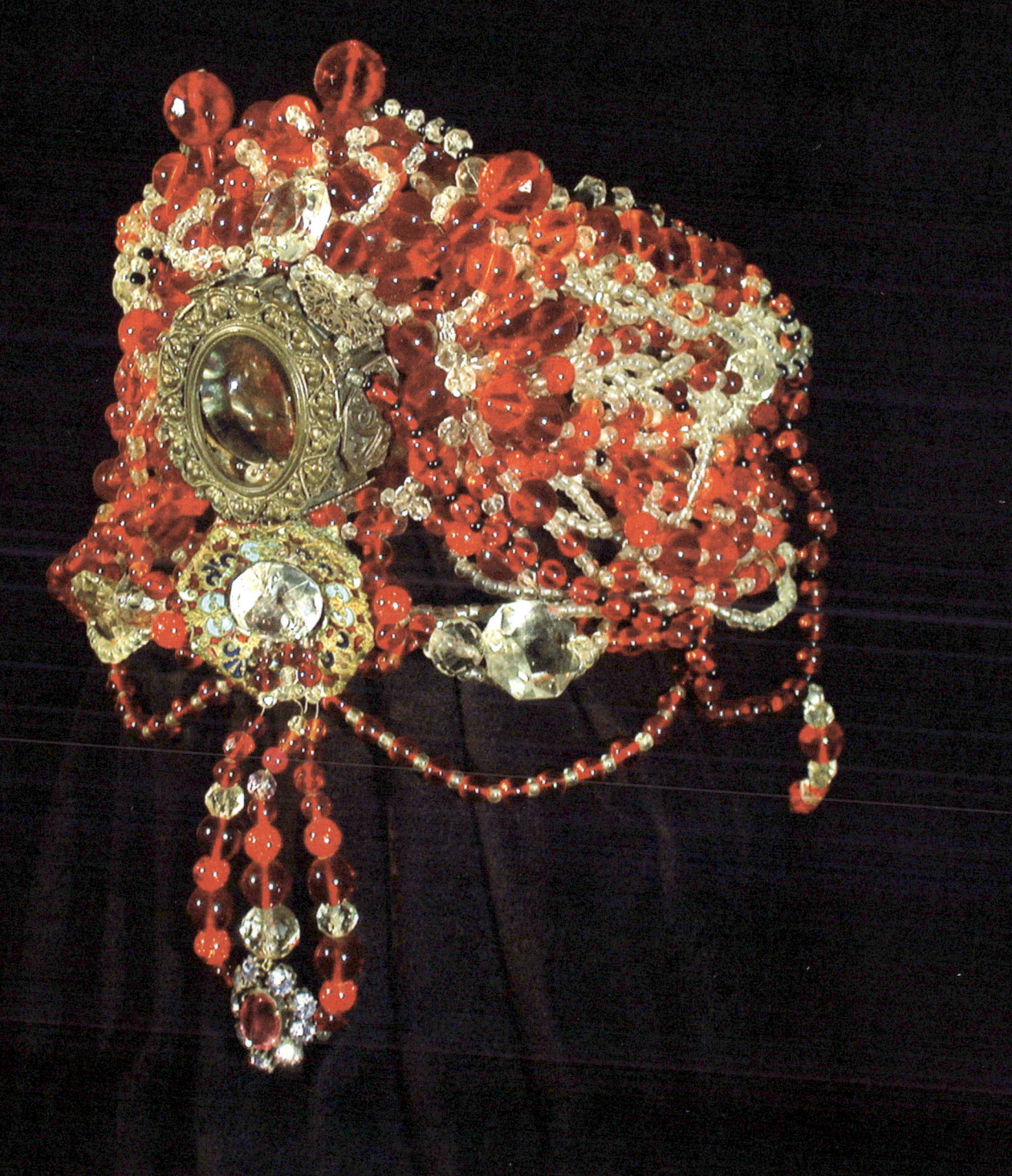

Tiare, 1992–1993. Glass beads, bronze, enamelled bronze, metal wire, approx. 27 × 20 × 26 cm.
Collection Valérie & Dennis Zegerius, Monaco

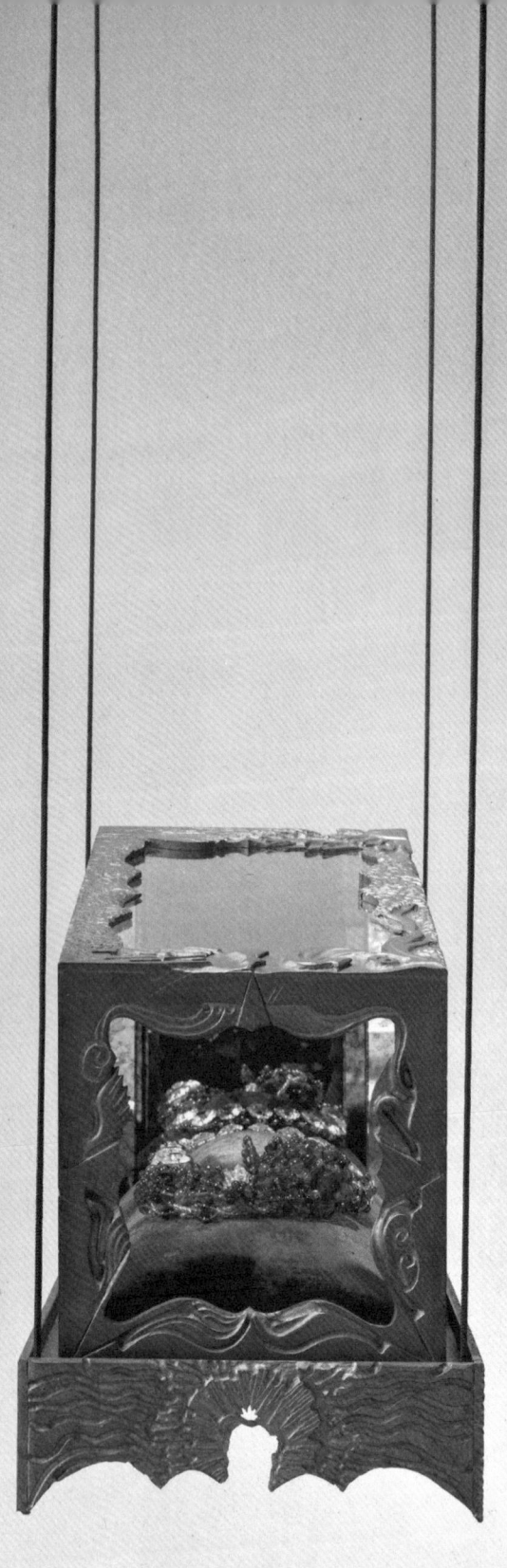

Reliquaire, 1992–1993, from the *Reliquaires* series. Wood, paint, glass, mirror, velvet, cotton cords, glass beads, tassels, metal wire, 52 × 55.5 × 36 cm

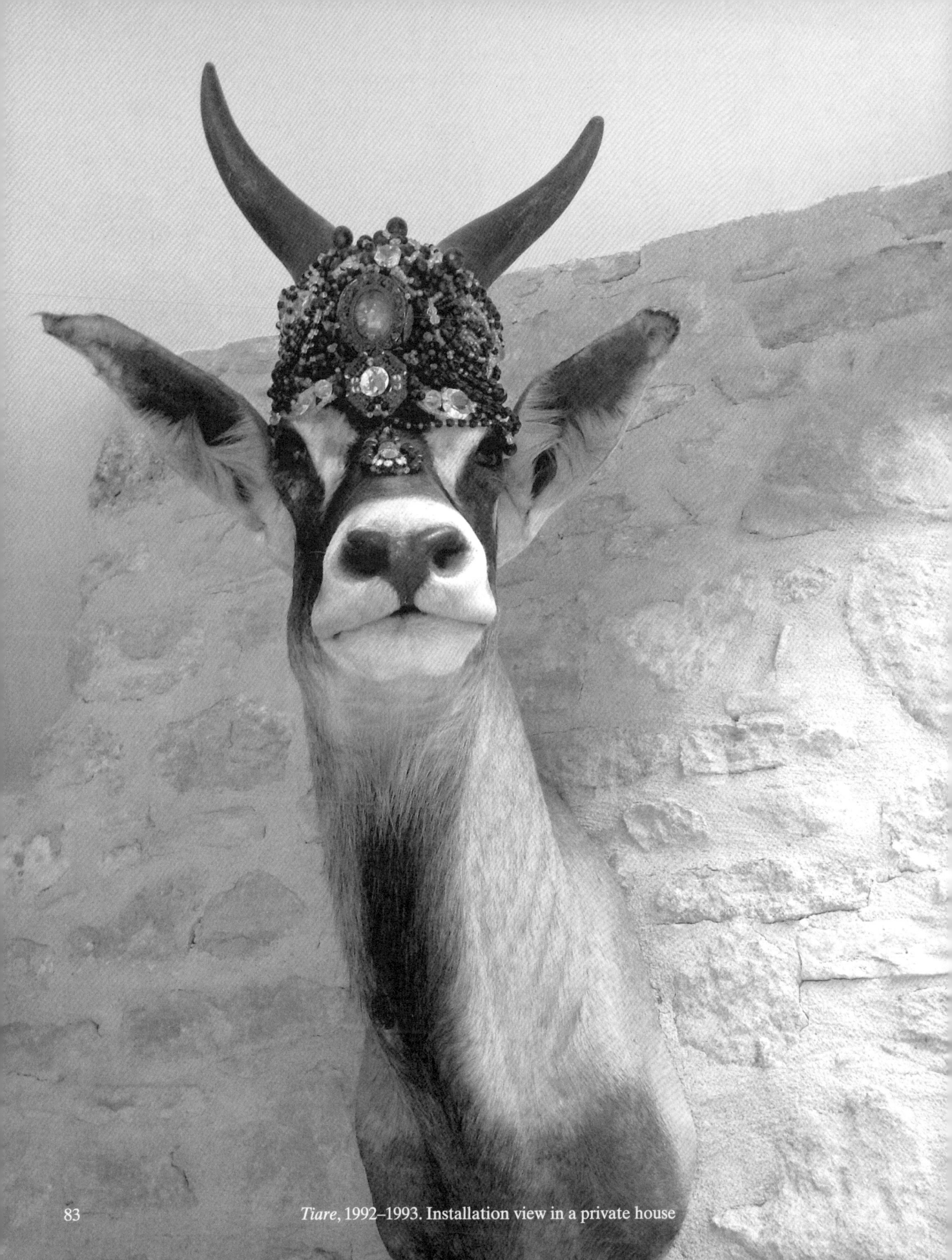

Tiare, 1992–1993. Installation view in a private house

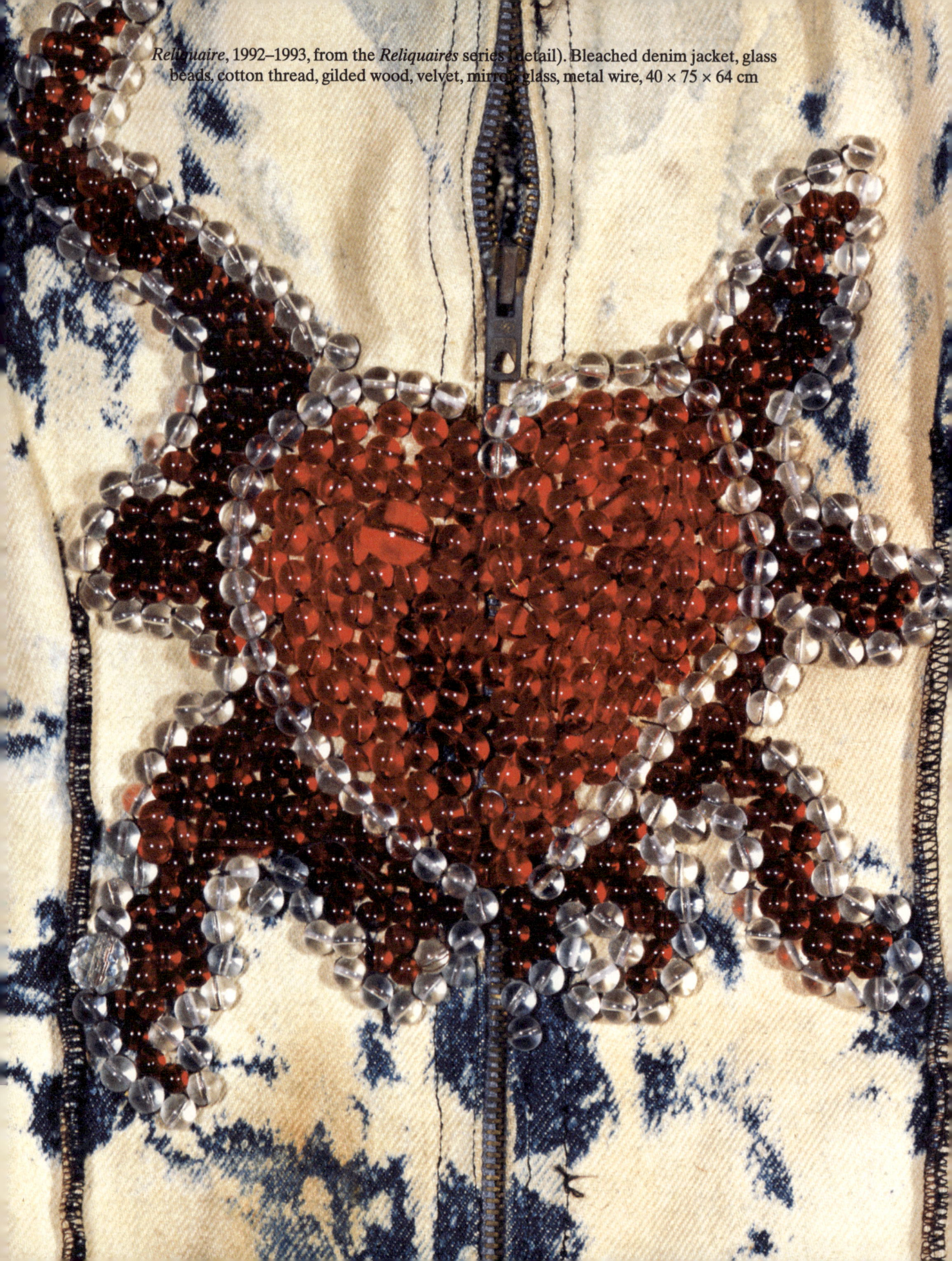
Reliquaire, 1992–1993, from the *Reliquaires* series (detail). Bleached denim jacket, glass beads, cotton thread, gilded wood, velvet, mirror glass, metal wire, 40 × 75 × 64 cm

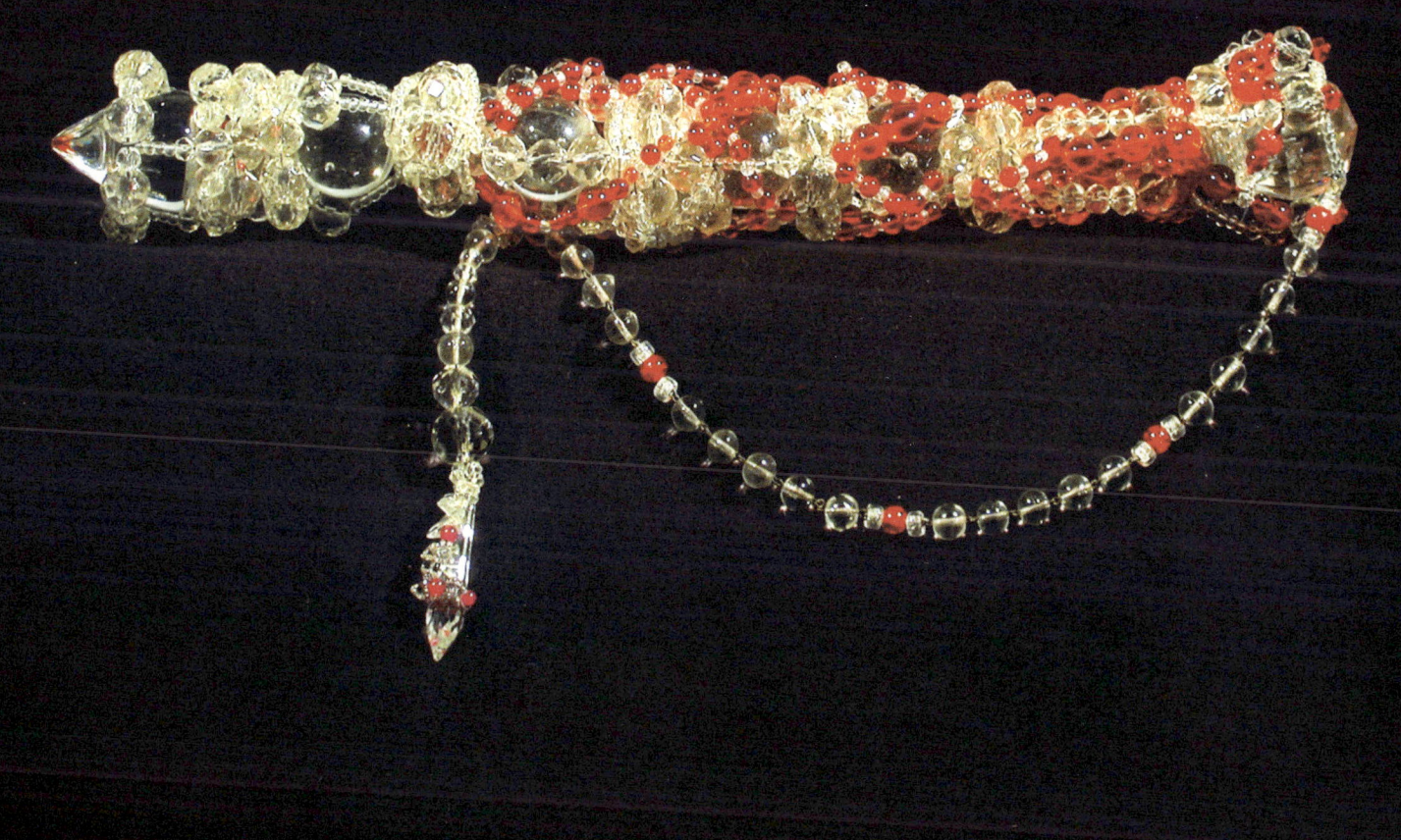

Sceptre, 1992–1993. Glass beads, tassels, rock crystal, metal wire, 50 × 7 × 23 cm.
Collection Neal Baer, New York / Paris

Untitled (Bye Bye Jeff), 1998. Glass, crystal, carnelian, glass beads, wire and metal rods, cotton thread, plastic, 32 × 20 × 19 cm

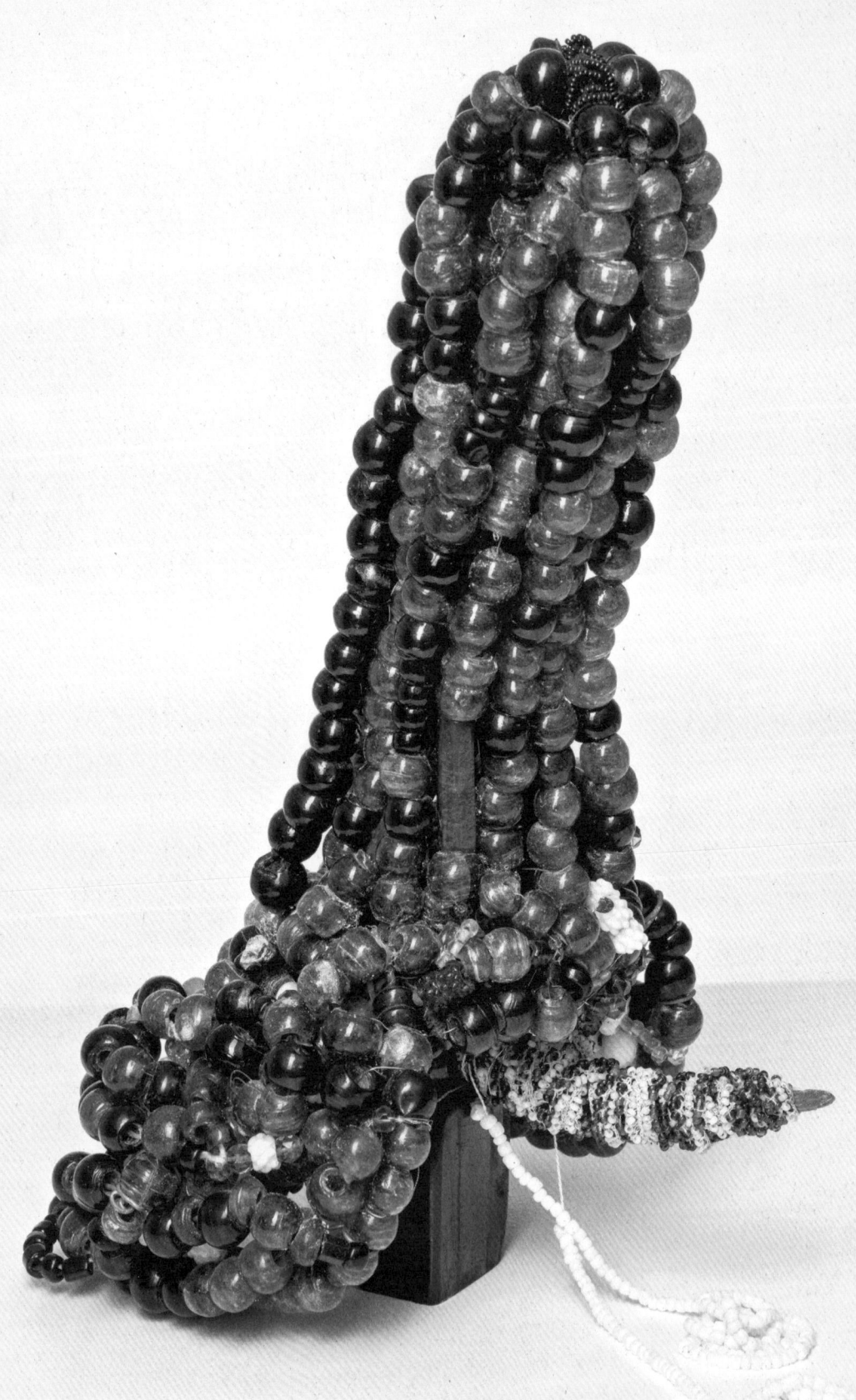

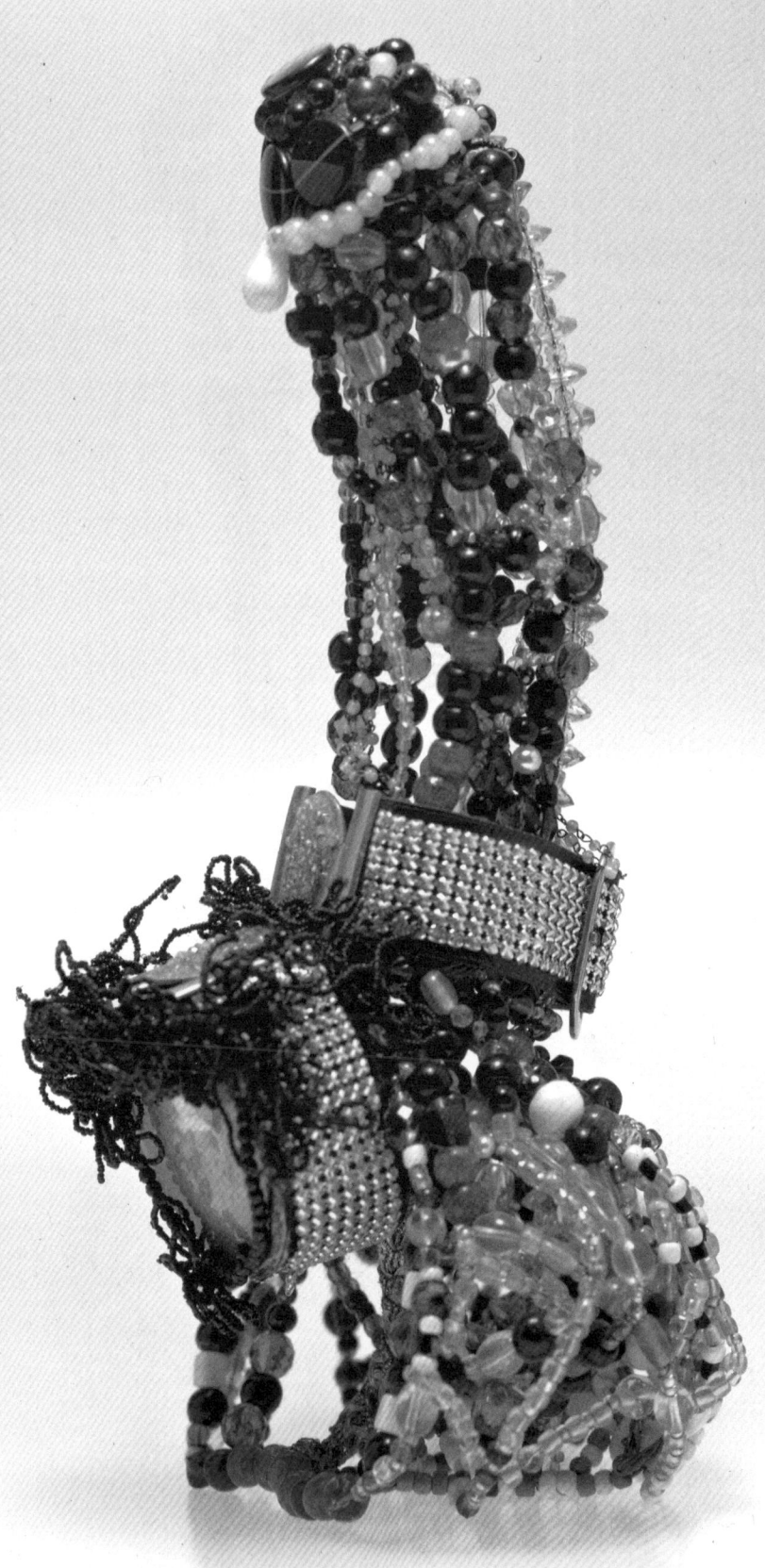

87 *Amour*, 1998. Beads, crystal, coral, metal, 48 × 20 × 23 cm. Collection Roselyne & Patrick Michaud, Nice

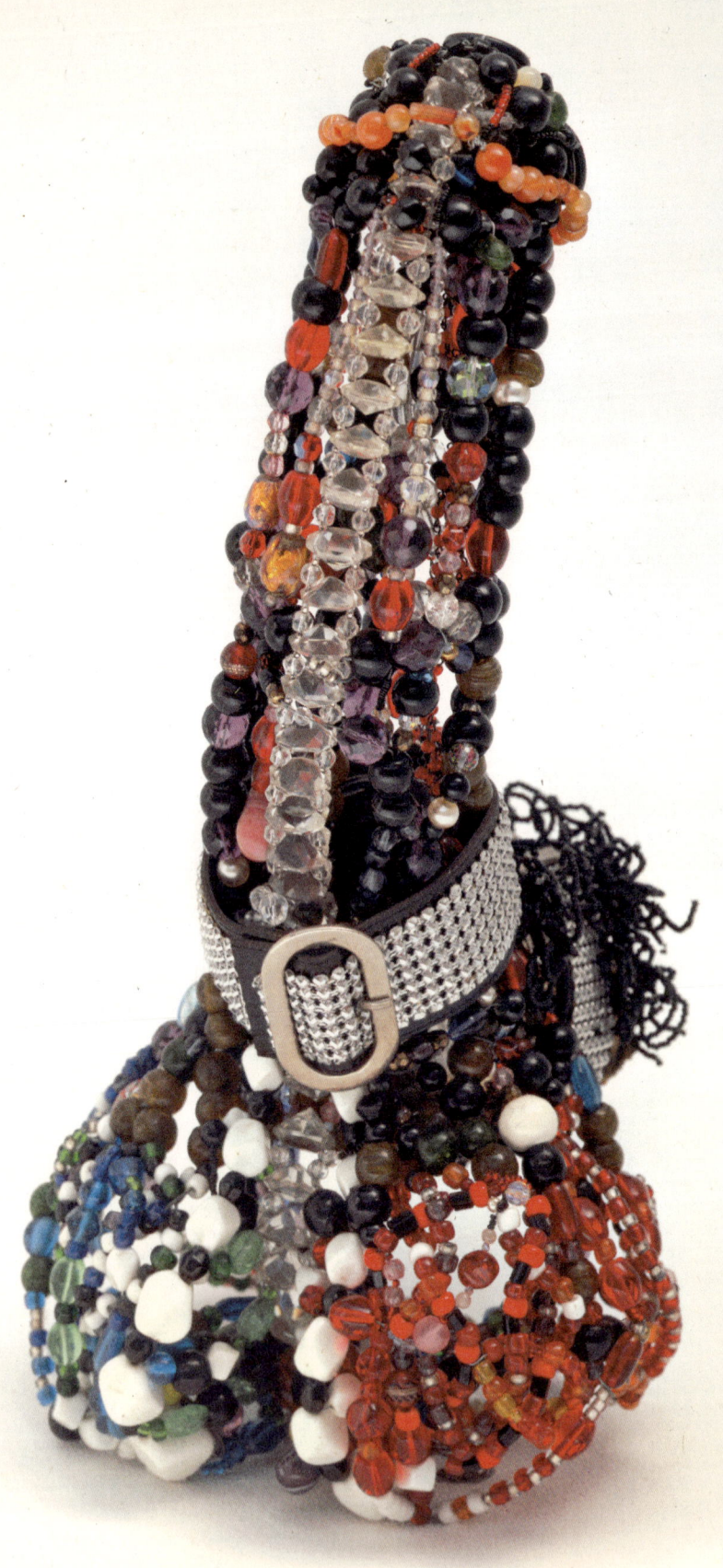

Amour, 1998. Beads, crystal, coral, metal, 48 × 20 × 23 cm. Collection Roselyne & Patrick Michaud, Nice

89 *Untitled (Bye Bye Jeff)*, 1998. Glass, crystal, carnelian, glass beads, wire and metal rods, cotton thread, plastic, 32 × 20 × 19 cm

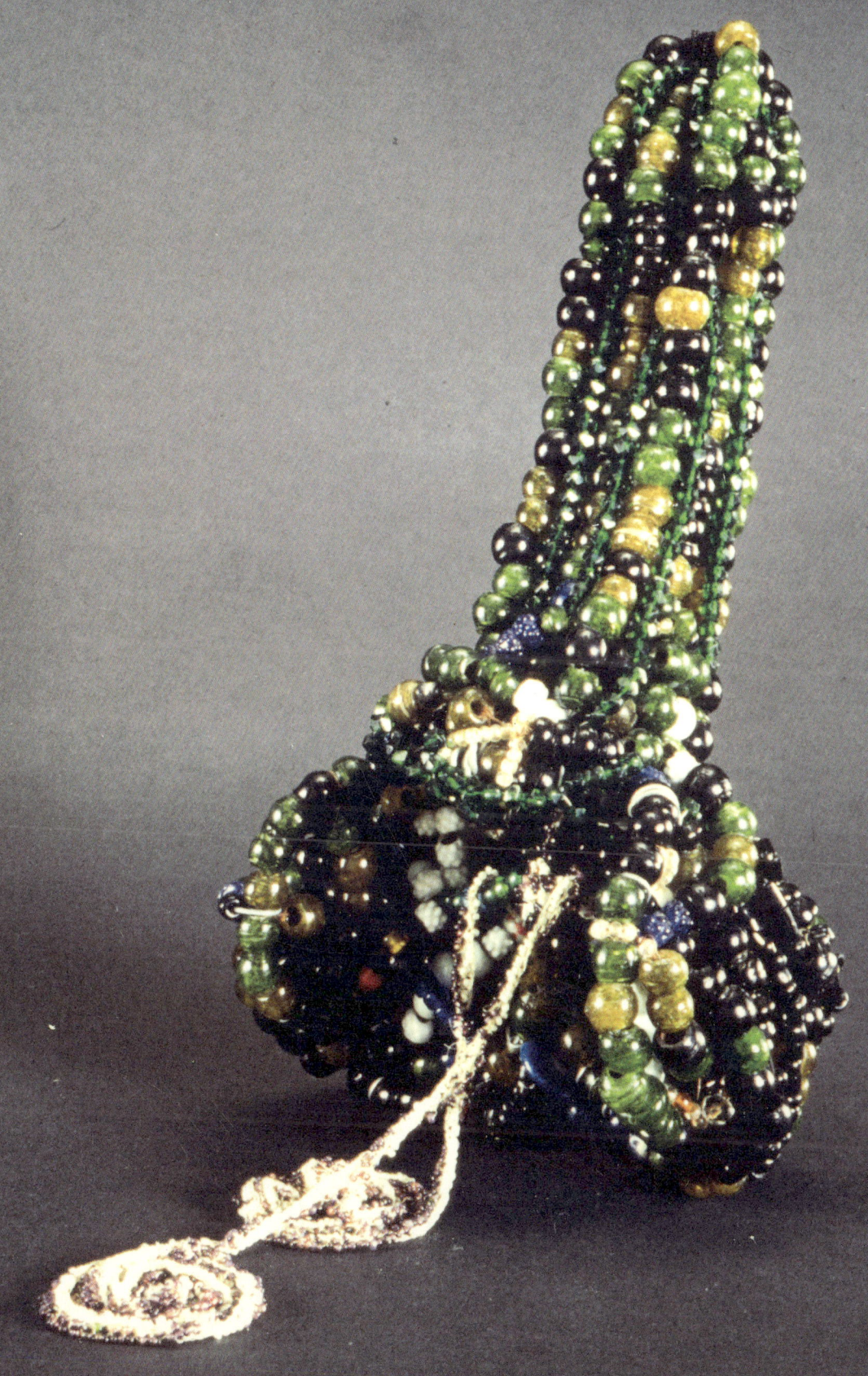

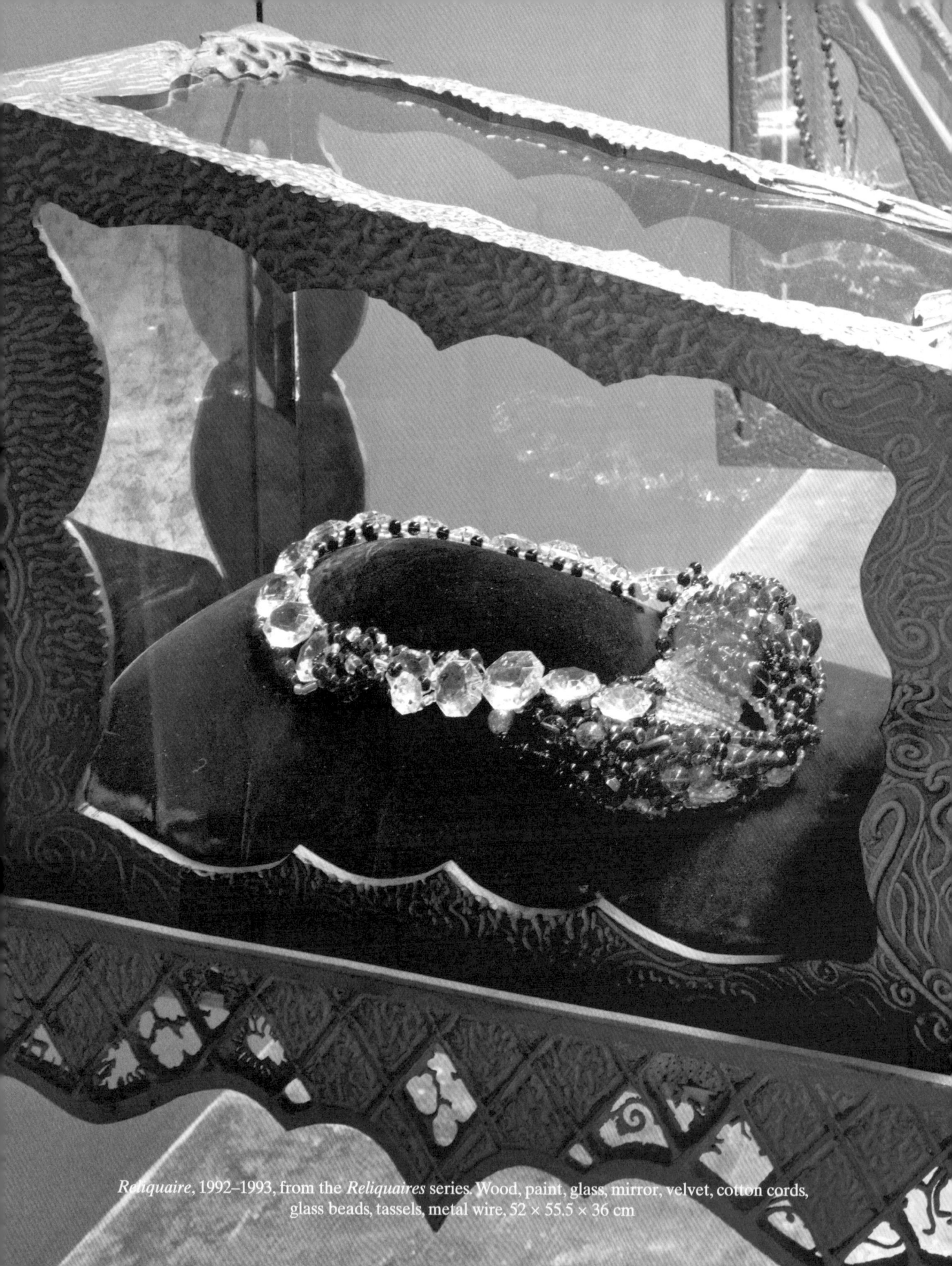
Reliquaire, 1992–1993, from the *Reliquaires* series. Wood, paint, glass, mirror, velvet, cotton cords, glass beads, tassels, metal wire, 52 × 55.5 × 36 cm

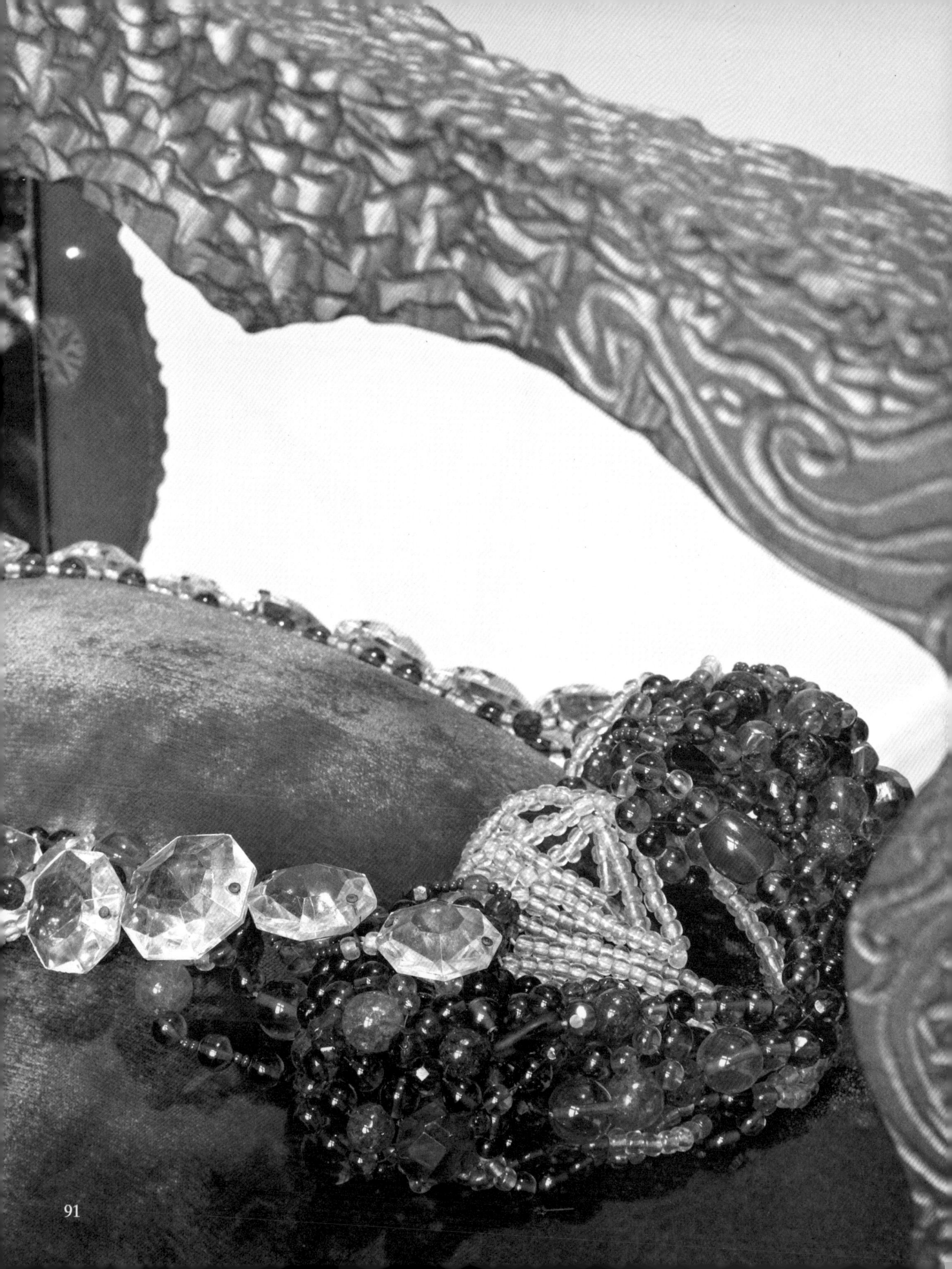

Untitled, 2000. Naturalized bird's head, feathers, glass, trimmings, marble, 57 × 28 cm

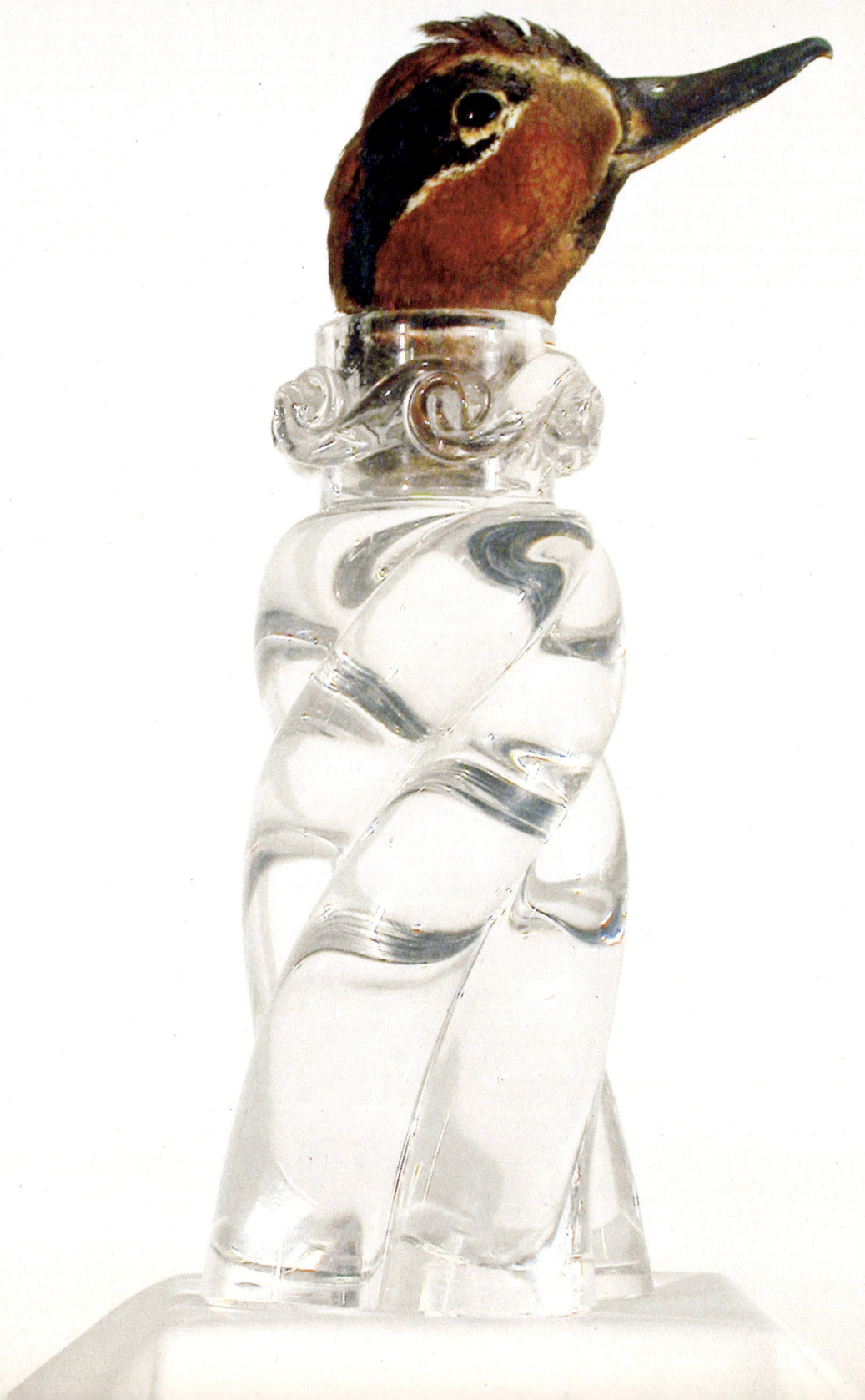

93 *Untitled*, 2000. Naturalized teal head, Baccarat crystal, 21 × 8 cm. Collection Patricia Laigneau, Paris

Reliquaire, 1992–1993, from the *Reliquaires* series. Glass beads, tassels, rhinestones, gilded wood, mirror, glass, metal wire, 63 × 34.5 × 34.5 cm

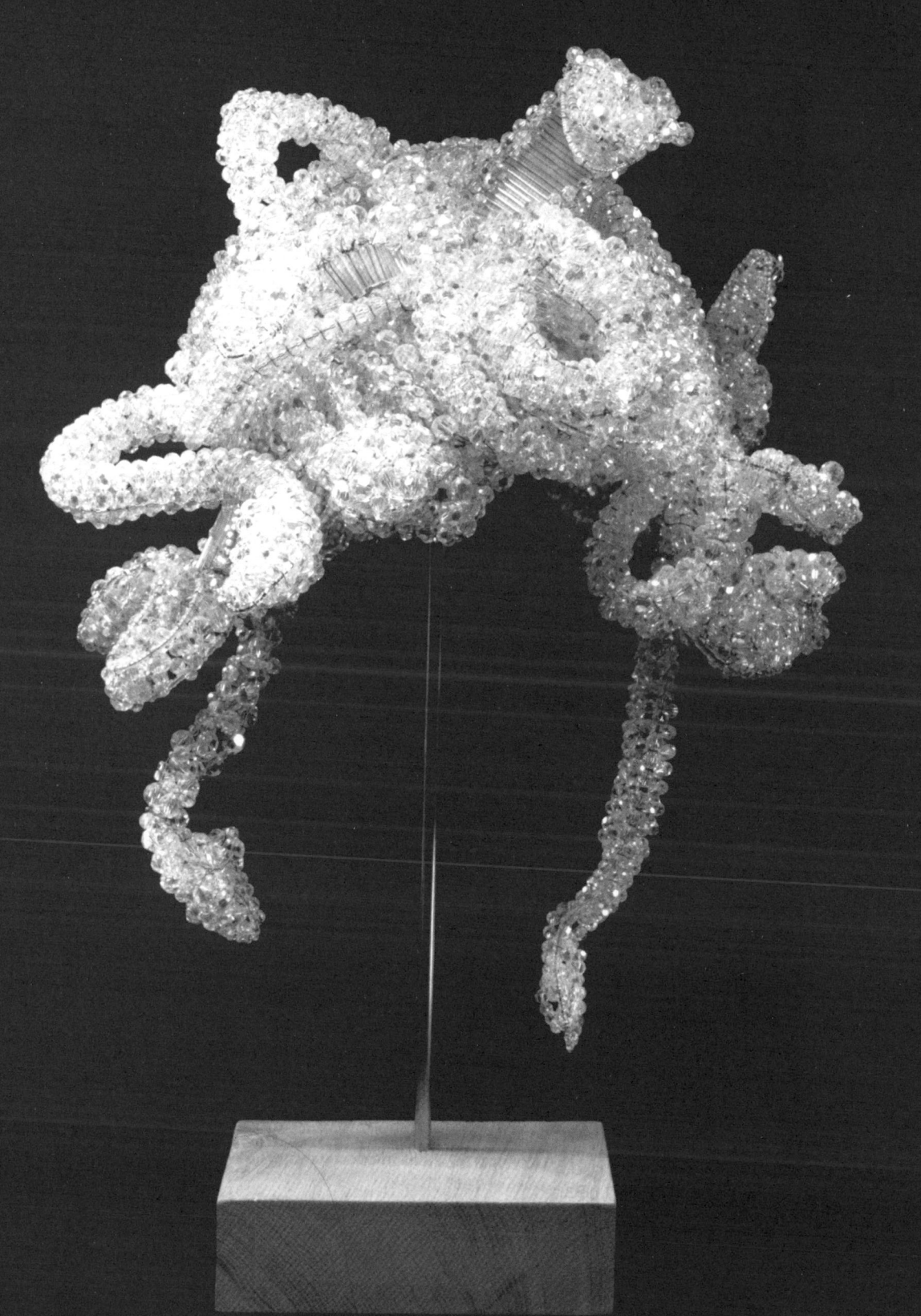

Untitled (Medusa Helmet), 1997. Swarovski crystal beads "aurora borealis," fabric, metallic wire, 37 × 33 × 33 cm. Collection Josiane Merino, Monaco

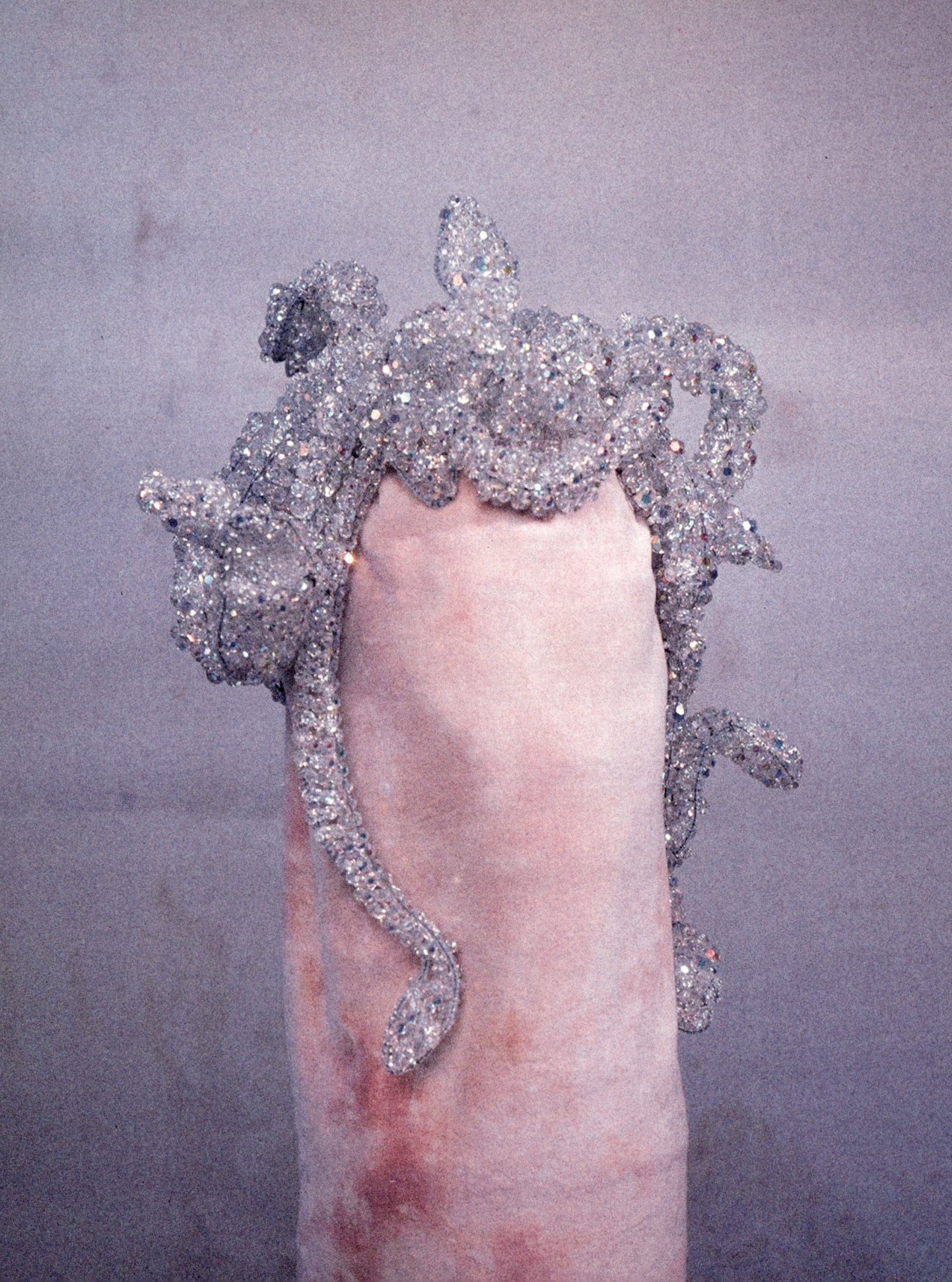

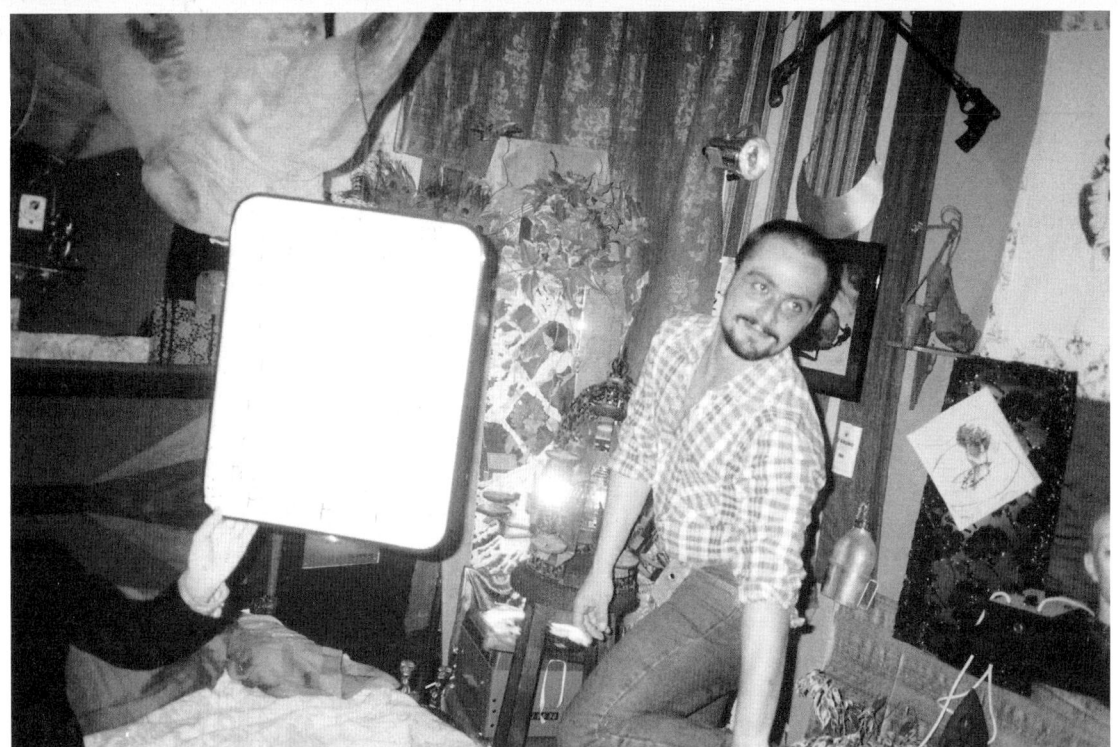
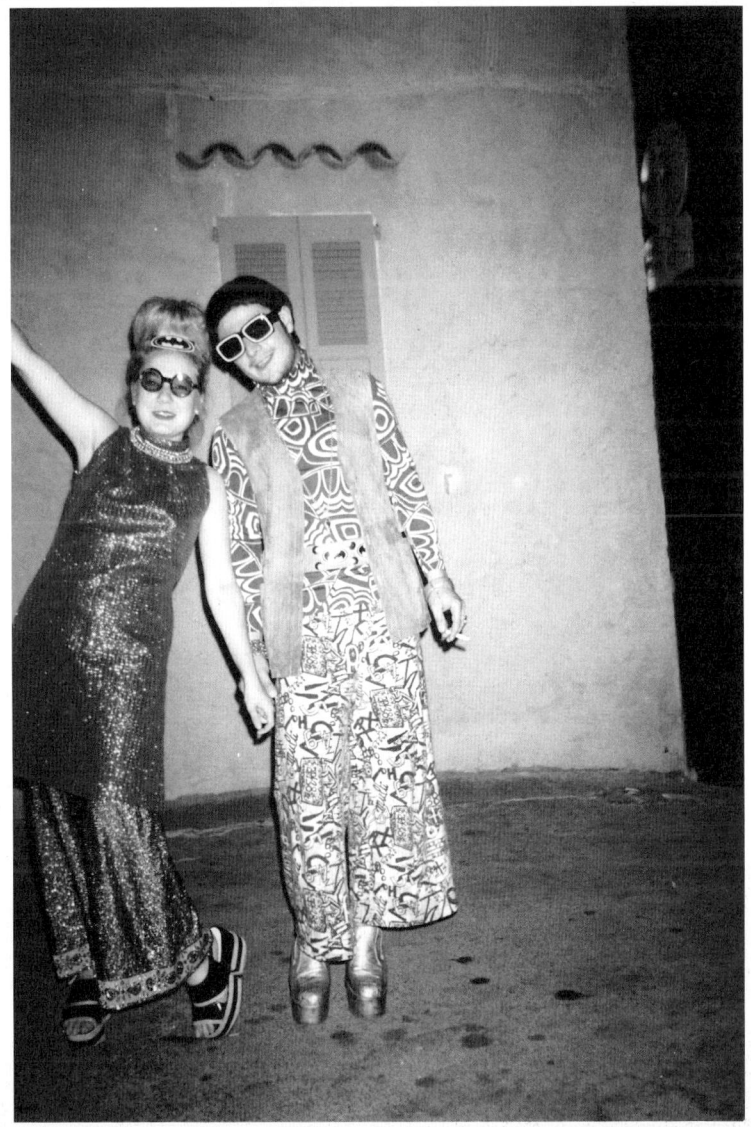

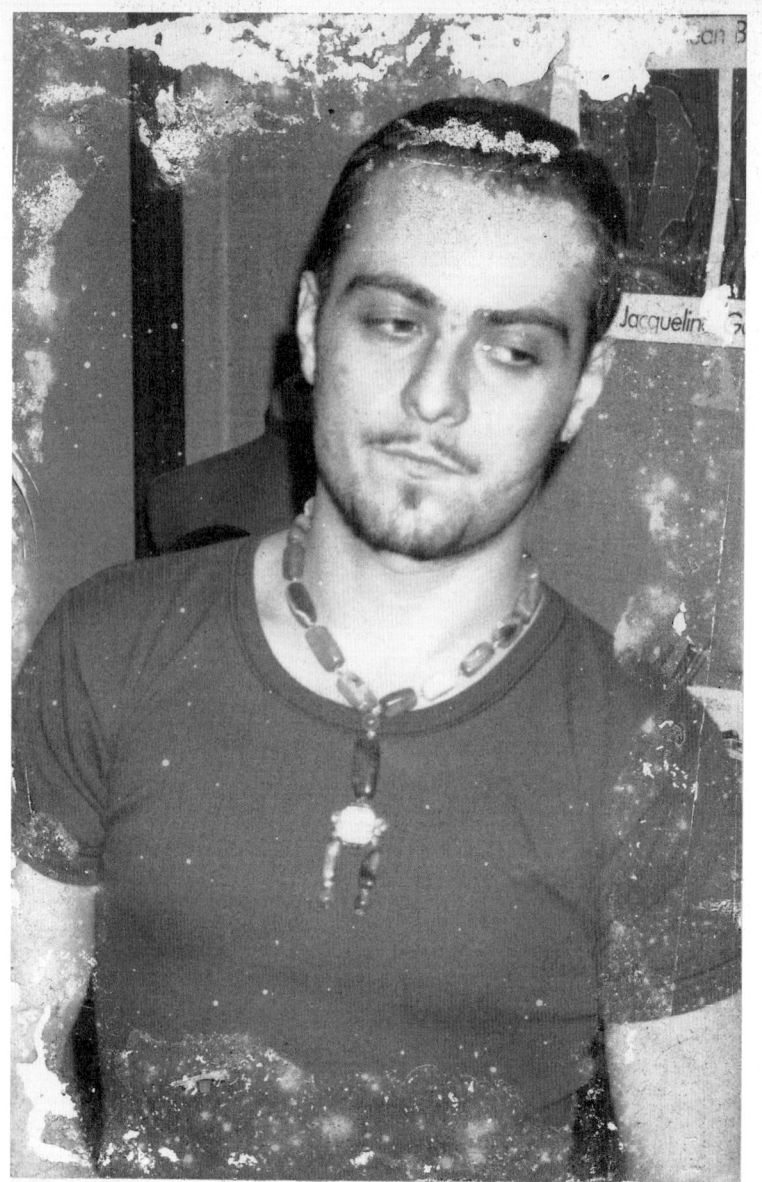
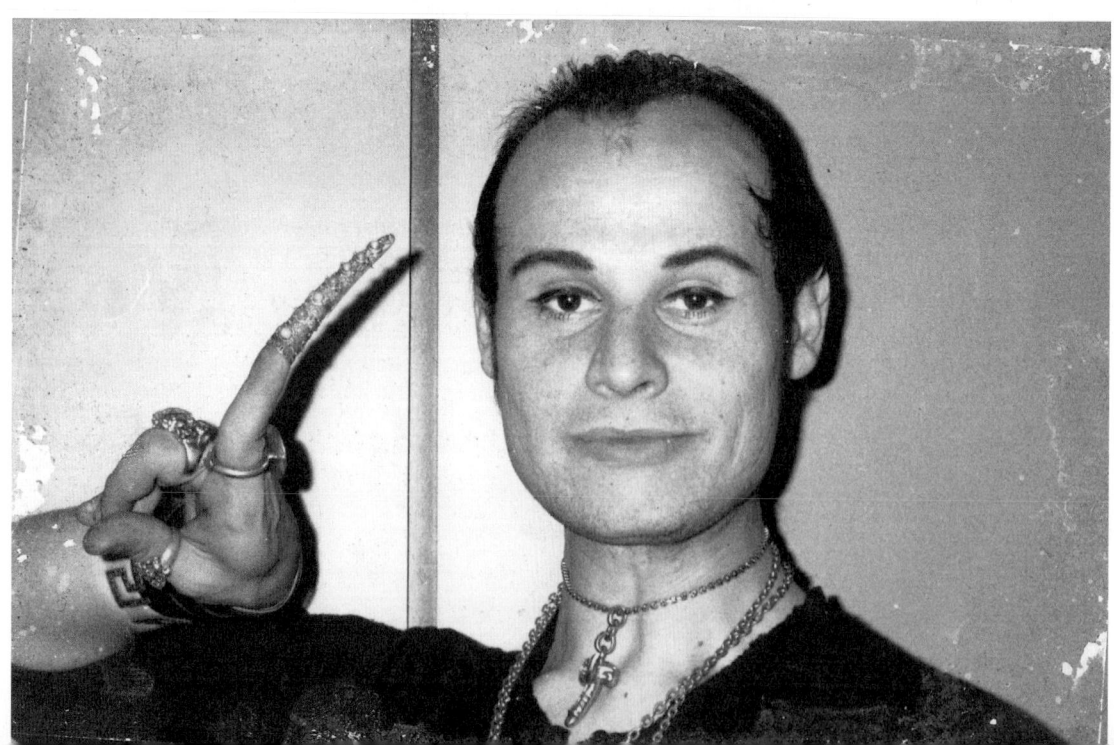

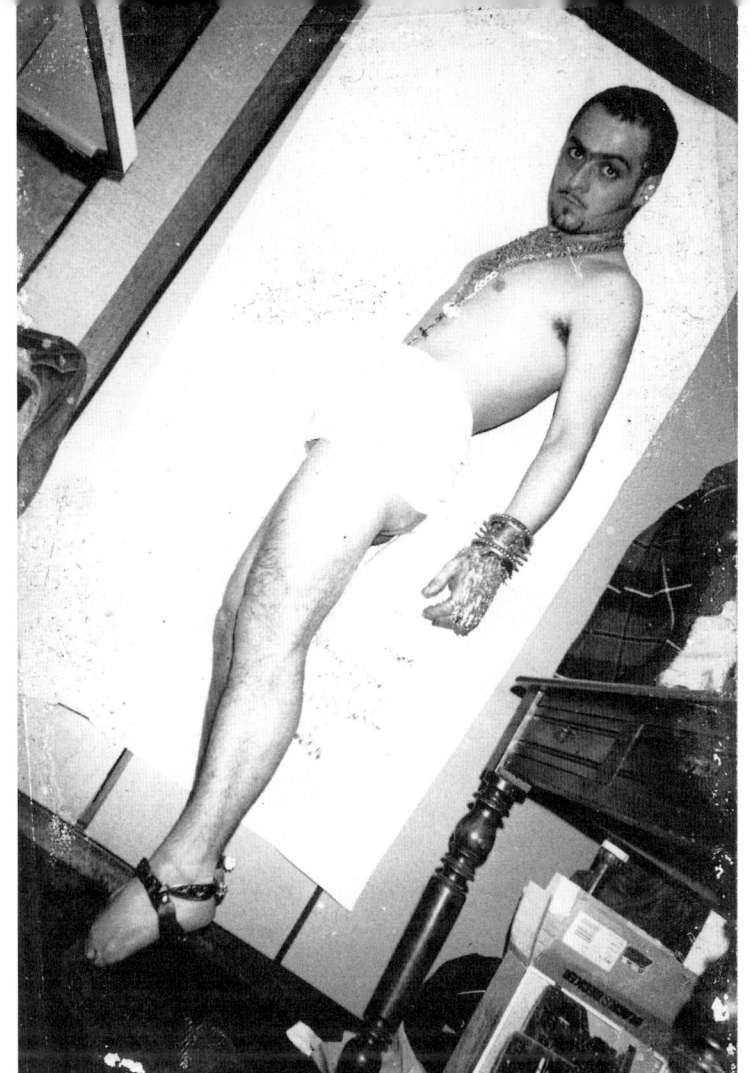
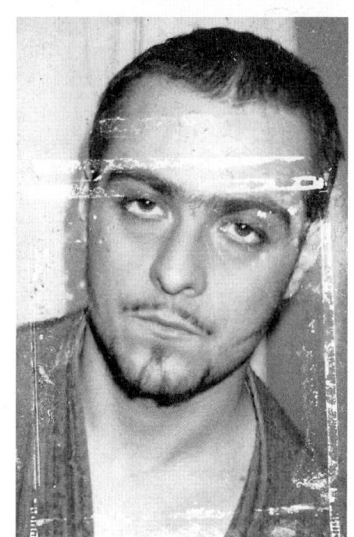
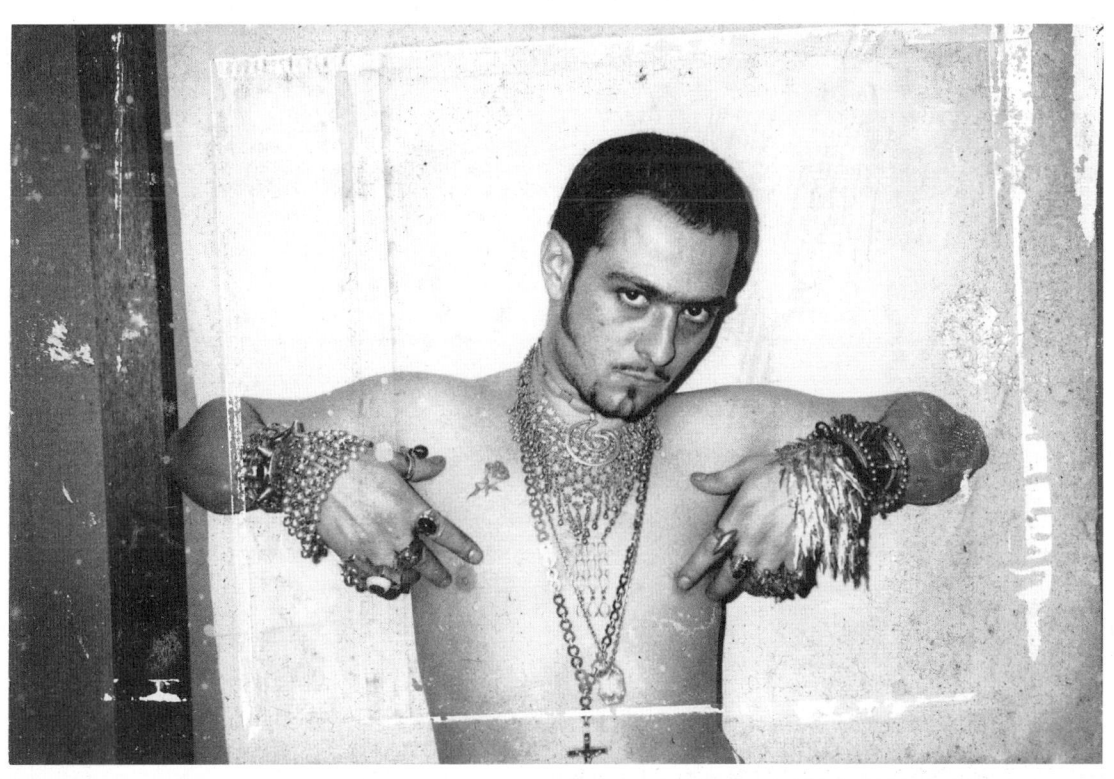

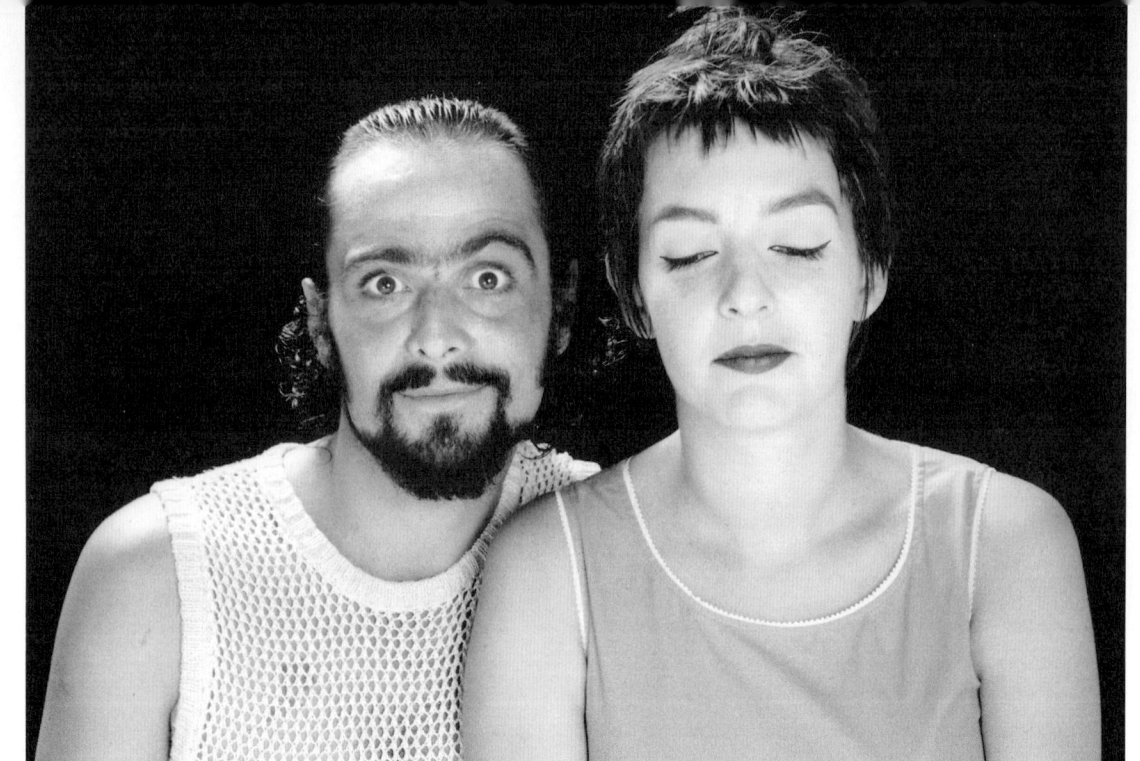
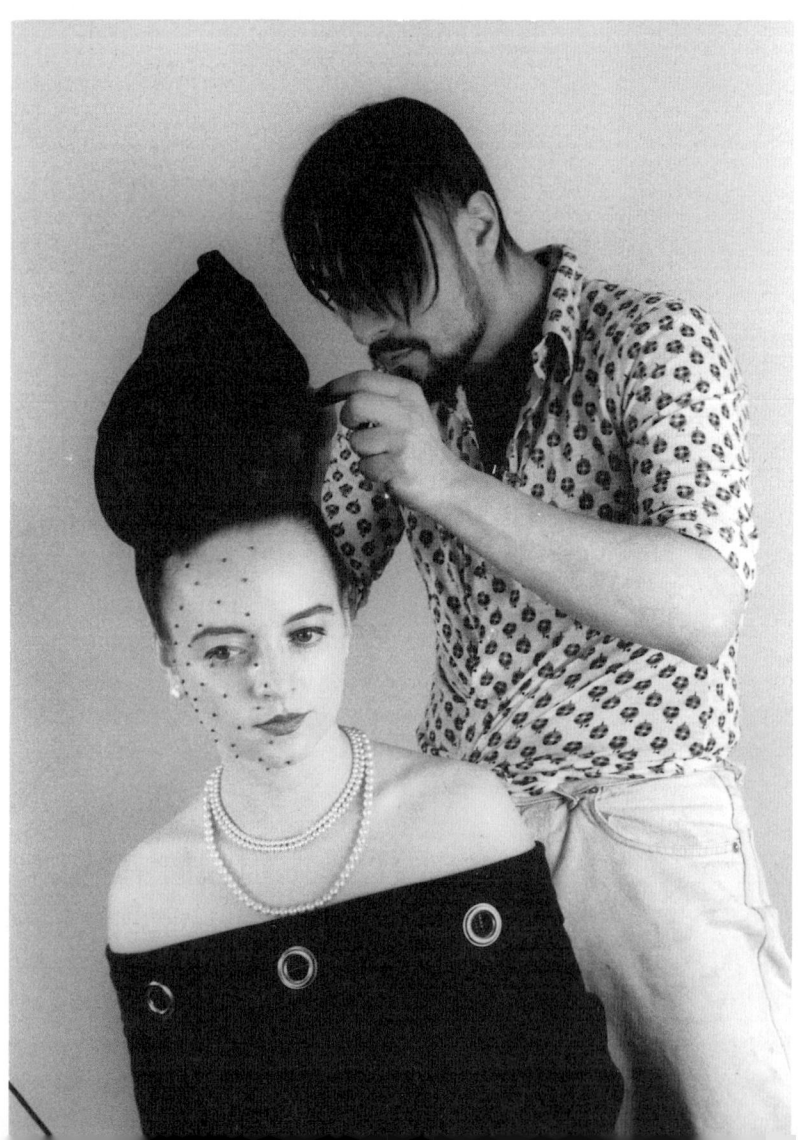

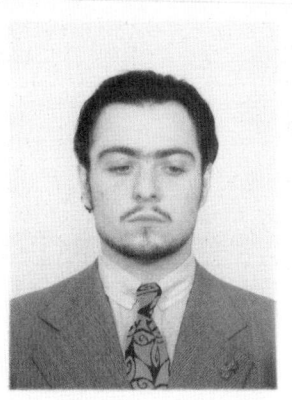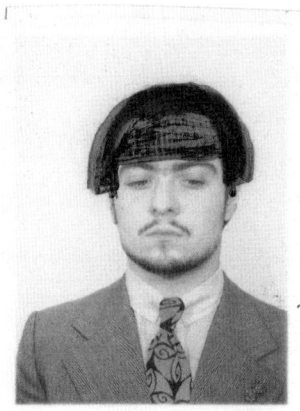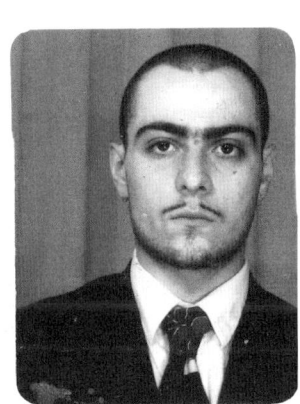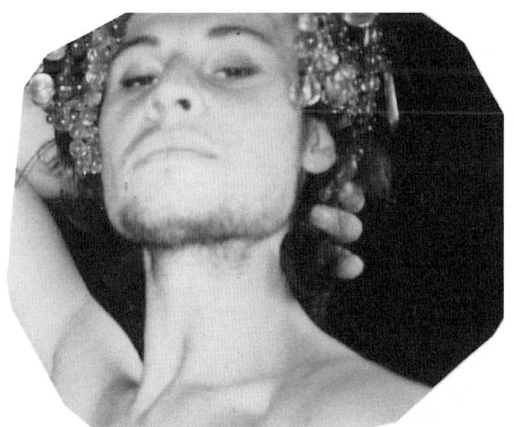

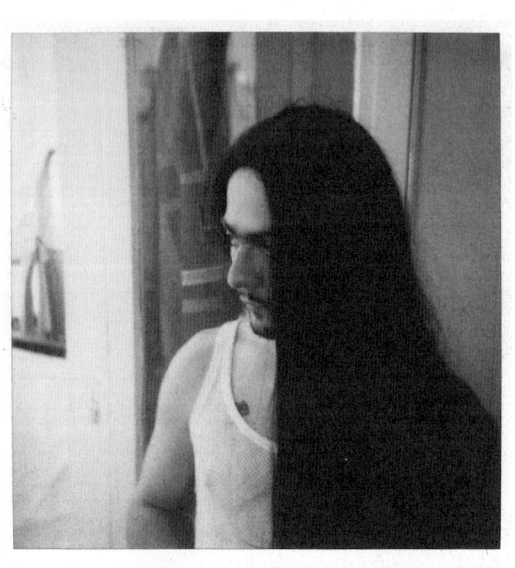
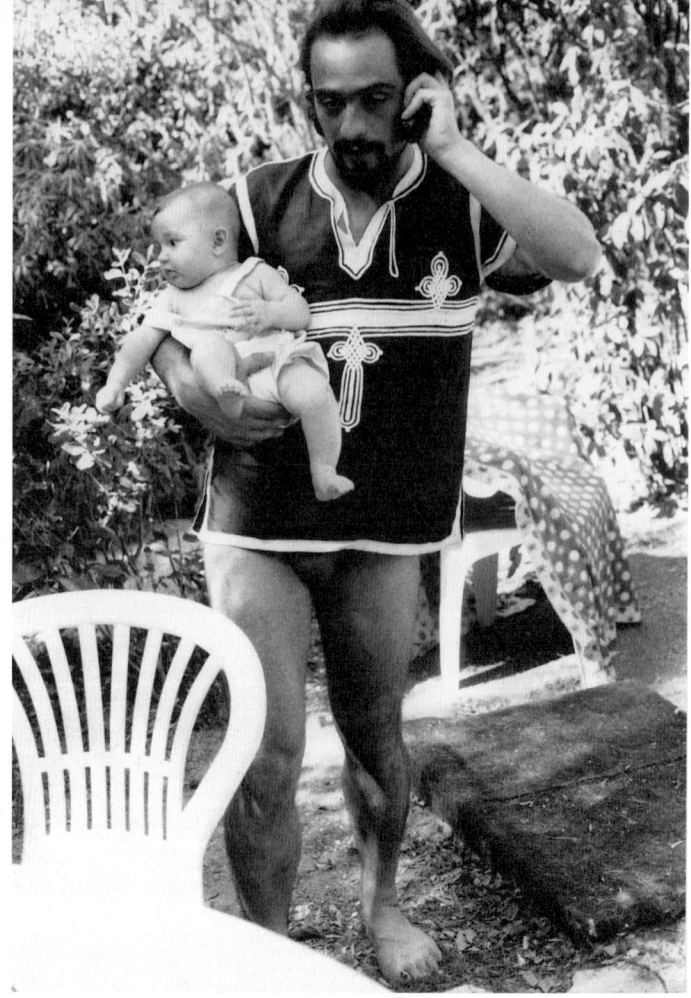
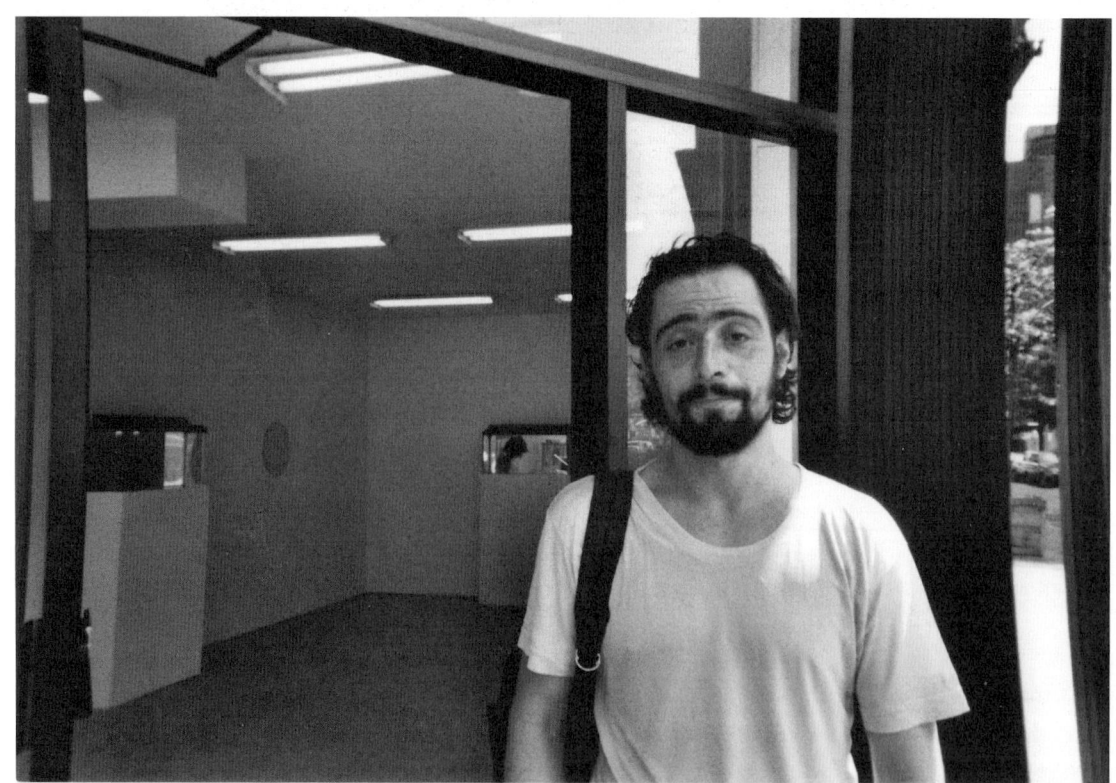

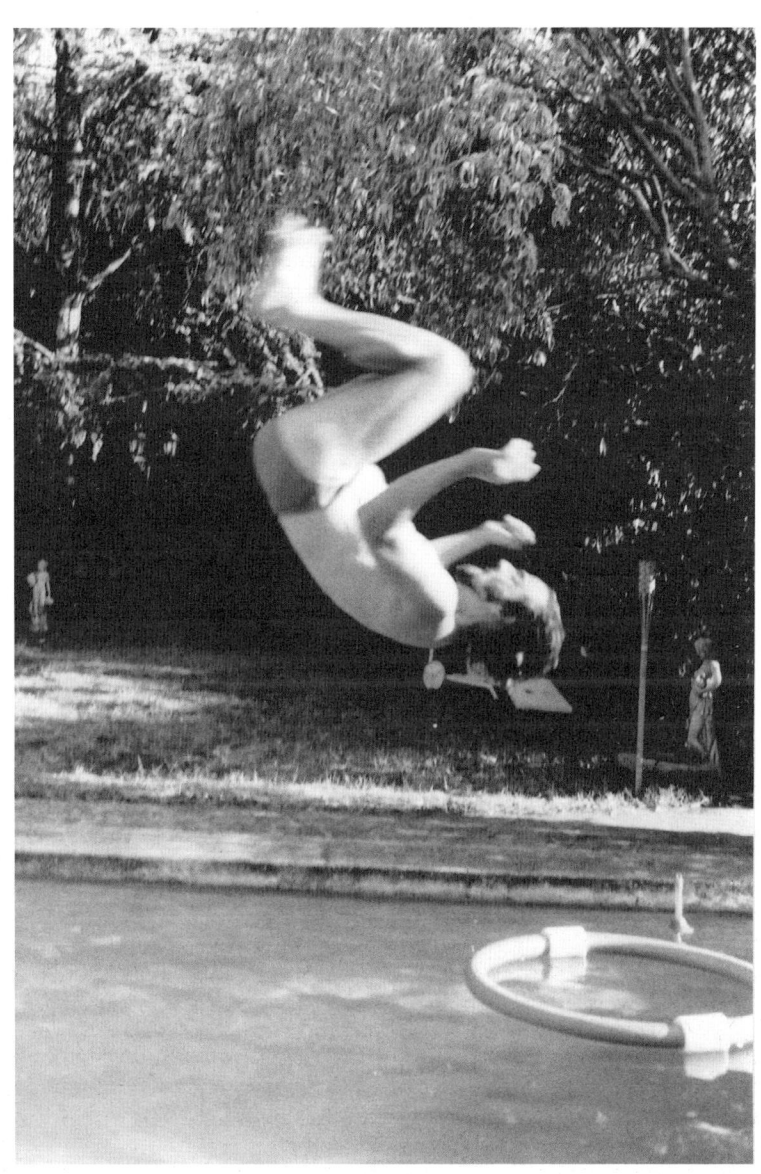

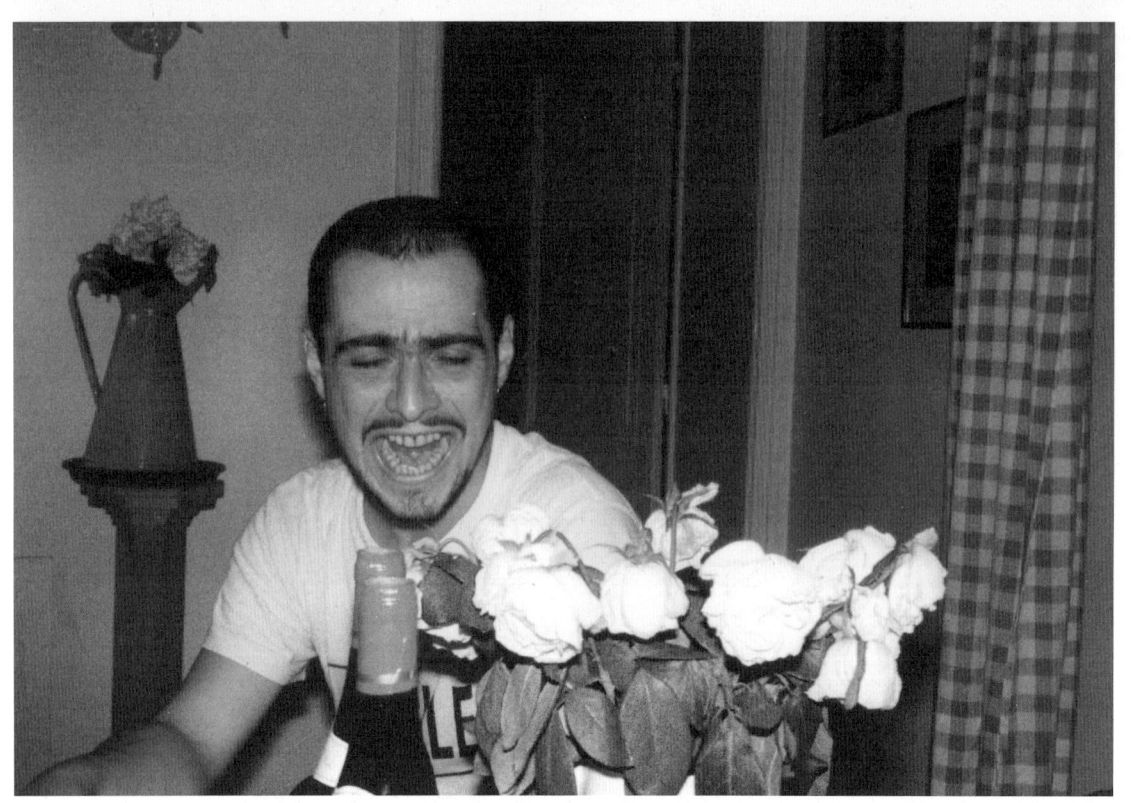
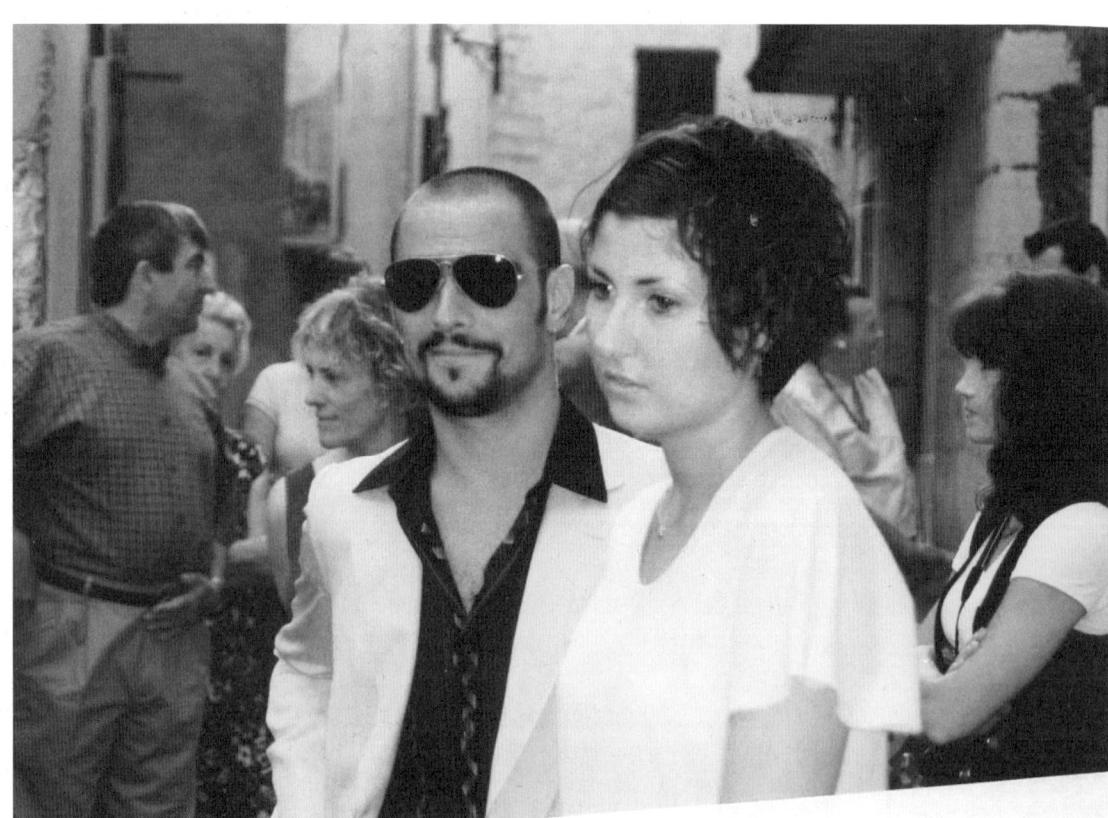

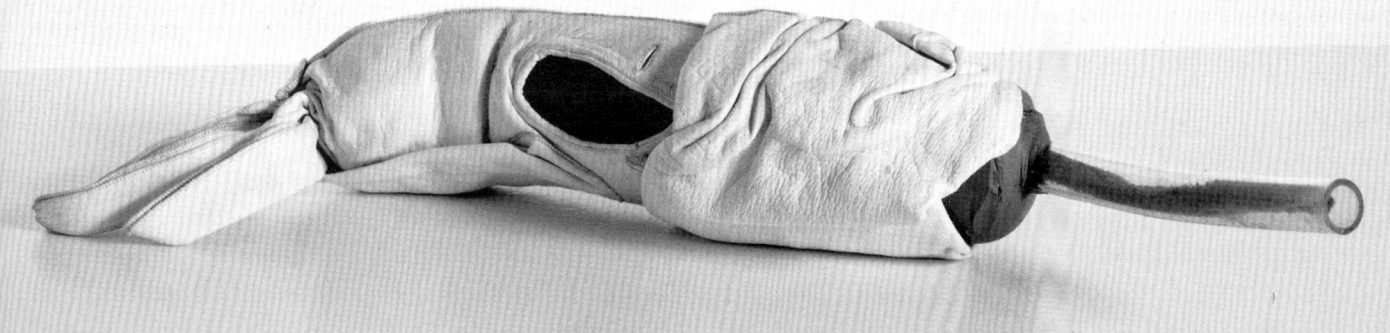

Untitled, 2000, from the *Gloves* series. White kid glove, plastic tube, red cotton cord, brown silicone, 36 × 11 × 7 cm

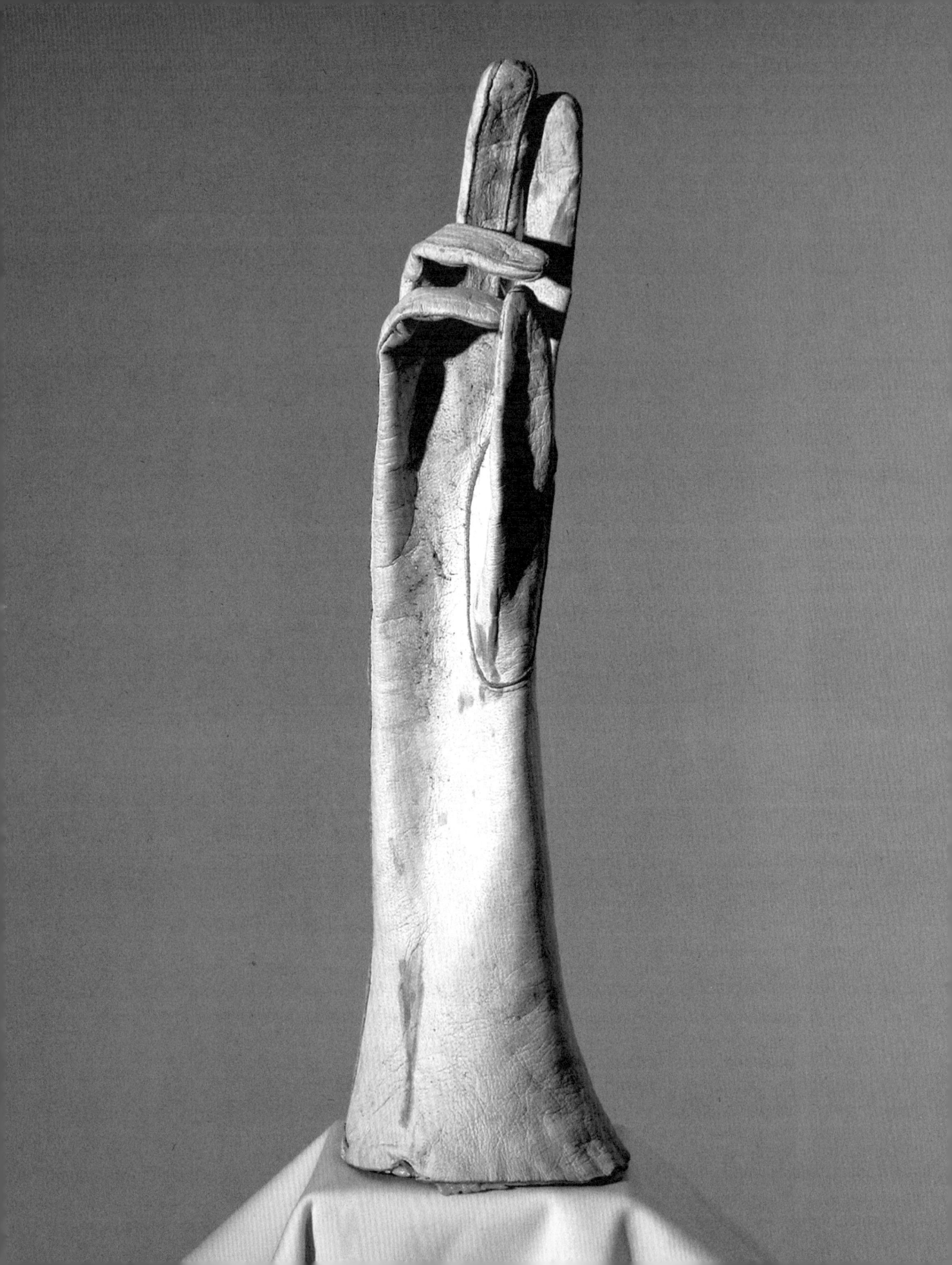

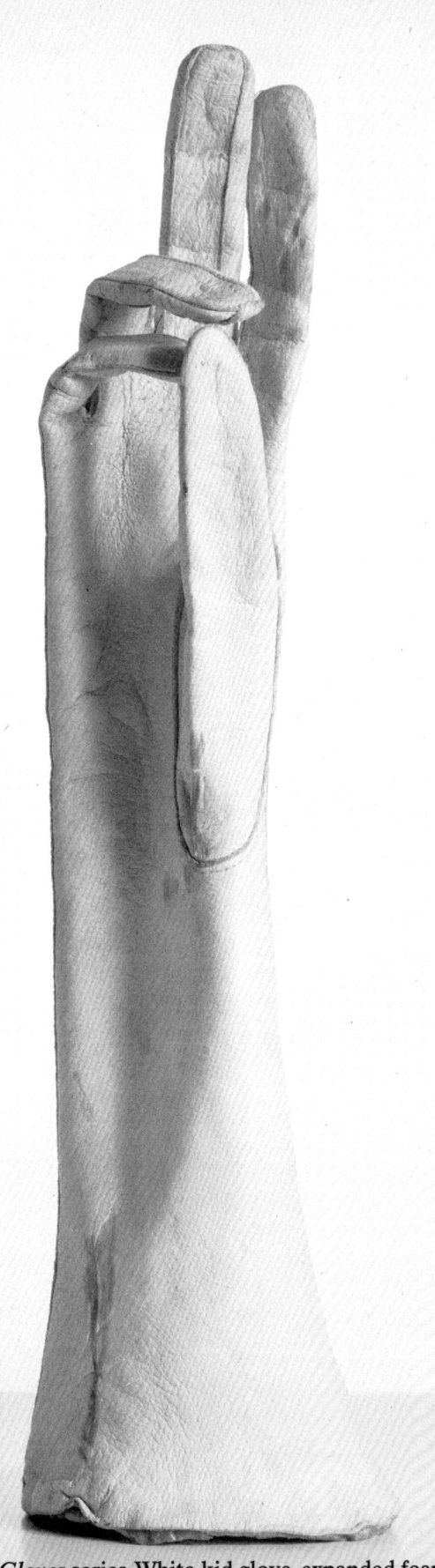

107 *Untitled*, 2000, from the *Gloves* series. White kid glove, expanded foam, 34 × 10 cm

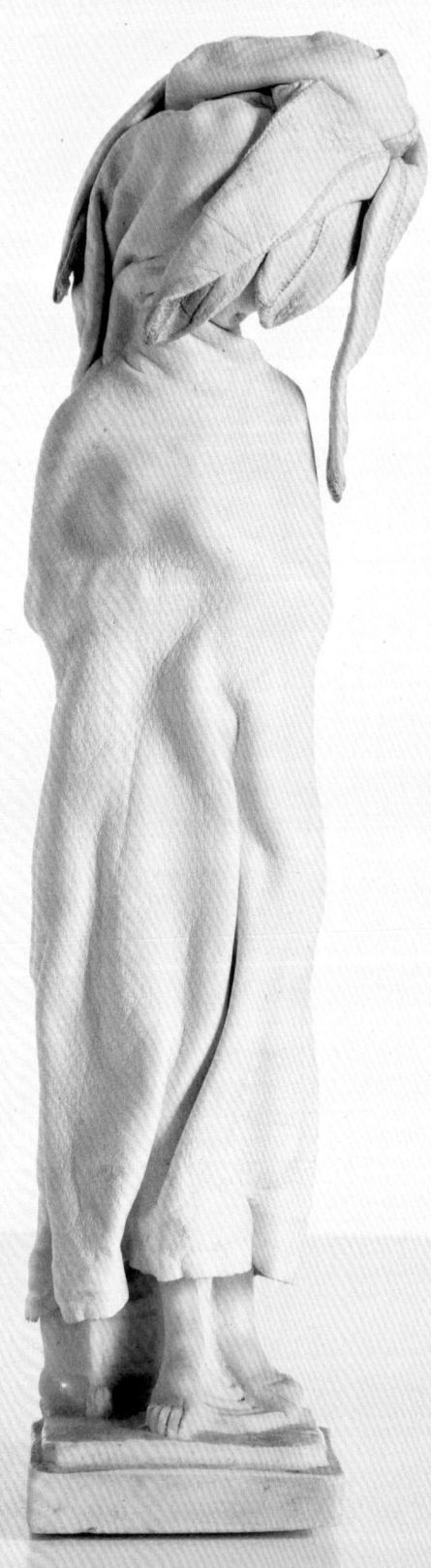

Untitled, 2000, from the *Gloves* series. White kid glove, statuette in synthetic stone, 23.5 × 7 cm

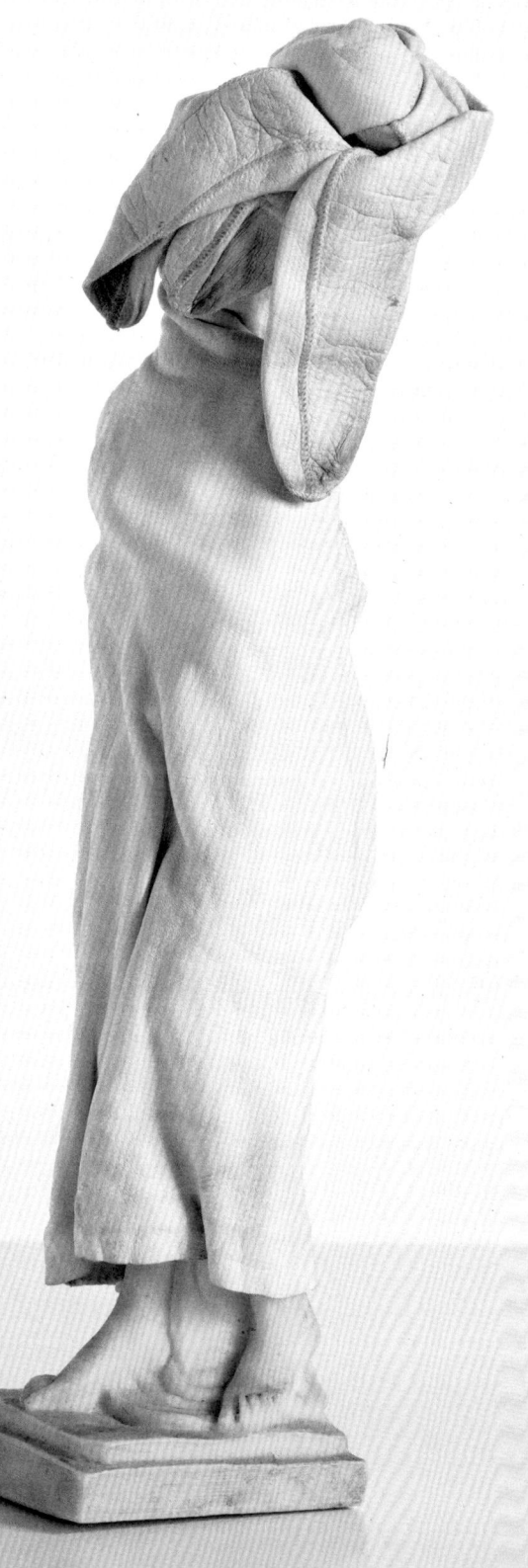

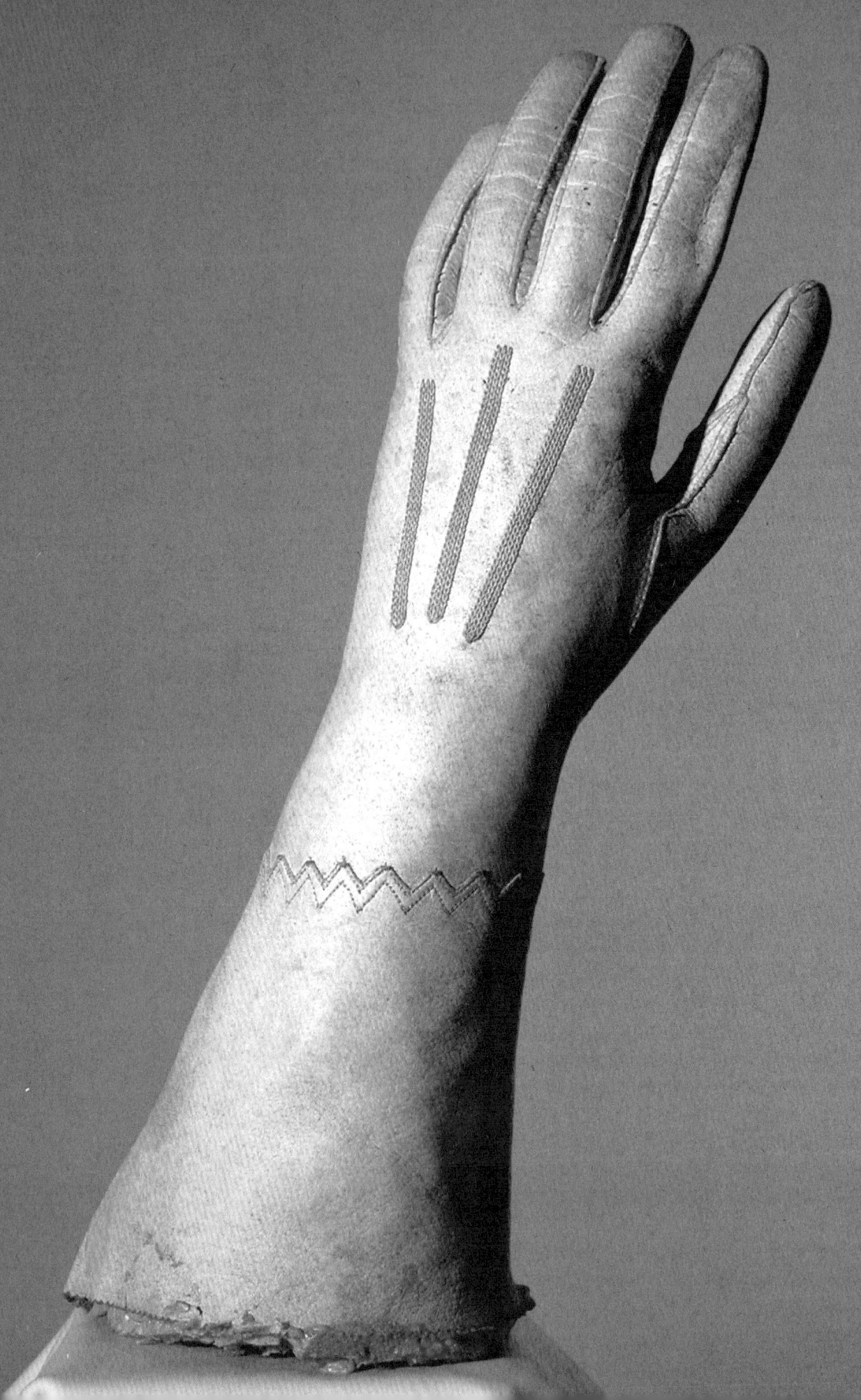

Untitled, 2000, from the *Gloves* series. White kid glove, expanded foam, 30 × 10.5 cm

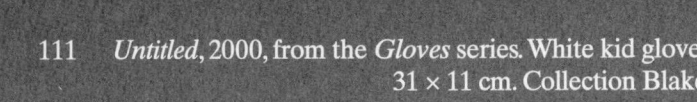

111   *Untitled*, 2000, from the *Gloves* series. White kid glove, white mink, chestnut hair, cut stone, expanded foam, 31 × 11 cm. Collection Blake Byrne, Los Angeles / Paris

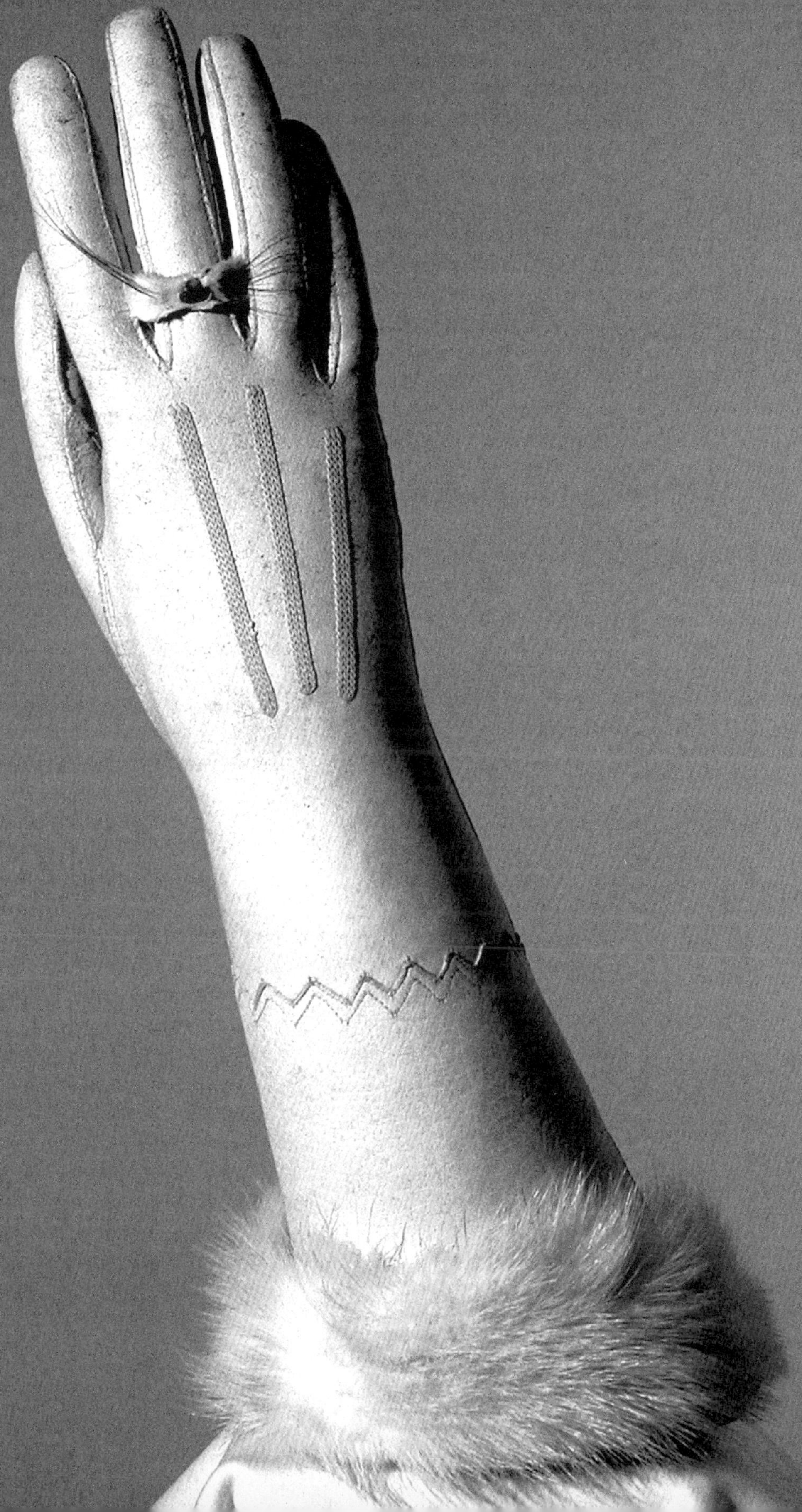

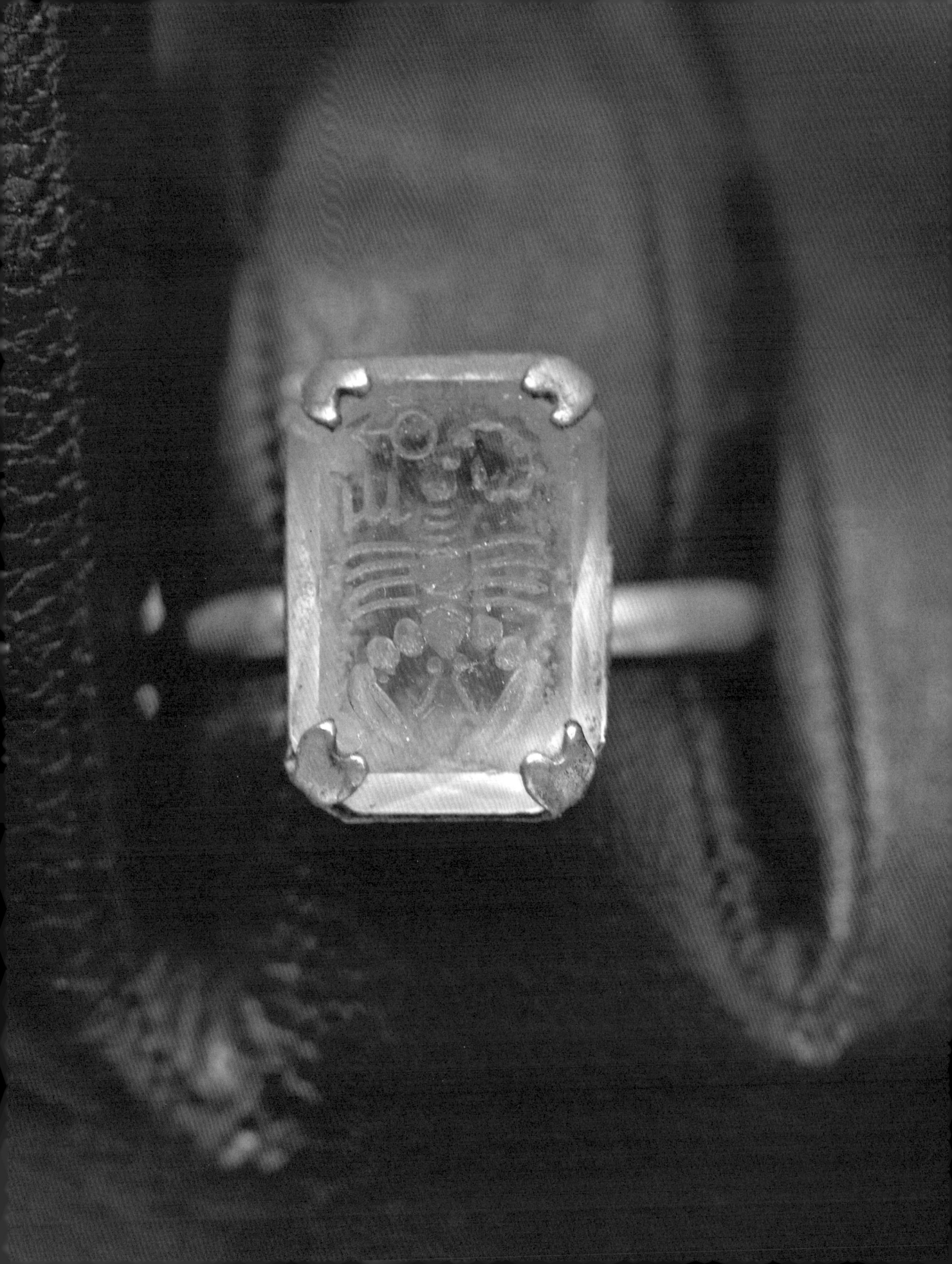

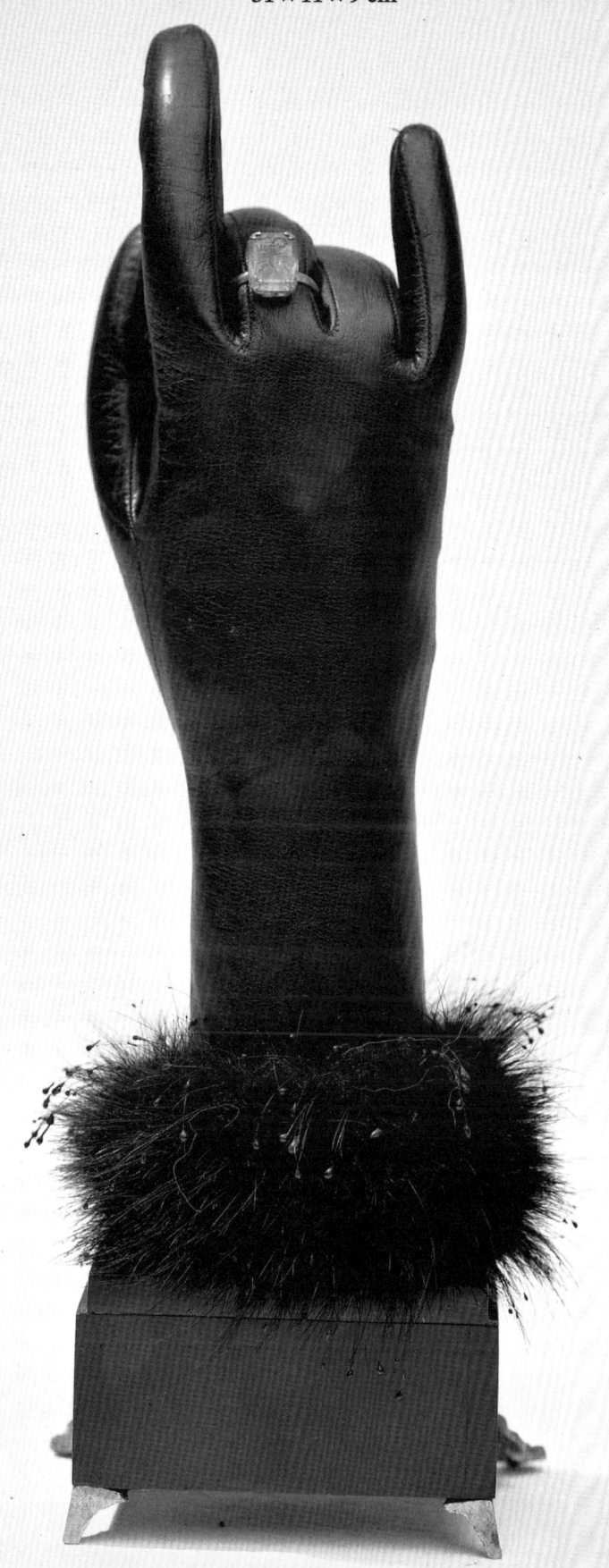

113   *Untitled*, 2000, from the *Gloves* series. Kid glove, ring with citrine, mink, sealing wax, marble, bronze, 31 × 11 × 9 cm

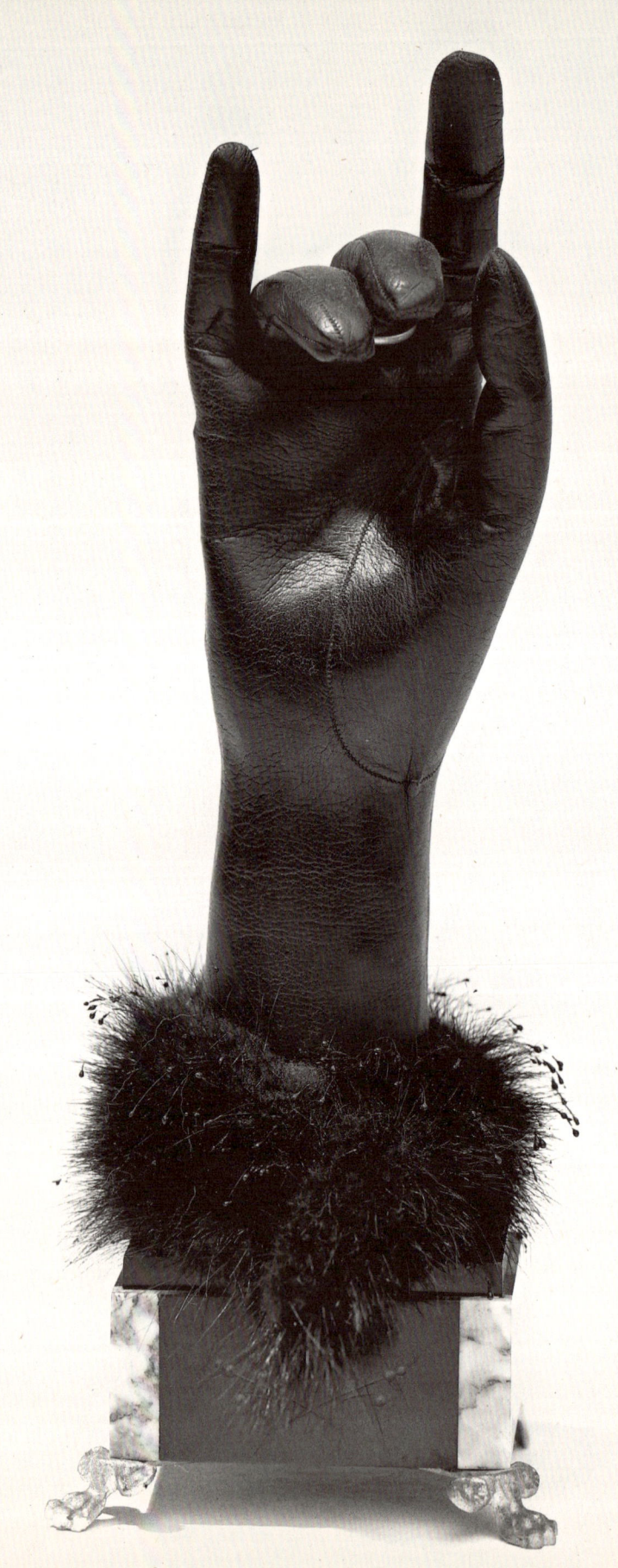

115 *Untitled*, 2000, from the *Gloves* series. Chainmail glove, metallic porcelain, silver, steel, cotton, 22.5 × 9 × 5.5 cm

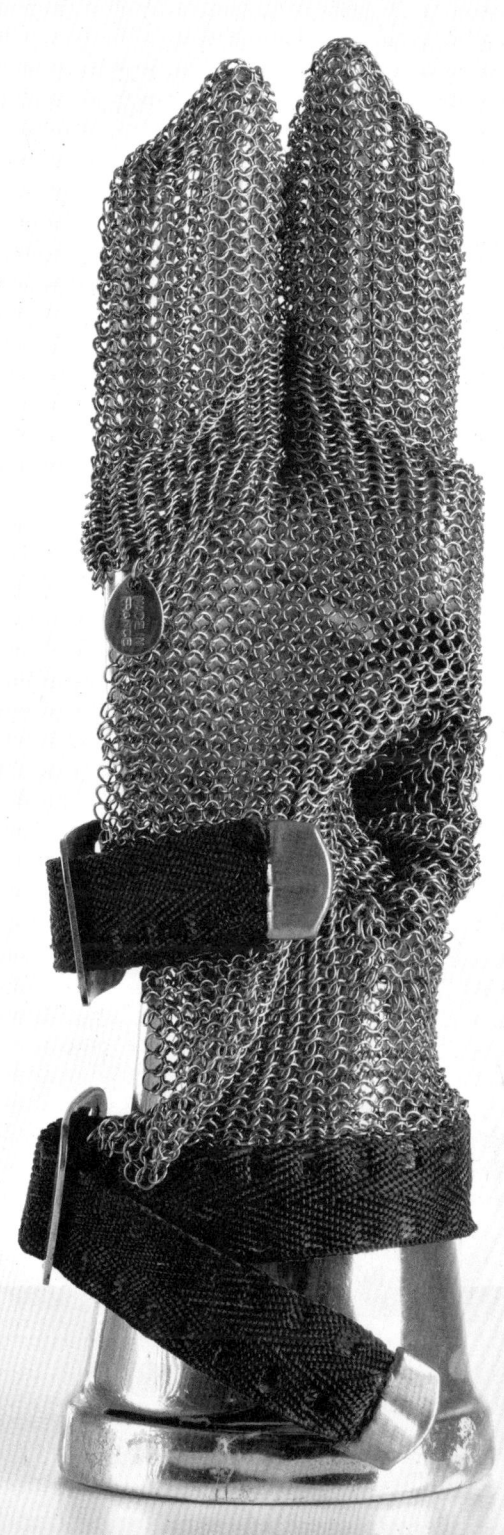

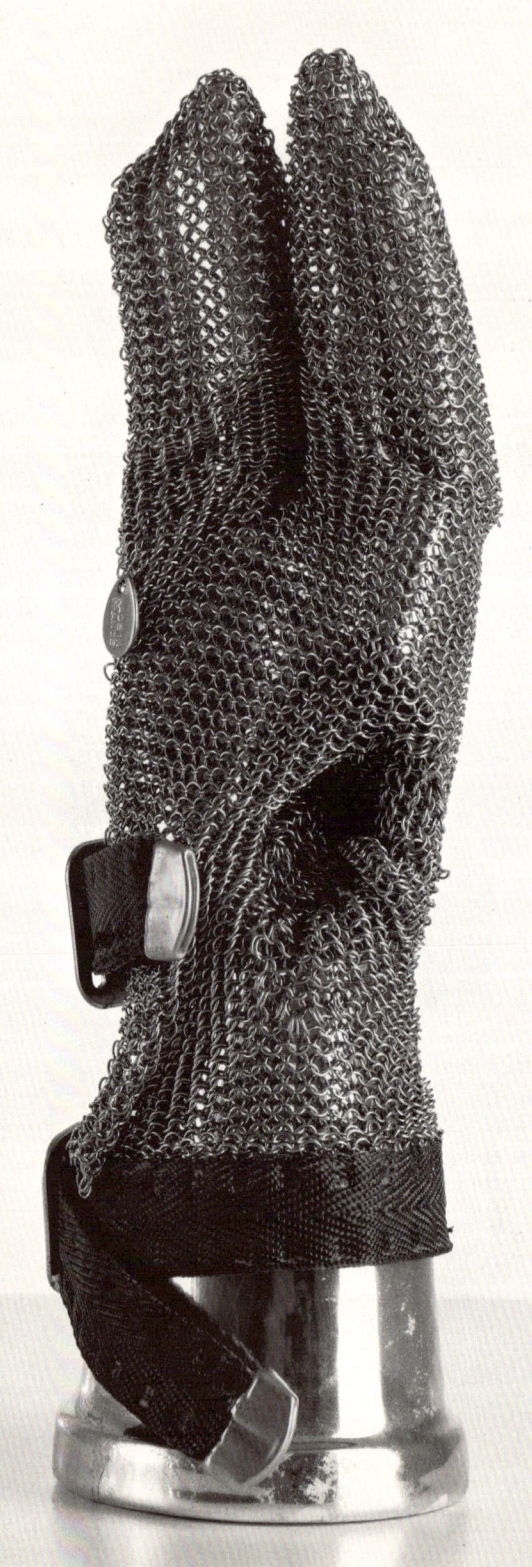

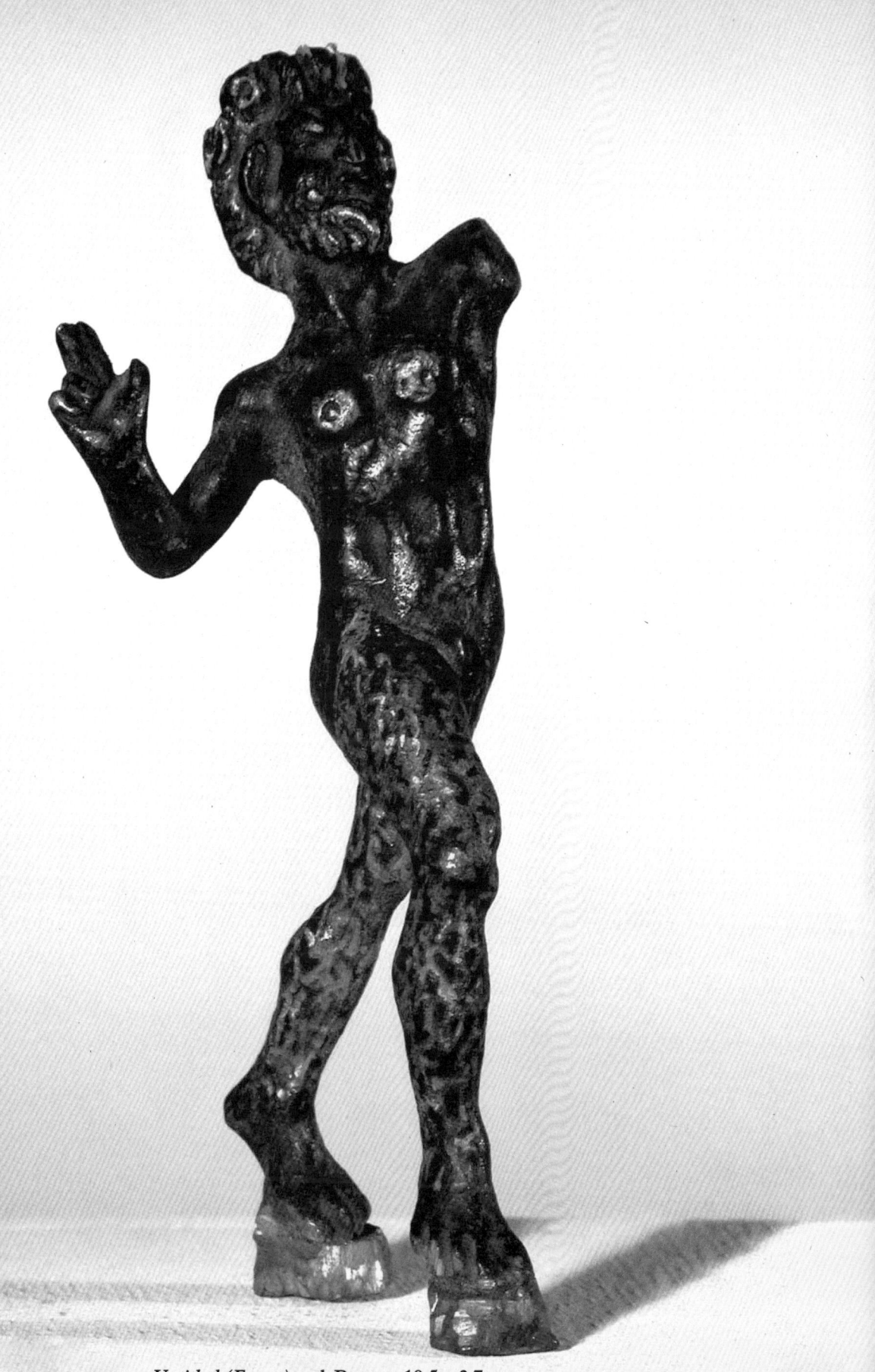

Untitled (Faune), n.d. Bronze, 10.5 × 3.7 cm

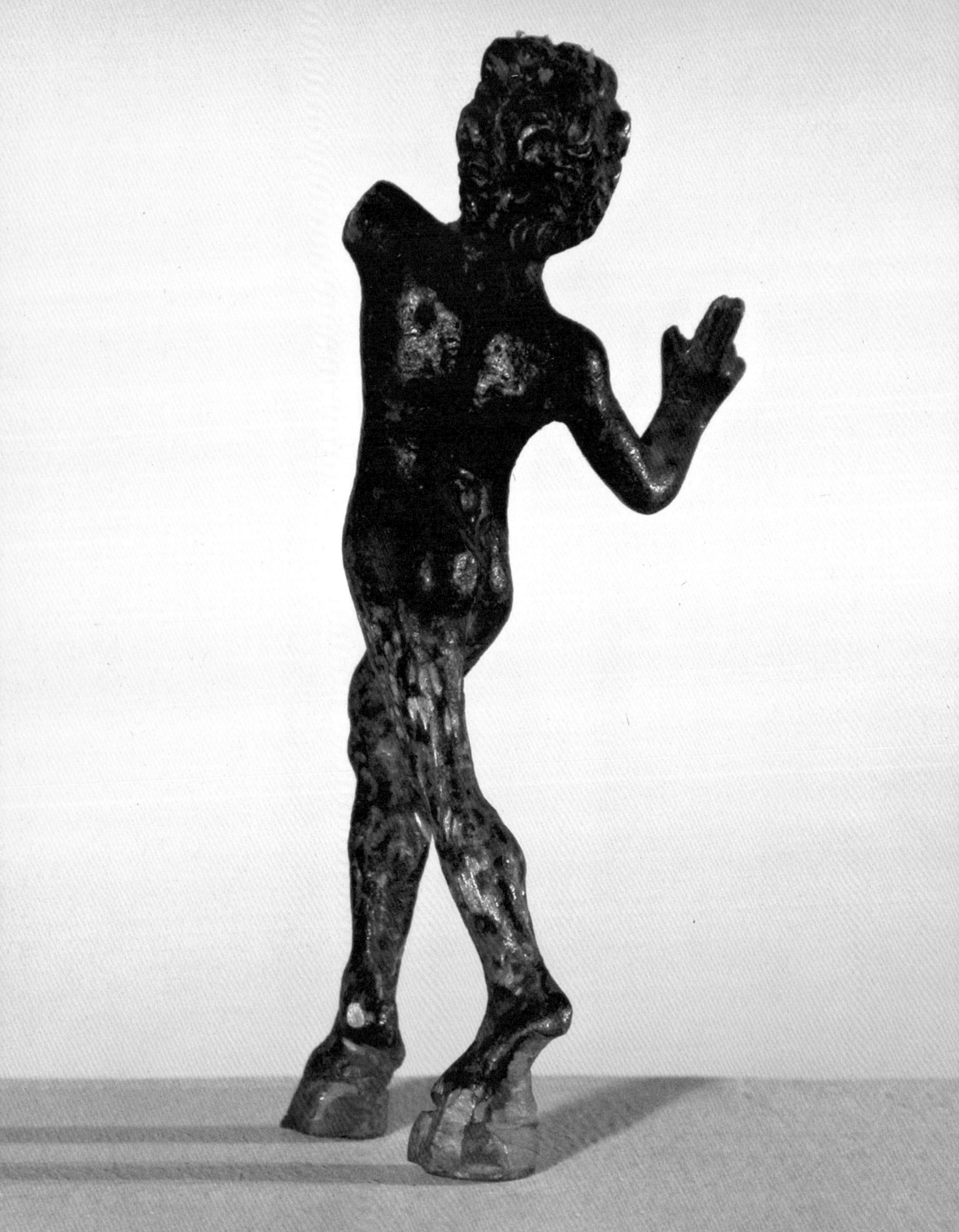

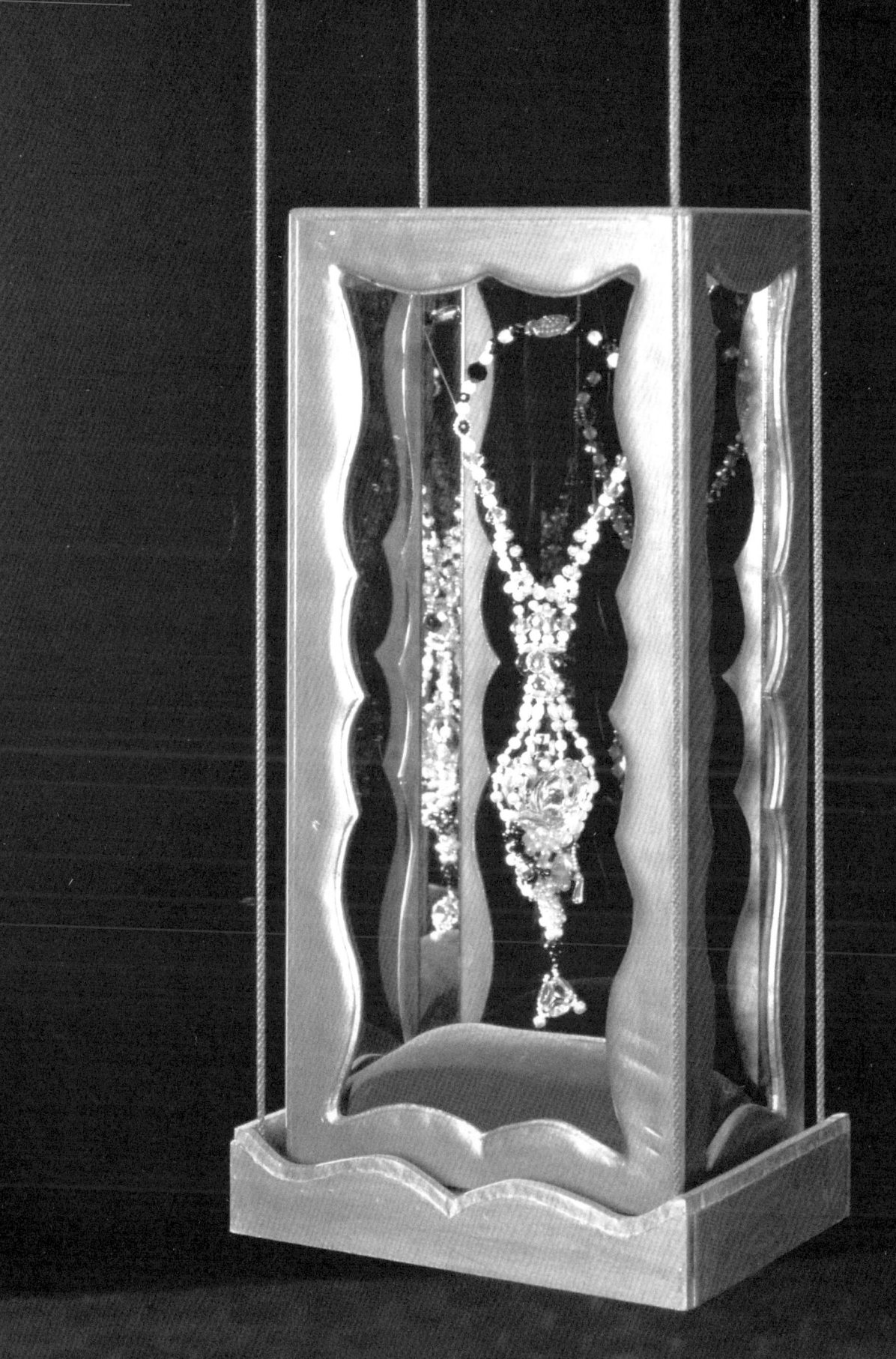

Reliquaire, 1992–1993, from the *Reliquaires* series. Glass beads, tassels, rhinestones, gilded wood, mirror, glass, metal wire, 65 × 31.5 × 20 cm

Untitled (Viva la Muerte), 1995. Glass beads, nylon, wood, 220 × 90 cm

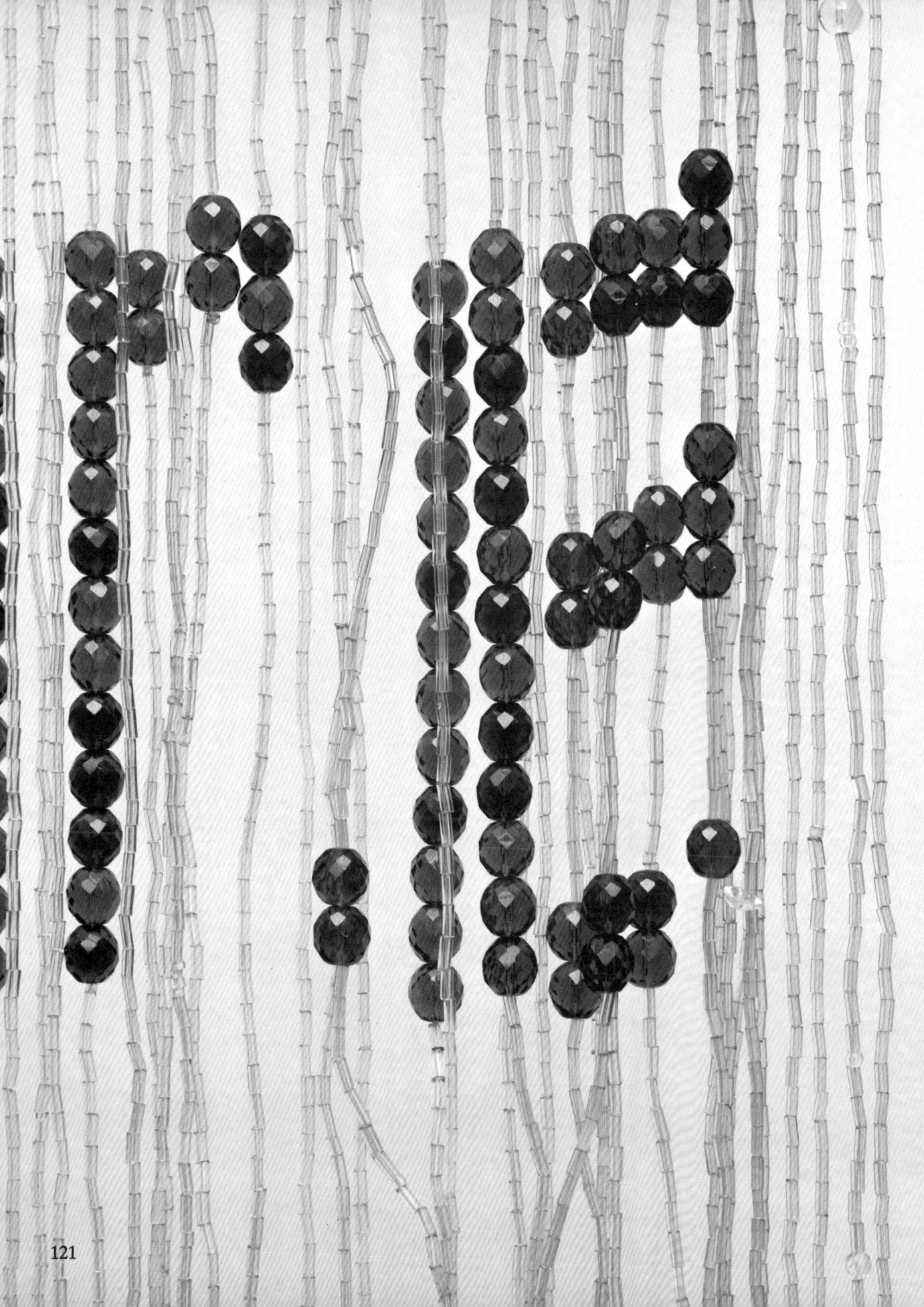

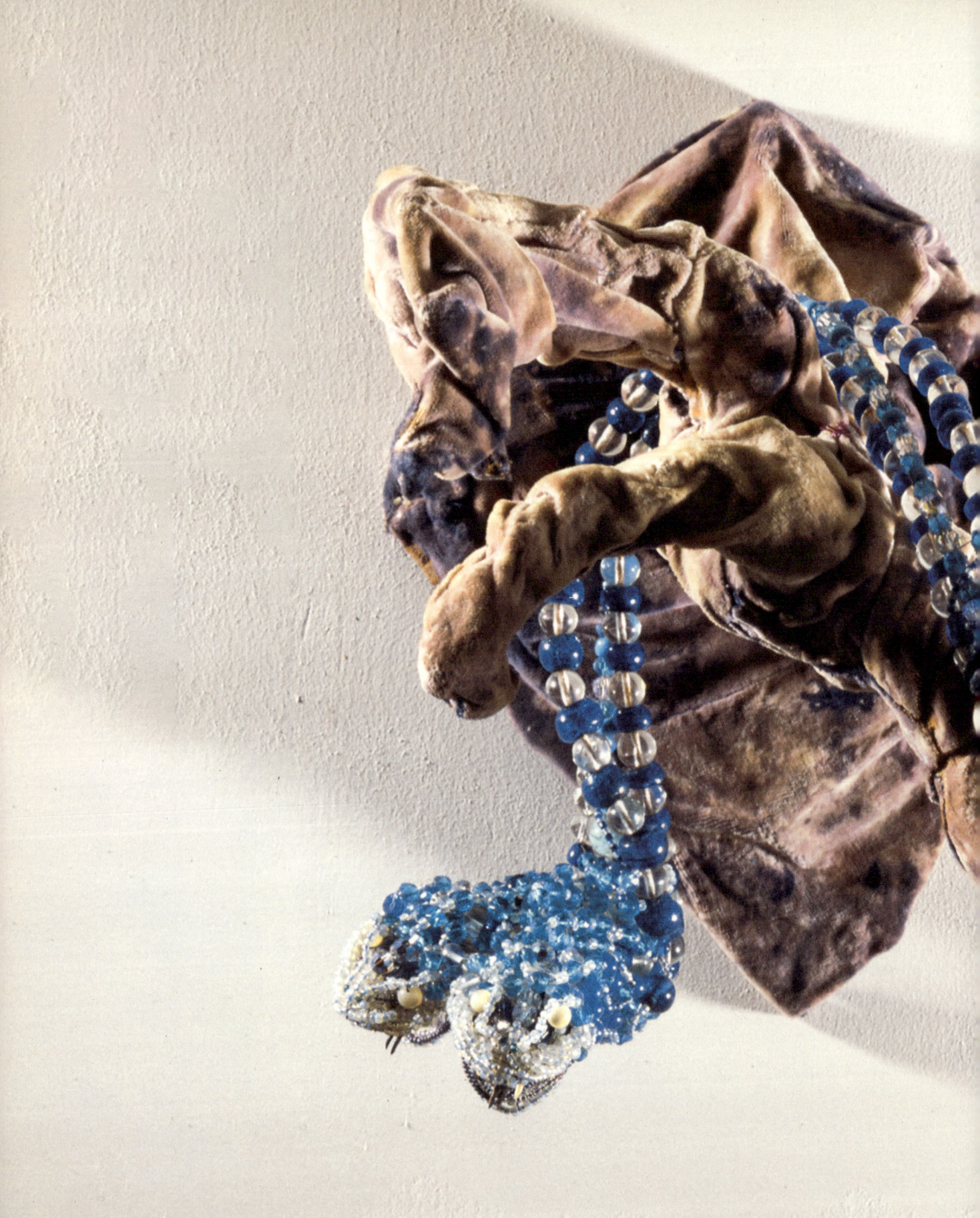

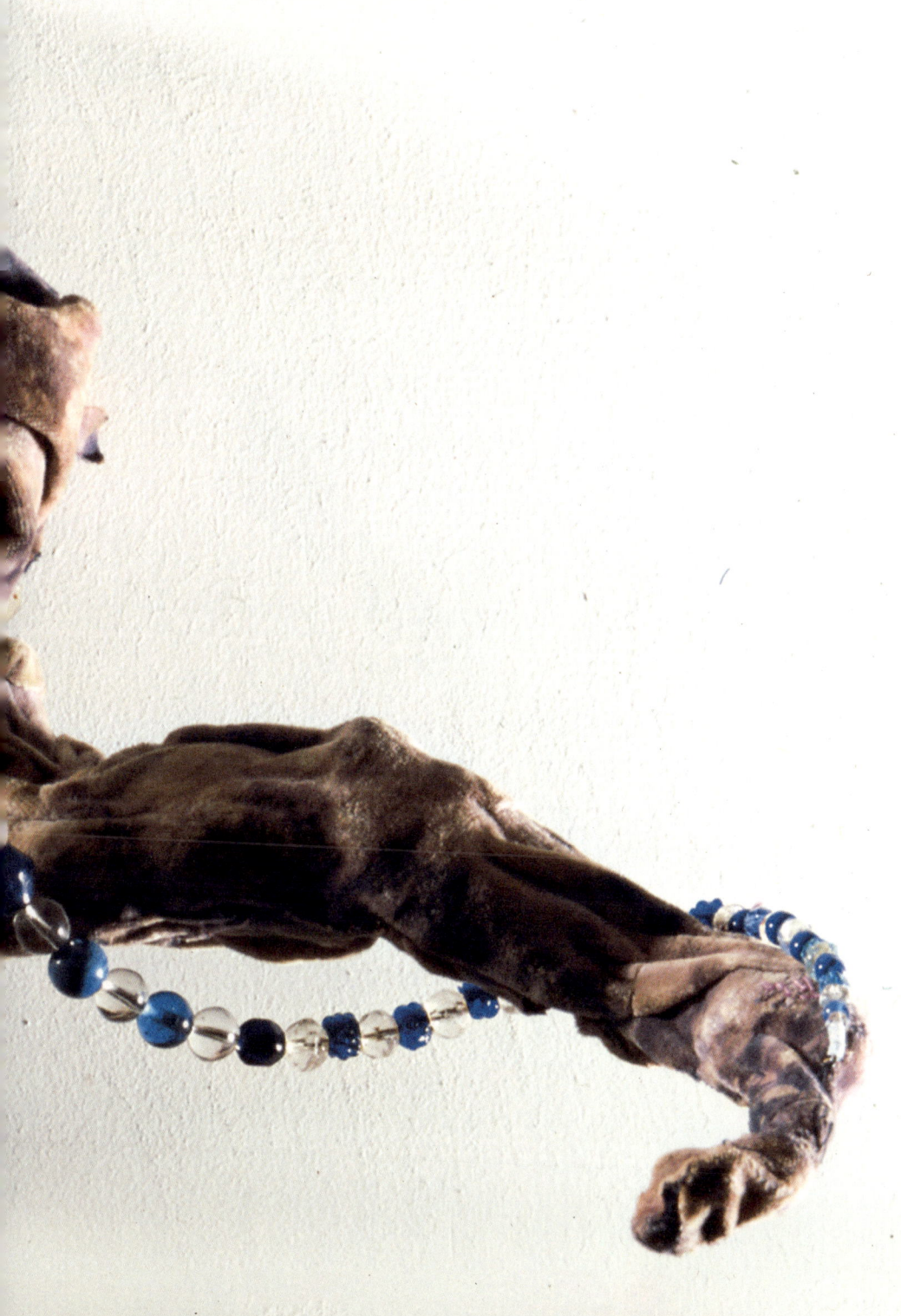

123 *Snake necklace*, 1997. Metal rods, wire, glass beads, crystal, opals, ivory, black coral, wood, vine shoots, bleached velvet, silicone, 25 × 48 × 39 cm (snake 87 × 10 cm). Collection Vincent Bazin, Grenoble

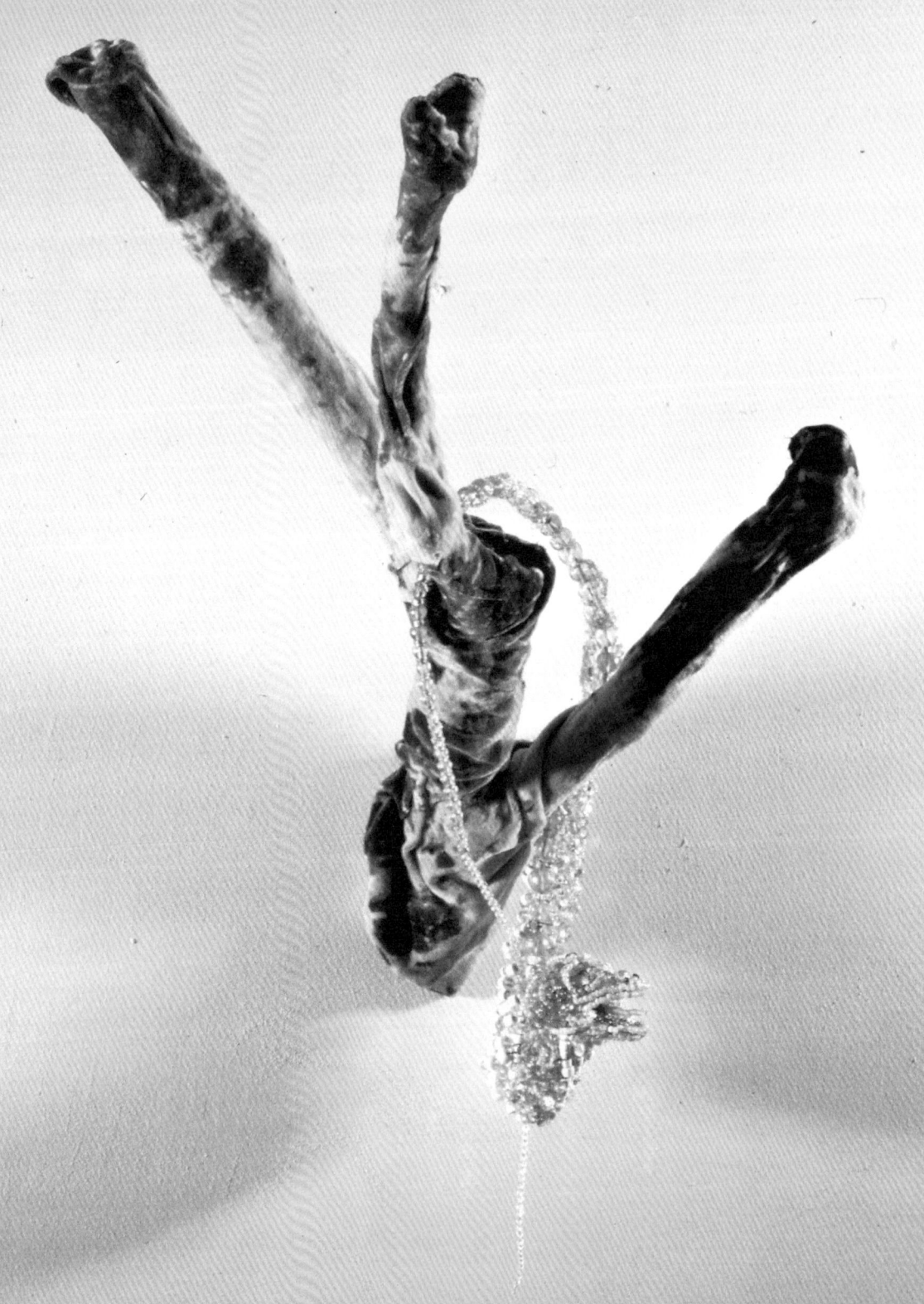

Untitled, 1997. Pearls, opals, coral, metallic thread, vine tendrils, velvet. Collection Josiane Merino, Monaco

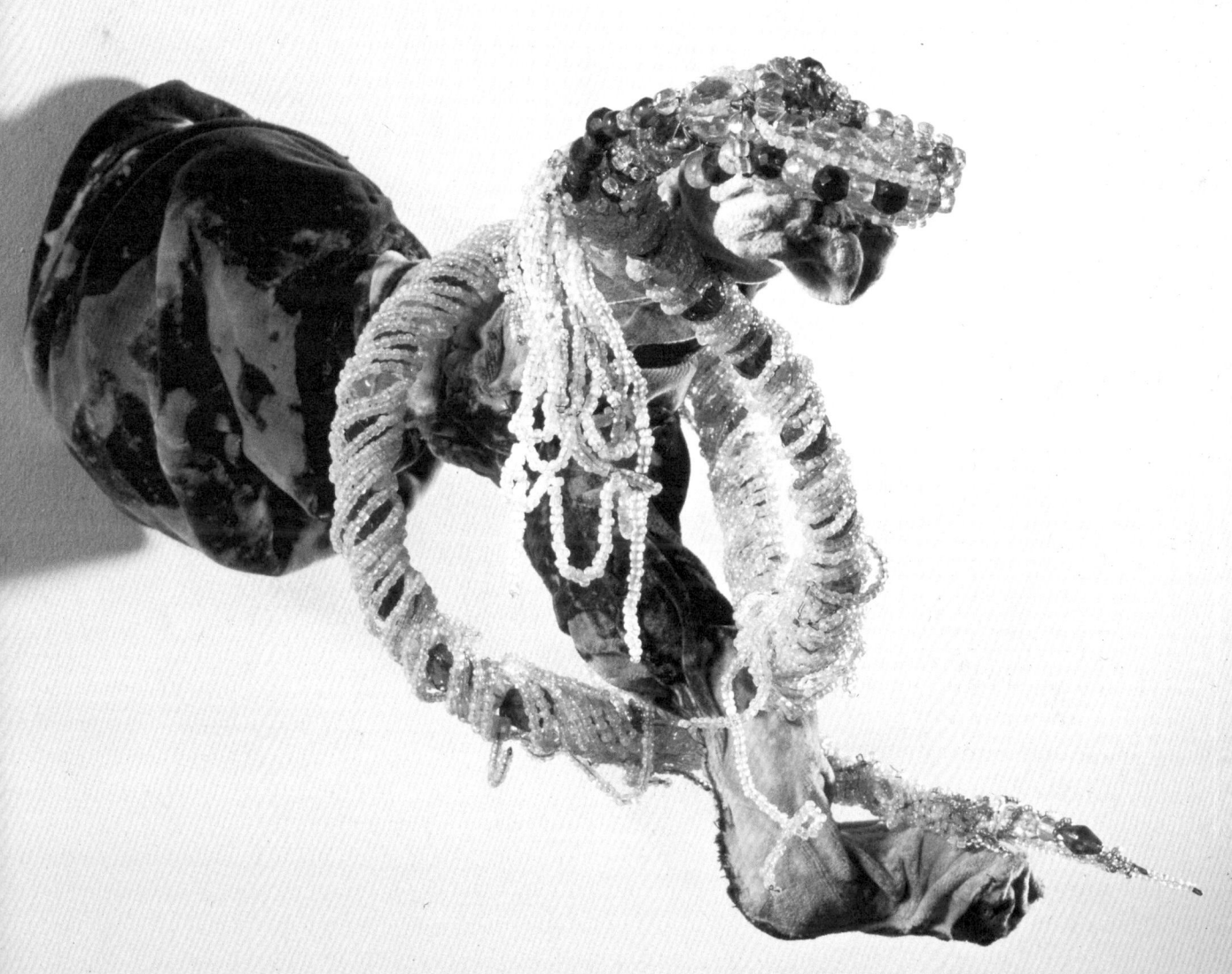

Serpent / The Moult, 1997. Glass beads, tassels, crystal beads, wood, vine shoot, velvet, silicone, wire and metal rods, 30 × 40 × 55 cm

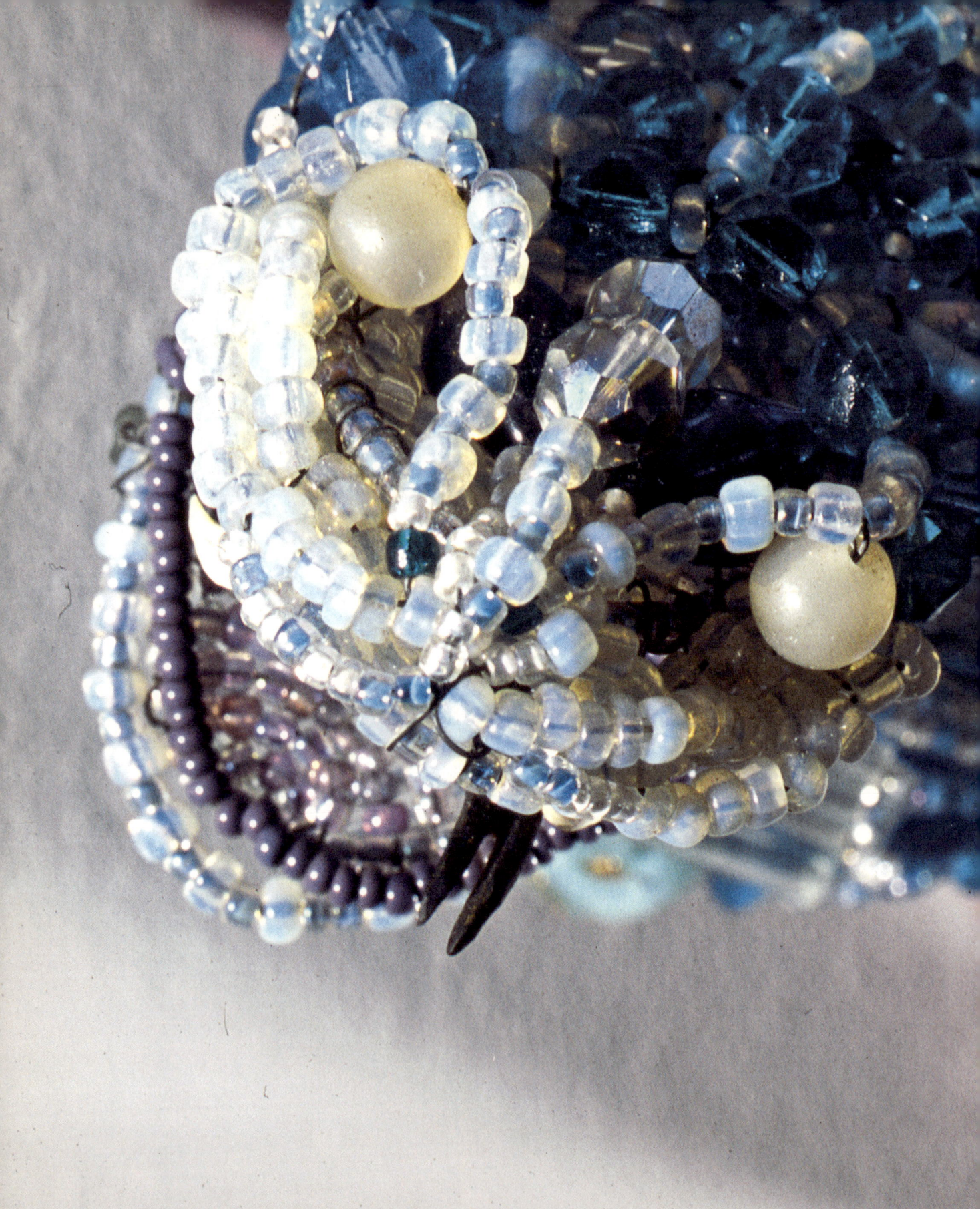

Snake necklace, 1997. Metal rods, wire, glass beads, crystal, opals, ivory, black coral, wood, vine shoots, bleached velvet, silicone, 25 × 48 × 39 cm (snake 87 × 10 cm). Collection Vincent Bazin, Grenoble

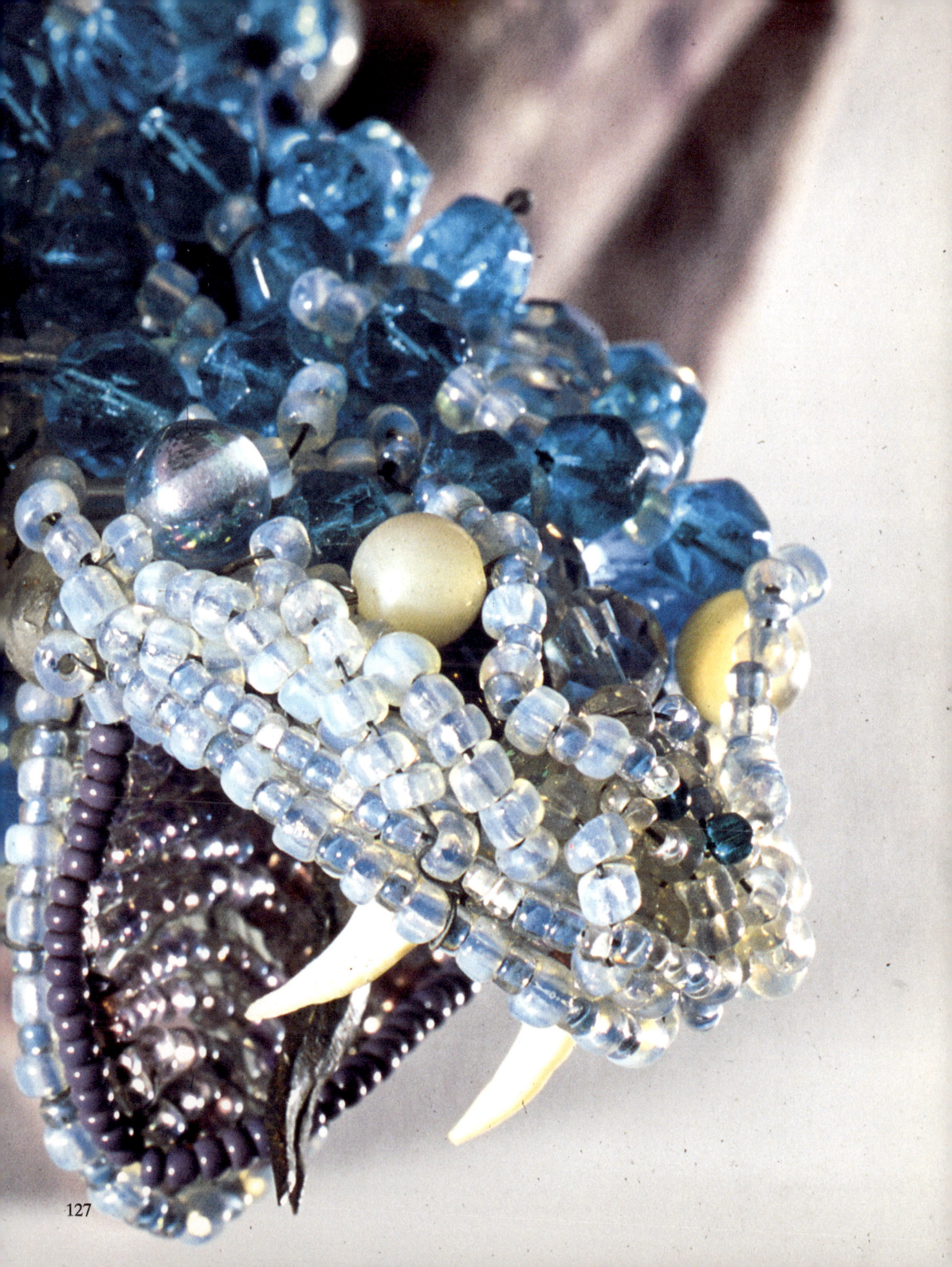

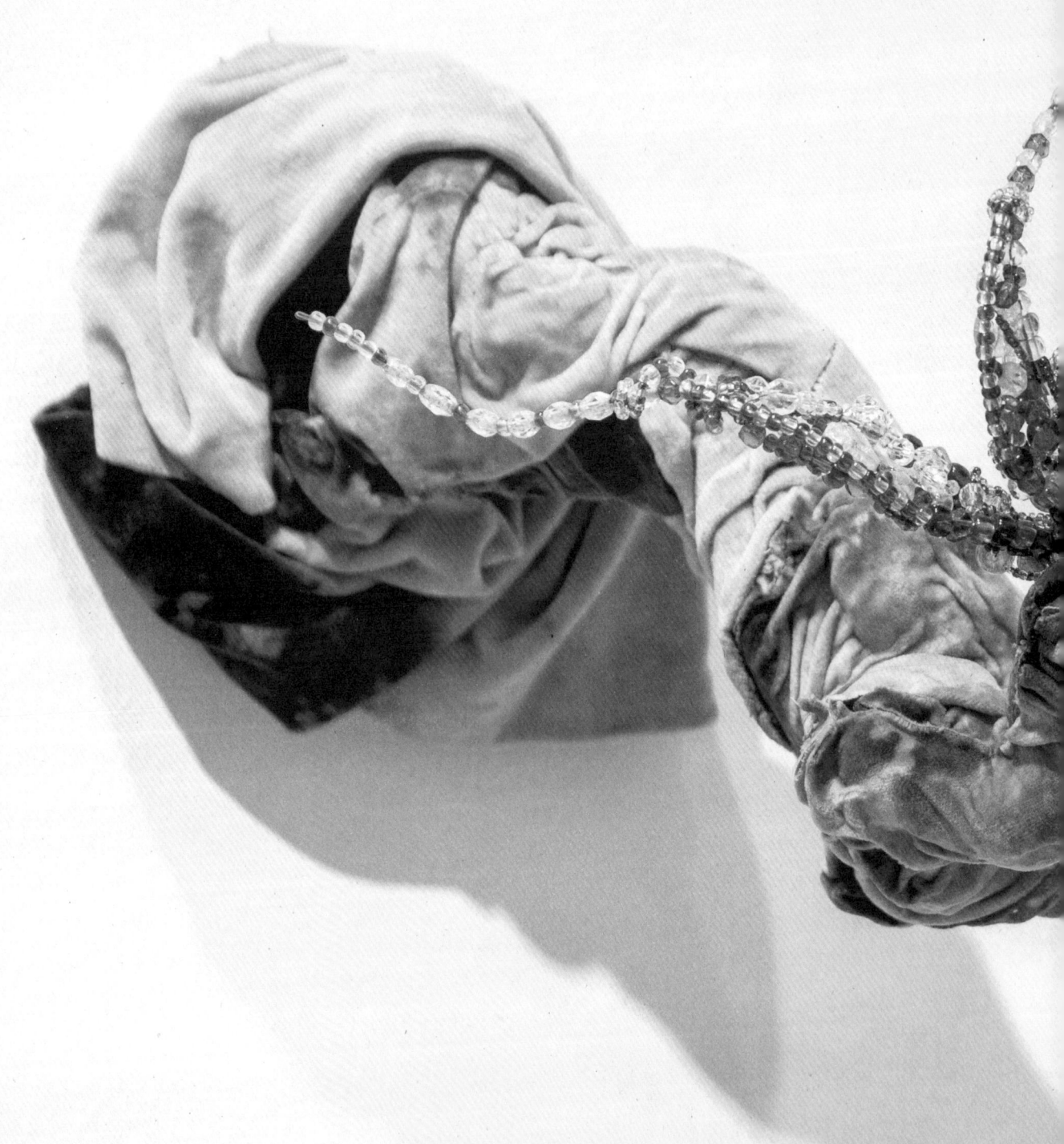

Serpent Ouroboros, 1997. Glass beads, tassels, crystal beads, wood, vine shoot, velvet, silicone, wire and metallic rods, 40 × 40 × 50 cm. Collection MAMAC, Nice

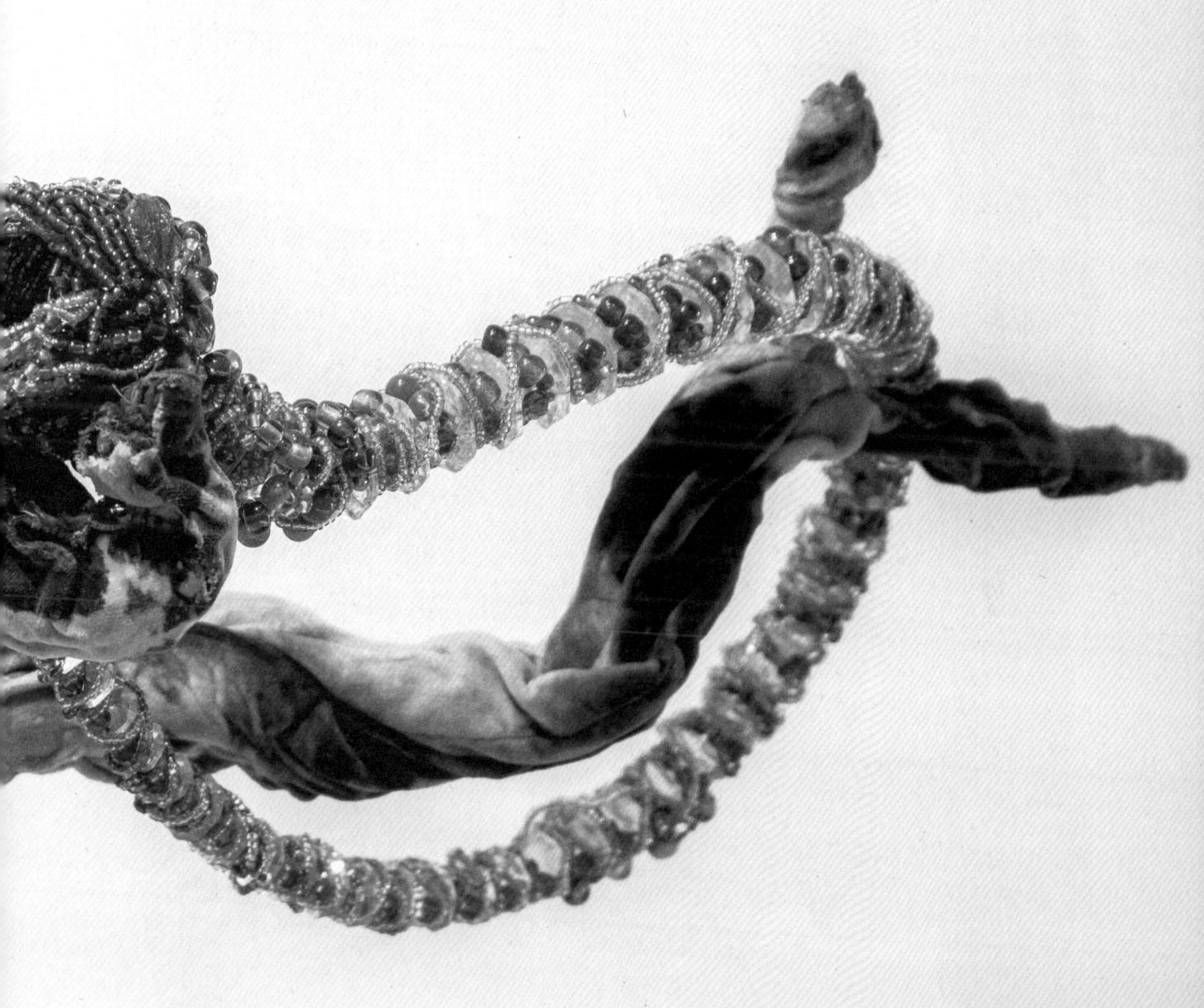

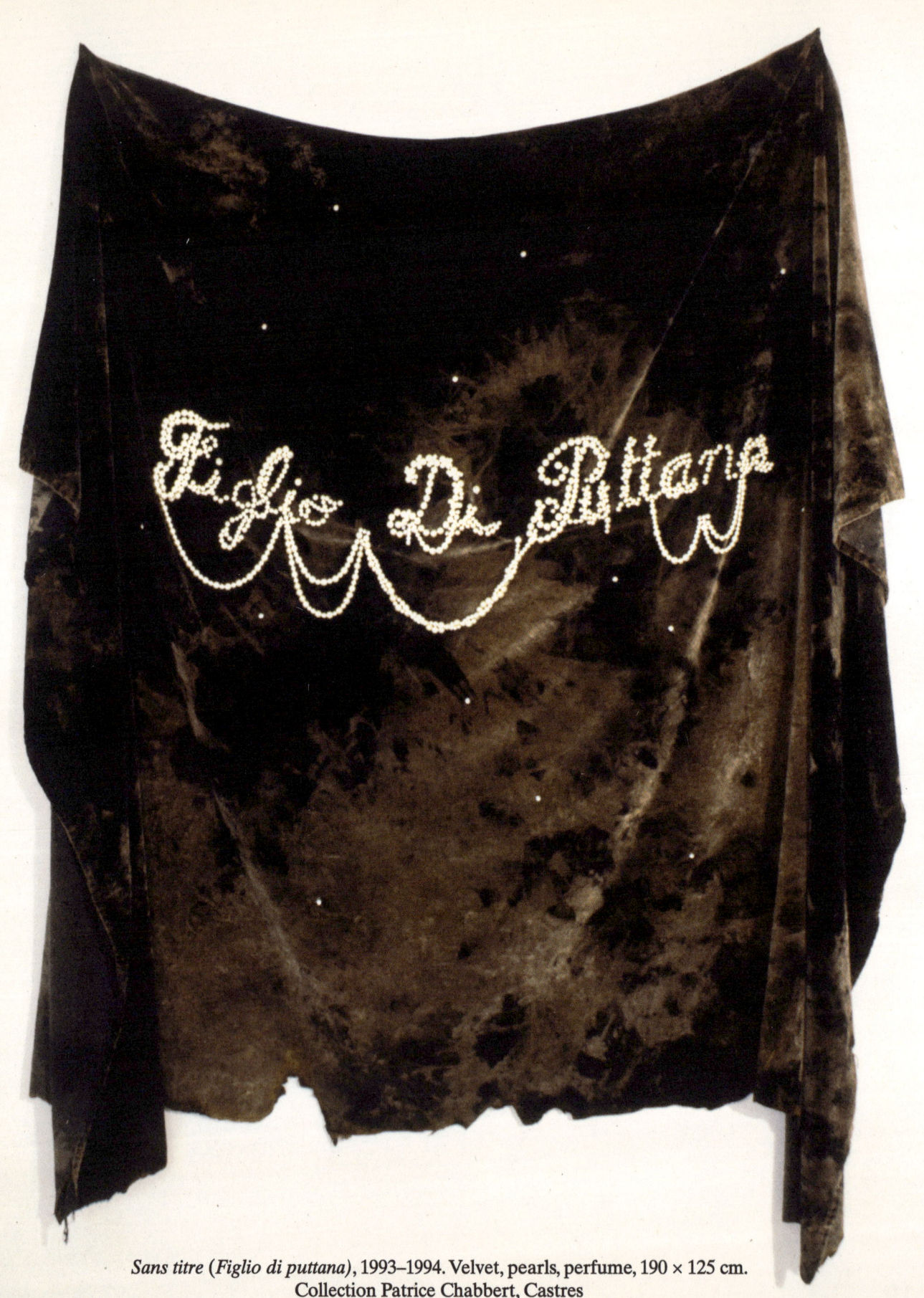

Sans titre (*Figlio di puttana*), 1993–1994. Velvet, pearls, perfume, 190 × 125 cm.
Collection Patrice Chabbert, Castres

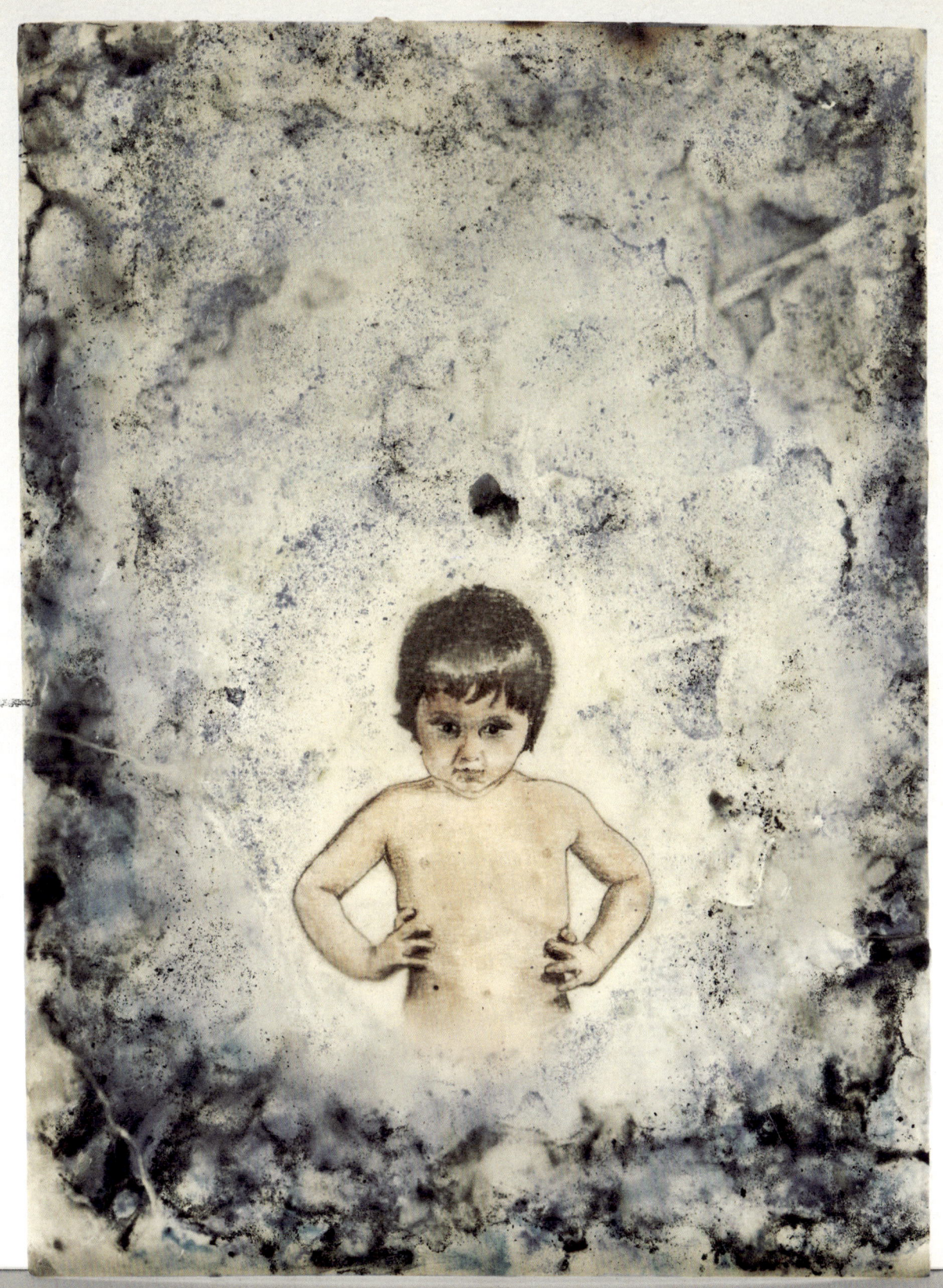

Untitled, 1996, from the *Wax* series. Pencil on paper, pigment, kerosene wax, 24 × 32 cm.
Collection Florence Bonnefous, Pantin

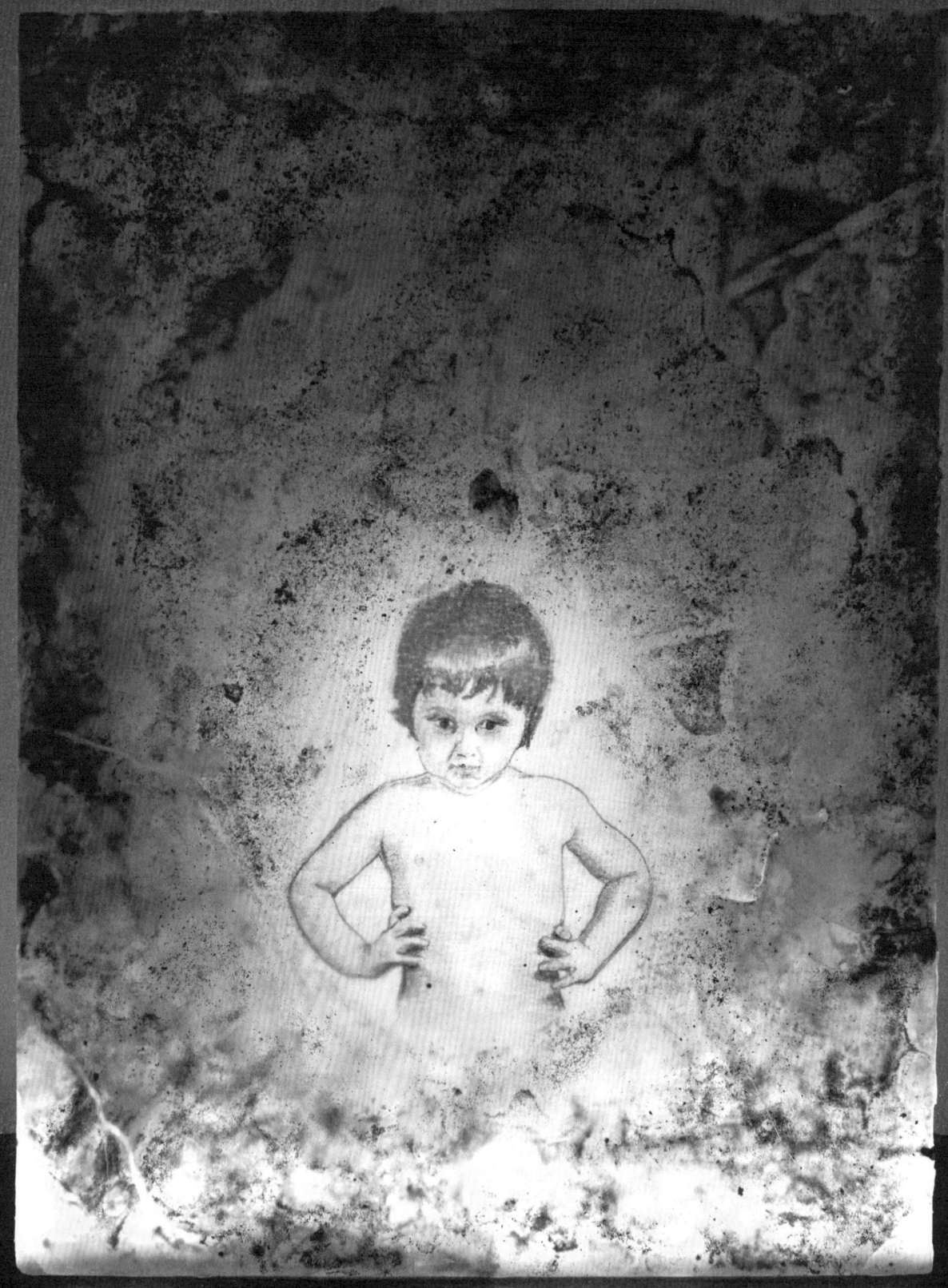

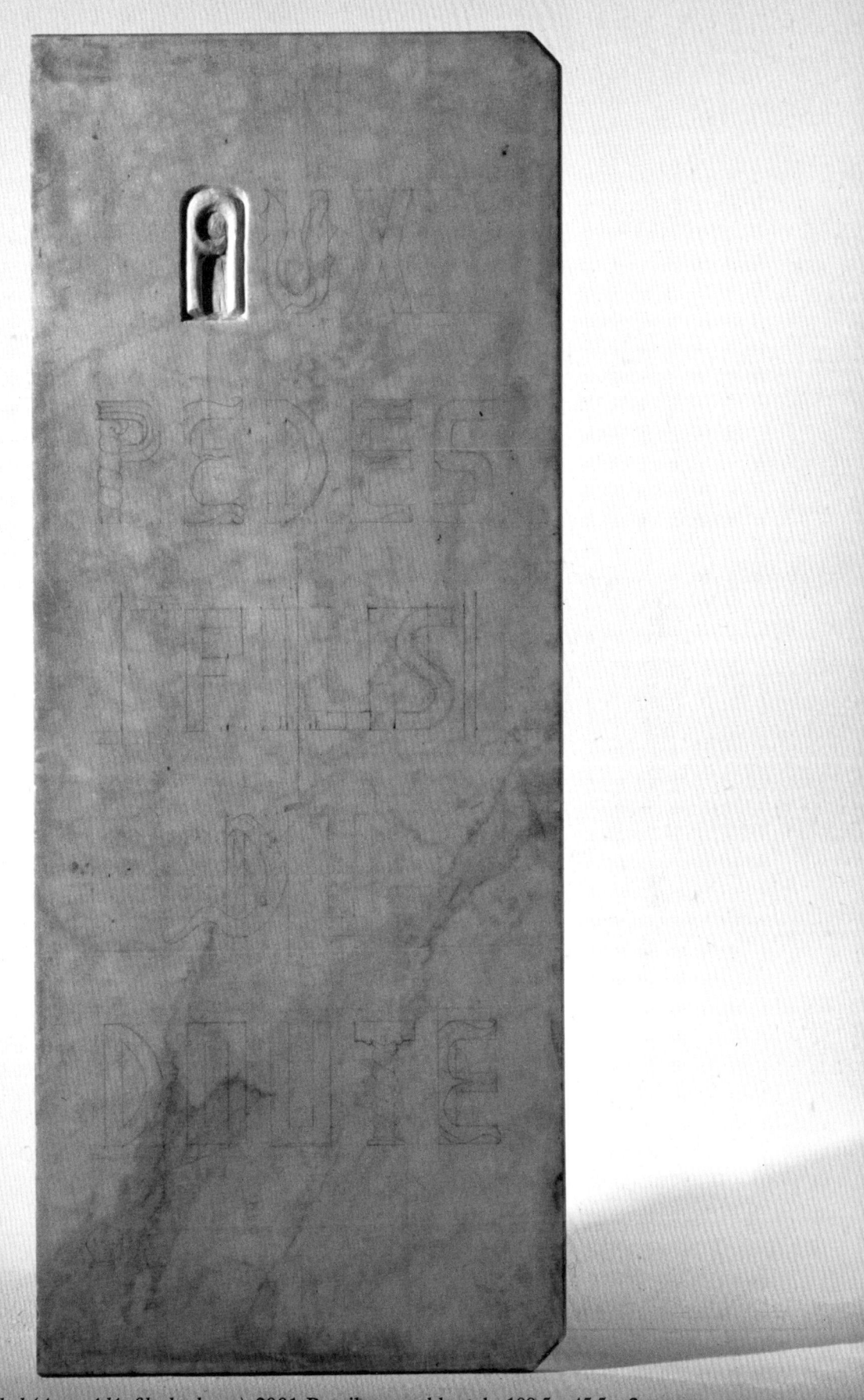

133　　*Untitled (Aux pédés fils du doute)*, 2001. Pencil on marble stele, 109.5 × 45.5 × 2 cm

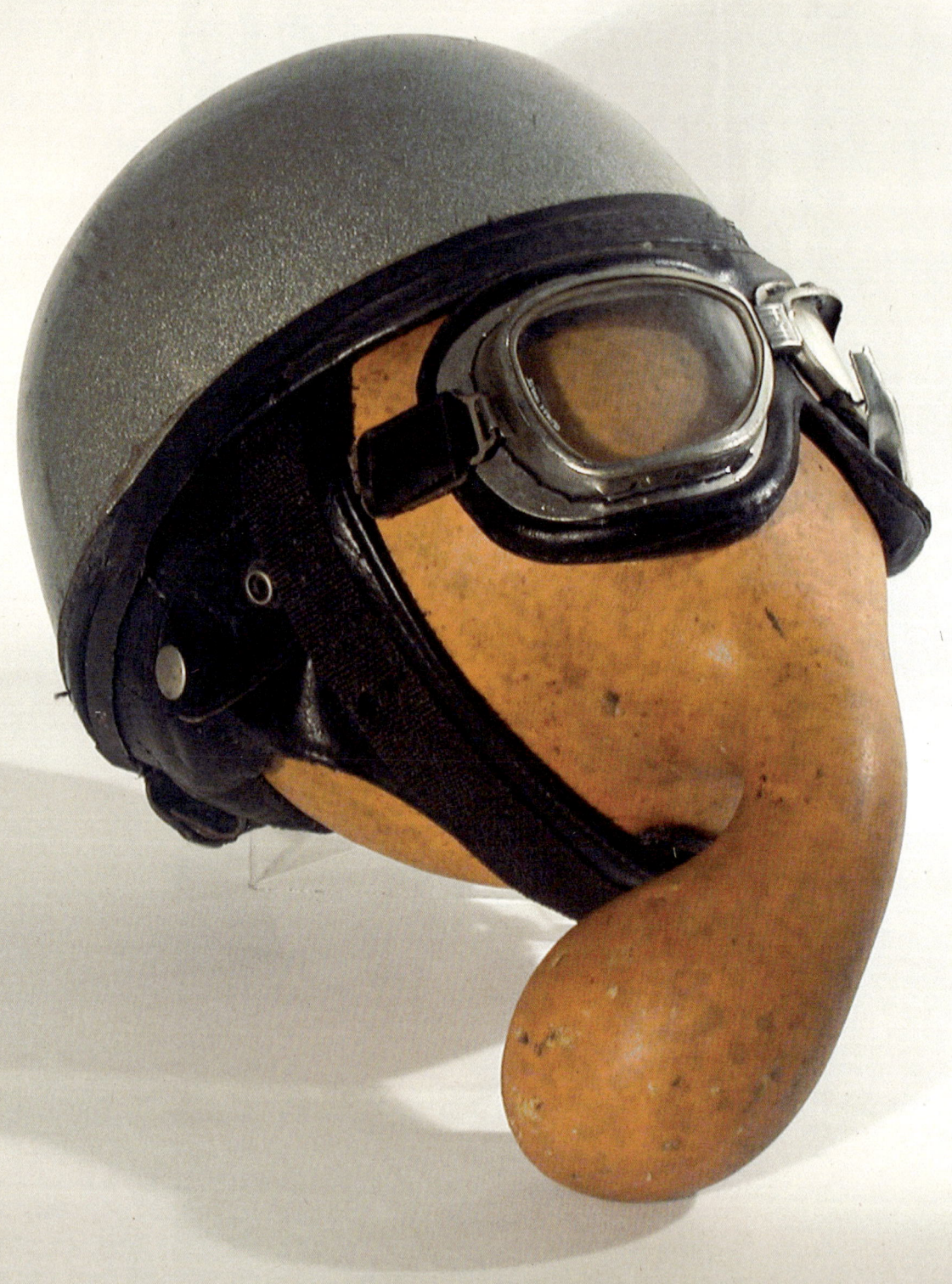

Untitled, n.d. Dried squash, helmet and motorcycle glasses, copper, metal, fiberglass, plastic, 38 × 18 × 26 cm

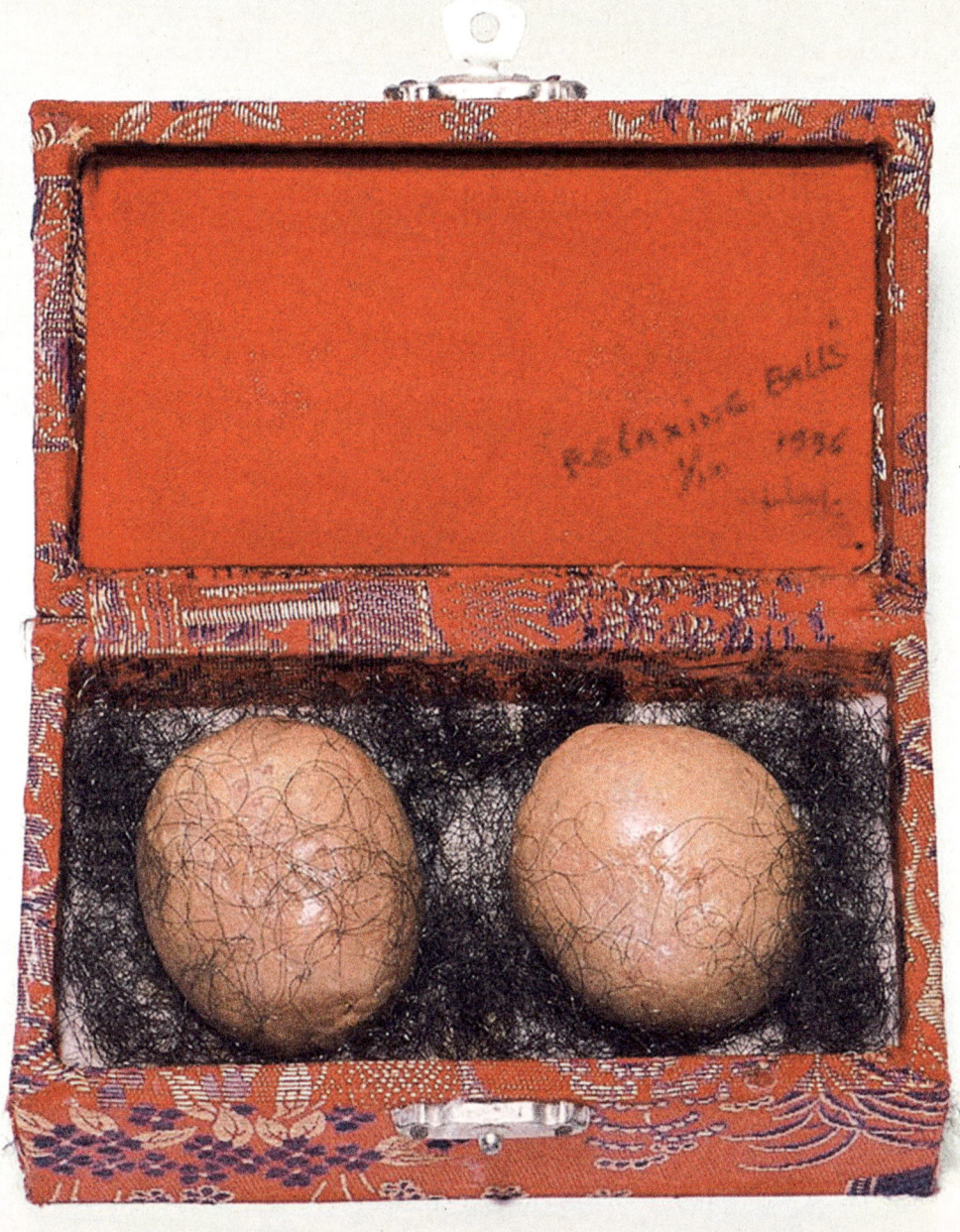

Relaxing Balls, 1996. Wood, silk, metal, fabrics, wax, body hair, 12.5 × 7.5 × 5.5 cm.
Collection Didier Bisson, Paris

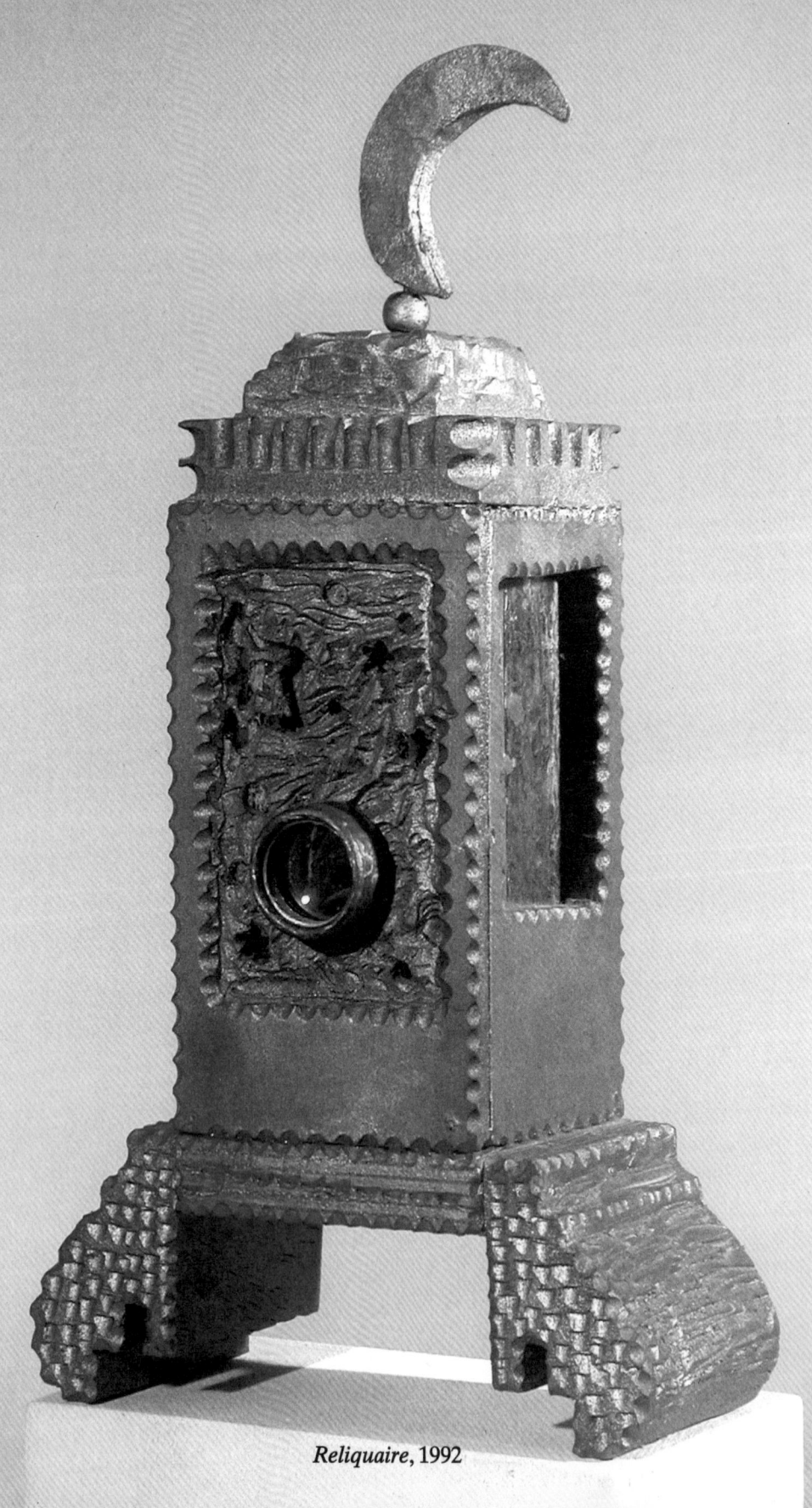
Reliquaire, 1992

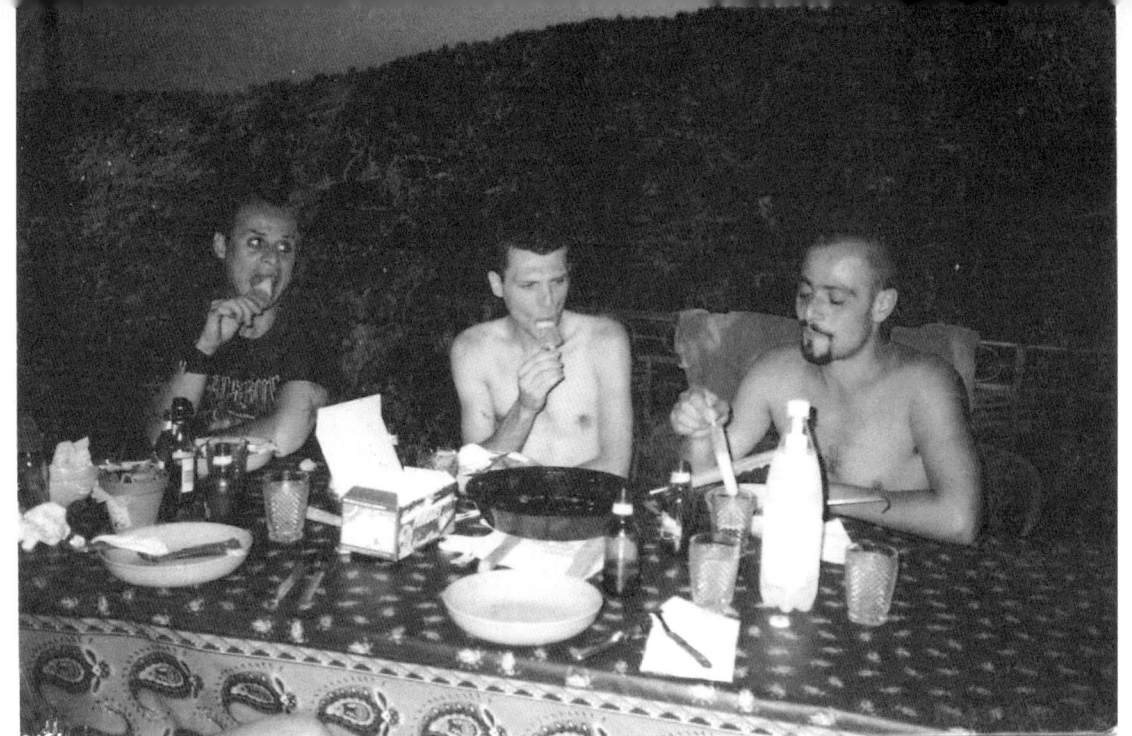
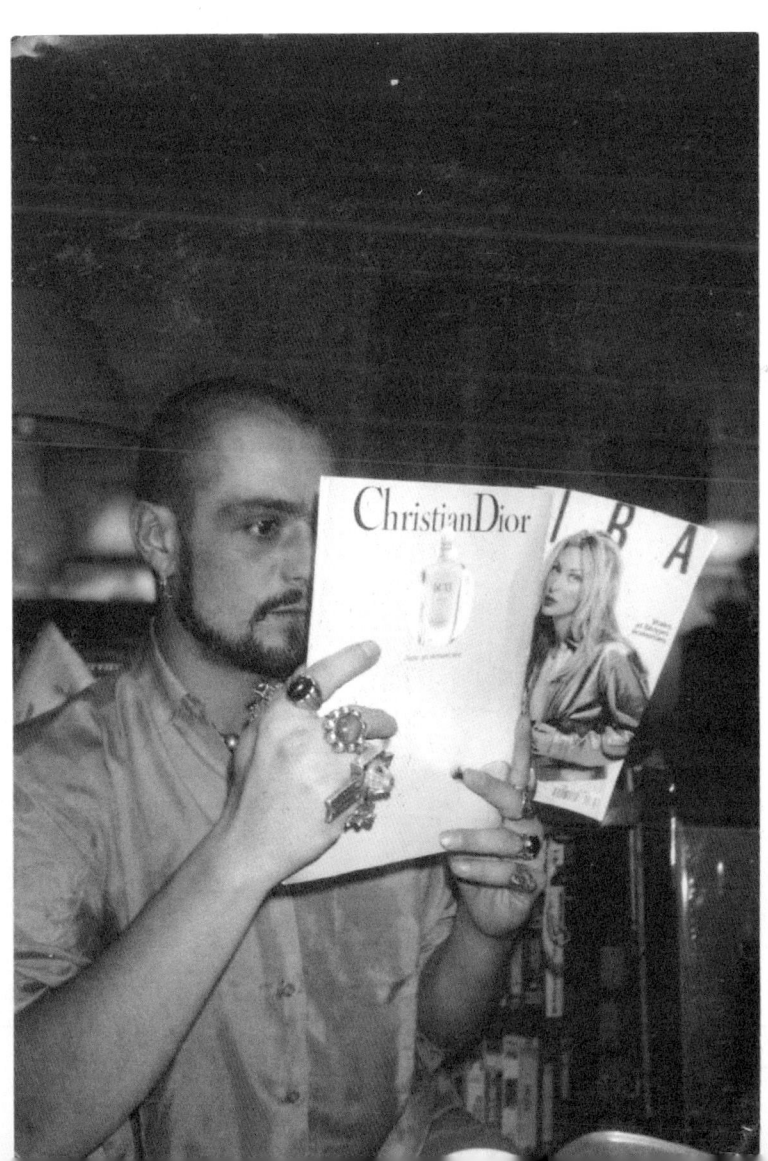

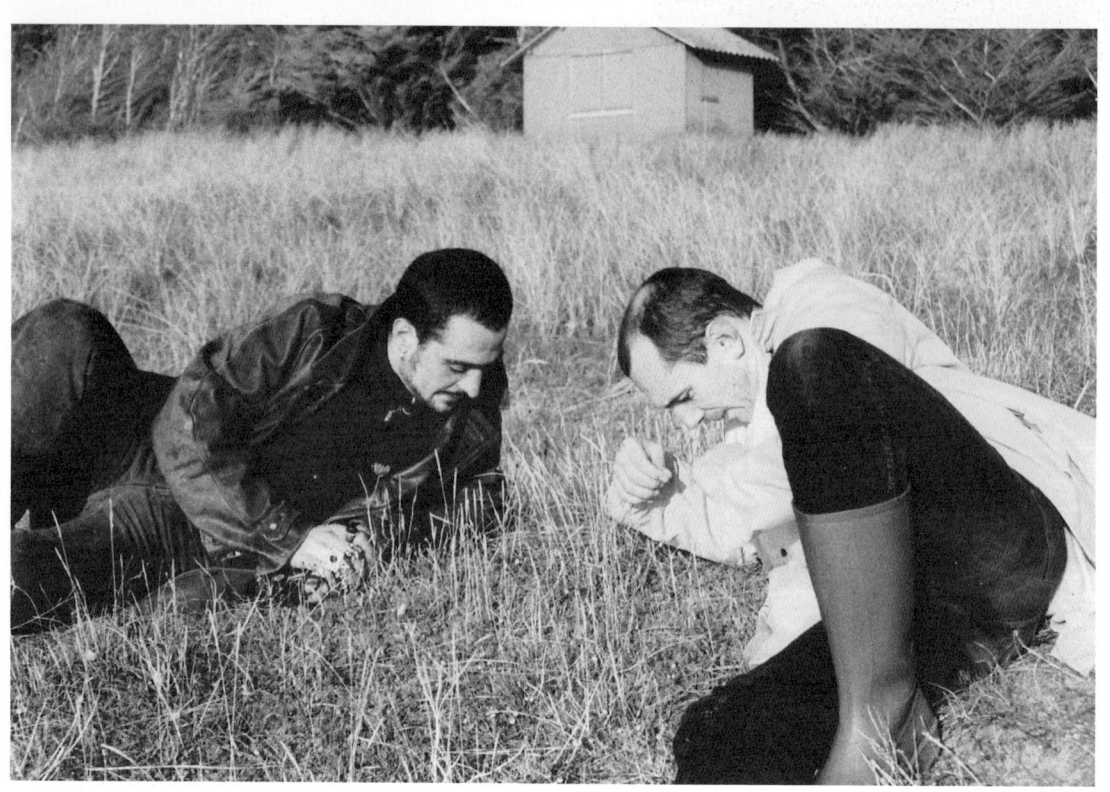

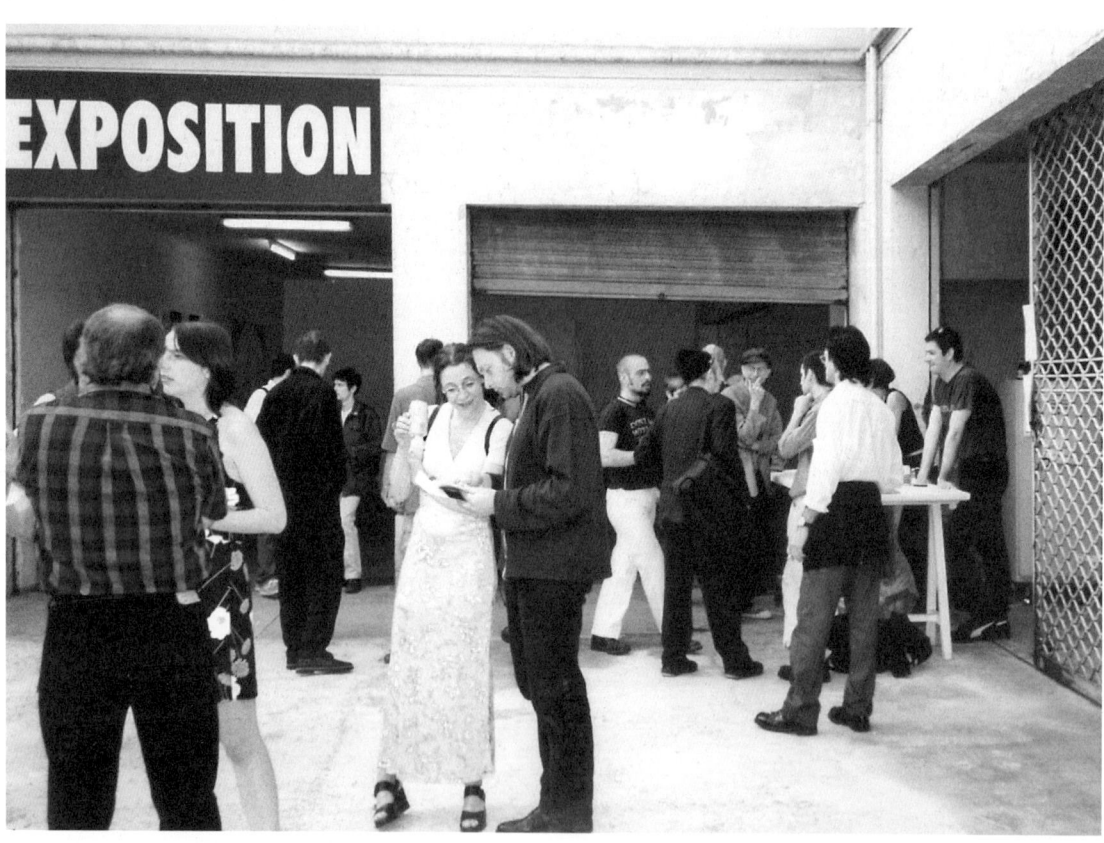

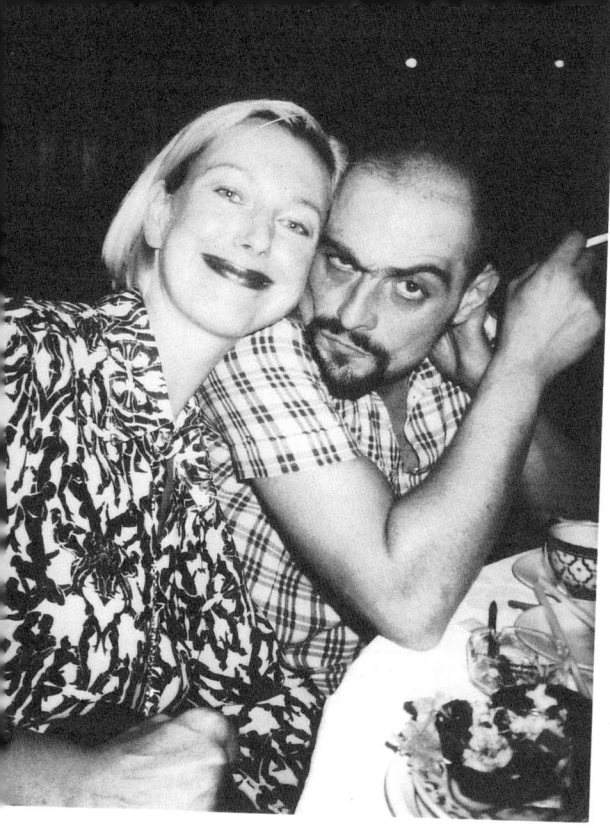
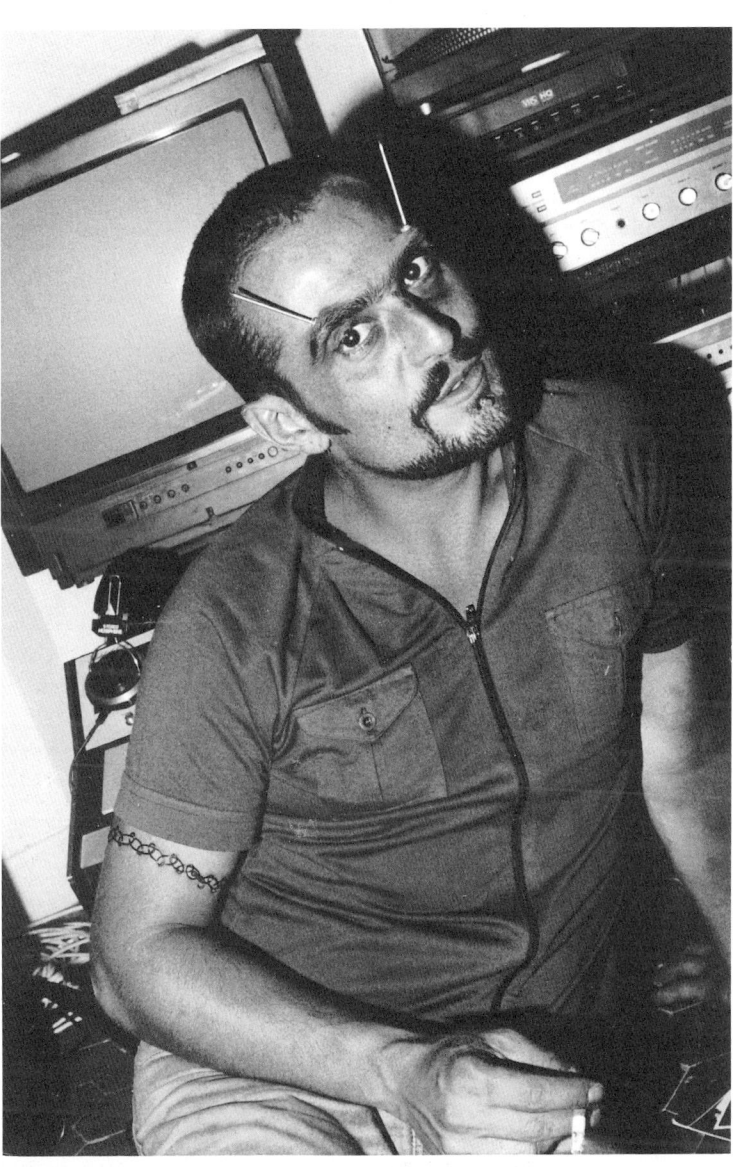

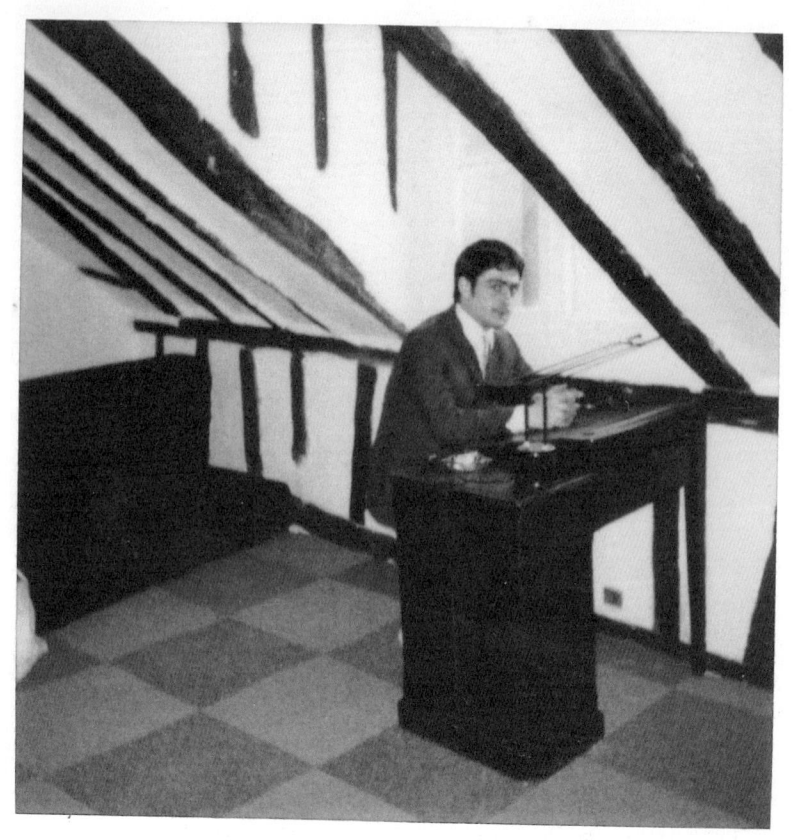

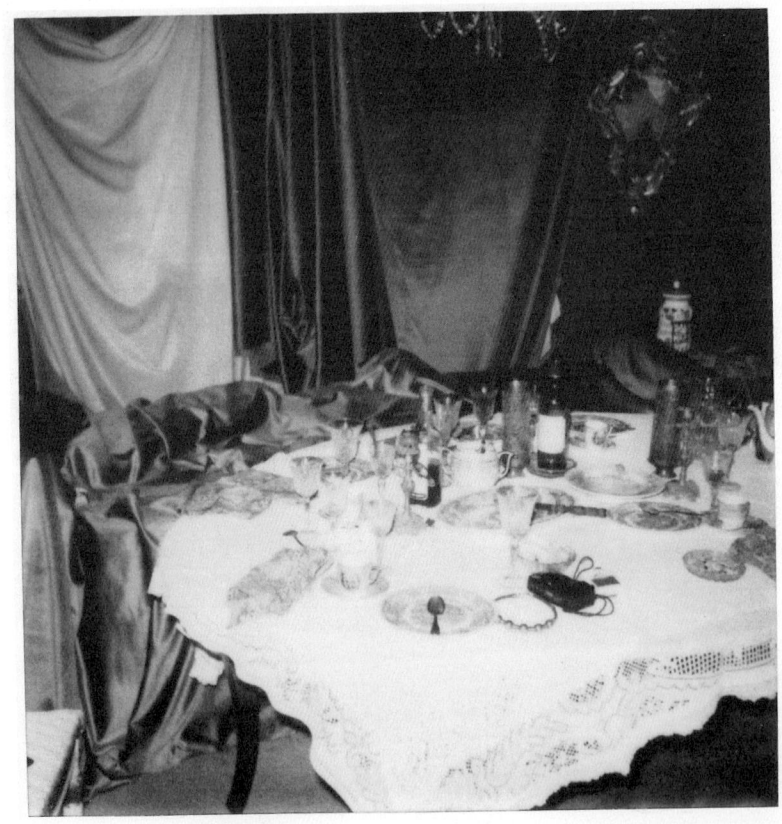

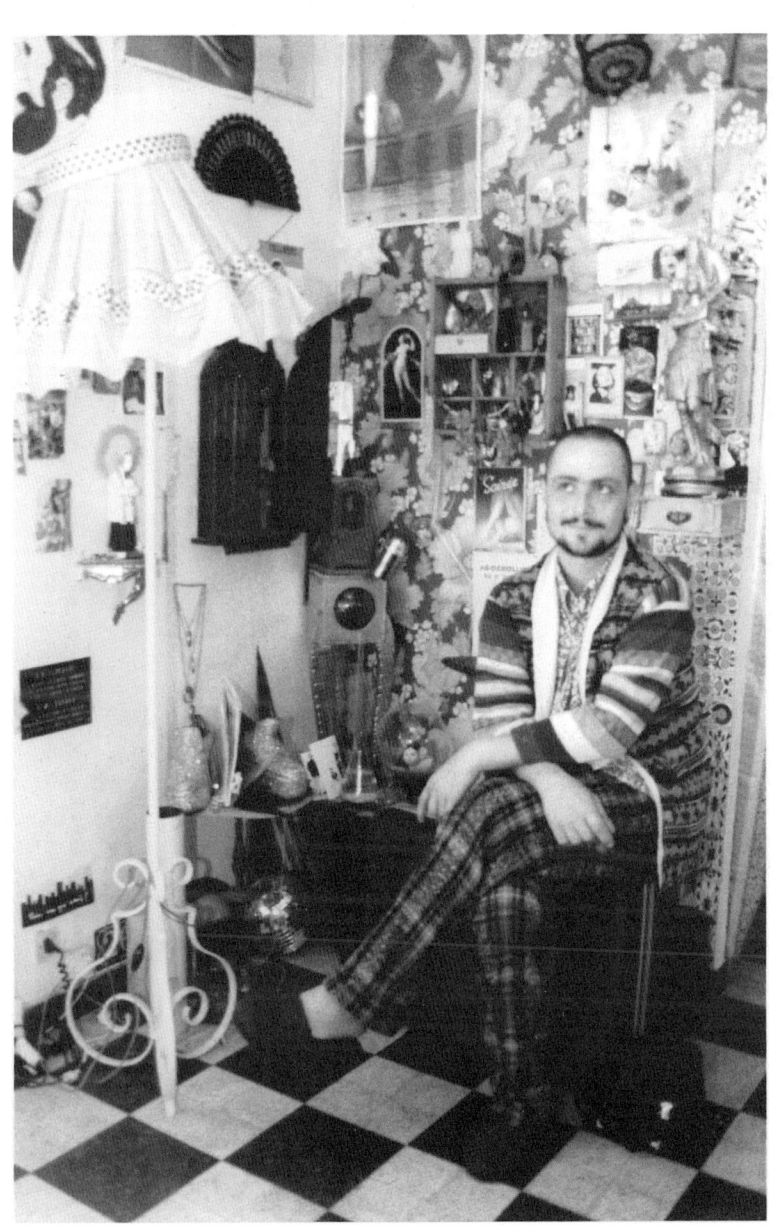

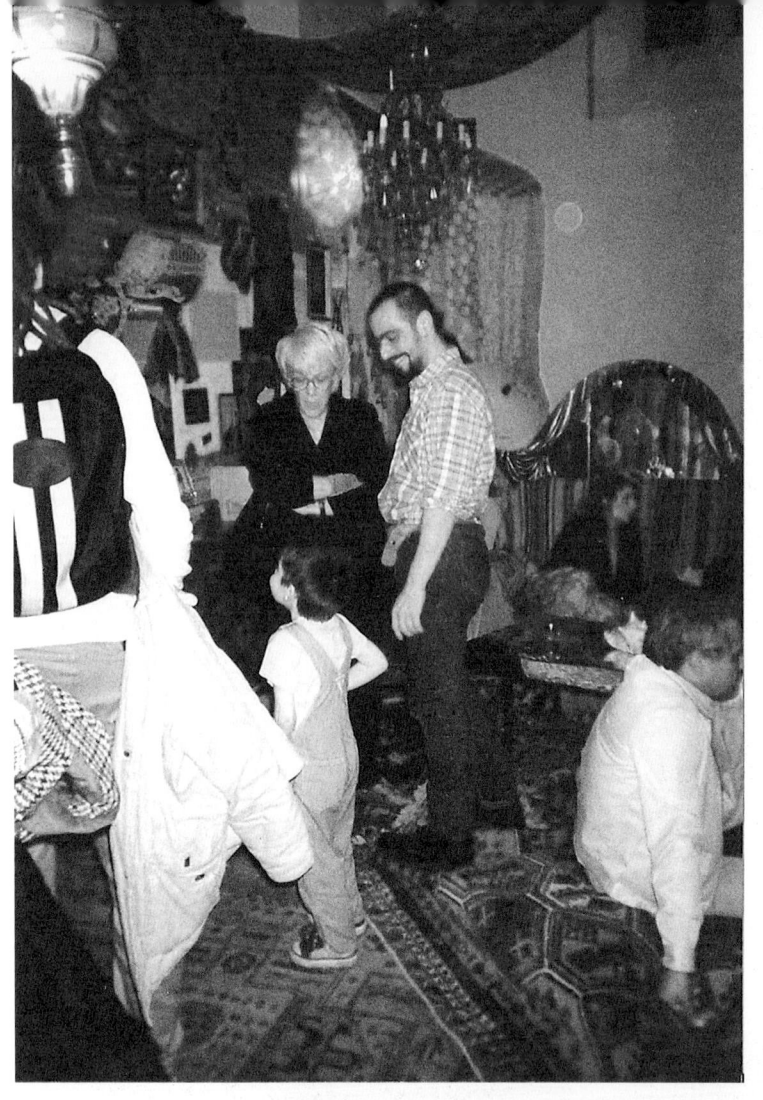
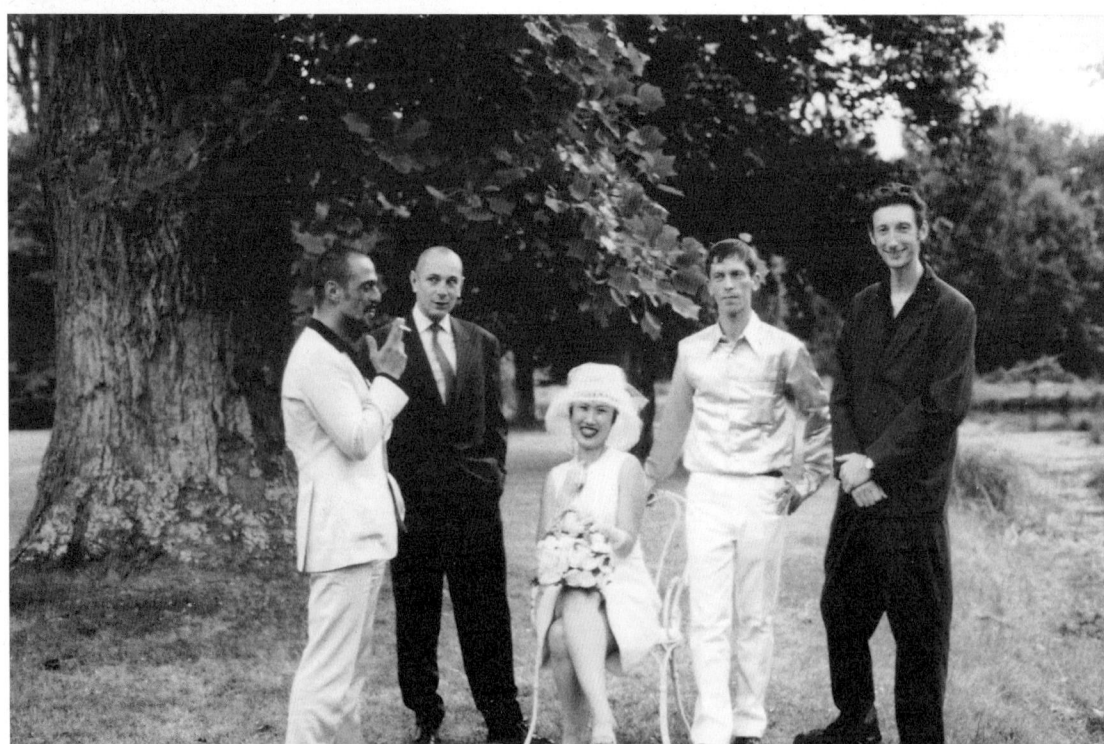

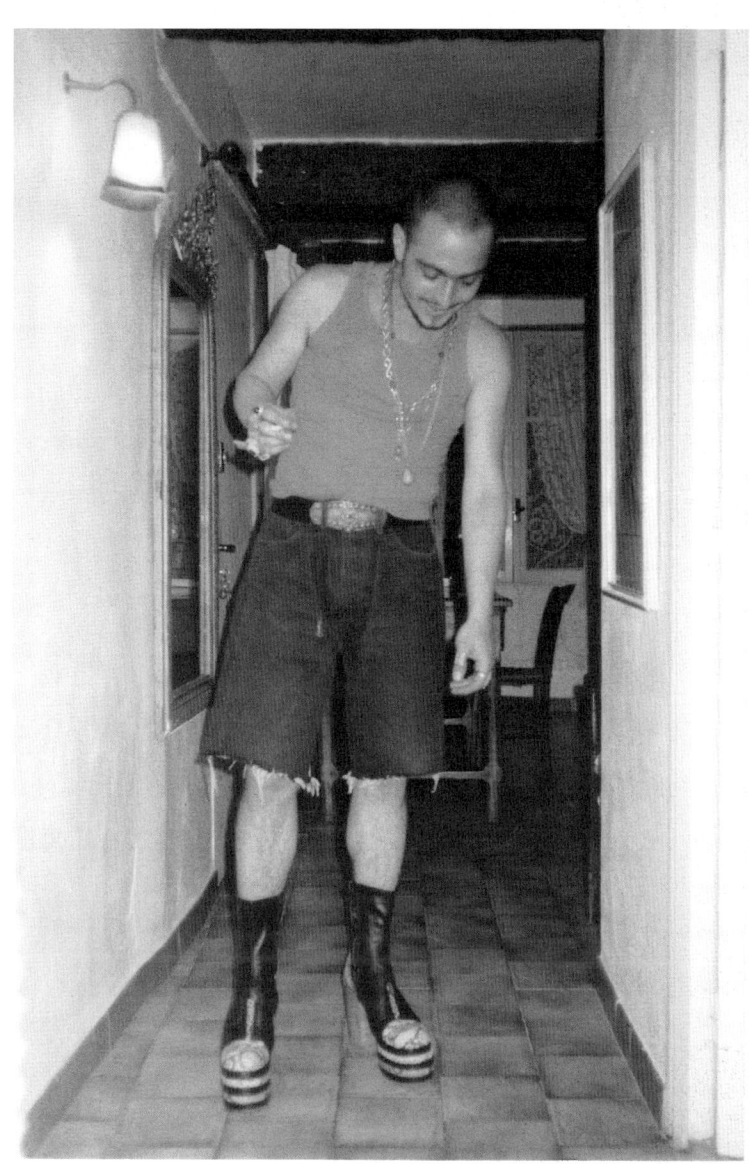
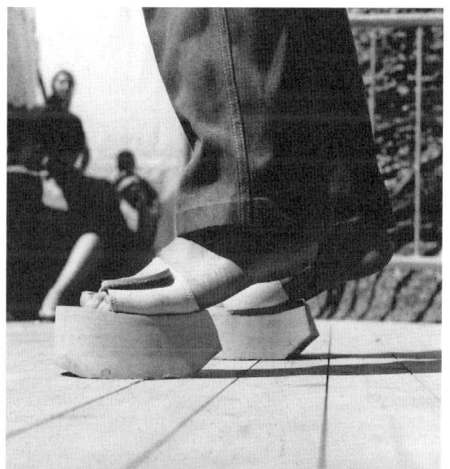
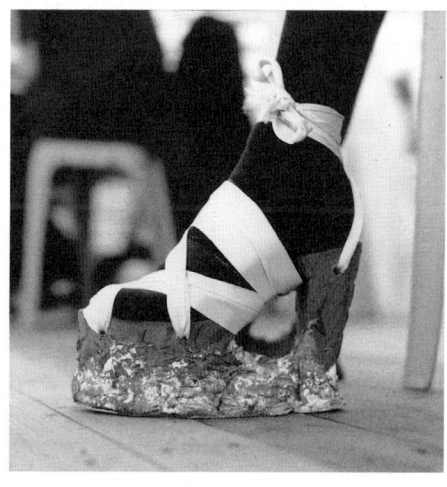

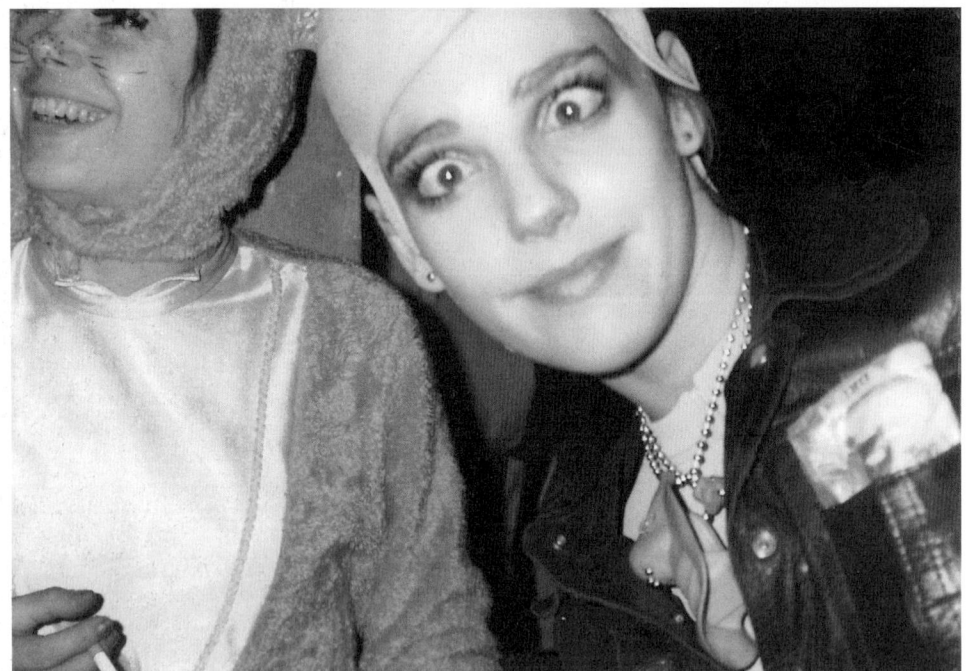

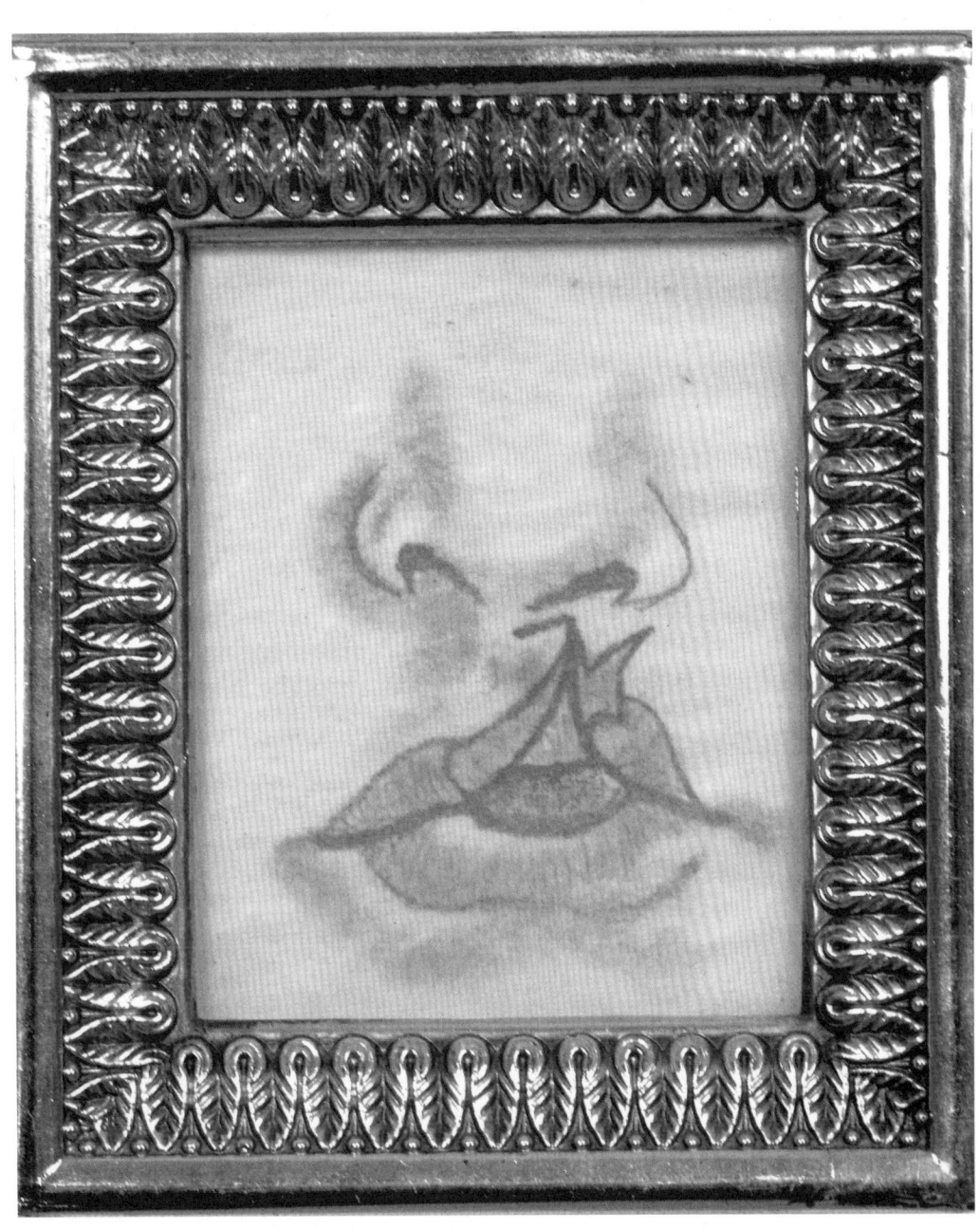

Untitled, 1994–1995. Triptych, pencil on paper. Collection Frieda Schumann, Paris

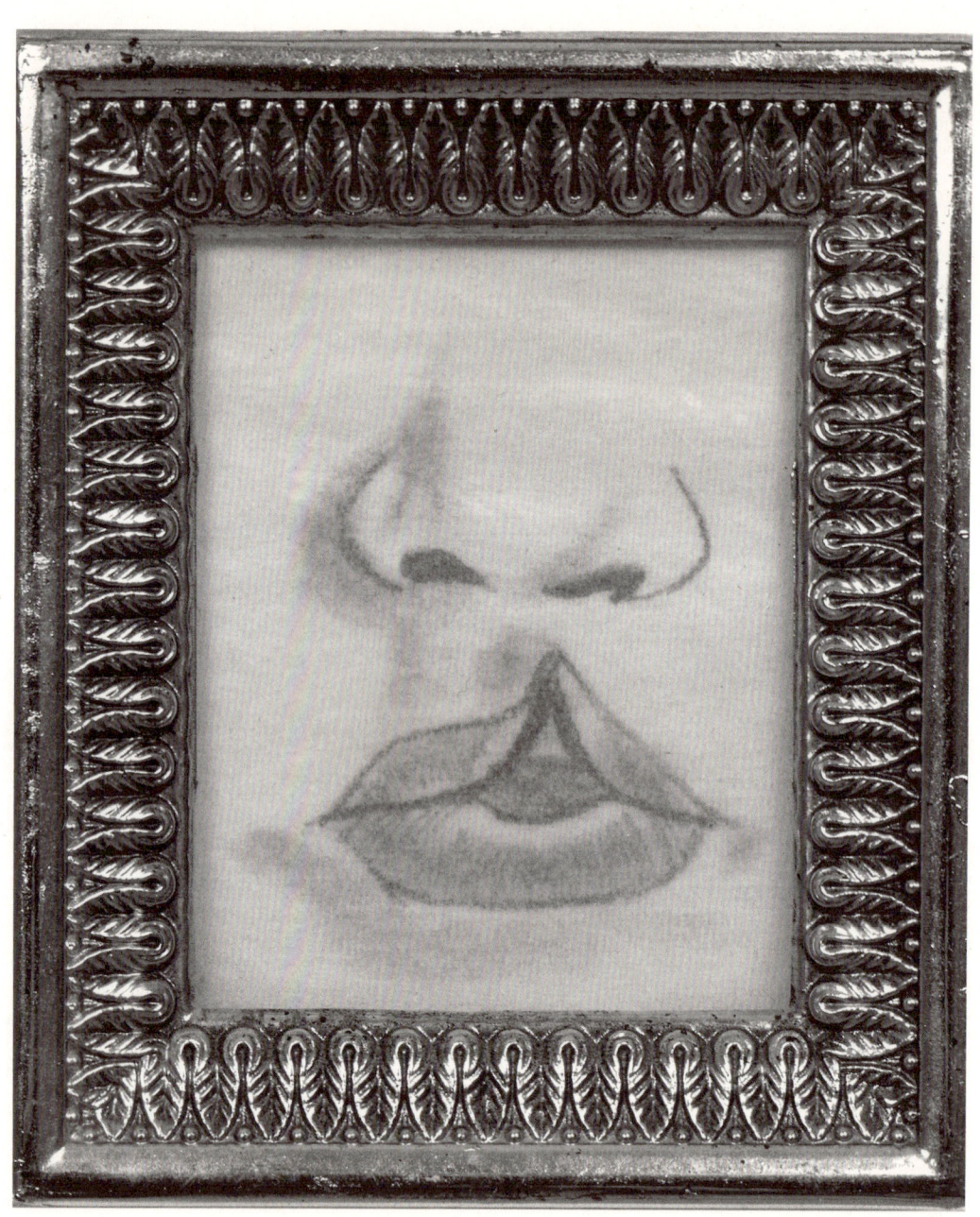

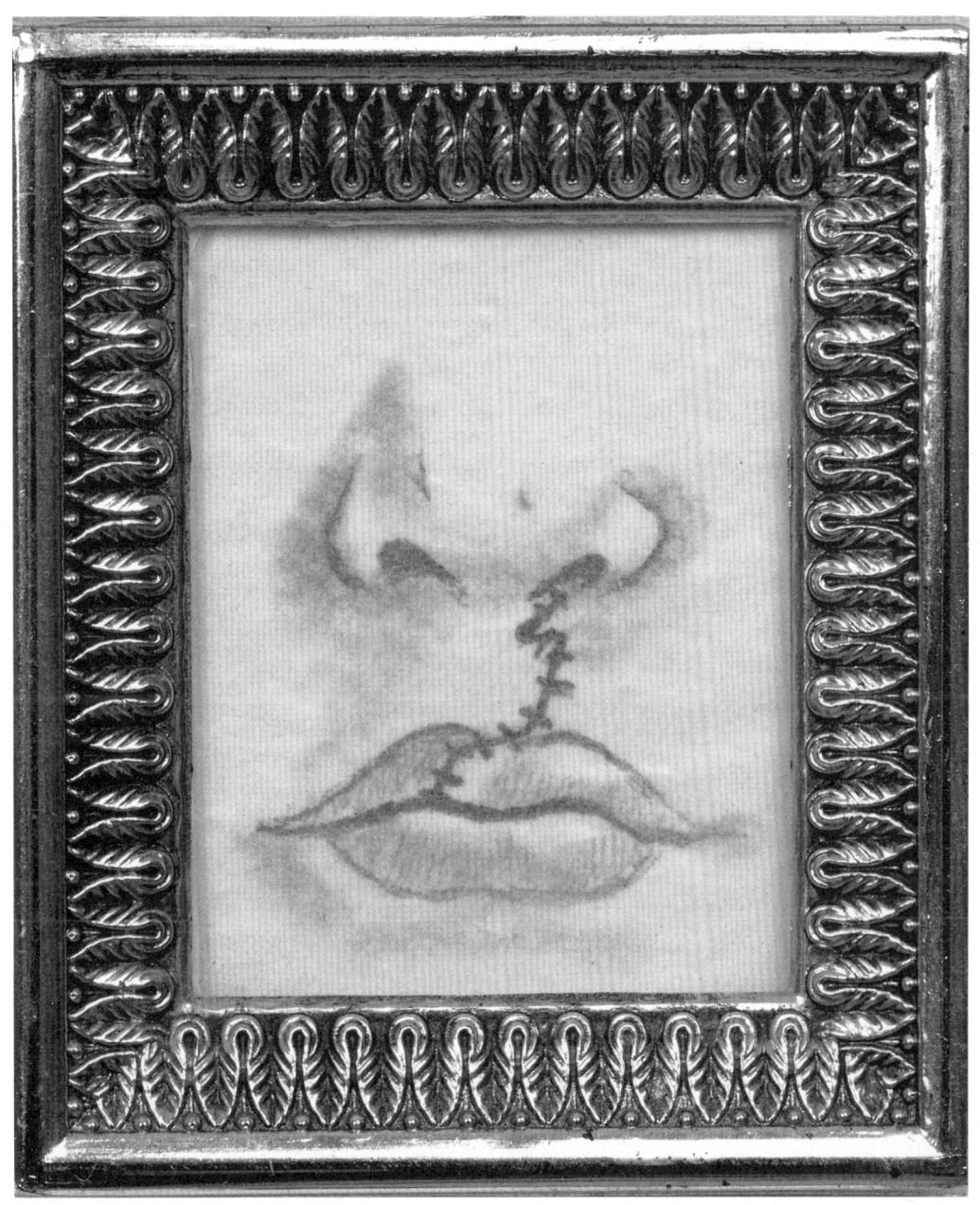

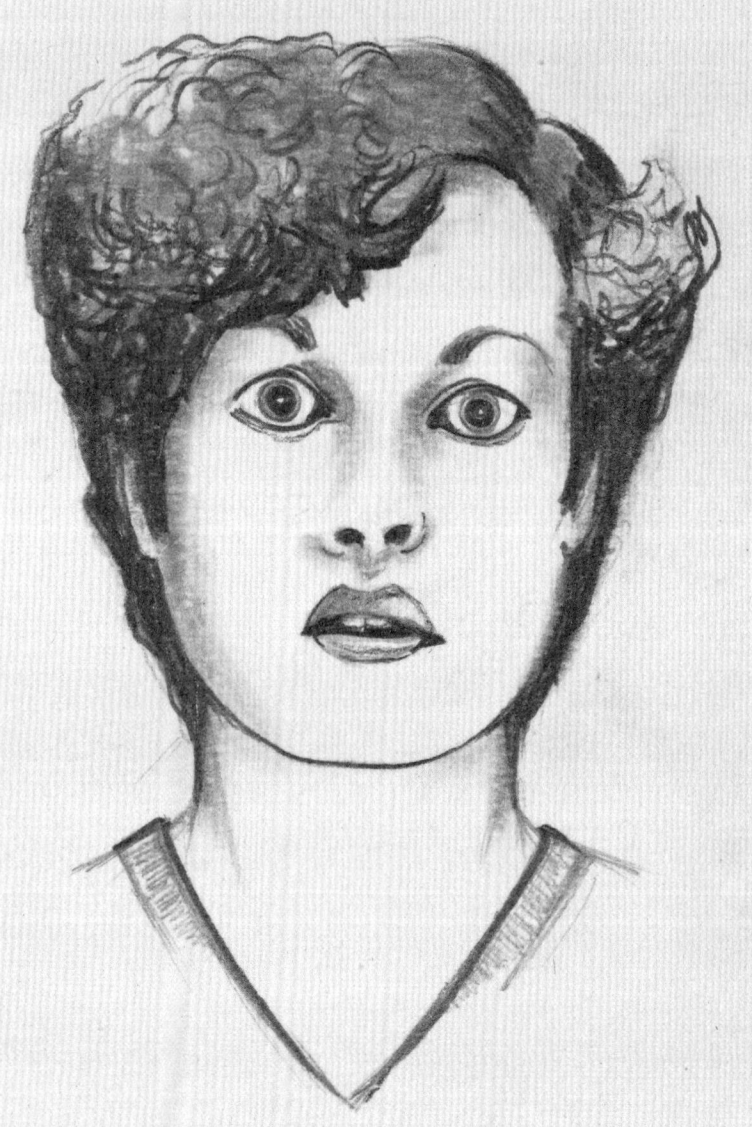

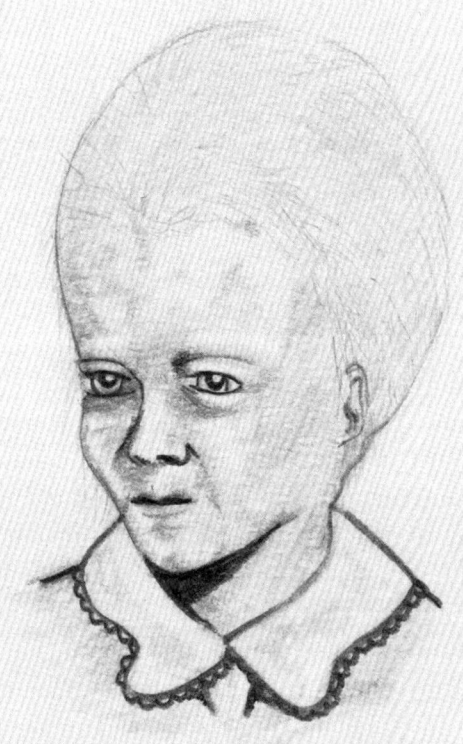

149 *Sans titre (We gonna have a good time)*, 1994. Framed crayon on paper, 39.5 × 31.5 cm

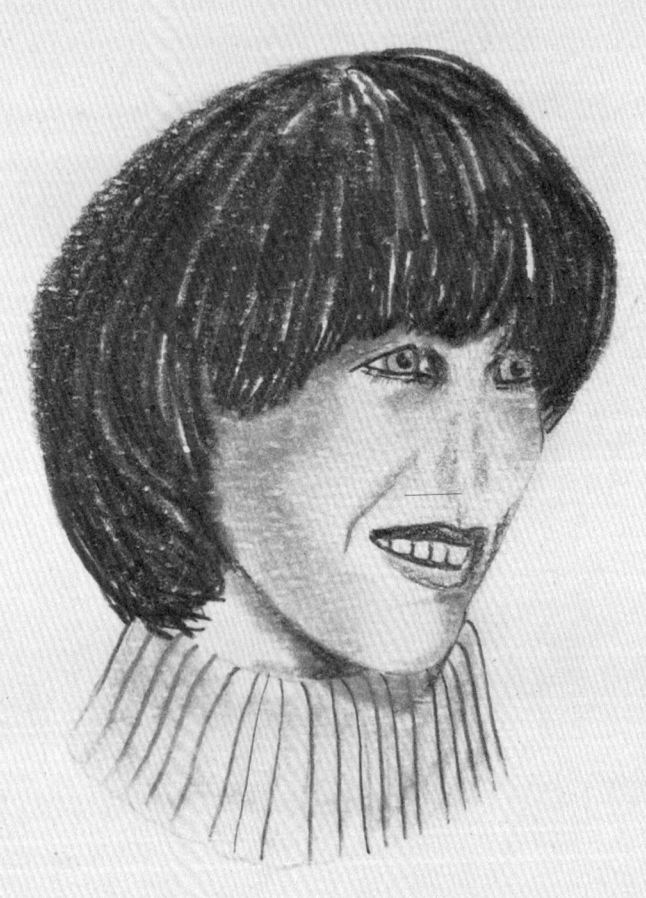

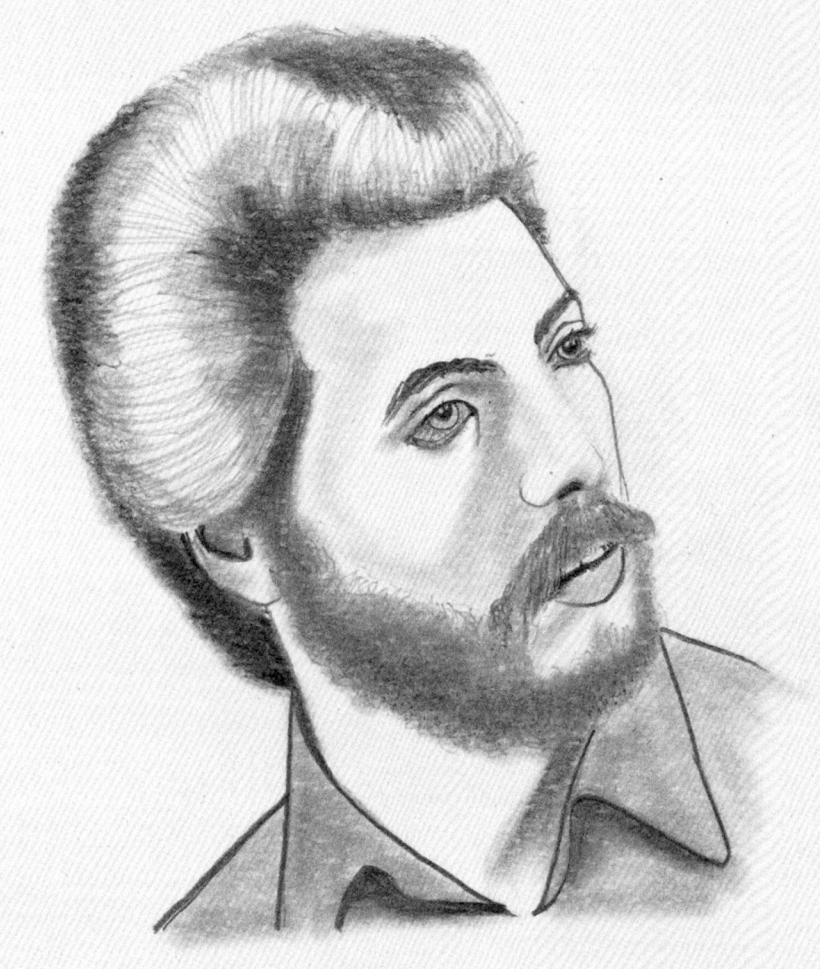

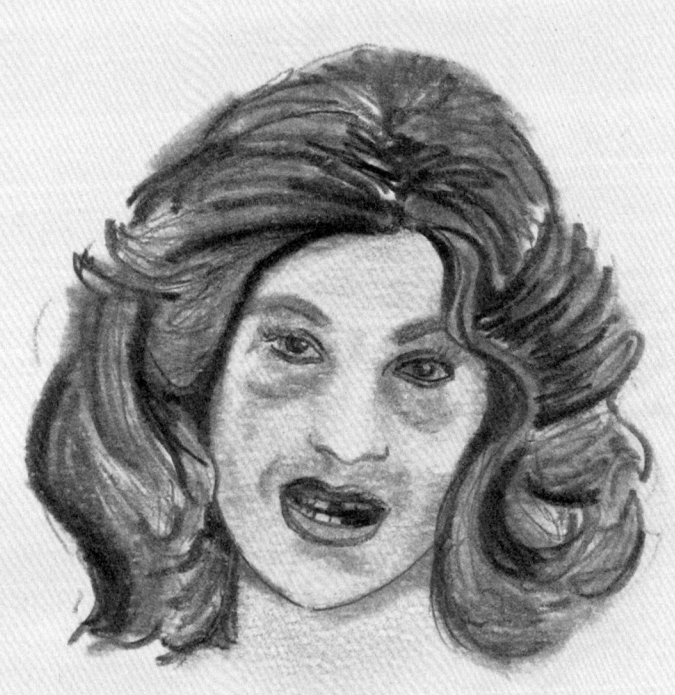

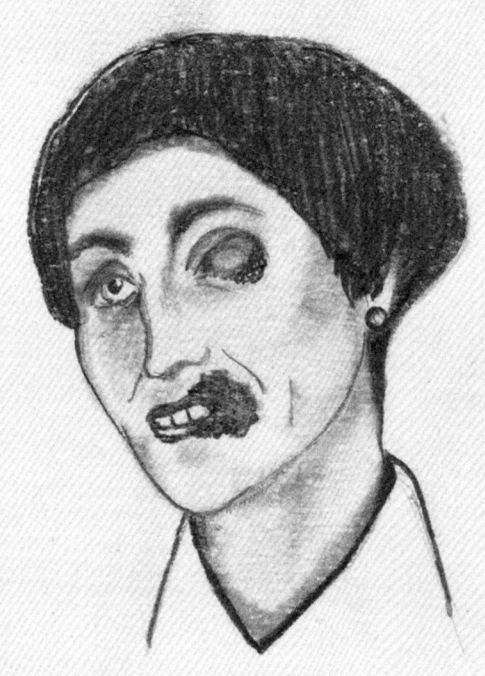

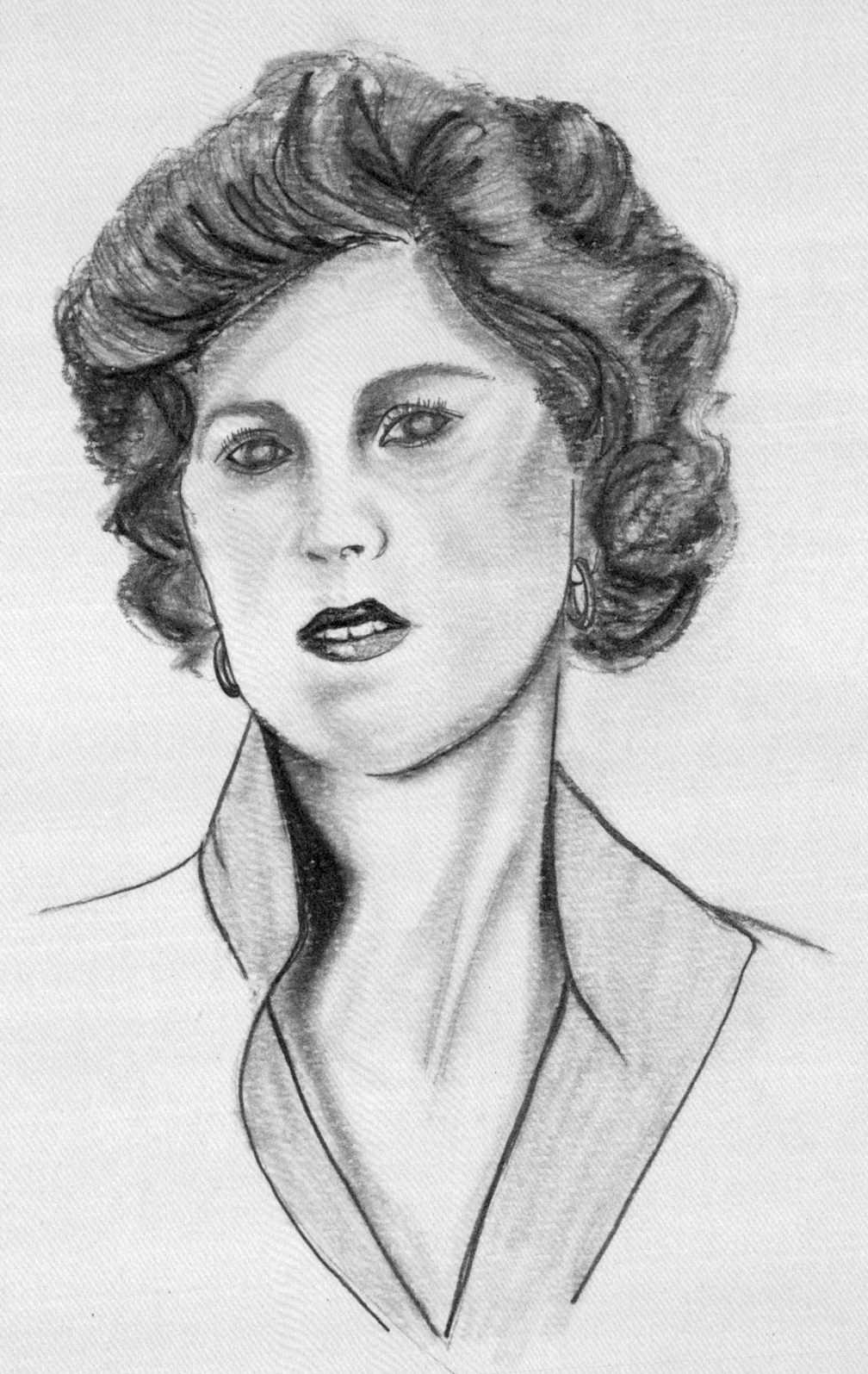

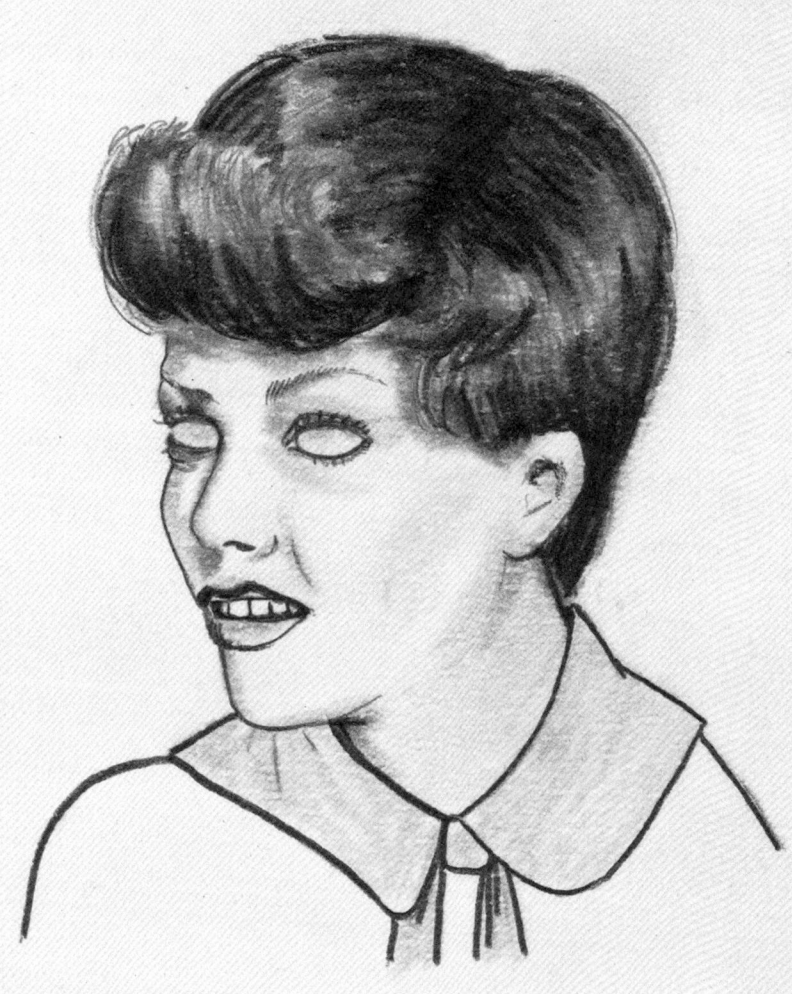

Sans titre (We gonna have a good time), 1994. Framed crayon on paper, 39.5 × 31.5 cm. Collection Hopi Lebel, Paris

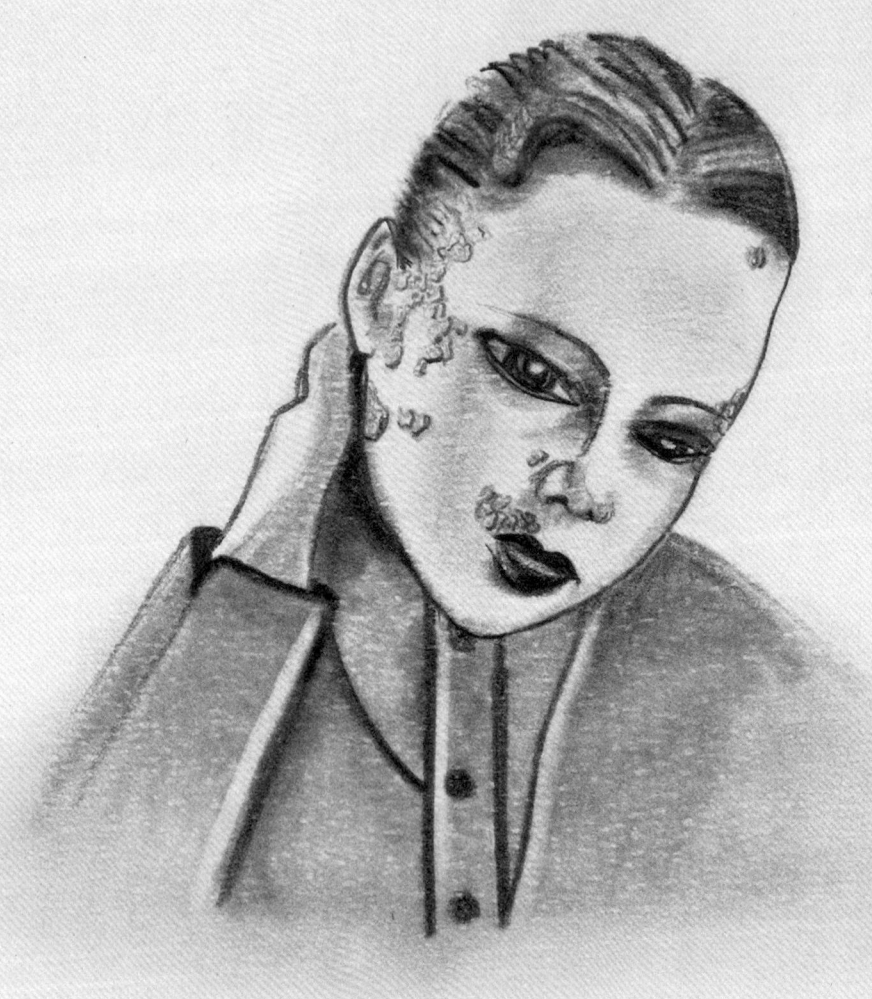
Sans titre (We gonna have a good time), 1994. Framed crayon on paper, 39.5 × 31.5 cm

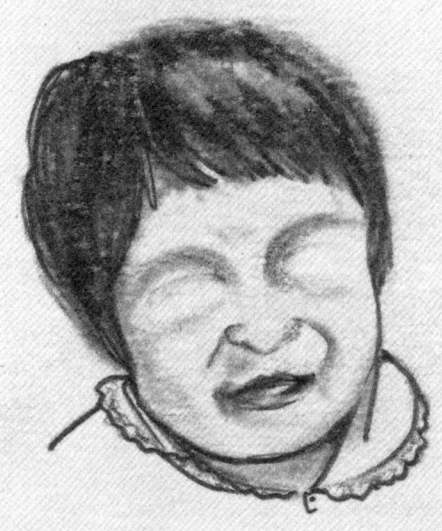

Sans titre (We gonna have a good time), 1994. Framed crayon on paper, 39.5 × 31.5 cm.
Collection Frieda Schumann, Paris

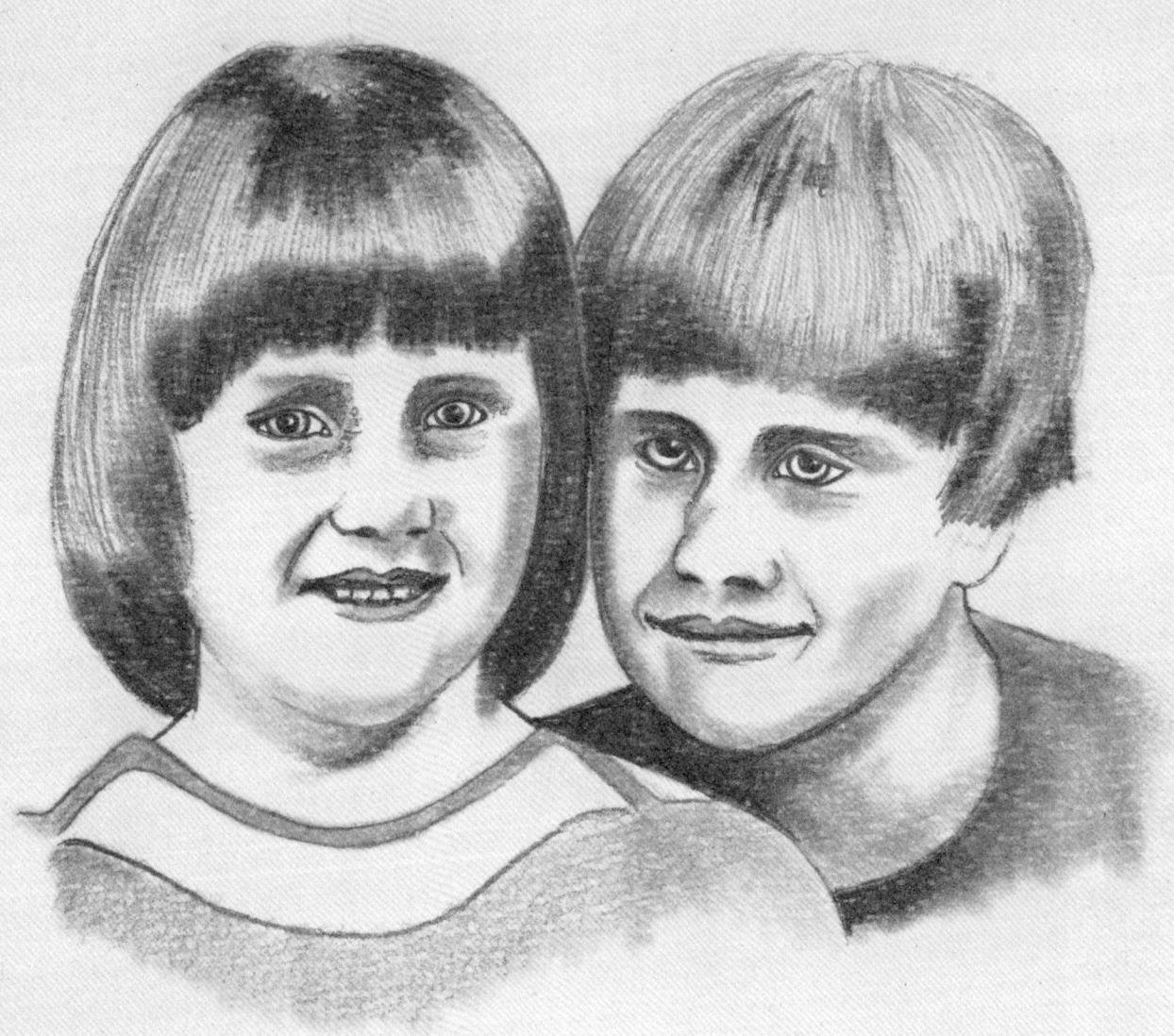

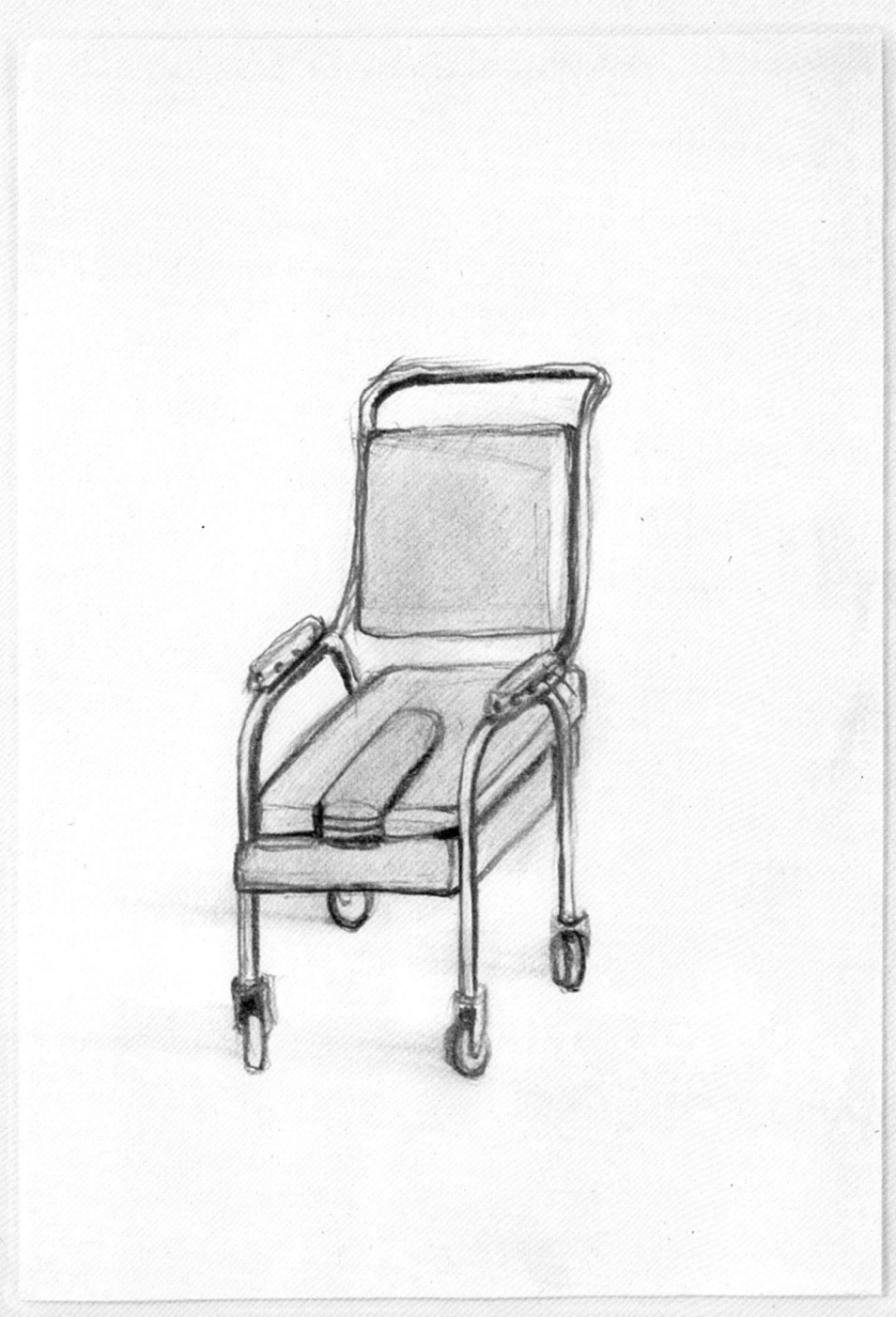

Untitled, 2002, from the *Last drawings* series. Graphite on white machine paper, 29.7 × 21 cm

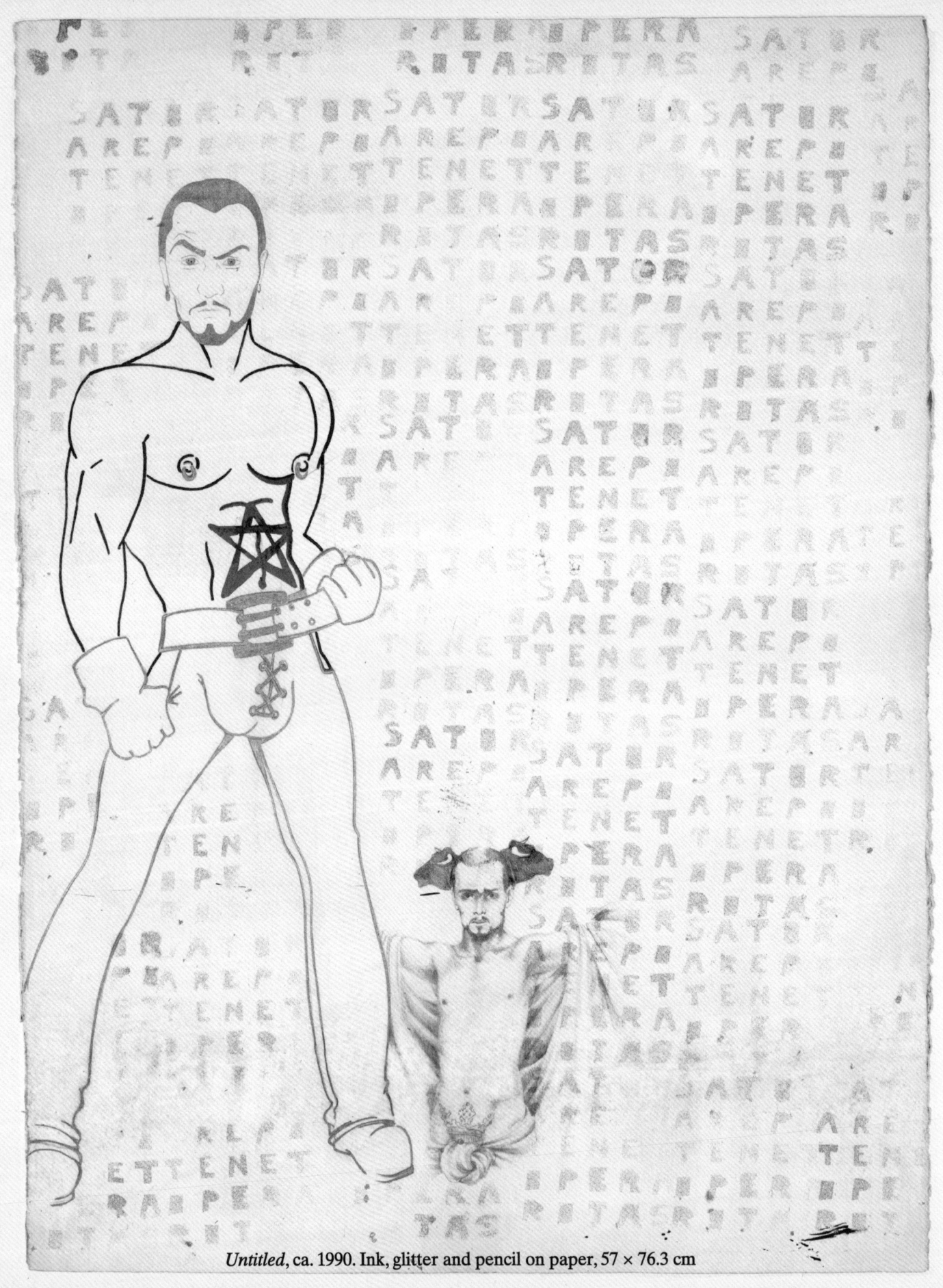

Untitled, ca. 1990. Ink, glitter and pencil on paper, 57 × 76.3 cm

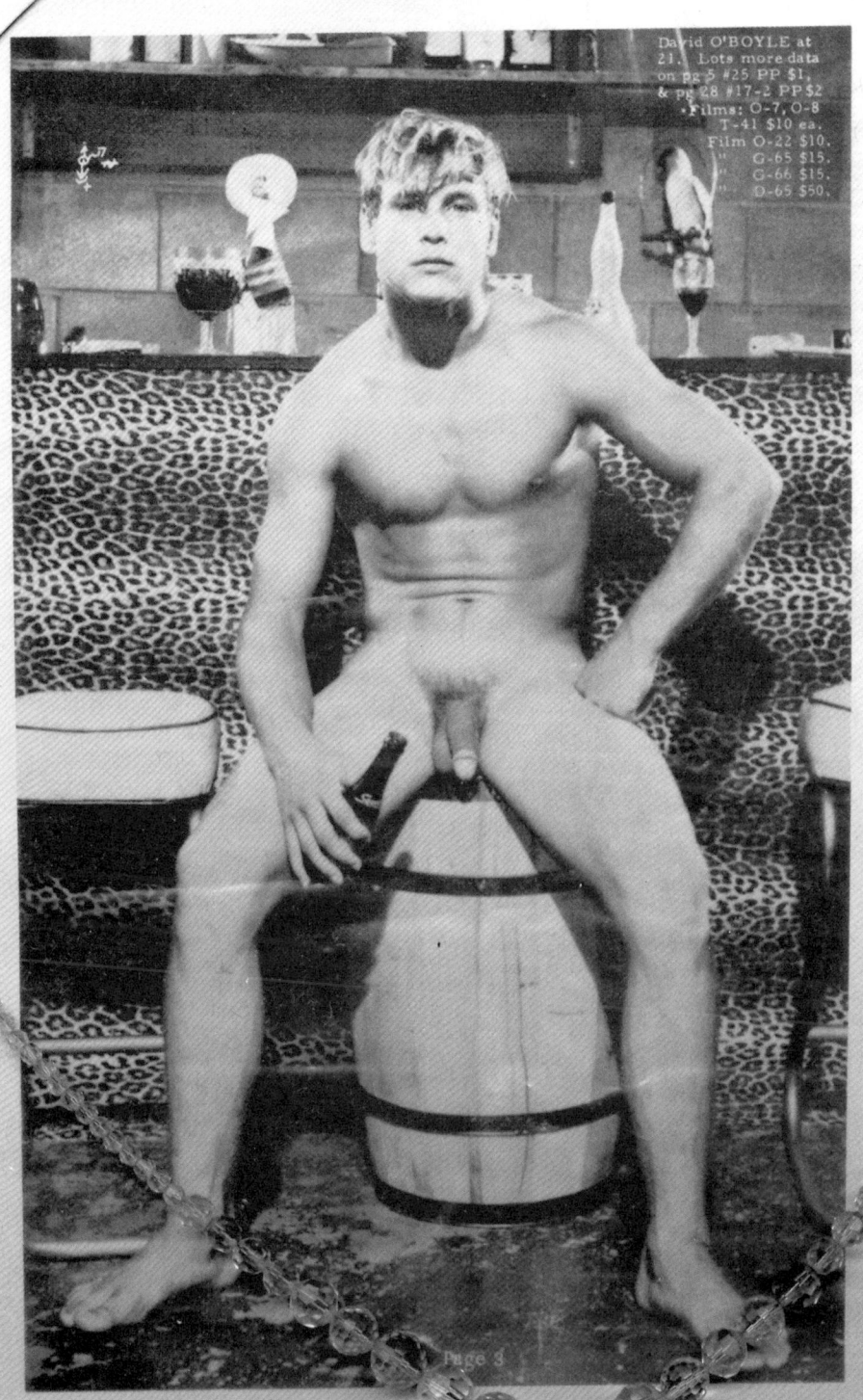

Page from *Physique Pictorial*, Vol. 27, July 1975
Photo: Bob Mizer

Untitled, n.d. Unnumbered jewel, glass pearls on a noose string; packaging: plastic bag with cut out Xerox

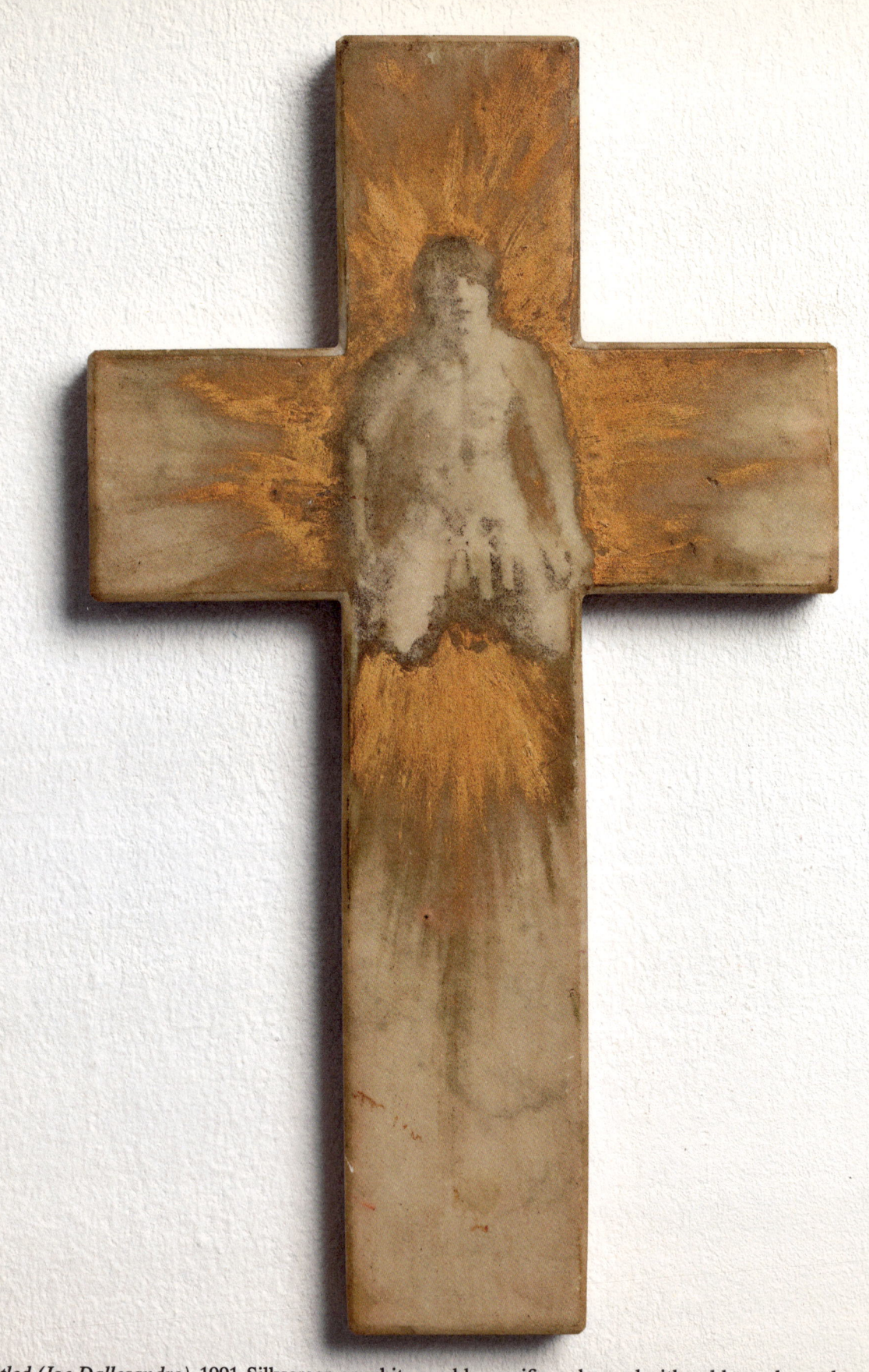

Untitled (Joe Dallesandro), 1991. Silkscreen on white marble crucifix, enhanced with gold powder and wax, 30 × 18 × 2 cm. Collection Patrick le Nézet, Nice

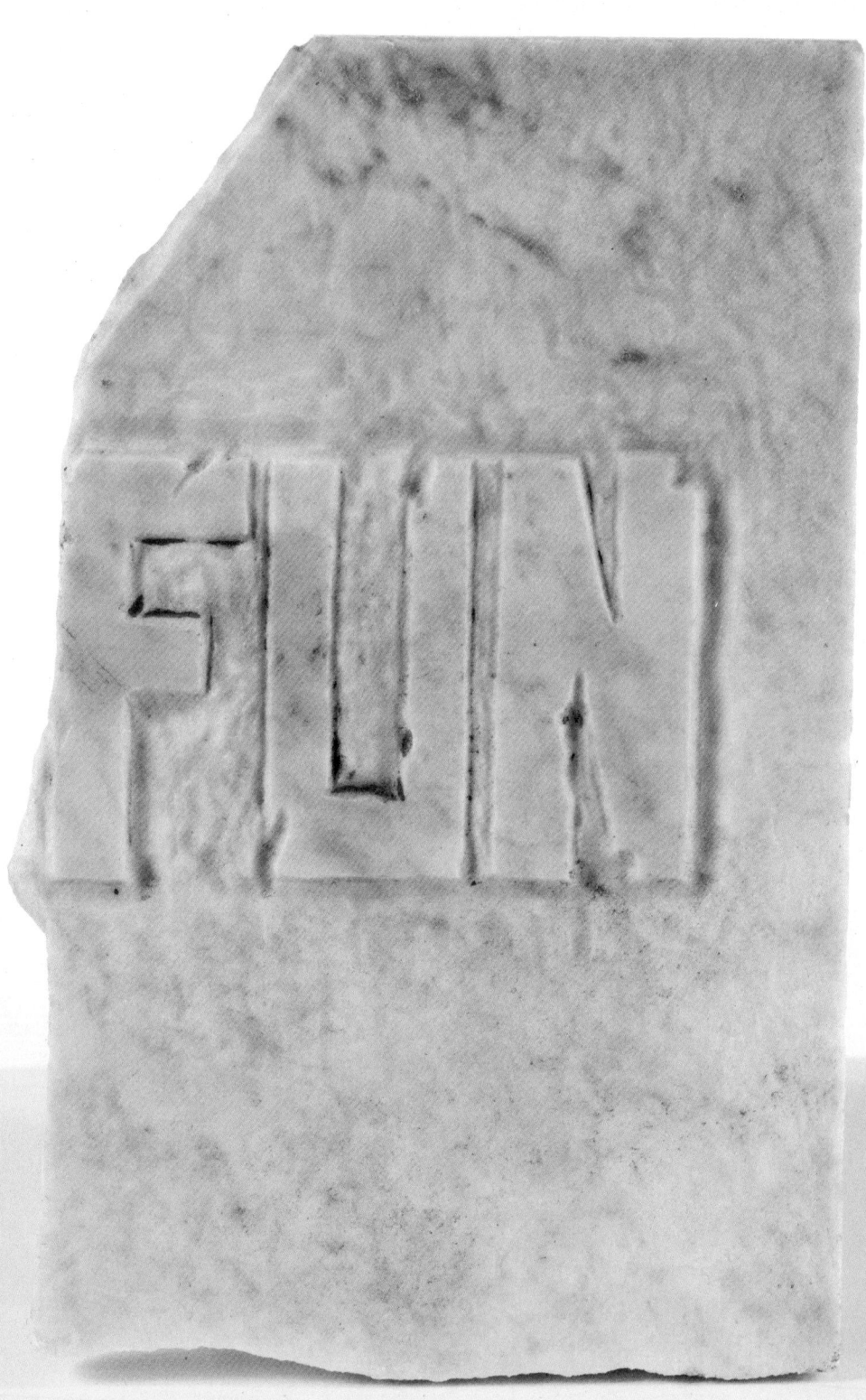

Untitled (Fun), 1995. Engraved white marble and pencil, 25.5 × 16 × 1.5 cm.
Collection Roselyne & Patrick Michaud, Nice

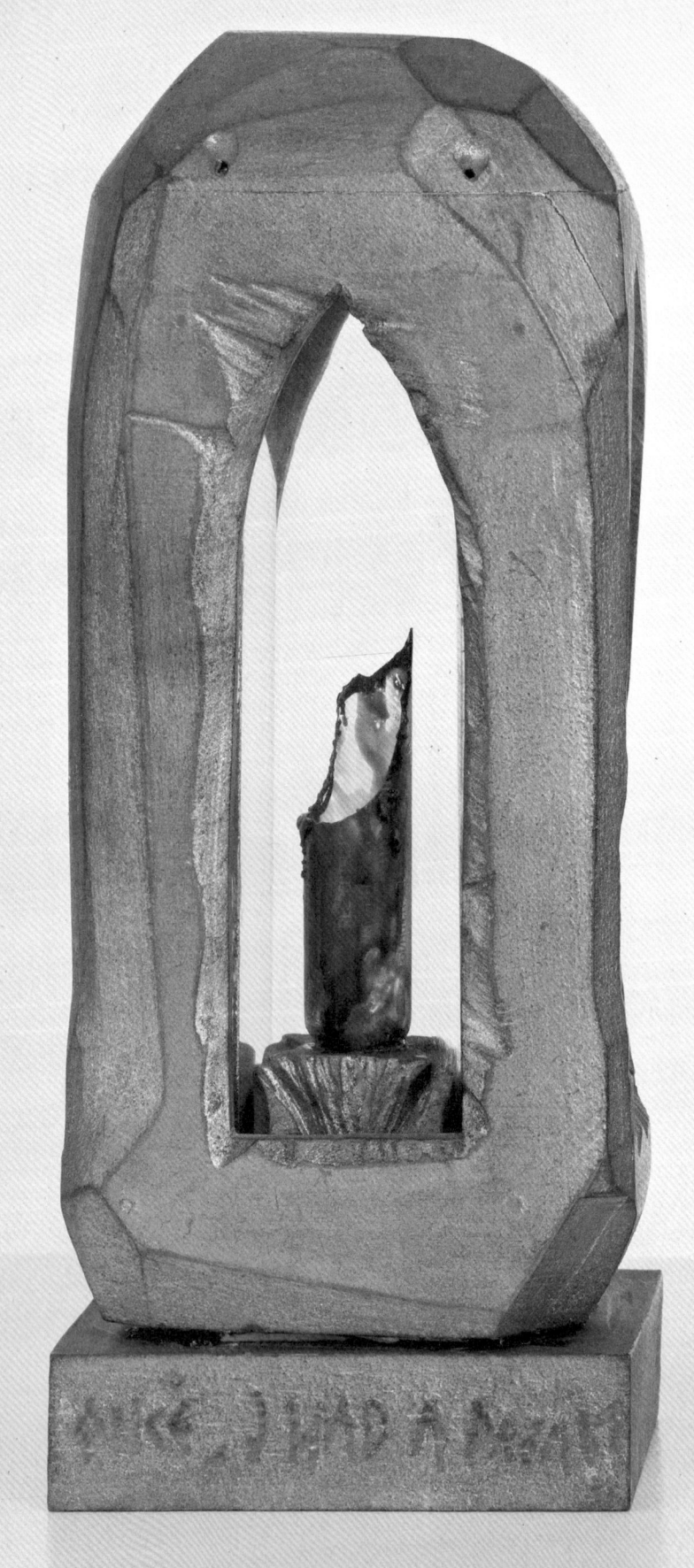

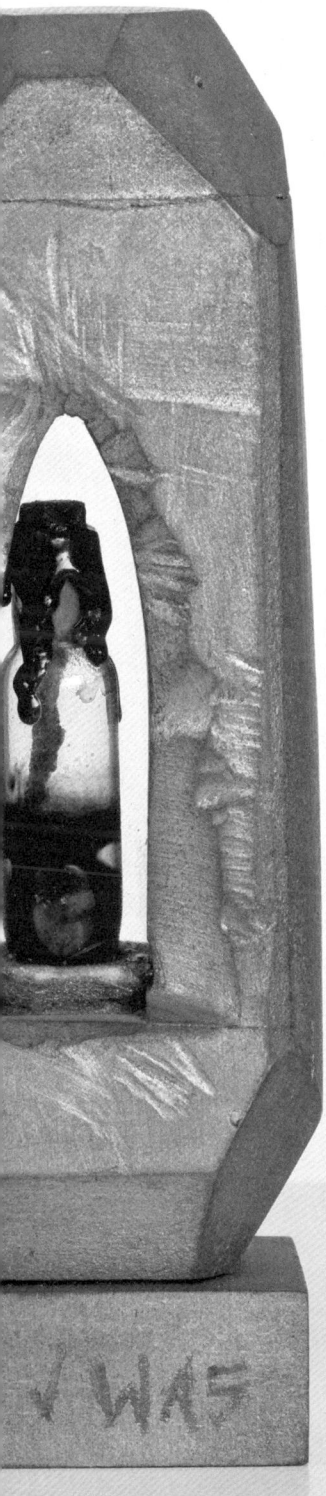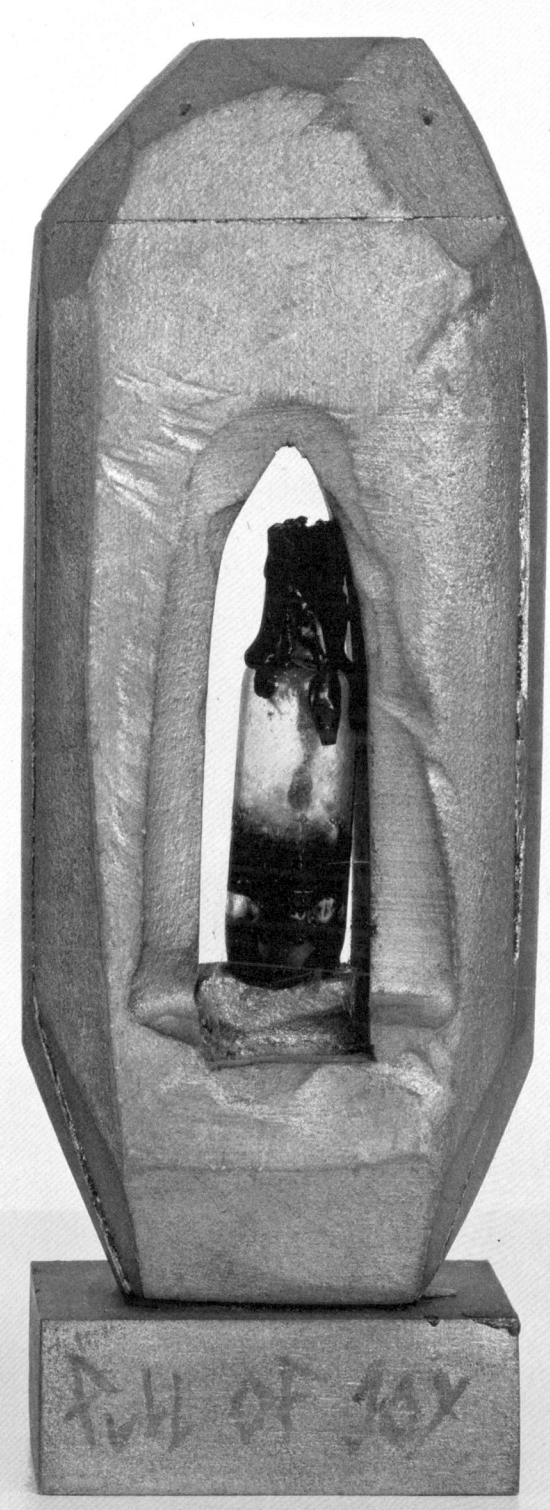

165 *Untitled (Reliquaire)*, 1992. Wood, paint, glass, mirror, beads, lamp, 30.6 × 16.6 × 8.7 cm

Untitled, n.d. Steel cylinder, Plexiglas, glass eye and phosphorescent paste, 24 × 6 cm

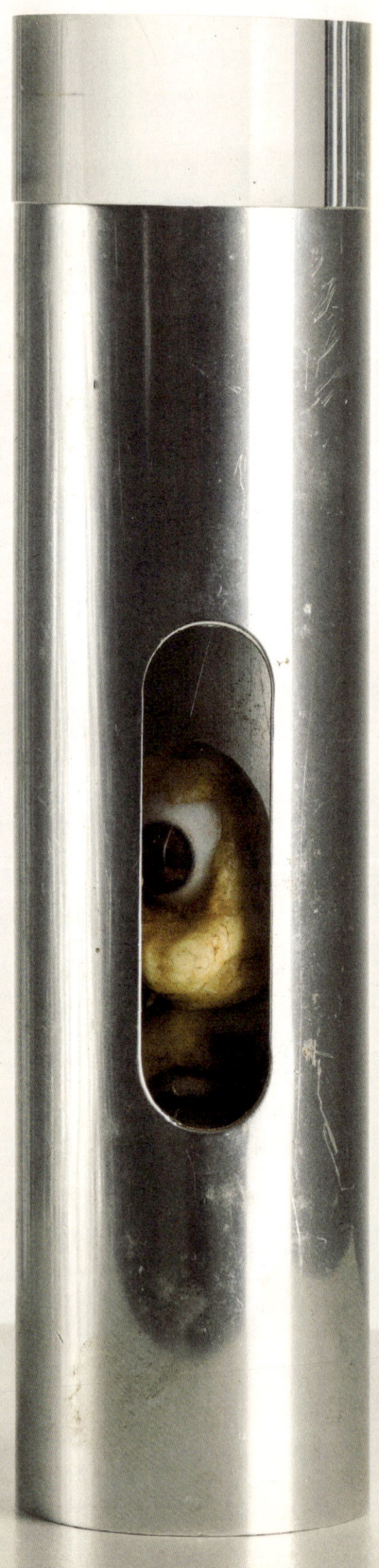

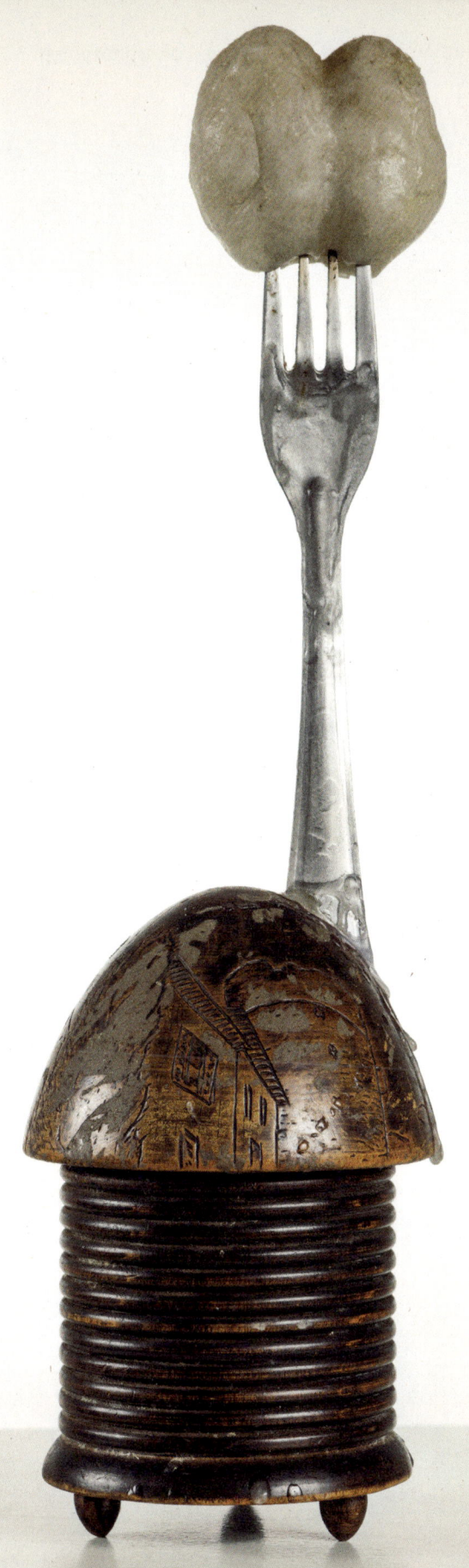

Untitled, 2000. Wood, stainless steel, silk cocoon, wax, 30.5 × 8 cm

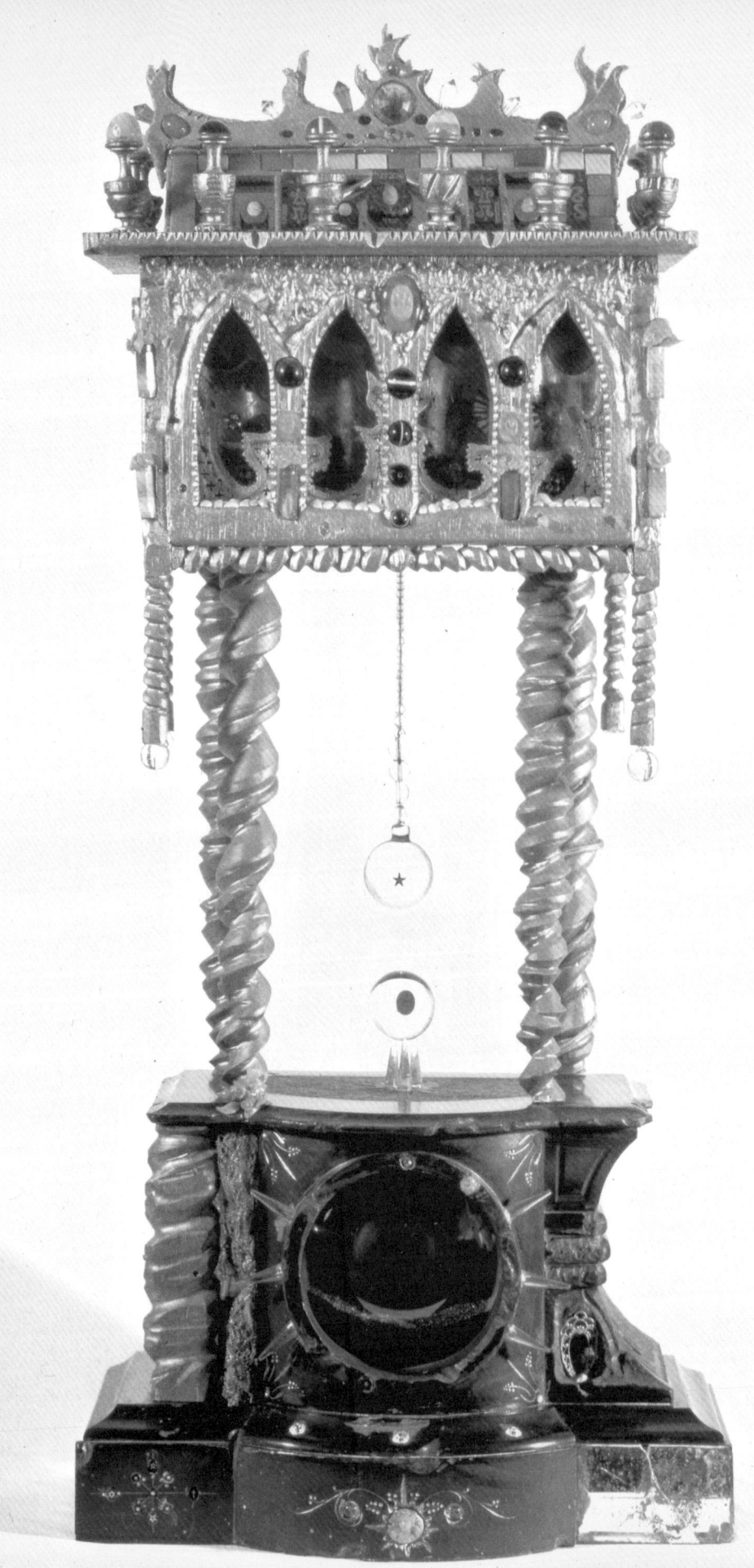

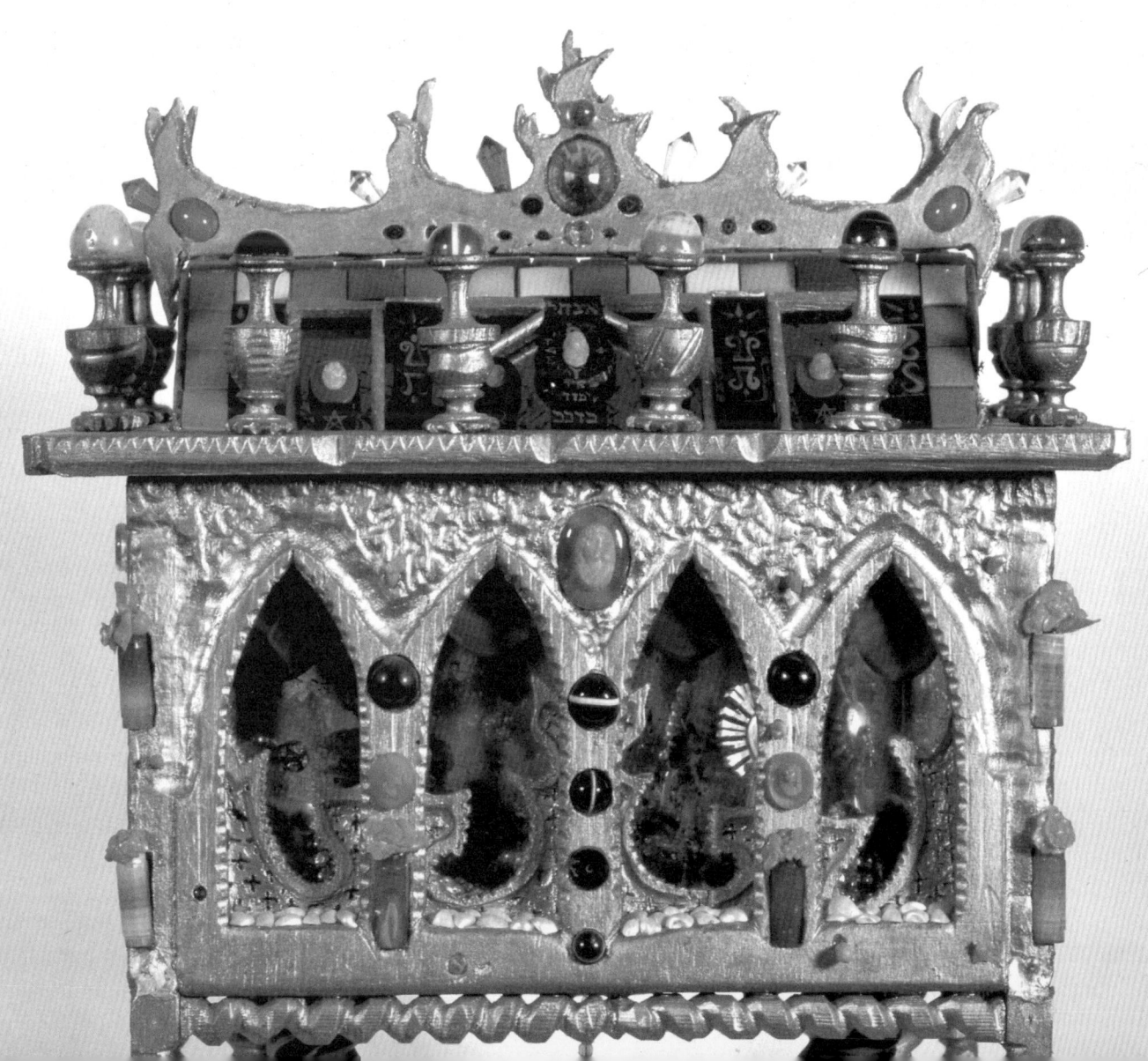

169   *Untitled (Temple)*, 1994–1995. Semi-precious and synthetic stones, coral, rhinestones, mother-of-pearl, lace, plastic, marble, mirror, metallic wire, bronze, glass paint, metal, gilded painted wood, glass, 80 × 35 × 22 cm. Collection Josiane Merino, Monaco

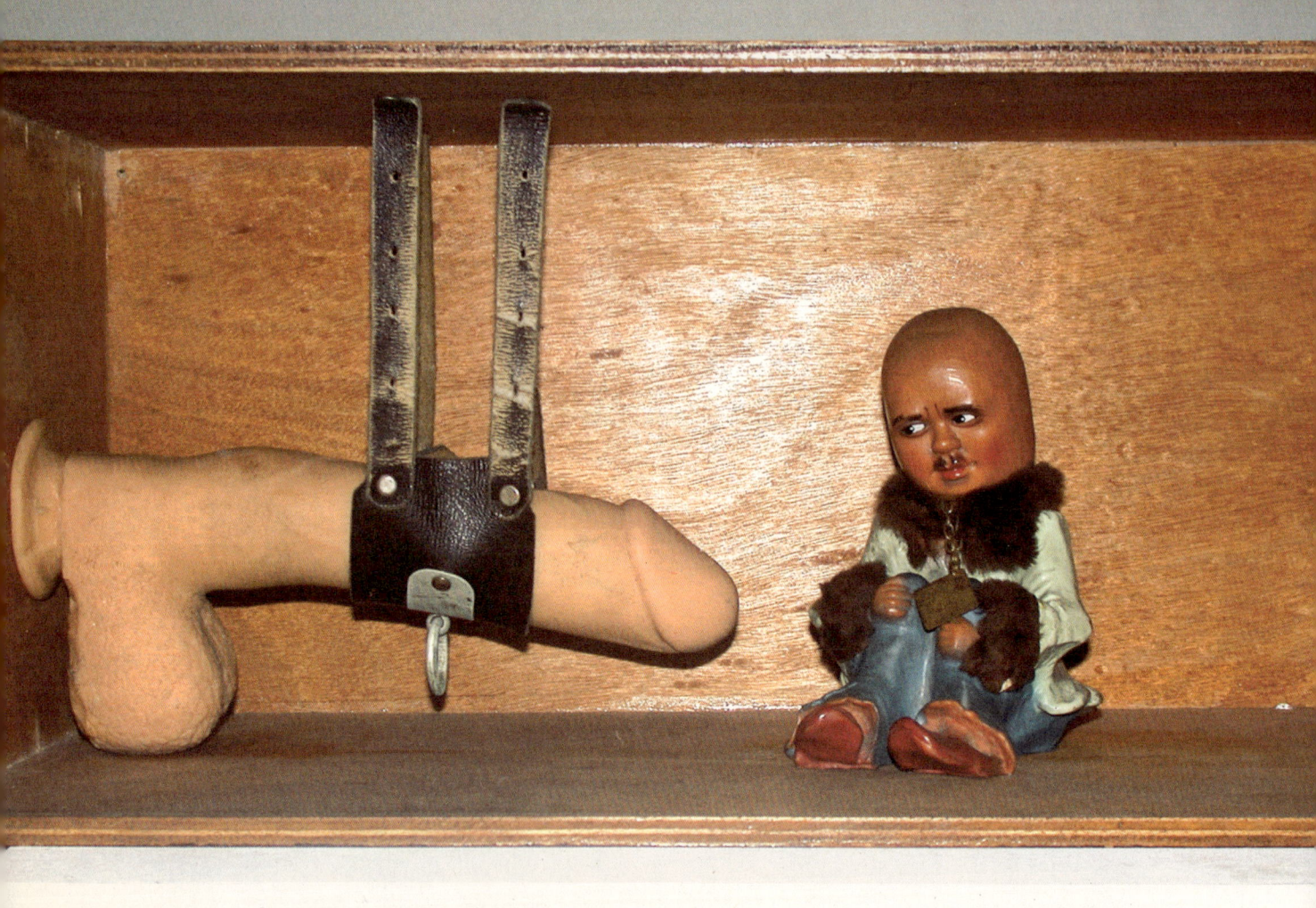

Untitled, n.d. Wooden case, glass and fabric figurine, Jeff Stryker dildo (a gift from Paul McCarthy, formerly part of *Dead Viking*, 1992), leather and metal hook, 25 × 62 × 29 cm. Collection Pascal Fazzini, Nice

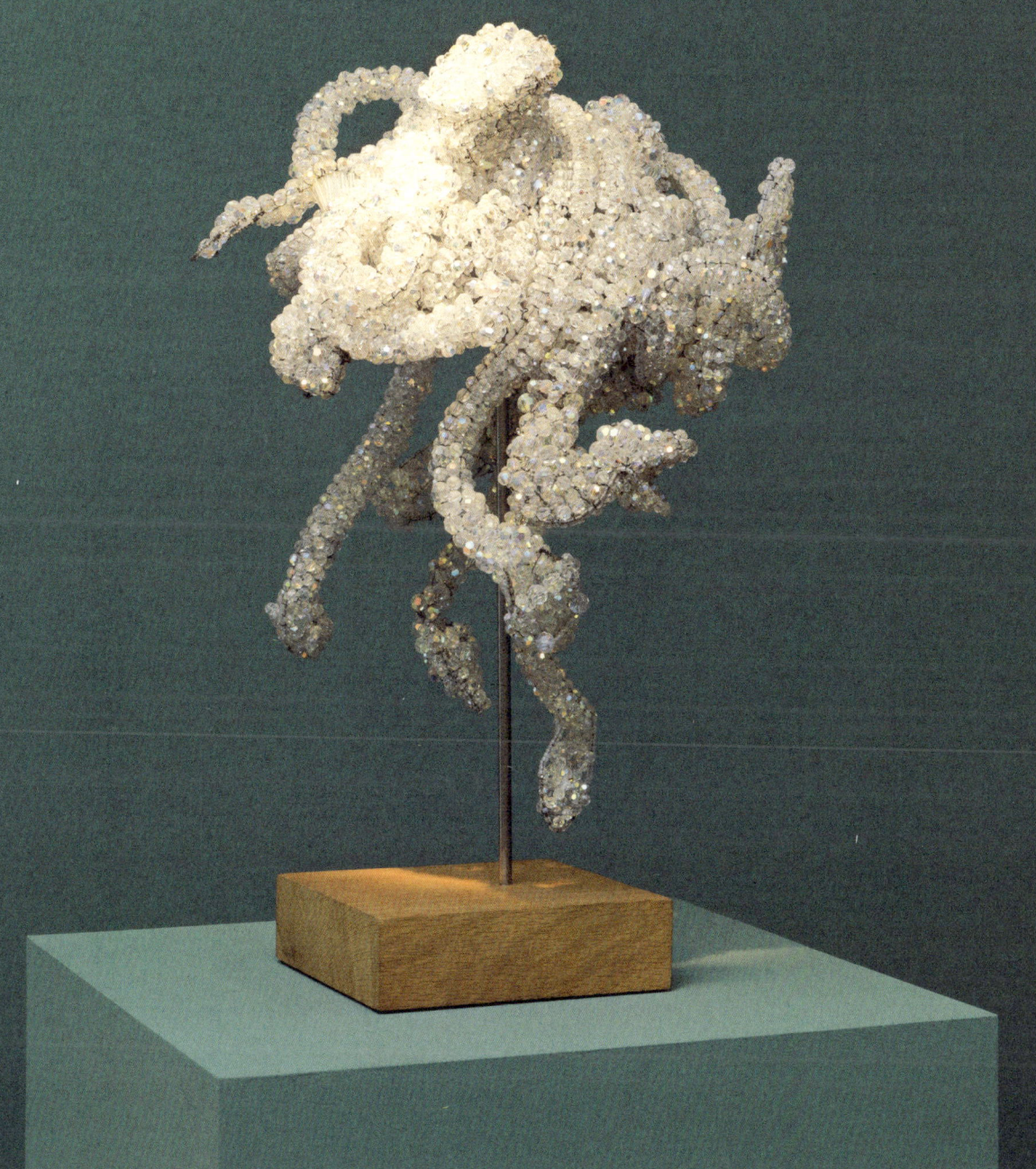

Untitled (Medusa Helmet), 1997. Swarovski crystal beads "aurora borealis," fabric, metallic wire, 37 × 33 × 33 cm. Collection Josiane Merino, Monaco

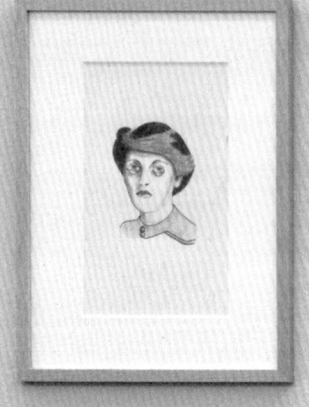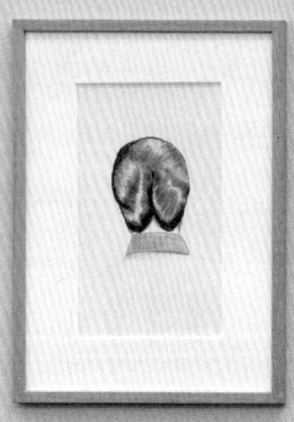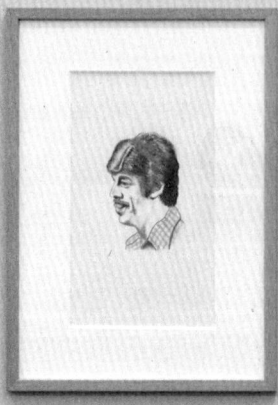

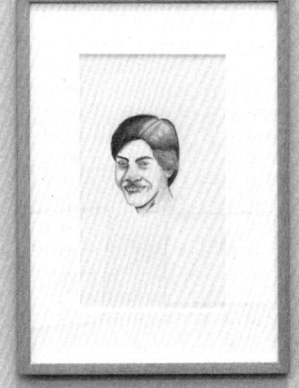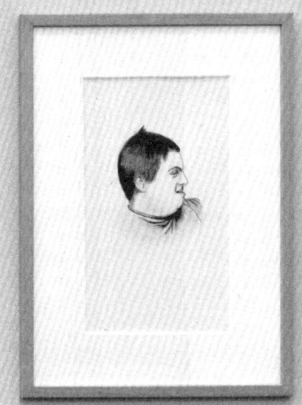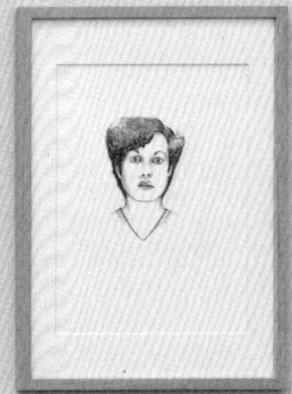

Exhibition view, *Bruno Pélassy*, February 12–May 1, 2016, MAMCO Genève

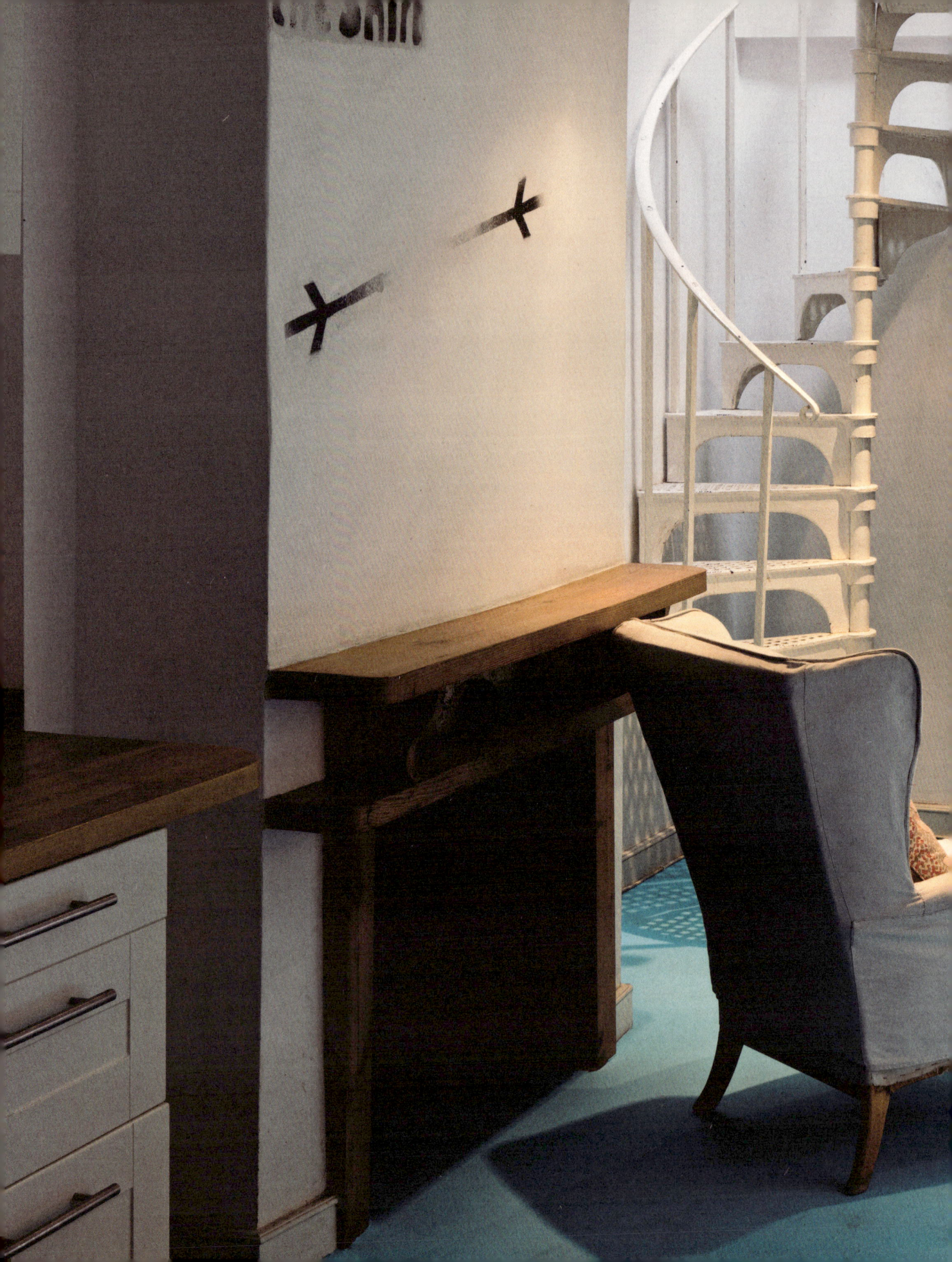

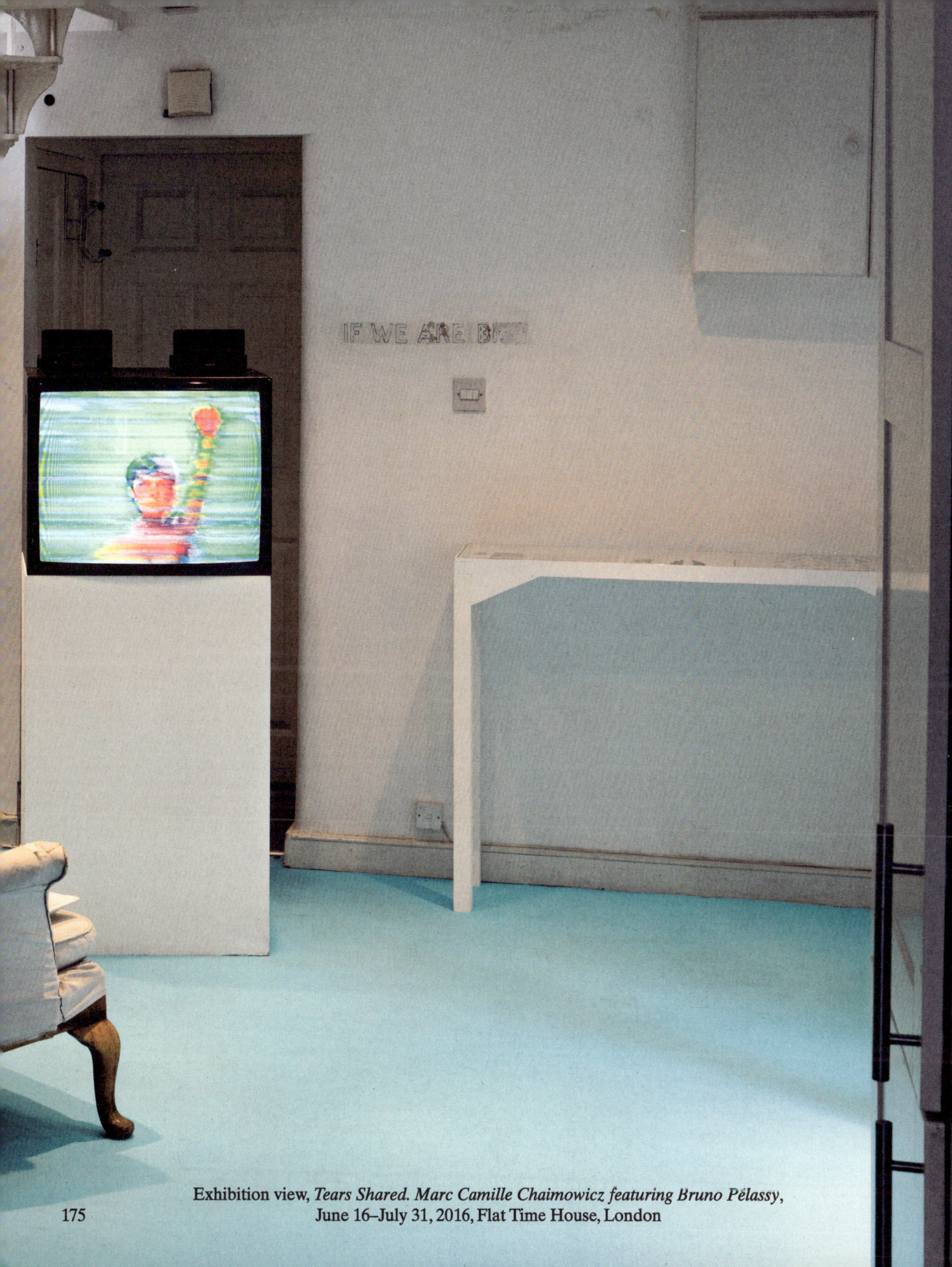

Exhibition view, *Tears Shared. Marc Camille Chaimowicz featuring Bruno Pélassy*, June 16–July 31, 2016, Flat Time House, London

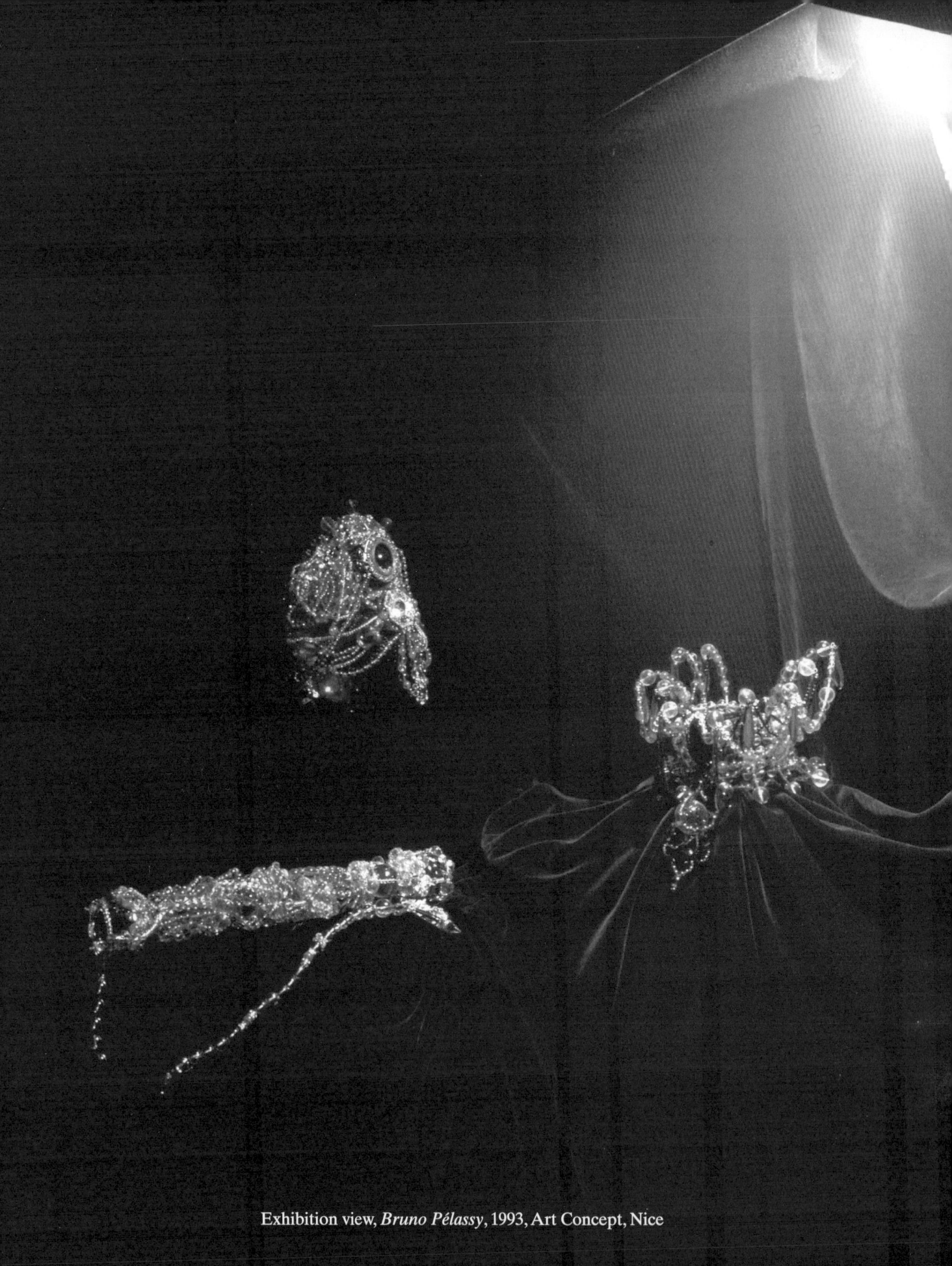

Exhibition view, *Bruno Pélassy*, 1993, Art Concept, Nice

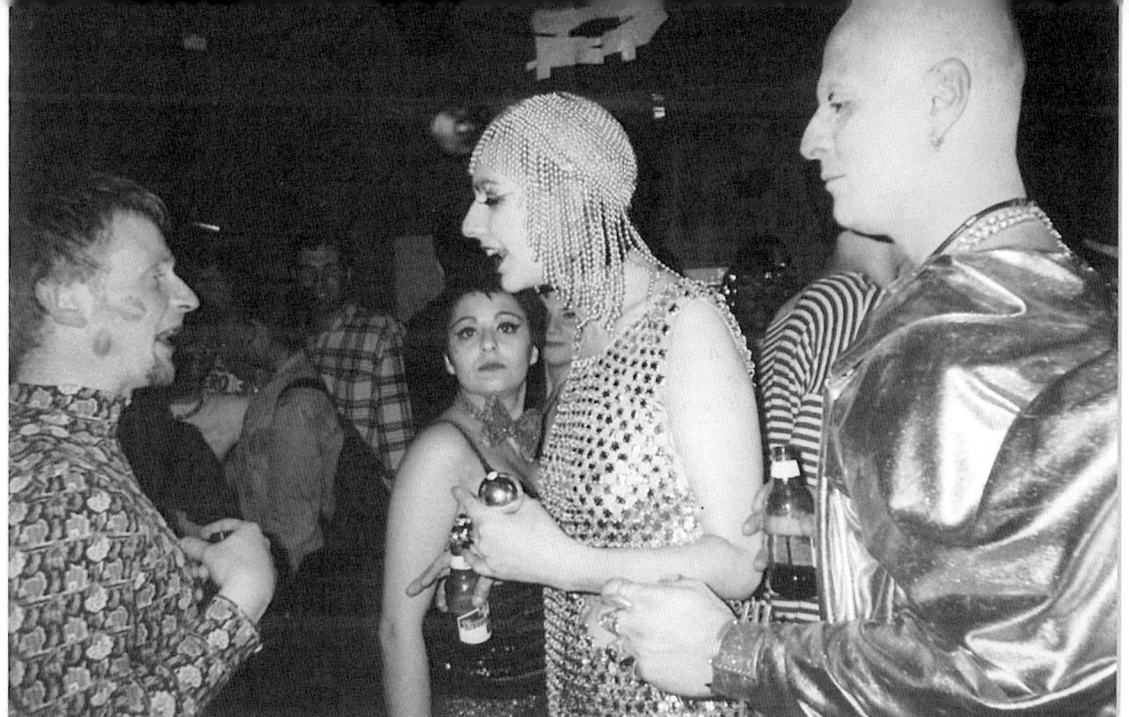
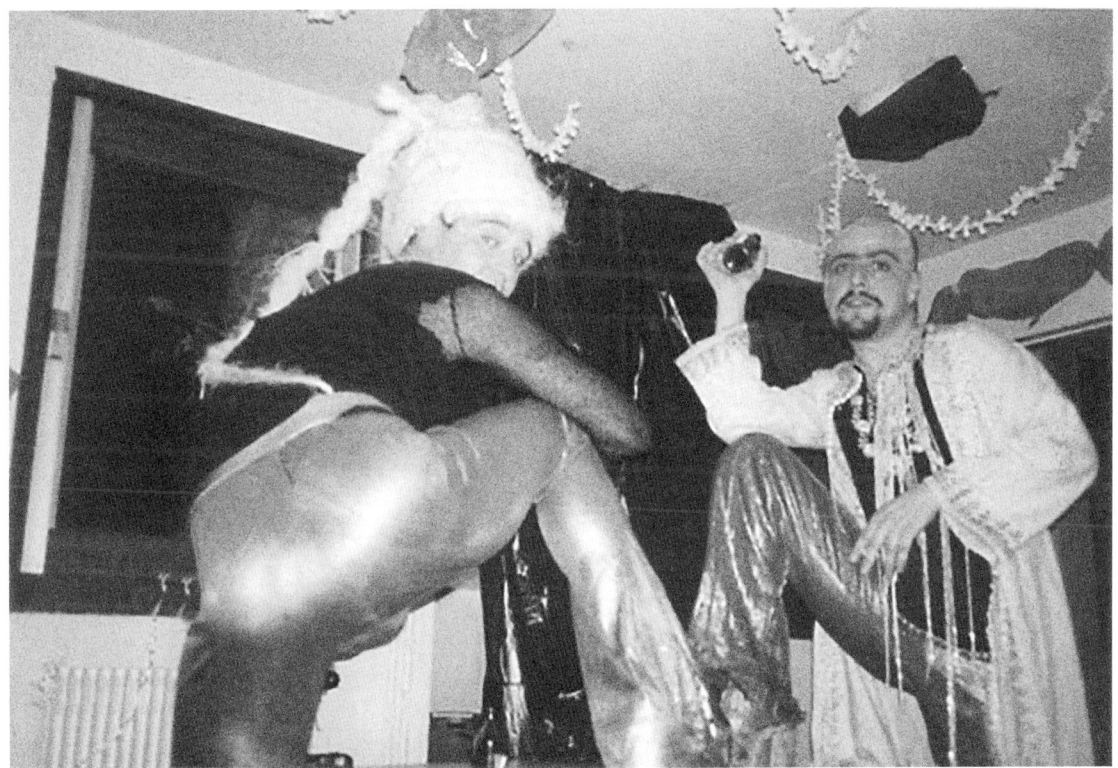

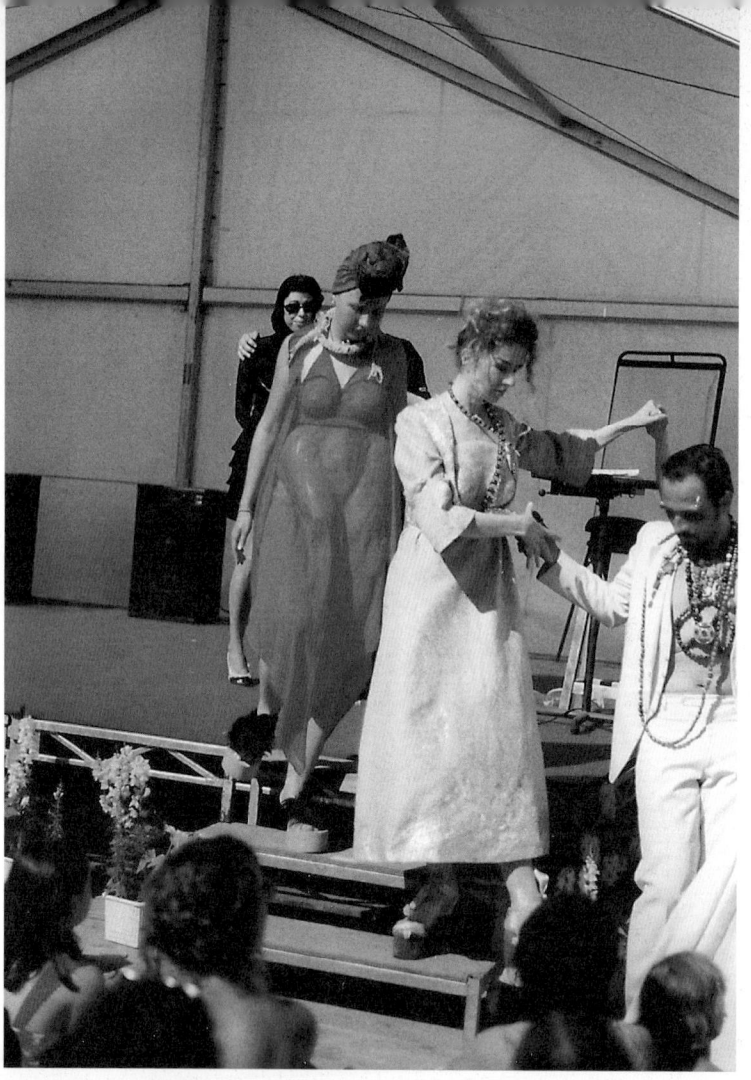
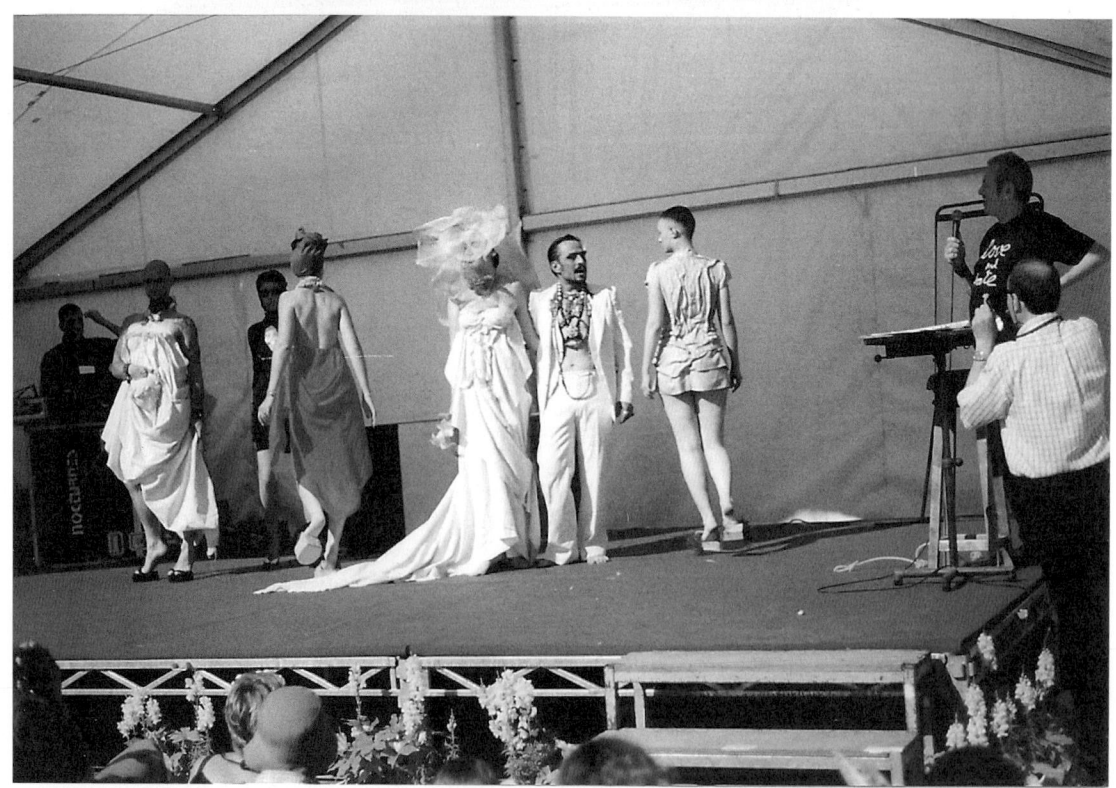

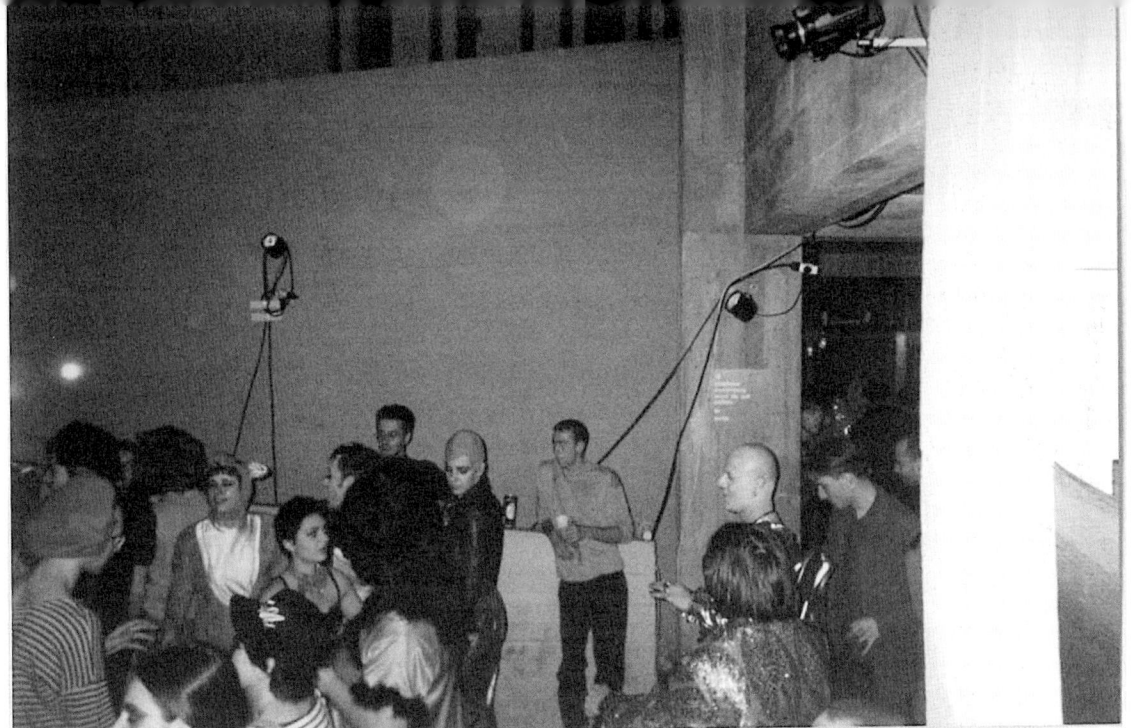
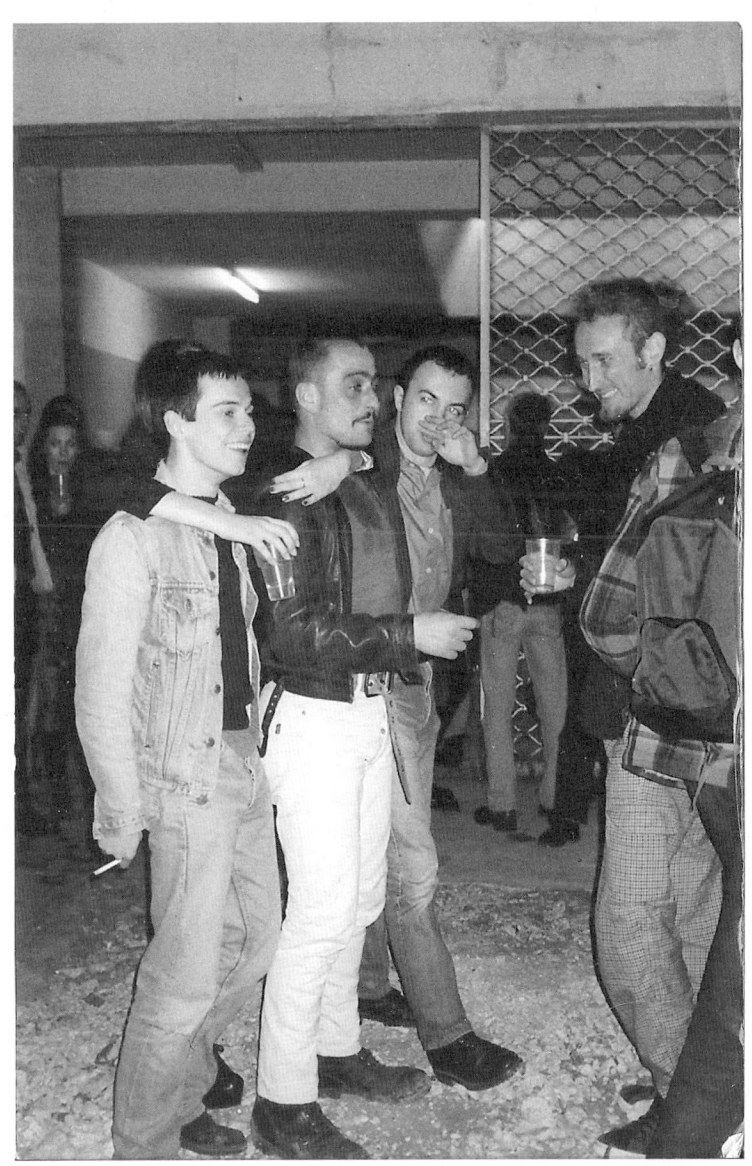

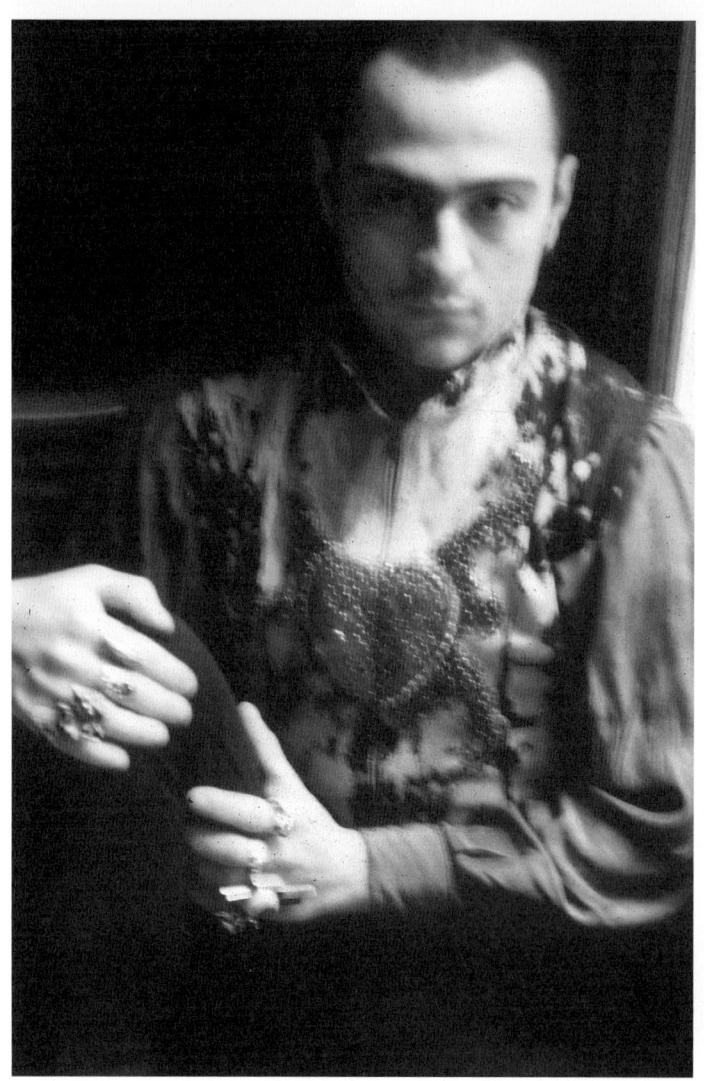
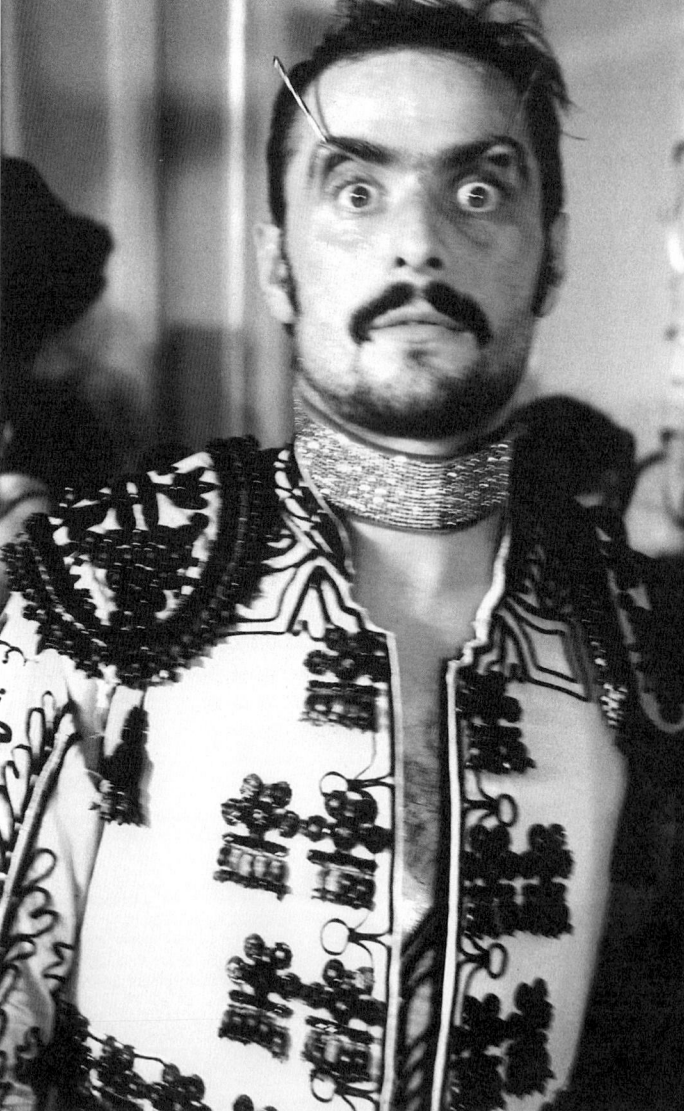

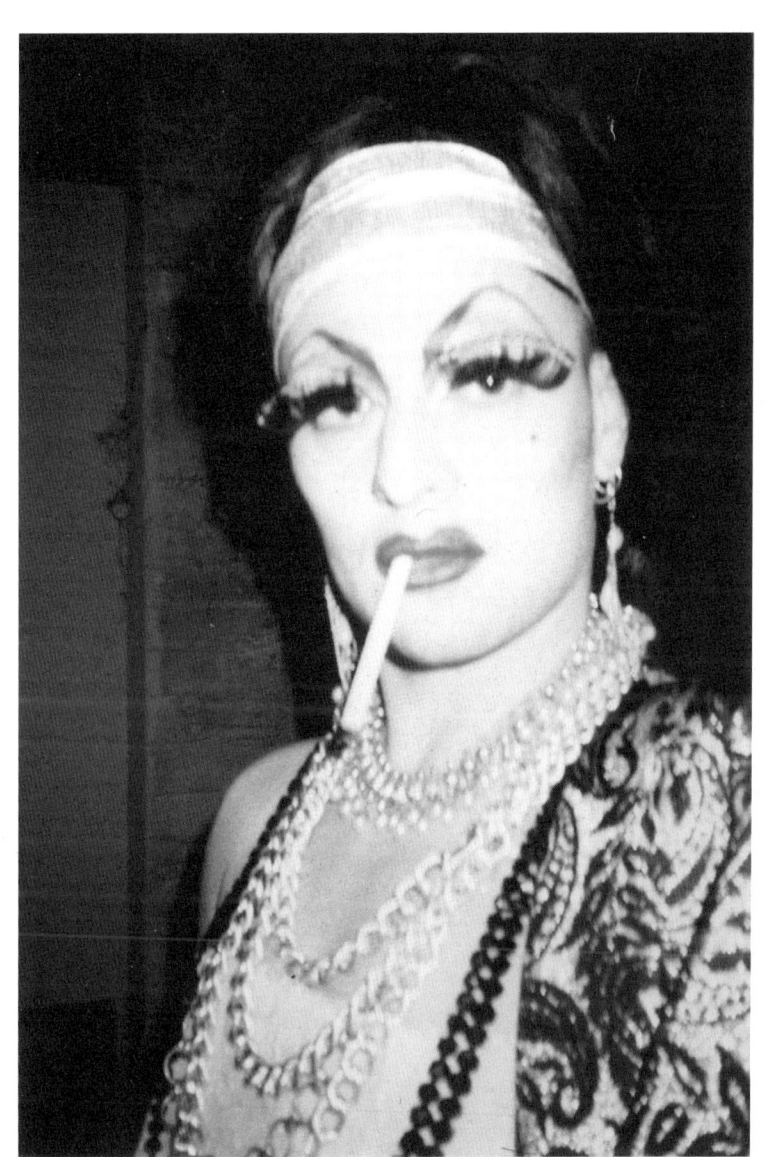

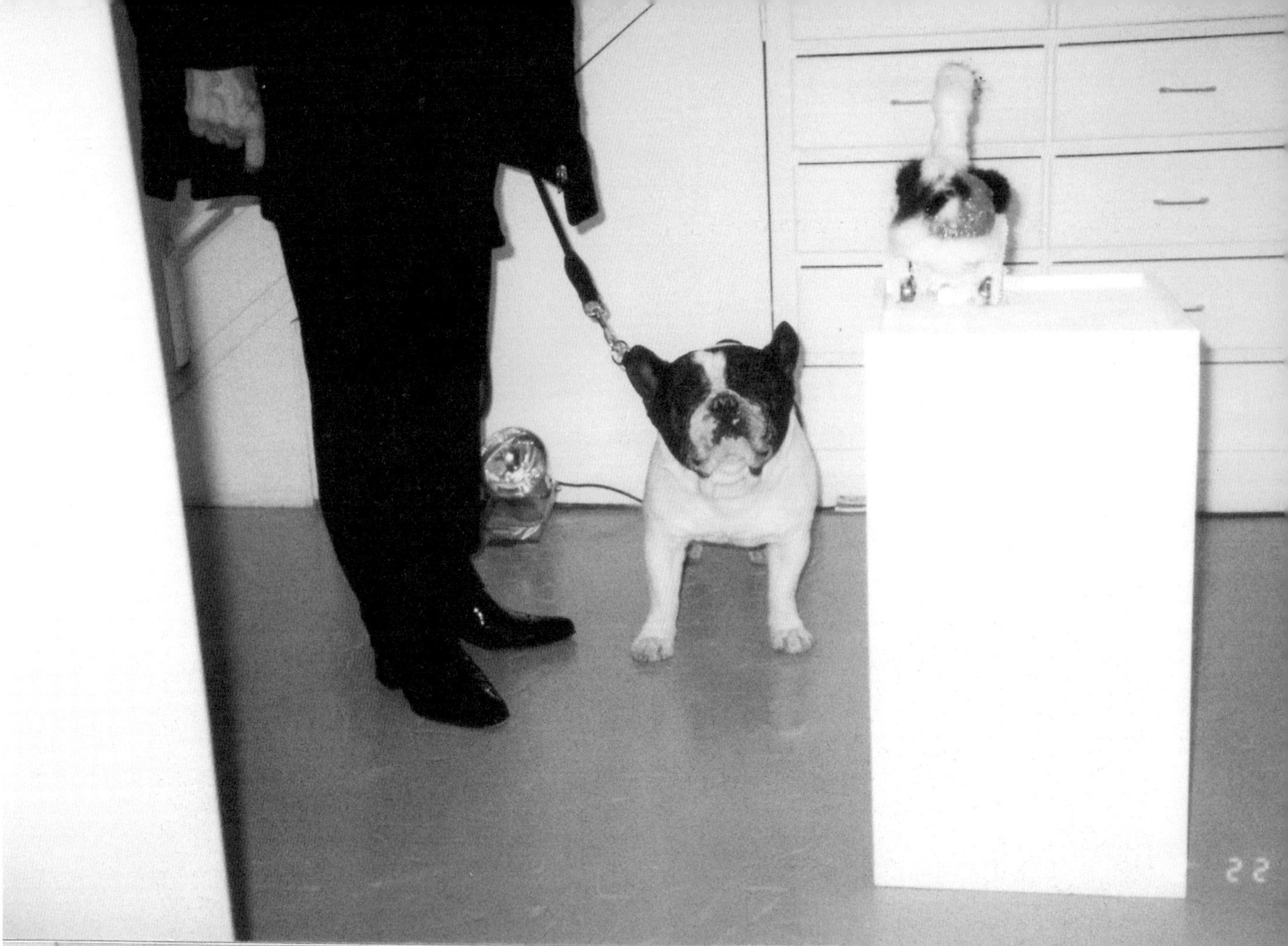

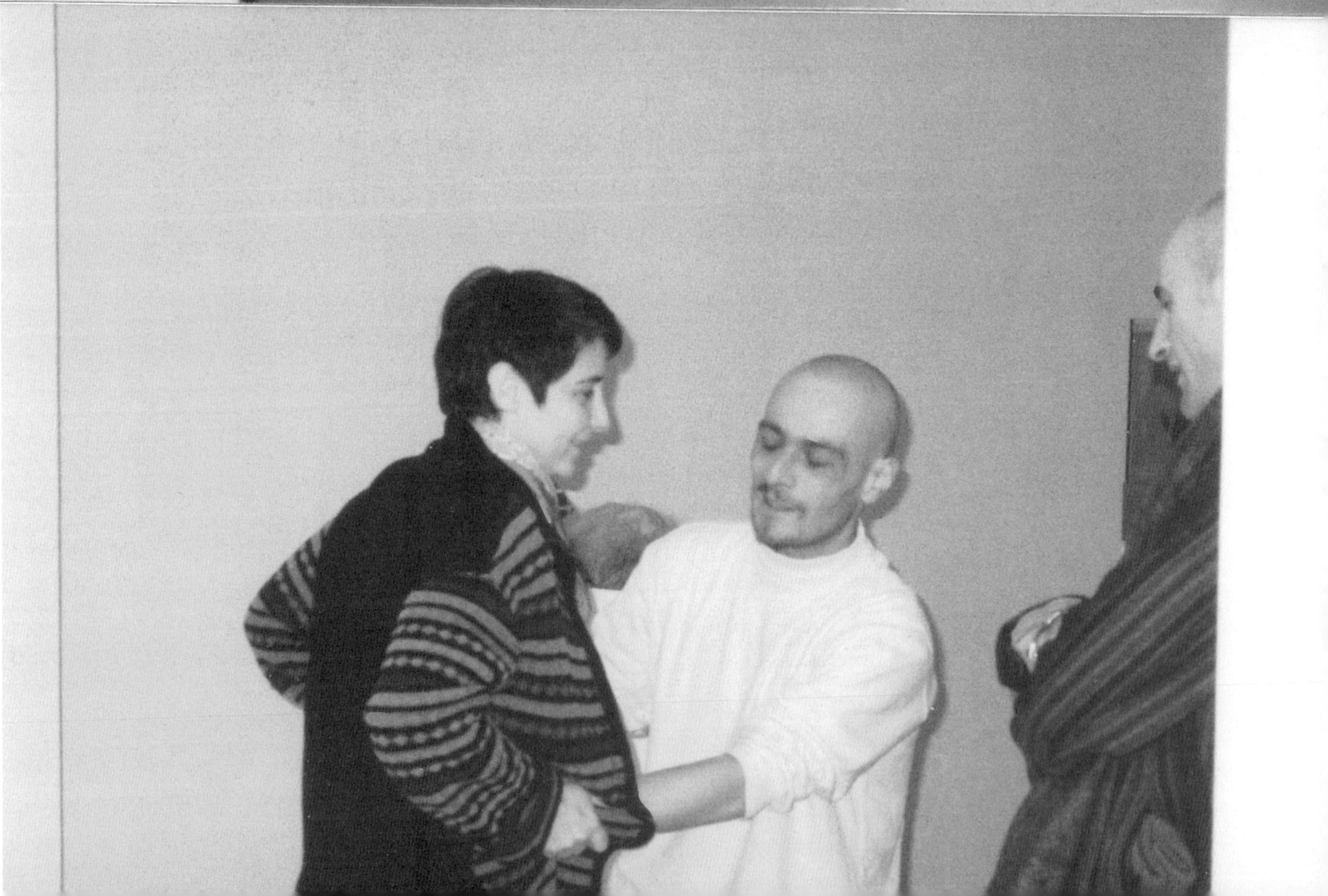

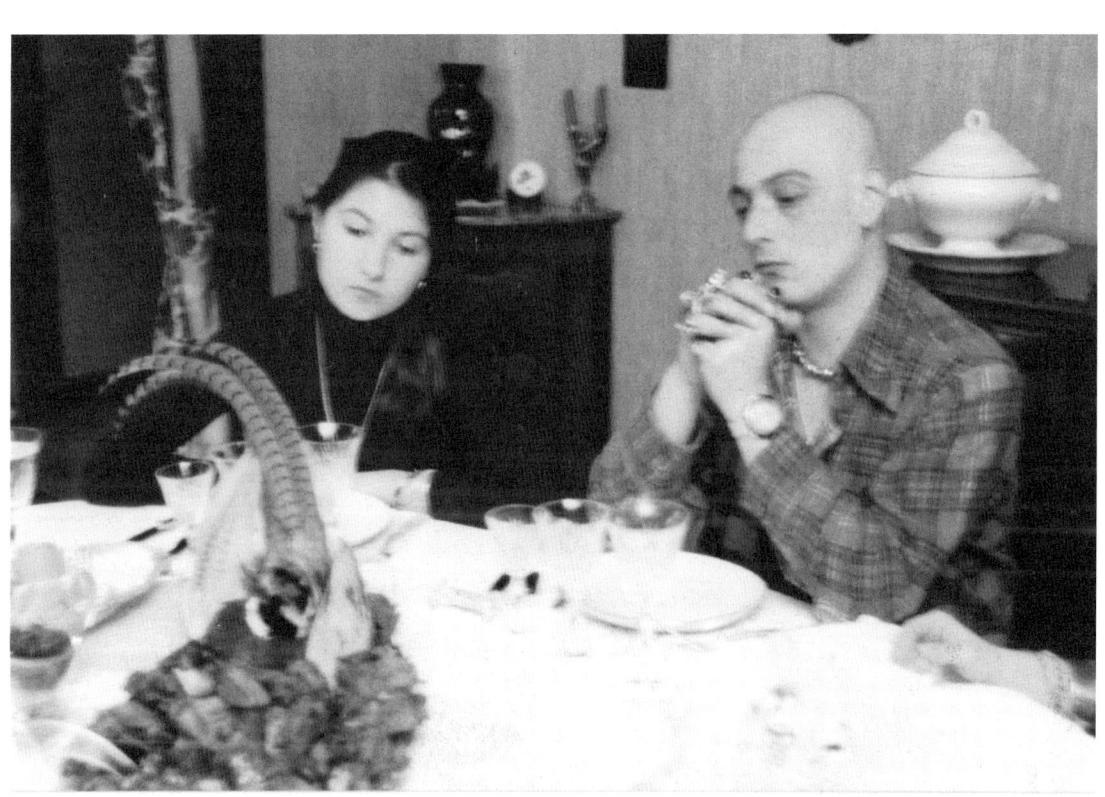

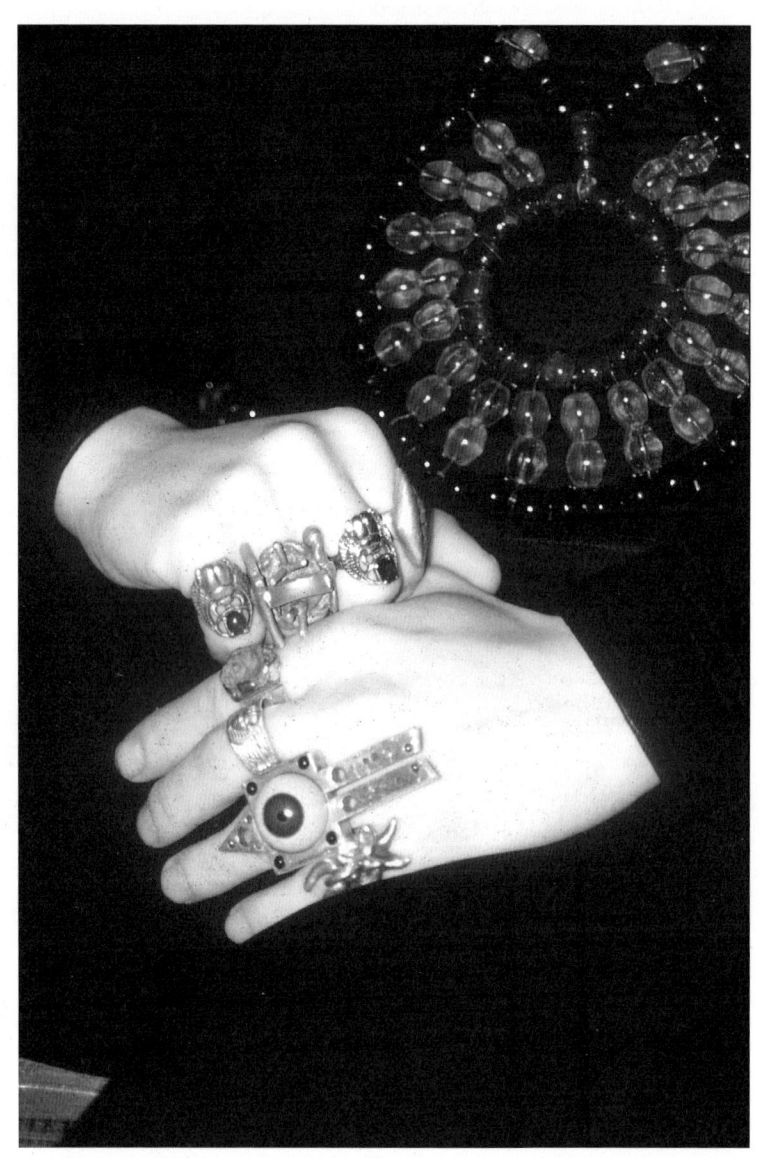

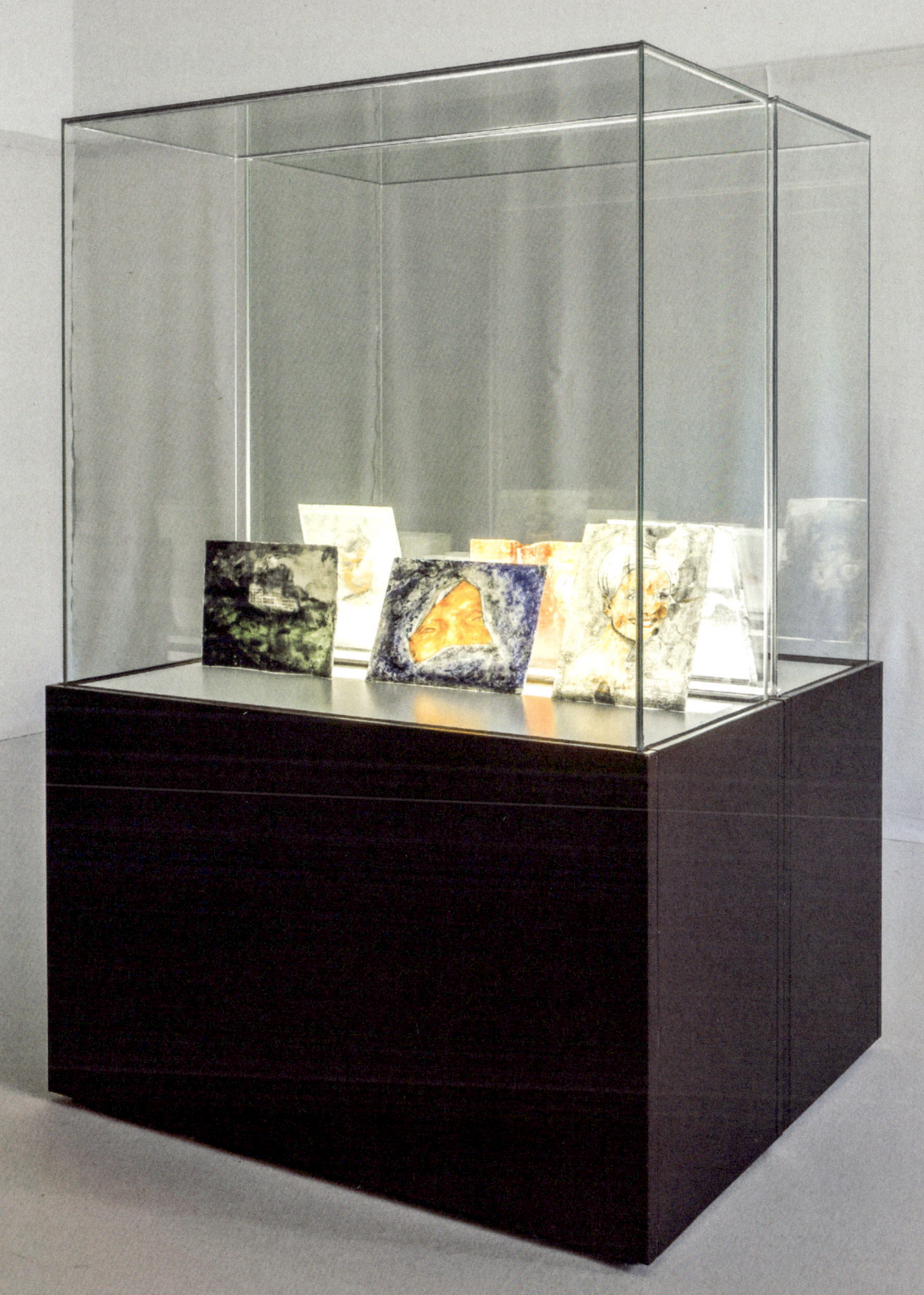

Exhibition view, *Bruno Pélassy and the Order of the Starfish*, October 20, 2023–January 14, 2024, Haus am Waldsee, Berlin

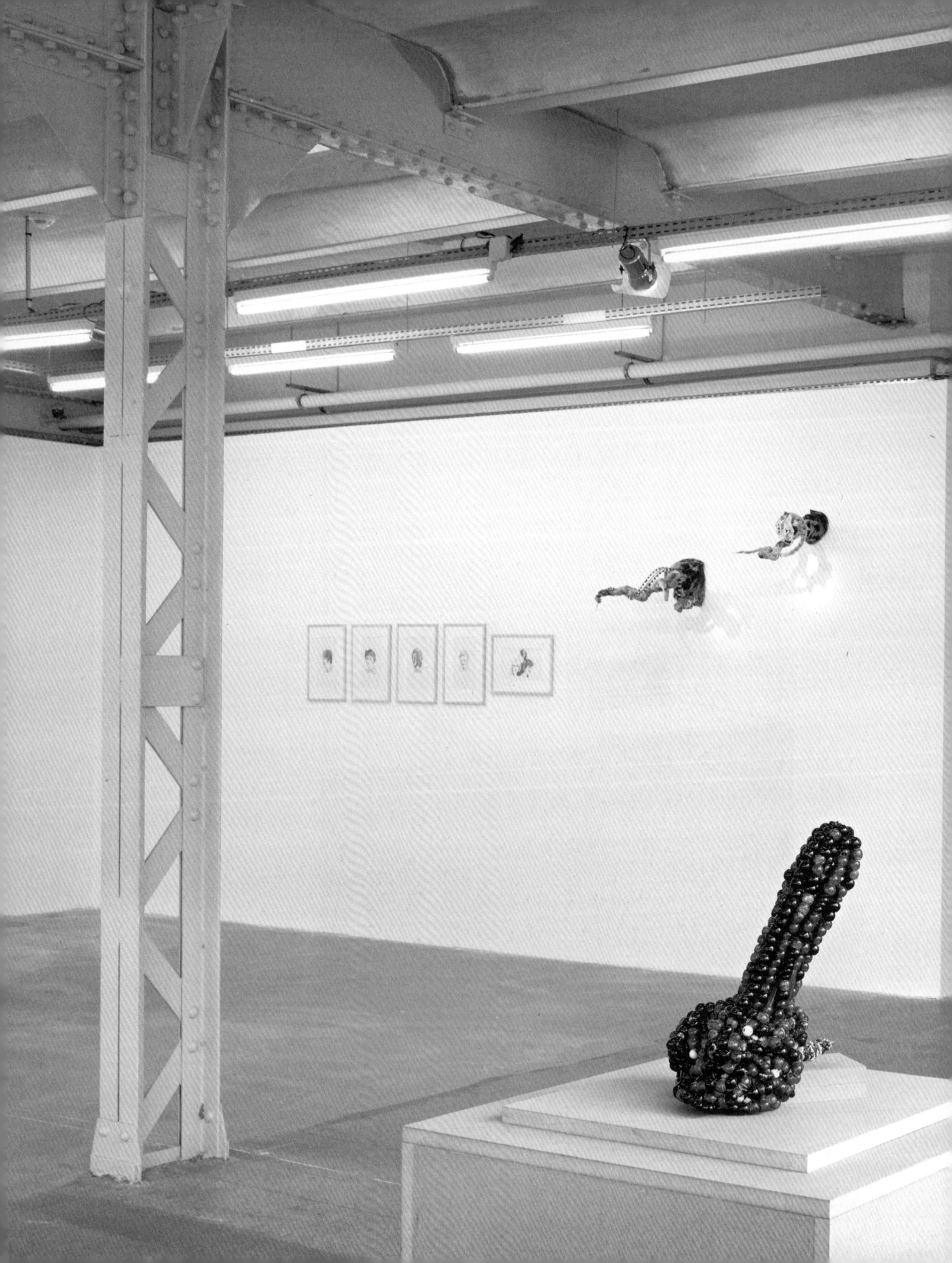

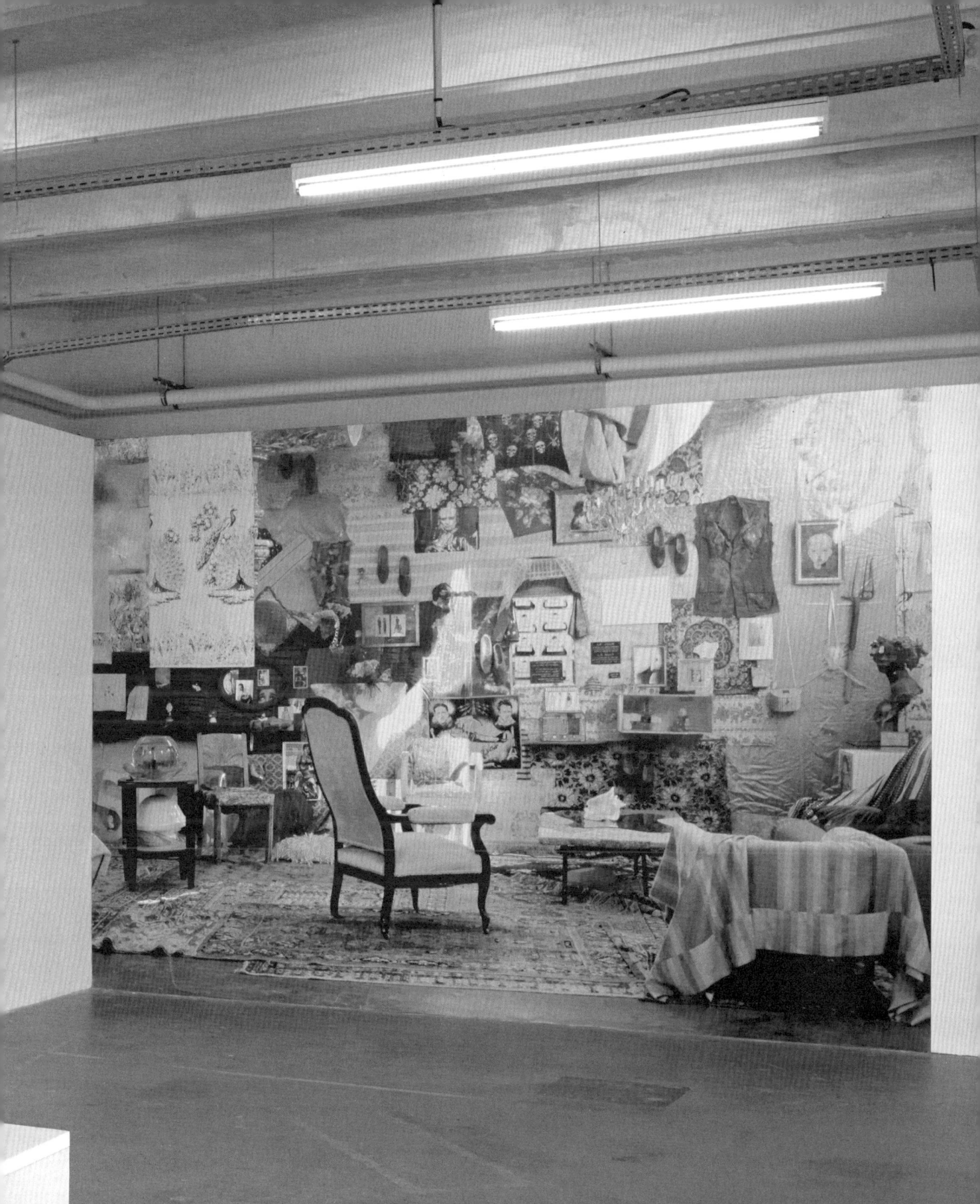

Exhibition view, *Bruno Pélassy*, January 16–March 22, 2015, Le Crédac, Ivry-sur-Seine

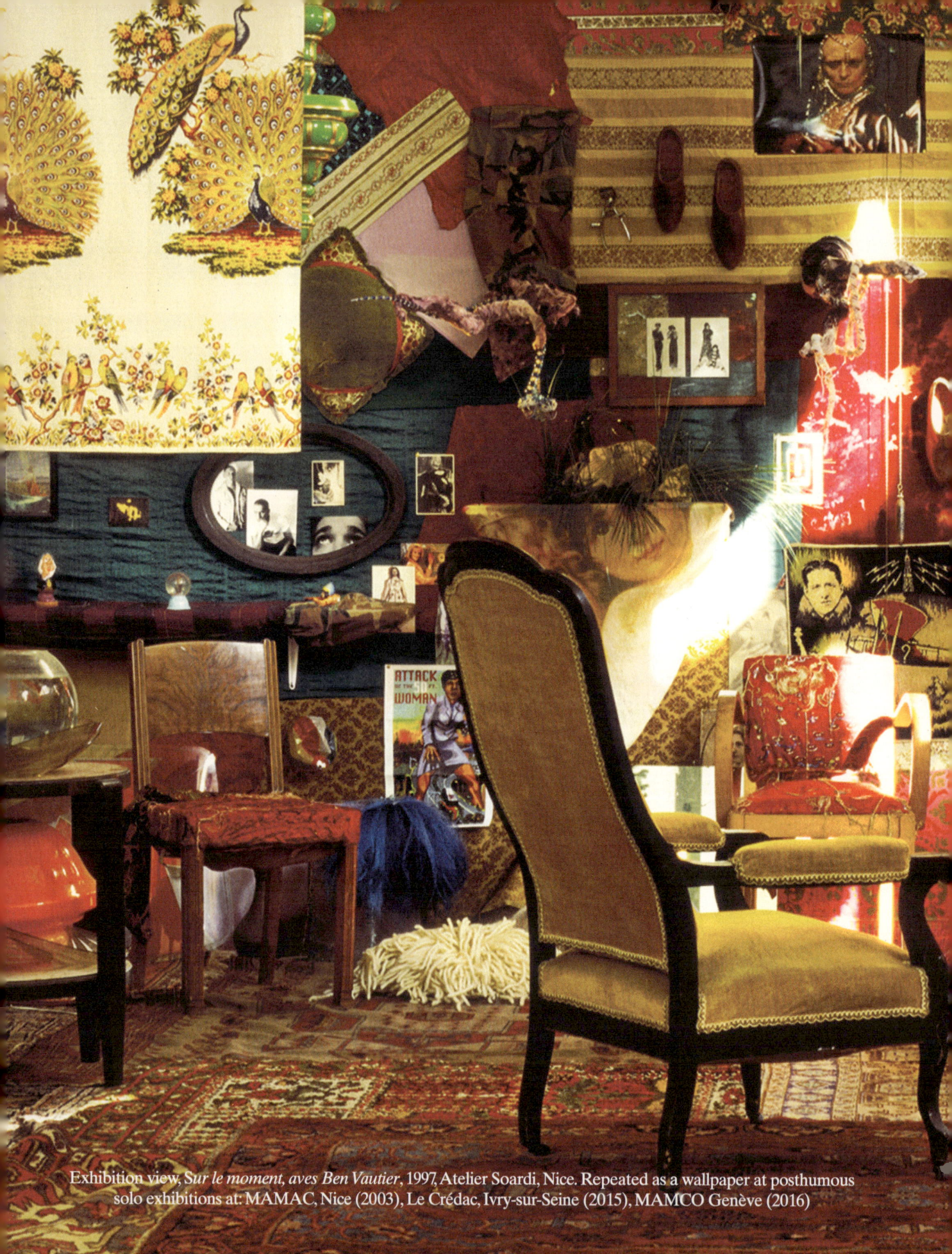

Exhibition view, *Sur le moment, aves Ben Vautier*, 1997, Atelier Soardi, Nice. Repeated as a wallpaper at posthumous solo exhibitions at: MAMAC, Nice (2003), Le Crédac, Ivry-sur-Seine (2015), MAMCO Genève (2016)

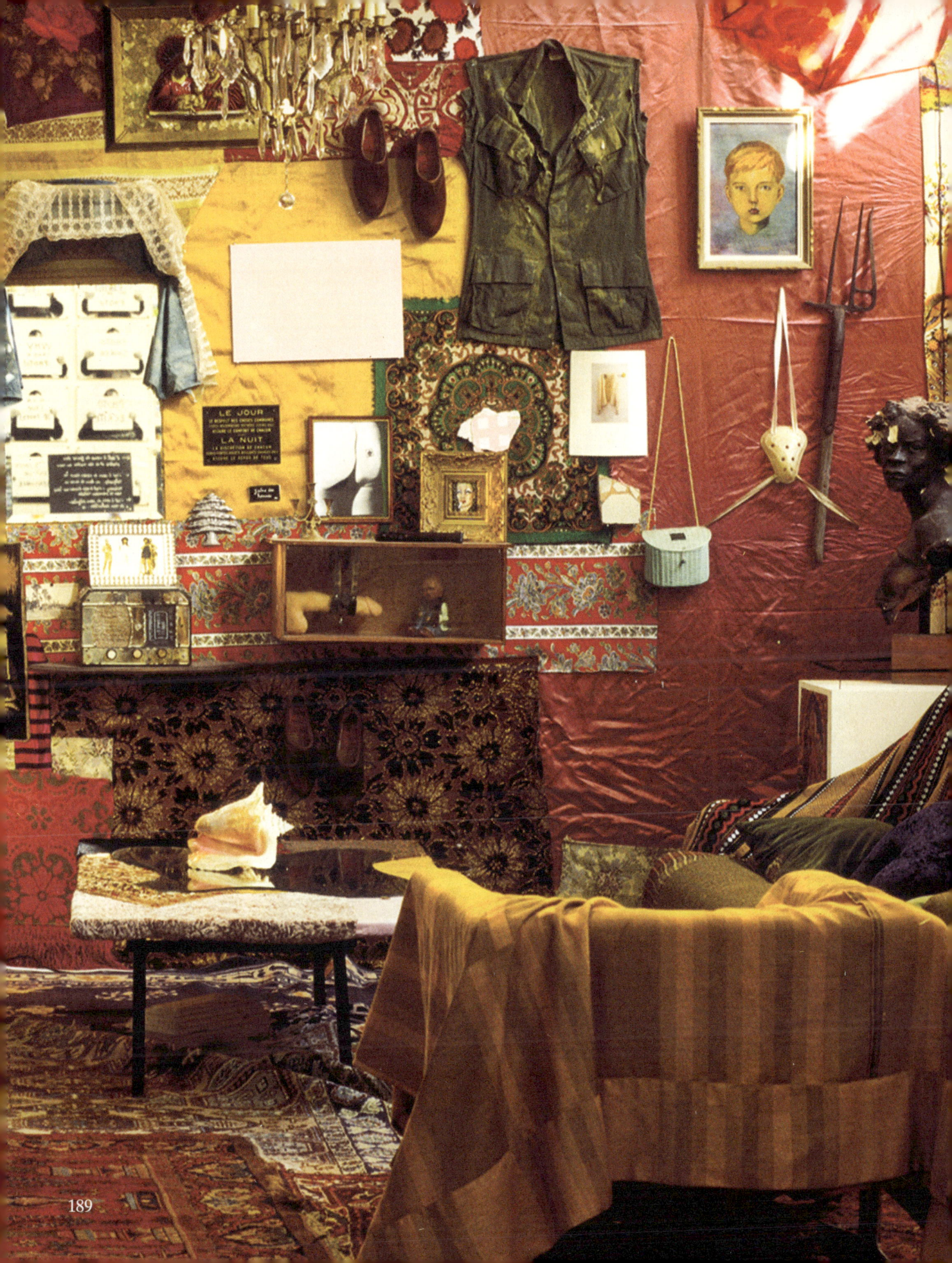

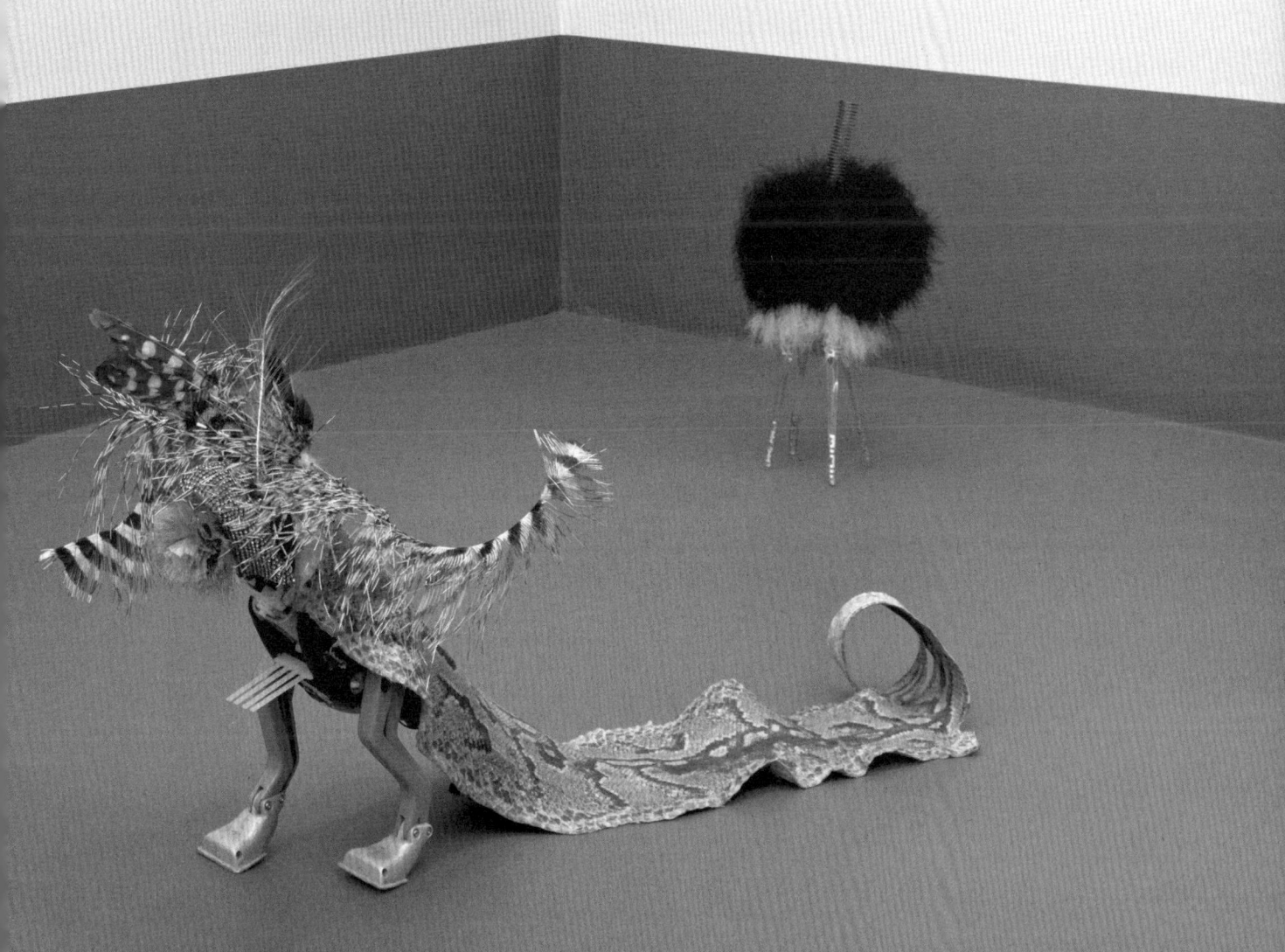

Exhibition view, *Bruno Pélassy*, February 12–May 1, 2016, MAMCO Genève

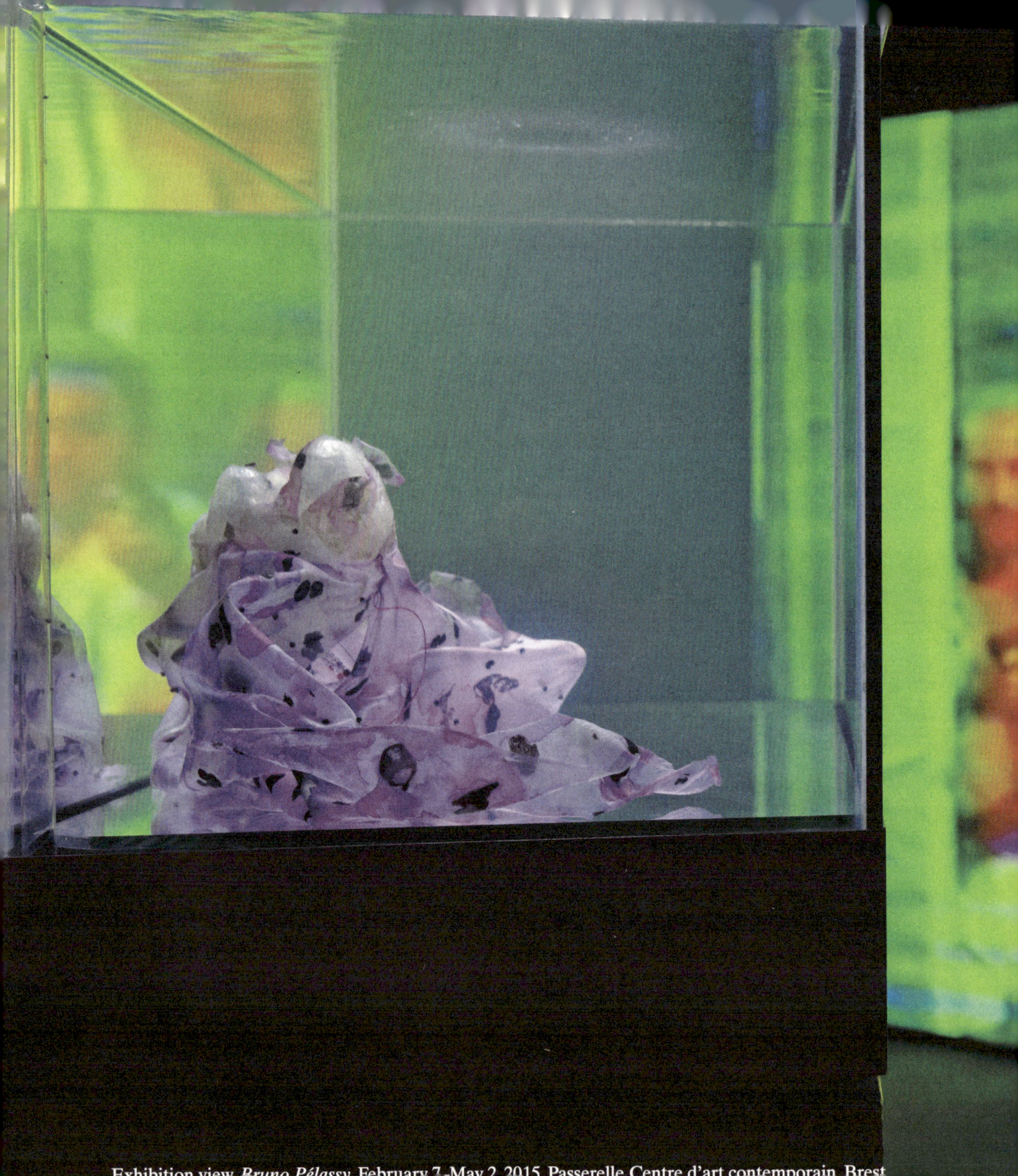

Exhibition view, *Bruno Pélassy*, February 7–May 2, 2015, Passerelle Centre d'art contemporain, Brest

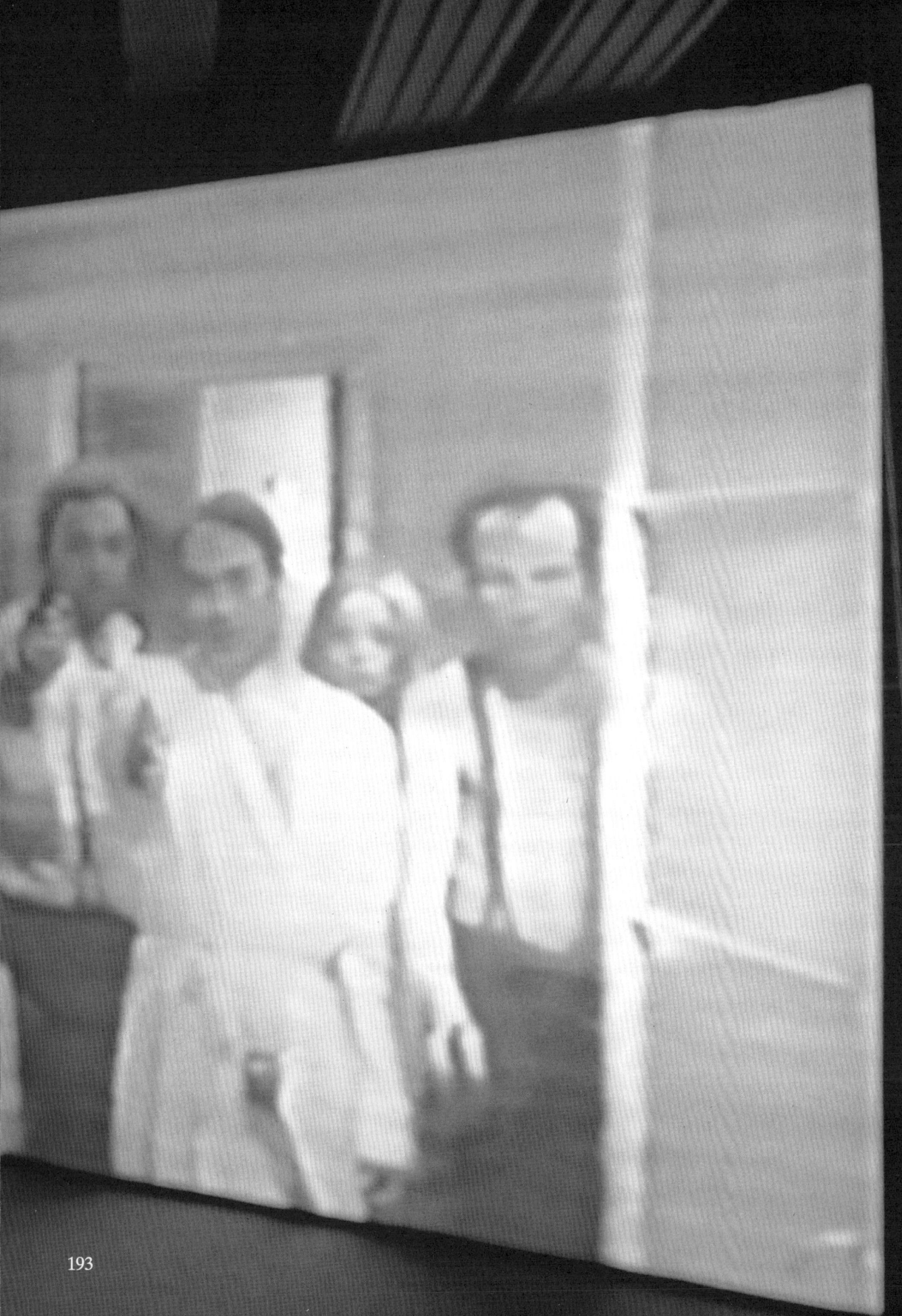

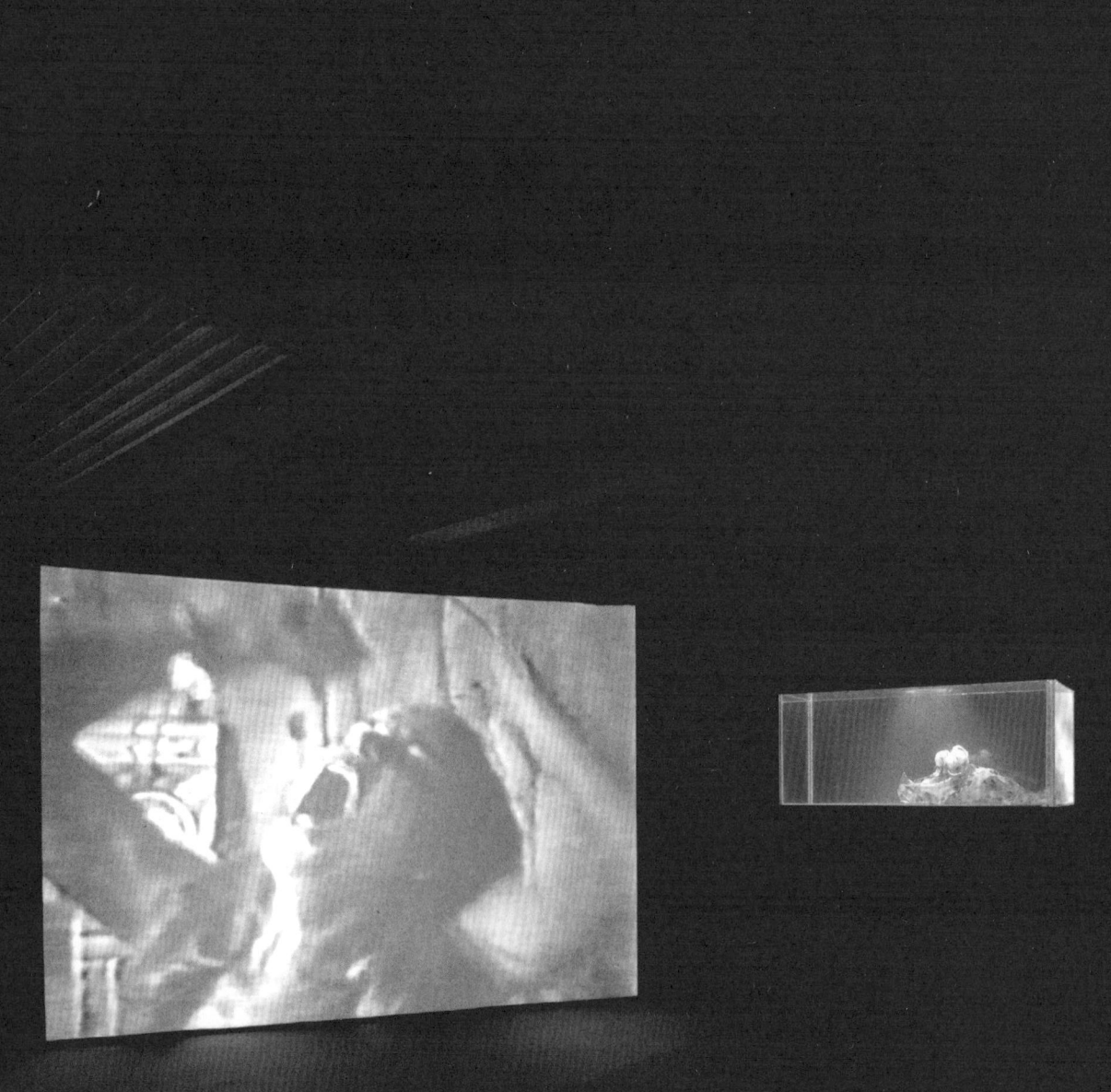

Ligne du Temps

Florence Bonnefous

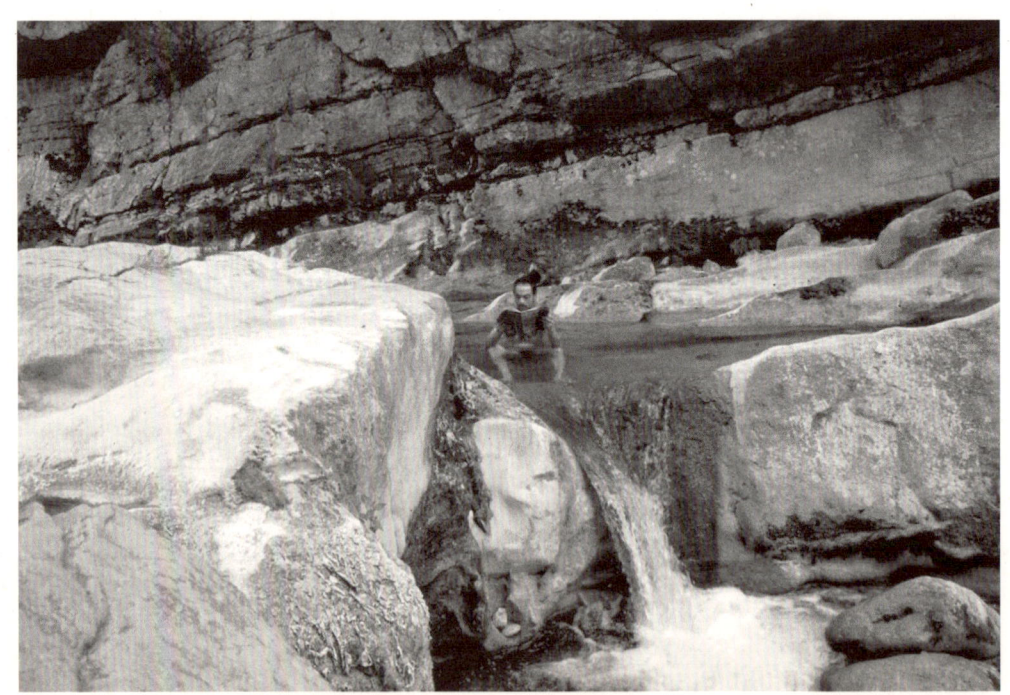

Bruno Pélassy is born on May 20, 1966, in Vientiane, Laos, the child of a French military family.

The family moves back to France in the summer of 1967. They spend several years in Metz, then move to Nice in 1971. Bruno choses a maharaja costume for his first fancy-dress party at the Rothschild nursery school.

After high school, he enrolls at the Atelier Mode Fleuri Delaporte in Paris's 15th arrondissement to study fashion design.

In 1986, under the aegis of his school, he participates in a fashion show at the Palais Royal amid the Daniel Buren columns. Many photographers are in attendance. Brigitte, his elder sister, reports that a famous fashion house later plagiarized the showpiece of Pélassy's collection.

In 1987, he finds out he is HIV positive. At the time, he is living on rue du Croissant in the 2nd arrondissement and working in a studio at the Hôpital Éphémère. He moves back and forth between Paris and Nice until 1992.

In the early 1990s, Bruno begins drawing and making his first jewelry pieces, mixing glass beads and black leather, and starts collaborating occasionally with Swarovski. He is strongly influenced by the films of Rainer Werner Fassbinder, Derek Jarman, and James Bidgood (Anonymous), as well as the actor Joe Dallesandro, the excesses of Jean Lorrain, and the powerful writings of Bernard-Marie Koltès. He draws his inspiration from a very camp, gay world. These artists become his extended family, his pantheon—and they will all die from AIDS.

In Nice, he starts spending time at the Villa Arson and the Saint-Tropez bar.

In 1992, he participates in his first group exhibition, *POTLATCH*, in Nice.

In 1993 he has his first solo exhibition at Galerie Art Concept in Nice.
He presents a series of reliquaries containing, among other things, a memorable bleached-denim jacket adorned with huge red glass beads. These works are to be worn, like heavy jewels on fancy occasions, and then re-enshrined in their carved and gilded wooden boxes. The installation is immersed in thick wreaths of incense.

In 1994, Bruno meets critic and curator Laura Cottingham and artist Paul McCarthy in Nice, and artist Monica Majoli in Los Angeles; he is in the latter city accompanying gallery Air de Paris's exhibition at the Gramercy Art Fair at the Château Marmont. His first, dazzling American tour.

Back in France, he produces a series of drawings entitled *We gonna have a good time*, which combine images from a 1970s hairdressing book with imagery from a medical textbook on facial diseases. With the same biting humor, he also creates his first *Bestioles* (Beasties), a series of wigs concealing toy robots that animate them in an erratic, jerky way.

In the same year, he is admitted to the Hôpital Saint Louis in Paris, suffering from lung cancer. He leaves Paris for good and moves to an apartment on Boulevard Raimbaldi in Nice. This is where he begins making *Sans titre, Sang titre, Cent titres*, a long film entirely made up of pirated fragments of other films and television programs. He spends his days in front of a television connected to two VHS player-recorders, with stacks of VHS videocassettes piled up on the floor surrounding him. His low-tech sampling artwork flourishes into a unique masterpiece of juxtaposition that is damaged whenever it is played.

In 1996, the *Cires* (Wax Pieces) series feature portraits—for instance of the actor Brad Davis or self-portraits as a young boy—sealed in candle wax. Light, heat, pain.

In 1997, Bruno returns to his *Bestioles*, (pro)creating a bestiary of small, impatient, irritated sculptures that seek to escape from whatever space is dedicated to them. He also sculpts beautiful, ever-erect phalluses out of glass beads. Late in the year, the shambles that is Bruno's studio is spilled out and rearranged in an art gallery for an exhibition with Ben Vautier at Galerie Soardi in Nice. He collaborates with Natacha Lesueur on a series of photographs of his feet filling and deforming cut-out stilettos. He immerses his *Créatures*—swaying works illuminated from the rear made of pearls, silk, and silicone—in aquariums' purified water.

In his last years, Bruno is considerably diminished by AIDS-related illnesses, and yet his vital energy and kindness remain astonishing as his work begins to travel to Rotterdam, Berlin, Dubrovnik, Lausanne, and beyond.

His last solo exhibition is held at Galerie Vigna in Nice in 2001 and is beautifully entitled *Shim*. Double gender.

Bruno Pélassy dies on August 11, 2002. His first retrospective exhibition is held at MAMAC, Nice, the following year, collectively curated by his friends Didier Bisson, Florence Bonnefous, Brice Dellsperger, and Natacha Lesueur, as well as the Pélassy family and many others.

Bookshelf

Bruno Pélassy

- HENRY MILLER — PLEXUS
- JEAN DUPERRAY — DORA PROVIDENCE
- Daniel Cohen — RICHESSE DU MONDE, PAUVRETÉS DES NATIONS
- RENÉ DELPECHE — Ces filles que l'on dit de joie
- Barbey d'Aurevilly — Les Diaboliques
- MARCEL PROUST — SODOME ET GOMORRHE II
- CONSTANTIN CAVAFY — POÈMES ANCIENS OU RETROUVÉS
- Copi — Virginia Woolf a encore frappé
- COPI / UNE LANGOUSTE POUR DEUX
- william burroughs — le festin nu
- ARTHUR KOESTLER — LE ZÉRO ET L'INFINI

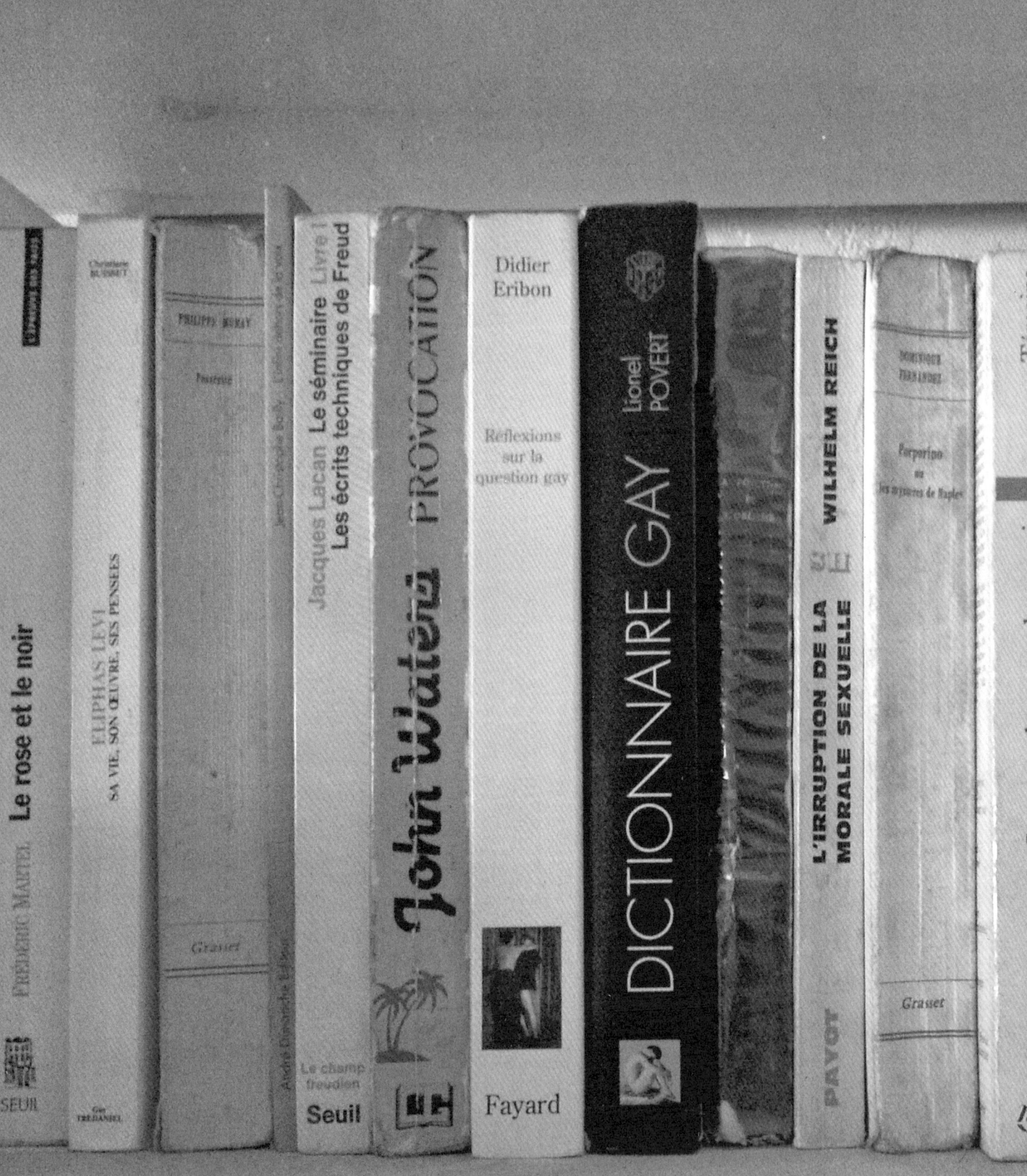

- Carlos Castaneda — Histoires de pouvoir — Témoins — nrf
- 1989/27
- 1988/23
- MARCEL ISY-SCHWART — INCROYABLE AMÉRIQUE
- Carrière
- L'ISLAM Religion de la Science
- Bêchir Torki — Echecs et mythe — ARRABAL
- Henri de Régnier — Histoires incertaines
- J. D'AGRAIVES — SUR LA PISTE DES DIEUX — Éditions ...
- Collection ATOPIA — Dom CALMET — DISSERTATION sur les Revenants en corps les Excommuniés les Oupires ou Vampires Brucolaques etc. (1751) — J. Millon
- Frédéric Nietzsche — Zarathoustra
- MARCEL JOUHANDEAU — Mémorial IV — APPRENTIS ET GARÇONS — nrf — Gallimard
- GEORGES PEREC — L'infra-ordinaire — SEUIL

- Florence Tamagne — *Histoire de l'homosexualité en Europe* — Seuil
- Pier Paolo Pasolini — *Lettres luthériennes* — Solo / Seuil
- *Les Mille et Une Nuits* — Contes arabes traduits par Galland — Librairie Garnier, Paris
- François Coppée — *Choix de Poésies* — 12 fr.
- [Les Poésies de Hérédia?]
- Marcus Herrenschmidt — *Le sexe inconnu*
- Pierre Loti — *Un pèlerin d'Angkor*
- [Paul Bourget — Le Justicier] — Plon
- Ginsberg — *kaddish*
- Paul Diel — *Le symbolisme dans la Bible* — P 20

In 2023, Anna Gritz organized *Bruno Pélassy and the Order of the Starfish* at Haus am Waldsee, the institutional premiere of Pélassy's work in Germany. With Marie Canet, a curator and critic who teaches aesthetics at the Villa Arson, Nice, and Florence Bonnefous, co-owner of the gallery Air de Paris, they began laying plans for Pélassy's first monograph. Florence was a longtime friend of Bruno's—they both lived in Nice in the late 1990s—and she now represents his work in collaboration with his estate. In 2024, editor and curator Alice Dusapin joined Villa Arson as head of the publishing department and initiated a collection entitled PasSage, dedicated to the production of monographs on artistic figures who have left a significant mark through their work and presence at Villa Arson. This is a collection of books published not in connection with exhibitions, but simply as reminders that the works of these passengers shine beyond what we believe to be "the moment."

This is certainly true of Bruno Pélassy, whose legacy is still very much alive in this new generation of young artists. His relationship with Nice is a significant one. This monograph brings together Pélassy's personal archives, works, and exhibition installation views, and includes commissioned texts by Marie Canet, critic Laura Cottingham, and editor Baptiste Pinteaux. Laura met Bruno and Florence at the Villa Arson, where she did a residency in 1997, and Baptiste often collaborates with Florence and Alice; they are all friends.

This book is copublished by Mousse Publishing, thanks to the trust and joy of Ilaria Bombelli, Barbara Casavecchia, and graphic designer Massimiliano Pace; Haus am Waldsee, which provided a significant part of the production and support required for such a monograph; Air de Paris and the estate of Bruno Pélassy; and finally Villa Arson, as the first title of its PasSage collection.

We believe this book carries a representation of friendships, and we are glad it is now in the world and in the present.

Ilaria Bombelli,
Florence Bonnefous,
Alice Dusapin,
Anna Gritz

This monograph was inspired by the exhibition *Bruno Pélassy and the Order of the Starfish* at Haus am Waldsee, Berlin, curated by Anna Gritz and on view October 20, 2023, through January 14, 2024. The exhibition also presented contributions by Marc Camille Chaimowicz, Beth Collar, Jesse Darling, Brice Dellsperger, Leonor Fini, Ull Hohn, Natacha Lesueur, Jean Painlevé & Geneviève Hamon, James Richards, and Soshiro Matsubara.

HAUS AM WALDSEE E.V.
Director
Anna Gritz
Managing director
Tobias Bader
Curator
Beatrice Hilke
Curatorial assistant
Pia-Marie Remmers
Press and communications
Erik Günther
Digital communications
Sarah Mohr
Visitor and event manager
Regina Schreieder
Accounting
Wiebke Sünderhauf
Education
Luise Bichler with Linus Cuno von Aufsess, Simon Balzat, Pia Gottschalk, Eileen Kesseler, Mette Kleinsteuber, Lea Meder, Johanna Pistorius, Claire Rüffer, Anna Schulte
Gardener
Nele Schinz
Front desk and invigilators
Michael Gottberg, Samer Ismail, Jeannette Mügge, Swenja Schmidt
Intern
Martina Kutsch
Install team
Justus Ruben Muthmann (Leitung / head of install), Yasuaki Hamada, Carl-Oskar Jonsson, Philipp Köstermenke, Antonia Nannt, Carol Peters

HAUS AM WALDSEE IS LED BY HAUS AM WALDSEE E.V.
Board
Jakob Braeuer, Kaspar v. Erffa, Leonie v. Gadow

THE EXHIBITION WAS SUPPORTED BY

Haus am Waldsee
Freunde und Förderer

Between Bridges

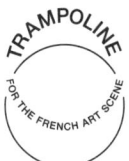 Phileas THE AUSTRIAN OFFICE FOR CONTEMPORARY ART

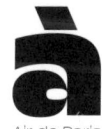

Bundesministerium
Kunst, Kultur,
öffentlicher Dienst und Sport

Air de Paris

HAUS AM WALDSEE IS SUPPORTED BY

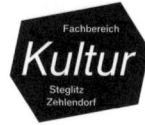

Published by
Mousse Publishing
Contrappunto s.r.l.
Via Pier Candido Decembrio 28
20137, Milan – Italy

Haus am Waldsee
Argentinische Allee 30
14163 Berlin – Germany

Villa Arson (collection PasSage)
20 avenue Stephen Liégeard
06100 Nice – France

Available through
Mousse Publishing, Milan
moussemagazine.it

Edited by
Ilaria Bombelli, Florence Bonnefous,
Alice Dusapin, Anna Gritz

Book Design
Massimiliano Pace

Translations
James Horton, Thomas Laval,
Callisto McNulty

Copyediting & Proofreading
Laura Bouillic, Emma Passarella,
Lindsey Westbrook

First edition
2024

Printed in Italy by Grafiche Antiga

ISBN 9788867496556

€ 40 / $ 45

VILLA ARSON
Head
Sylvain Lizon
Director of the art center
Marie-Ann Yemsi
Head of publishing
Alice Dusapin

All images courtesy of Air de Paris /
Famille Pélassy, unless otherwise indicated.

Photo credits
AAA Production/Michel Coen
p. 41, 42, 43, 45, 46, 50, 51, 87, 88, 93, 110, 111, 113, 114
Muriel Anssens
p. 34, 35, 36, 37, 38, 39, 44, 47, 80, 81, 84, 120, 121, 123, 127, 124, 125, 129, 133
Marc Domage
p. 33, 96, 131, 132, 145, 148, 155, 157, 160, 162
Natacha Lesueur
p. 188
Aurélien Mole
p. 192, 193, 194
André Morin
p. 186, 187
Jean Marc Pharisien
p. 176
Plastiques Photography
p. 175
Frank Sperling
p. 27, 28, 31, 32, 36, 37, 49, 56, 82, 86, 89, 90, 91, 94, 105, 106, 107, 108, 109, 115, 116, 119, 159, 163, 165, 166, 167
Loic Thebaud
p. 48
Julien Veran
p. 54, 55
Annik Wetter
p. 171, 173, 191

© 2024 Mousse Publishing, Haus am Waldsee, Villa Arson, Air de Paris, Bruno Pélassy family, and the authors of the texts: Marie Canet, Laura Cottingham, Baptiste Pinteaux

The publishers and Air de Paris would like to thank Brigitte Pélassy, Paulette & Roger Pélassy, and all the people who appear in the photos of the artist's life, or who took them. There are too many of Bruno's friends to name them all here, but may this book revive their beautiful memories of him.

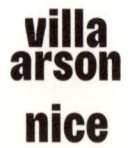 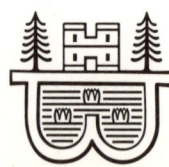 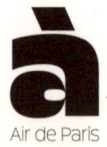